CHINA'S TRANSITION TO A NEW PHASE OF DEVELOPMENT

Other titles in the China Update Book Series include:

The titles are available online at press.anu.edu.au/publications/series/china-update

CHINA'S TRANSITION TO A NEW PHASE OF DEVELOPMENT

EDITED BY LIGANG SONG AND YIXIAO ZHOU

Australian
National
University

ANU PRESS

社会科学文献出版社
SOCIAL SCIENCES ACADEMIC PRESS (CHINA)

Australian
National
University

ANU PRESS

Published by ANU Press
The Australian National University
Canberra ACT 2600, Australia
Email: anupress@anu.edu.au

Available to download for free at press.anu.edu.au

A catalogue record for this book is available from the National Library of Australia

ISBN (print): 9781760465575
ISBN (online): 9781760465582

WorldCat (print): 1350161737
WorldCat (online): 1350161736

DOI: 10.22459/CTNPD.2022

Cover design and layout by ANU Press

Contents

List of figures

List of tables

Abbreviations

AI	artificial intelligence
BRICS	Brazil, Russia, India, China and South Africa
CCP	Chinese Communist Party
CGE	computable general equilibrium
CPTPP	Comprehensive and Progressive Agreement for Trans-Pacific Partnership
ETS	emissions-trading scheme
FTA	free-trade agreement
G7	Group of Seven
G8	Group of Eight
GDELT	Global Database of Events, Language and Tone
GDP	gross domestic product
GFC	Global Financial Crisis
GHG	greenhouse gas
GW	gigawatt
IMF	International Monetary Fund
MW	megawatt
NATO	North Atlantic Treaty Organization
NBS	National Bureau of Statistics
OECD	Organisation for Economic Co-operation and Development
PPP	purchasing power parity
PRI	political relations index
R&D	research and development
RCEP	Regional Comprehensive Economic Partnership Agreement
RMB	renminbi
SMEs	small and medium-sized enterprises

SOE	state-owned enterprise
UK	United Kingdom
UN	United Nations
UNFCCC	United Nations Framework Convention on Climate Change
US	United States
WTO	World Trade Organization

List of contributors

Vishesh Argawal
The World Bank

Cheng Li
Chinese Academy of Social Sciences

Shenghao Feng
University of International Business
and Economics

Jane Golley
The Australian National University

Yiping Huang
Peking University

James Laurenceson
University of Technology Sydney

Li Shi
Zhejiang University

Justin Yifu Lin
Peking University

Xiujian Peng
Victoria University

Tunye Qiu
The Australian National University

Haocheng Shang
Peking University

Xunpeng Shi
University of Technology Sydney

Ligang Song
The Australian National University

Fang-Fang Tang
Peking University

Wang Wei
Development Research Centre of the
State Council

Wing Thye Woo
UN Sustainable Development
Solutions Network

Qiyuan Xu
Chinese Academy of Social Sciences

Xiang Yu
Chinese Academy of Social Sciences

Zhan Peng
Zhejiang University

Dandan Zhang
Peking University

Kunling Zhang
Beijing Normal University

Xiaojing Zhang
Chinese Academy of Social Sciences

Yongsheng Zhang
Chinese Academy of Social Sciences

Yixiao Zhou
The Australian National University

Acknowledgements

The China Economy Program (CEP) at the Crawford School of Public Policy, The Australian National University (ANU), acknowledges the financial support provided by BHP for the China Update 2022. We thank CEP Project Manager Timothy Cronin, from the Crawford School, for his programming support and editing assistance. We sincerely thank our chapter authors for their valuable contributions. We would also like to thank colleagues from ANU Press, notably Elouise Ball and Teresa Prowse, for their expeditious publication of this year's book. Our copyeditor, Jan Borrie, has consistently lent her professionalism and expertise to the China Update book series throughout the years, and her meticulous work is truly appreciated by the series' contributors. Thanks also go to our Crawford School colleagues, including David Sprinkle and Adelaide Haynes (as well as Luka Vertessy, from the ANU College of Asia and the Pacific), for their support in preparing for this year's update event. We thank the Social Sciences Academic Press of the Chinese Academy of Social Sciences, in Beijing, for translating and publishing the Chinese version of the book each year—making this important research available to a wider readership.

1

Managing China's transition to a new phase of economic growth and development

Ligang Song and Yixiao Zhou

Introduction

The Chinese economy is undergoing fundamental changes leading towards a major transition to a new phase of economic growth and development. This transition is a result of the need to elevate the standard of living to a new level in a more sustained model of economic growth and of the rapidly changing environment that has increased the complexity of implementing new reform measures and policies.

The transition is guided by a Chinese Government vision to build a modern socialist country by 2035 through economic growth and social development, achieve a high level of openness and a strong modern economy towards the middle of the century and build a more affluent society. This vision was apparent from the Chinese Communist Party's recent twentieth national congress.

China's strategic goals include building an integrated domestic market system through supply-side reform; enhancing institution-building and entrepreneurship; building an innovation-based economy centred on digital transformation; achieving peak carbon by 2030 and carbon neutrality by 2060 through an energy transformation to the use of new and renewable energies; achieving more equitable development with an emphasis on common prosperity; enhancing global and regional economic reintegration by cementing China's position as a hub for global value and supply chains and implementing the dual-circulation strategy; accelerating the pace of financial opening with the goal of achieving full convertibility of the renminbi through capital account liberation and the consolidation of its domestic banking system; and building a modern economy centred on new patterns of industrialisation, urbanisation and digitisation.

China is facing some severe headwinds in achieving its goals, including: the unfavourable global macroeconomic environment and financial conditions since the Global Financial Crisis (GFC) and the Covid-19 pandemic; the increasing financial risks due to high leverages among households, firms and local governments; readjustment in real estate sector development; very low fertility rates that are accelerating the pace of population ageing; deglobalisation and rising protectionism; economic and technological decoupling, which has hampered efforts towards global and regional integration, exacerbated by the weakening of the multilateral trading system (for example, the World Trade Organization); the enormous adjustment costs of adopting a low-carbon development strategy; the rising geopolitical tensions that have fractured the global system of trade flows, financial integration, payments for international settlements, cross-border investment flows and technological transfers and further disrupted global supply chains; not to mention the worsening global food and energy crises that have hampered global efforts to achieve poverty reduction and more equitable and sustainable growth and development.

These headwinds are forcing China to make changes to its model of growth and adjust its policies and long-term strategies for external economic activities such as international trade, investment, balance of payments, resources and technology. Key lessons can be learned from the experience of reform and opening in the past and new opportunities will be created in confronting these challenges. Taking full advantage of these opportunities holds the key for success. Some of the crucial issues China must manage in the difficult transition to the new phase of growth and development are described below.

Fundamental changes in growth drivers: Necessity and significance

In the past 10 years (2012–2022), China's annual GDP growth rate reached 6.6 per cent—the highest among the major world economies and higher than the global average of 2.6 per cent and the average for the developing world of 3.7 per cent over the same period. China's average contribution to global economic growth reached 38 per cent, surpassing the total contributions of the G7 countries during this period. In 2021, China's GDP accounted for 18.5 per cent of global GDP, rising from 11.3 per cent 10 years earlier. In the same year, China's total foreign trade value reached US$6.9 trillion—an increase of 56.8 per cent compared with 10 years earlier. China remains the second-largest economy and the largest trading nation in the world.

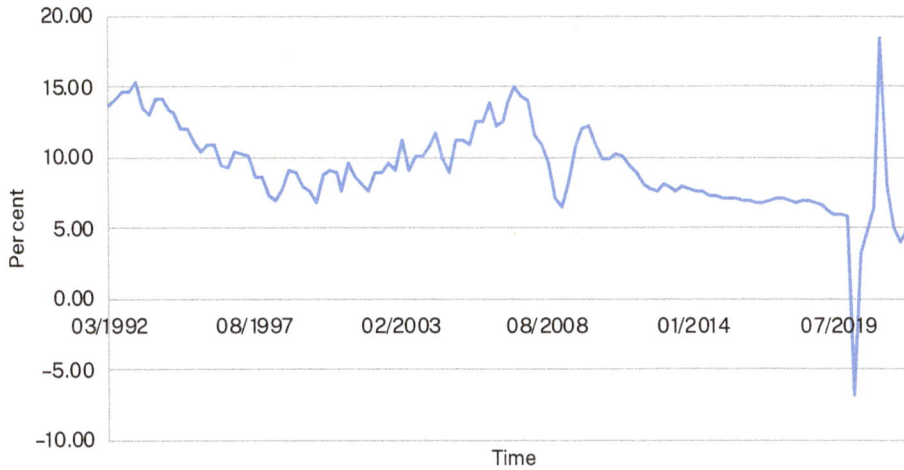

Figure 1.1 Quarterly real GDP growth rate of China, year on year, 1992Q1–2022Q2
Source: Authors' construction using data from the CEIC Database.

However, China's economic growth has been trending down, especially since the GFC in 2008 (Figure 1.1). The Chinese Government set a growth target of 5.5 per cent for 2022, but strict Covid-19 restrictions (which will not have a long-term impact on growth), a prolonged property slump and global recession risks challenge its efforts to boost economic growth. Assisted by government measures to revive economic activities, including monetary and fiscal policies and policies for stabilising the housing markets, China's GDP rose 3.9 per cent in the July–September quarter year on year, increasing from the 0.4 per cent pace in the second quarter. While investments in infrastructure and manufacturing are increasing, consumption remains subdued. Exports are continuing to rise but the growth rate has been slowing.

With its labour force peaking in 2011 and an ageing society, China's labour costs, caring responsibilities and demand for healthcare resources will increase, adding to the costs of operating the economy.

The Covid-19 pandemic, the resulting disruptions to supply chains, the rising costs of energy and food due to geopolitical tensions and the increasing financial fragility of global financial markets all point to slow growth of the global economy in 2022 and beyond. The International Monetary Fund has made downward adjustments to its forecasts for the global economy, raising the prospect of a global economic recession in 2023. The World Trade Organization (WTO) forecast a further weakening in global trade in the second half of 2022 and the Organisation for Economic Co-operation and Development (OECD) also predicted substantial drops in growth in the European Union and the United States in 2023. Given the contributions to global growth made by China in the past 10 years, maintaining its relatively high growth will be crucial not only for China, but also for the global economy.

This changing environment highlights the importance as well as the urgency of China accelerating the change in its drivers of growth. A key lesson from past development is to find effective ways of lifting productivity through efficient resource allocation and structural change. We explore this in detail along the four contributory factors of growth.

First, as growth theories have made clear that total factor productivity (TFP) growth is the ultimate driver of long-run economic growth, it is crucial to adjust policies and institutions to nurture TFP growth as the economic structure evolves, and to remove domestic factors and policy choices that contribute to the slowdown of TFP growth by deepening supply-side reform, focusing on state-owned enterprises (SOEs) and the process of 'creative destruction', the financial sector, factor markets and entrepreneurship. The government should continue to play a key role in leading the nation's drive to become more innovative, especially in those areas where uncertainties could prevent the private sector from investing.

Second, China's fertility rate has continued to fall in recent years. It now has an ageing society, as the share of the aged population (65 years and older) has surpassed 14 per cent of the total population. The rapid pace of ageing prompted the Chinese Government to adopt a series of policies, including the Two-Child Policy, hoping to raise fertility and increase the labour force in the long run. It is likely the government will remove its family planning policies altogether, returning families' right to reproduce in the hope that some kind of balance in the demographic structure will be restored in the long term. However, loosening birth-control policies alone may not be sufficient and other conditions will have to be changed to incentivise higher fertility, including financial subsidies to families that have more children. However, one concern about such incentives is that younger generations have shown a low propensity to reproduce despite such subsidies, as shown in the experiences of Japan and South Korea.

Third, although China has made significant achievements in enhancing education access and quality, there is still plenty of room to catch up with the education levels of advanced economies. Against the background of a falling labour force since 2012 (and of the total population from 2023), labour policies must focus more on quality than quantity. This will require increasing government expenditure on education and training and reform of the education system, including of curriculums for all levels of education, and boosting the development of vocational education. The first two will help improve the employability of graduates by resolving the mismatch between what is learned at schools and universities and what is required in the workplace. The last will not only fill the gaps in educational provision, but also equip young people with the skills to make them more employable.

There are two important areas of education policy. One is that China has a large labour force—about 800 million people in total. Upgrading the skills of the existing labour force is critical for enhancing firms' productivity, ongoing digital transformation of the economy and green growth. Enterprises must shoulder more responsibility for contributing to training and will reap the benefits as the quality of labour improves. The other area is to address the urban–rural divide in educational provision and quality by allocating more funding for rural and inland regions. Reforming China's fiscal system holds the key to securing funding from local public finance. Private sector participation in education investment is also an option for filling the investment gaps in educational provision in China.

Fourth, since the GFC, the predominant driver of economic growth in China has been capital deepening, as seen in the contribution of capital intensity growth to real GDP growth in Figure 1.2. While capital deepening boosts labour productivity as well as technological progress, as there is new embodied technology in new investment, when TFP growth slows and labour force expansion is constrained, continued capital deepening will encounter diminishing returns and become less effective in sustaining and boosting economic growth.

Another major concern is whether resources are allocated to the most efficient use and generate the maximum return. In the Chinese context, the comparison of returns to investment in the state economy with those in the private economy is important. While the state economy undertakes important functions such as maintaining employment stability, lowering income inequality and investing in infrastructure and research and development (R&D) projects with strong positive spillover effects, the relative productivity of the state sector versus the private sector is also an important consideration for optimal resource allocation between both sectors. Therefore, to drive and sustain economic growth, capital deepening must go hand-in-hand with reforms that boost TFP growth and resource allocation efficiency—which will become especially necessary as savings decrease due to the continuing fall in the labour force and population ageing.

China has made significant progress in both innovation inputs (Figure 1.3) and innovation performance (Figure 1.4). There is still a significant gap between China and the advanced economies in key determinants of innovation performance. Closing these gaps will further propel innovation activities in China, raising TFP and economic growth in the long run. The areas for future efforts include the following. More basic research (research activities can be categorised into three types: basic, applied and experimental development) is needed to sustain innovation and technological progress as China moves towards the world technology frontier; more efficient allocation of innovation funds is needed between SOEs and private firms, and between businesses, higher education institutions and research institutions. Further improvement in institutional quality through supply-side reforms is needed to nurture more R&D investment and innovation activities. Areas for improvement include strengthening intellectual property rights protection, the business environment and fair competition—all of which help enhance entrepreneurship and market-driven innovation. Last, improvement in the design of the national innovation system—for example, through incentives and wage increases for science and technology workers—will incentivise further innovation.

China's commitment to achieving peak carbon emissions by 2030 and carbon neutrality by 2060 requires a dramatic change in output structure, the energy mix, industrial location and production technologies. Moving towards decarbonisation represents the beginning of the decline of traditional industrialisation in China, which was powered by high investment, resource and energy intensities and high pollution. It also represents an opportunity for China to undertake a historic transformation of its economy towards more efficient and sustainable development. The combination of measures including structural reform, energy transformation, new technology and new patterns of international trade and wider cooperation offers hope for continued economic growth with greater environmental amenity and higher productivity (Song 2022).

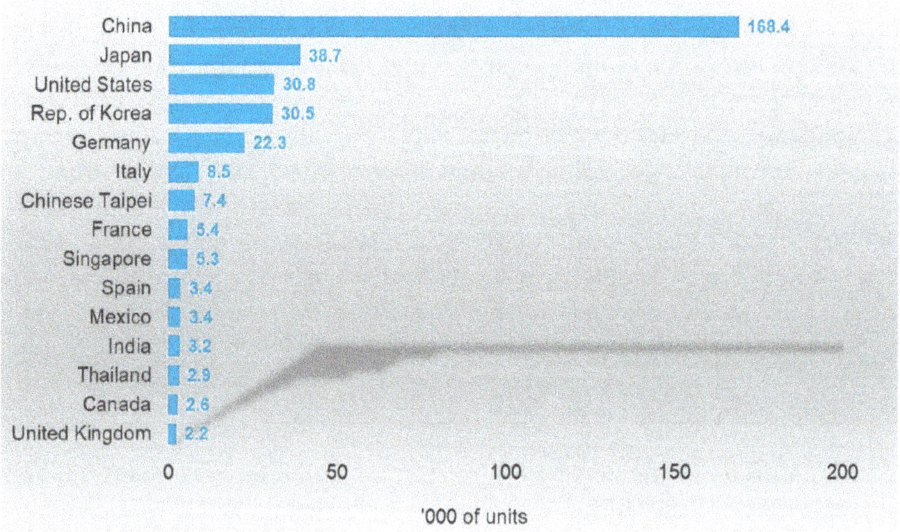

Figure 1.2 Annual installation of industrial robots, 15 largest markets, 2020
Source: International Federation of Robotics.

Billions of 2010 constant PPP dollars

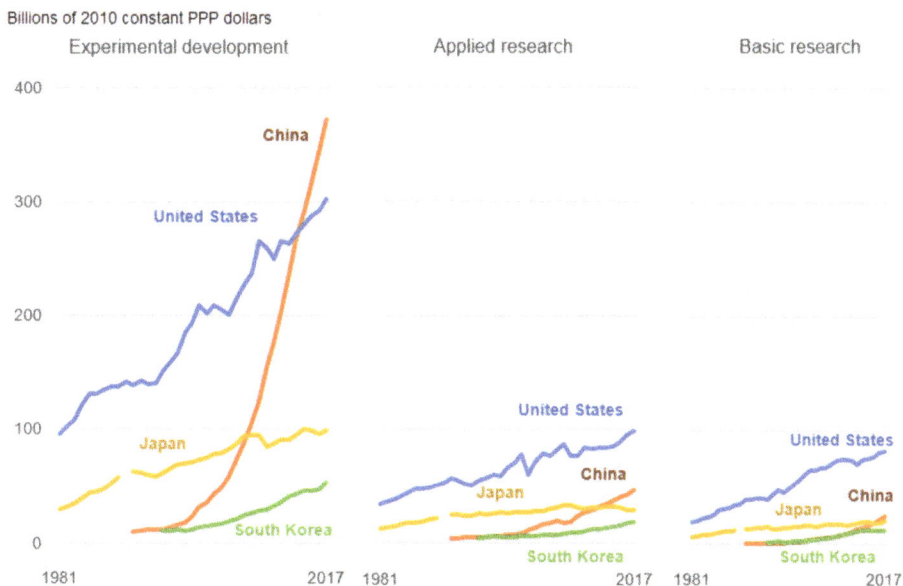

Figure 1.3 China leads the world in experimental development spending

Source: US National Science Foundation based on OECD statistics (available from: www.nsf.gov/statistics/2020/nsf20304/overview.htm).

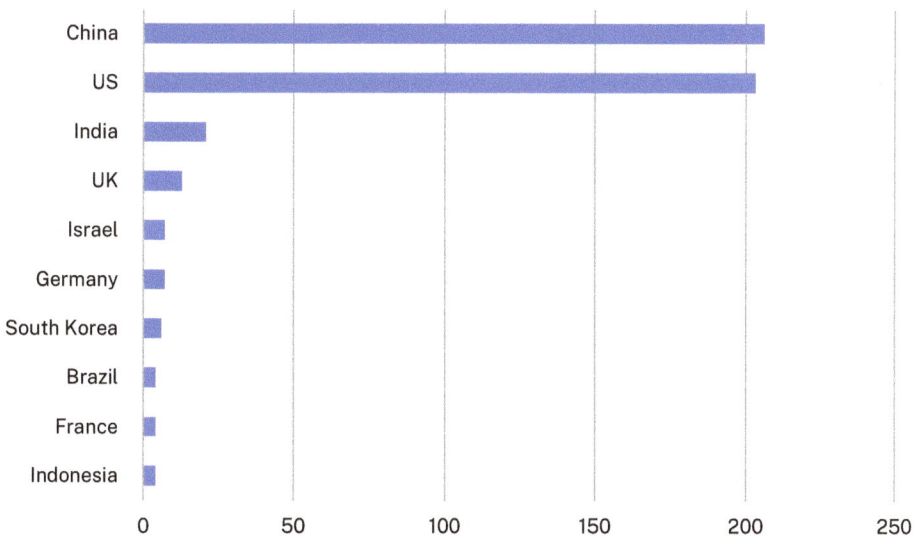

Figure 1.4 Top 10 countries for number of unicorn firms, 2019

Note: A 'unicorn' startup or company is a private company with a valuation of more than $1 billion. As of August 2020, there were more than 400 unicorns around the world.

Source: Hurun Institute.

Structural problems to be tackled in the next phase of growth

There are three structural problems that must be addressed to lower risks to growth: high debt and the associated financial risks, high income inequality and the deepening of integration with international markets. China's National Institution for Finance and Development (NIFD) estimated the country's overall debt to be 270.1 per cent of GDP at the end of 2020—up from 246.5 per cent at the end of 2019 (Figure 1.5). Although lower than the United States, China's debt-to-GDP ratio almost doubled in the decade after the GFC. Current deleveraging is focused on the non-financial corporate sector, where it is expected to fall by 6.5 percentage points, according to the NIFD. Reducing the stock debt is just the first step in creating a more sustainable debt model. Another important step is to remove implicit government guarantees for large institutions and allow creative destruction to reallocate resources from unproductive to more productive firms, thus enhancing the return on investment and economic growth and the ability to pay down the debt burden. This change could be seen in the Evergrande debt crisis that began in 2021.

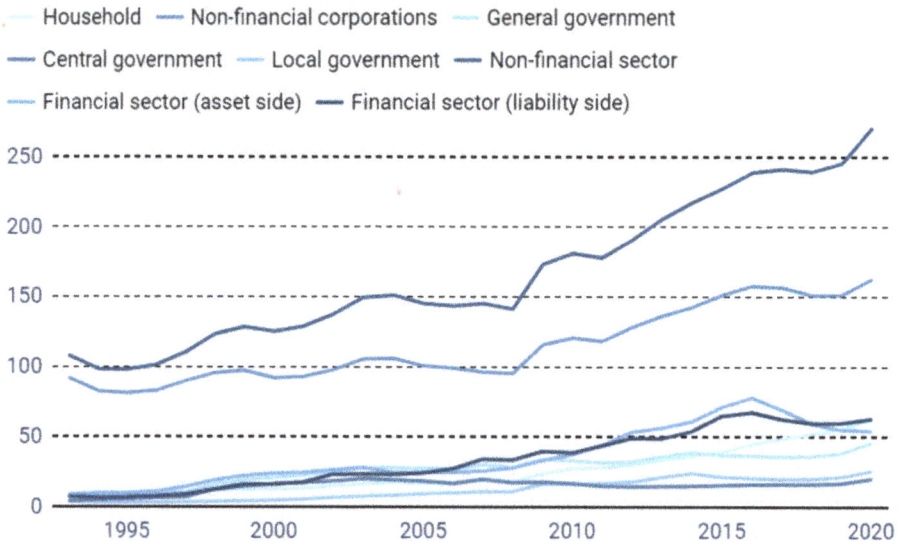

Figure 1.5 China's internal debt
Source: Authors' construction based on data from the CEIC Database.

The second structural problem is high income inequality (Figure 1.6). Piketty et al. (2019) find that China's inequality level was less than Europe's in the late 1970s—close to the most egalitarian Nordic countries—while it is now approaching US levels. The rapid increase in income inequality has put China among the most unequal countries in Asia and indeed the world. China is now among the least equal

25 per cent of countries worldwide—a group to which very few Asian countries belong. With a Gini coefficient of 0.47, China's level of income inequality is like that of several high-inequality Latin American countries (Sicular 2013) and approaching that of the United States (Piketty et al. 2019). Income inequality is an economic, political and social problem for China.

Income inequality rises with the increase in per capita income and can fall once a country reaches a certain level of per capita income. This pattern is commonly referred to as the inverted Kuznets U-curve (Kuznets 1955). This implies a causal relationship running from economic or income growth to income inequality. However, potential causes of income inequality can be very complex, involving factors such as technological and structural change, political and economic institutions, social norms, culture and geography. It is even more complex for China as it is not only a developing economy but also a transitional economy. A transitional economy emphasises economic incentives but is still nurturing market means of allocating resources and the redistribution function of government policies.

As Piketty (2014: 85) quoted Charles Dunoyer (1845) as saying: 'Reduce everything to equality and you will bring everything to a standstill.' However, there is evidence that overemphasising income equality at the expense of incentives and efficiency can compromise growth. Therefore, finding the right balance between efficiency and equity is one of the most challenging tasks for China's economic reform and public policy.

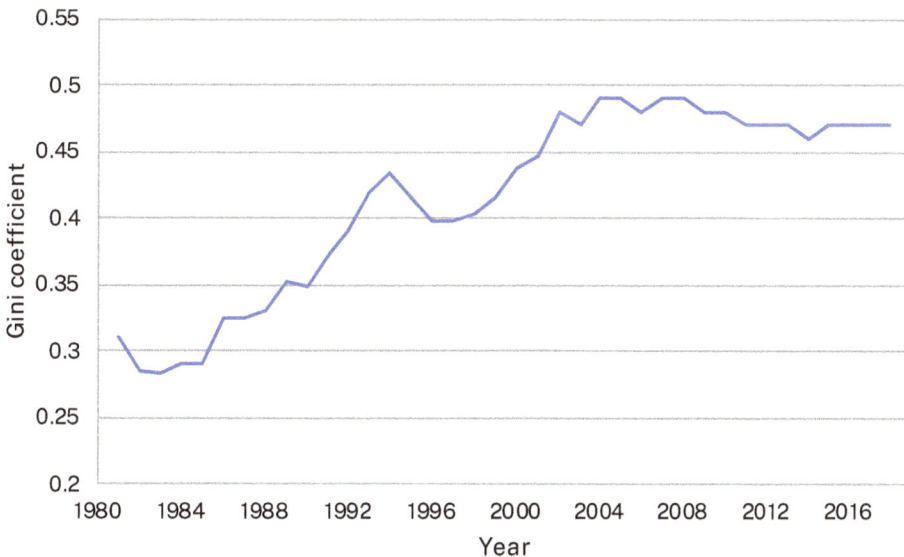

Figure 1.6 Gini coefficient in China, 1981–2018

Source: Zhou and Song (2016). Gini coefficients for the years 1981–2001 are from Ravallion and Chen (2007); for 2002 from WIND; 2003–18 from the National Bureau of Statistics of China.

To develop sound policies to alleviate income inequality, it is important to identify the roles and evolution of its various drivers such as the urban–rural income gap, intra-urban and intra-rural income gaps, the income gap due to incomplete economic reforms such as that between workers employed in monopolistic industries and those in more competitive sectors, regional inequality attributed to different levels of trade liberalisation, fiscal decentralisation and marketisation in various regions in China and the income gap due to different skill and education levels.

As well as rising income inequality, wealth concentration in China has sharply increased over the past decades. The share of wealth of the top 10 per cent of citizens rose from 40 per cent in 1995 to 67 per cent in 2015, while the wealth shares of the middle 40 per cent and bottom 50 per cent were much reduced. As a result, while wealth inequality was much lower in China than in the West in the mid-1990s, it is now between European and US levels. The wealth share of the top 10 per cent of Chinese (67 per cent in 2015) is approaching that of the United States (72 per cent) and is much higher than a country like France (50 per cent). The wealth share of the bottom 50 per cent is now barely higher than in rich countries, where it is usually around 0–5 per cent. According to Piketty et al. (2019), savings flows explain 50 to 60 per cent of the rise in the wealth–income ratio since 1978, while the increase in relative asset prices accounts for the remaining 40 to 50 per cent. That is, equity and housing prices have increased above and beyond the rise in consumer prices. These causes of rising inequality present a big challenge for China in pursuing its policy of 'common prosperity' to achieve more equal outcomes from growth and development.

The third structural problem is how China can integrate further with international markets. China has grown into a world manufacturing powerhouse, propelled by the lowering of institutional barriers to international trade and technological change that leads to declining transportation and communication costs and facilitates global value chains. In the future, China could move beyond being a manufacturing powerhouse to become a financial powerhouse as well. The economic fundamentals suggest this change would be beneficial for long-term growth in China, but the institutional challenges are significant.

Economic fundamentals favour a portfolio adjustment to China's market. First, let us look at the economic fundamentals. As China's exports to international markets become more uncertain due to trade conflicts resulting from rising protectionism, China must rely more on domestic investment and consumption to drive economic growth. However, this switch of GDP composition faces headwinds, including the ageing demographic structure. Population ageing has caused China's domestic savings rate to decline continuously from its peak of 50 per cent in 2010 to 45 per cent in 2019. This decline contributed to the fall in the net exports to GDP ratio following the GFC as well as tighter availability of investment funds and declining rates of domestic investment. To counteract these downward forces on investment, one possibility is for China to undertake reforms to boost the efficiency of fund allocation and thus raise investment returns. These reforms would go beyond financial market reforms and involve enhancing competitive neutrality and balancing out market forces and government intervention in investment decisions. The other possibility is for further financial opening and integration with the world capital market, which could lead to global portfolios balancing towards the Chinese financial market and greater foreign capital inflows to fund investment in China.

It could be an opportune time for China to implement financial integration as a long-term growth strategy. Aided by the inclusion of Chinese bonds in global benchmark indices and China's Bond Connect program, which allows foreign fund managers to trade in the country's debt markets without an onshore trading entity, there has been a strong pickup in foreign buying of Chinese bonds and an increase in exposure to Chinese debt in recent months. Foreign investors accounted for about 12 per cent of all purchases of Chinese Government and policy bank bonds in 2020. China's onshore fixed-income market is the second largest in the world, with a total of US$13.7 trillion in outstanding bonds as of December 2019, and the government is the major issuer of bonds (Figures 1.7 and 1.8).

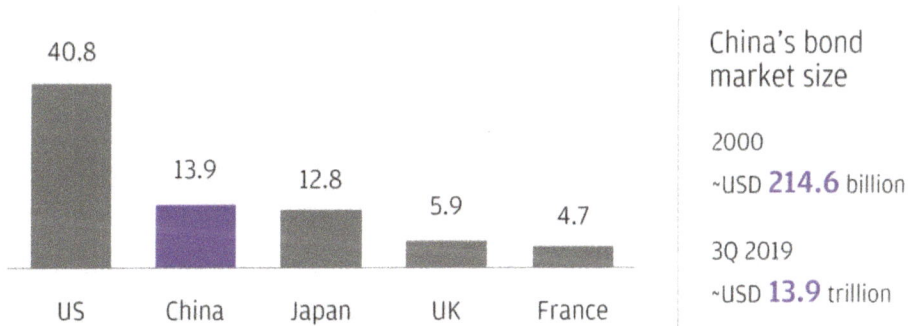

Figure 1.7 The world's top five bond markets (market size in US$ trillion)
Source: J.P.Morgan.

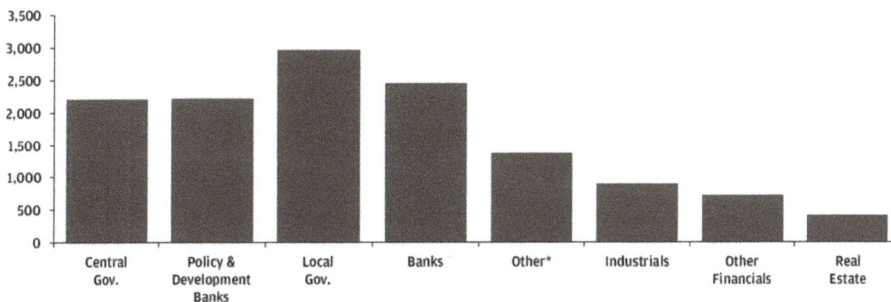

Figure 1.8 The government is the largest issuer of onshore bonds in China
Source: J.P.Morgan.

China's bond market is still developing and foreign investors face challenges. First, onshore bond market trading lacks market-makers to facilitate buying and selling and bonds are traded directly between parties on the interbank market. Although this could help preserve the lower volatility than traditional safe assets that is attracting foreign investors, it also means less liquidity compared with US Treasury Bonds and greater difficulty for investors to enter and exit the market quickly. Second, there is conjecture that the acceleration of financial opening is partly motivated by China's consideration to pre-empt possible US financial decoupling. With more integration into global financial markets, financial decoupling could be more difficult and the leverage of financial decoupling could decrease as well.

What does a financially integrated Chinese market mean for the global economy? Tyers and Zhou (2020) show that China's financial openness, as measured by cross-border flows and asset ownership, peaked during its growth surge in the 2000s, as did downward pressure on global interest rates and prices. Globally, China's growth surge raised asset prices, reduced yields and bolstered deflationary pressures, while improving aggregate economic welfare. Therefore, greater financial integration between China and the world will amplify the impacts on the global economy of China's economic growth and moderate the effects on China's domestic economy.

China's integration into the global financial system will require further financial reform and opening, including capital account liberalisation and full convertibility of the renminbi. At the same time, financial opening involves risks. China can reduce the potential risks by allowing more flexibility in renminbi exchange rates, building a more solid banking system with more stringent prudential regulations, reducing government debt at all levels through more stringent fiscal discipline and maintaining a balanced position in its international balance of payments. The last task could prove difficult given the falling domestic savings ratios due to population ageing. It could be too early to predict when China will become a net capital importer, but the prospect will have significant implications for China's long-term growth and development as well as global macroeconomic balances with respect to the relationship between savings and investments (and therefore the determination of global interest rates).

Finally, with China as the world's second largest economy and largest trading nation, it is in its fundamental interest and that of other countries to continue to champion regional and global economic reintegration in the post-Covid world, after the pandemic saw some countries pursue a strategy of self-sufficiency to safeguard supply security. Resisting the attempts of economic and technological decoupling will be crucial to help restore the global trading order in the process of economic recovery post pandemic (Song and Zhou 2020). China should actively participate in regional economic cooperation and global efforts to change the multilateral trading system (such as the WTO) to minimise the damage brought about by deglobalisation and to maximise the chances for international trade to continue as an engine for global economic growth.

Structure of the book

The *2022 China Update* examines the key characteristics of China's transition to a new phase of economic growth and development. It covers a range of diverse topics that reflect the complex and changing nature of the economy. It explores the critical questions of why China needs a new development paradigm and how best to achieve it. What are China's choices when faced with the restructuring of global industrial value chains? What roles will domestic consumption play in the next phase of China's development? What does digital transformation mean for the Chinese economy? What has been the impact of the Covid-19 pandemic on domestic income inequality and labour market outcomes? What pathways exist for China in its transition to carbon neutrality? How does China's emissions-trading market compare with that of Europe? What will be the impacts of China's carbon-neutrality strategy on the Australian economy? And what are the political factors influencing bilateral trade flows between China and its trading partners and what is at stake for China–US bilateral relations?

In Chapter 2, Justin Yifu Lin addresses the question of why China needs a new development paradigm—the dual-circulation strategy in which domestic circulation is the core element and domestic and international circulations promote each other. The fact is that 82.6 per cent of China's GDP in 2019 arose from domestic consumption, suggesting that internal circulation already dominates China's economy. Lin argues that the proportion of China's exports dropped from 35.4 per cent in 2006 to 17.4 per cent in 2019 because of the massive increase in its economic size and per capita income in the intervening years, as well as the rapid expansion of the service industry.

Even as China makes domestic circulation the core of development, it must simultaneously promote dual domestic and international circulation. This is because, from the perspective of the new structural economics, the products of industries with comparative advantages should not only circulate in the domestic market, but also enter the international market to realise economies of scale and accelerate economic growth and capital accumulation. This means that to reduce the cost of economic development, China should make greater use of all kinds of goods, including natural resources, capital and technology, which can be provided by the international market at a lower cost than domestic production.

On China's potential for future growth and development, the chapter argues that future development potential depends not on current income levels, but on the gap between China and developed countries such as the United States. Although China's population is beginning to age, its per capita GDP is only 22.6 per cent of that of the United States. Technological innovation and industrial upgrading can make use of the latecomer advantage and reallocate labour from low value-added to high value-added industries to improve labour productivity. The room for such adjustments is still very large. So, it is possible for China to achieve an average annual growth rate of about 6 per cent in the period 2021–35. The most important thing is for China to recognise its potential, do its own thing well and deepen both reform and opening.

In Chapter 3, Xiaojing Zhang and Cheng Li apply a national balance sheet approach to understanding China's economic development in terms of its aggregate sectors such as wealth accumulation, structural distribution and macro financial risks over the past decades. Their findings show that China has continued to make phenomenal progress in accumulating wealth and playing the role of net provider of savings to the rest of the world over the reform period. China's wealth expansion has generally outpaced GDP growth.

Their findings also show that China's strong propensity for saving and upward asset revaluation has contributed to the expansion of national wealth. On the one hand, the high savings rate corresponds to rapid fixed-capital formation, thereby leading to continuous incremental growth in non-financial assets. Apart from savings, the revaluation of assets, including land and housing, serves as another important driver of rapid growth in China's aggregate wealth.

The results from an international comparison show that, in 2018, China's GDP reached 65 per cent of that in the United States and its level of wealth reached 80 per cent of that in the United States. China's wealth exceeded that of Japan, Germany, France and the United Kingdom combined, while its GDP was only slightly smaller than the sum of these four countries. This indicates that China has made even greater strides in its economic catch-up from a stock perspective than a flow perspective. This suggests that China's overall national strength, as measured by wealth, ranks second in the world behind only the United States and the gap between the two countries has become even narrower than GDP figures would suggest.

However, as argued by the authors, China's wealth data become far less rosy than aggregate indicators would suggest due to problems including so-called zombie firms and implicit local government debt, wealth inequality and the efficiency of wealth accumulation. At the same time, China's wealth distribution is skewed in favour of the government sector. Their data show that there has been a slowing accumulation of household financial assets because of China's underdeveloped direct financing market and the decreasing share of stocks and equities held by the household sector since 2013. The authors look at financial risks from the balance sheet perspective and conclude that, despite the successes in reducing financial risks, China's overall macroeconomic risks remain alarmingly high and tend to concentrate in government and other public institutions.

To reduce financial risks, the chapter argues that China should: create a well-functioning property system for the paid acquisition and use of natural resources; improve the exit mechanism for the state sector from the economy; optimise the associated layout of state-owned assets/capital in favour of market efficiency; and reform the distribution of aggregate wealth/income in favour of households, especially low and middle-income families, to improve the allocative efficiency of economic resources and the promotion of private consumption. The chapter concludes by noting that it is important to neutralise implicit government guarantees in favour of a 'sustainable' debt accumulation path featuring market-based risk pricing. This also requires a mix of policies aimed at restructuring bankrupt SOEs and hardening and enforcing the budgetary discipline of local governments.

China has been undergoing some fundamental changes in applying digital technology in the economy. In Chapter 4, Yiping Huang discusses the platform economy, which refers to the new economic model that relies on network infrastructure such as cloud computing, the internet and mobile technology and uses digital technology such as artificial intelligence, R&D, big-data analysis and blockchain to match transactions, transmit content and manage processes. The chapter shows that the development of China's platform economy is a product not only of digital technological progress, but also of market-oriented reforms, as all the top platforms are privately owned. Measured by the number of world-leading platforms in 2019, each with a market valuation of more than US$10 billion, China's platform economy is now the second largest in the world, second only to the United States.

The chapter highlights the main factors in China's success in developing its platform economy, including, first, the development of good digital infrastructure, which provides the technological basis for digital platforms to connect with huge numbers of users anytime and anywhere. The second is the huge population, which makes some digital economic innovations more feasible and efficient. The third factor is relatively weak protection of individual rights. The downside of this weak protection is widespread illegal collection and analysis of personal data and violation of individuals' privacy. The fourth factor is segregation from the international market, which protects domestic platforms from international competition and provides space for them to innovate and grow. Of all these factors, the third is already changing and the fourth must change eventually. Therefore, maintaining the innovative capability of platform enterprises and ensuring sustainable growth of the platform economy in China are important challenges for both enterprises and the government.

The chapter argues that the platform enterprises have already brought about some fundamental changes to the Chinese economy, including their roles in supporting innovation, promoting growth, improving efficiency and providing jobs. At the same time, there are some new challenges for emerging platform enterprises, including unfair competition that harms consumers. Some platforms use their vast market power to crowd out competitors or stifle innovation by means of 'killer' mergers and acquisitions to eliminate competitors.

The chapter then reaches the following conclusions: first, China has developed a large platform economy within a relatively short period, but most domestic platforms do not enjoy technological advantages. Second, some key characteristics of the platform economy have mixed impacts on economic operations. Third, the original intention of China's 'strong regulation' was to achieve orderly and healthy development, but 'campaign-style' regulation and regulatory competition have already caused many problems. Fourth, within the broad governance structure, there should be some separation of economic regulation and antitrust policies, with the former maintaining efficient market functions and the latter repairing functions in that market. Finally, the chapter argues that China must establish a comprehensive governance system for the platform economy and suggests actively participating in the formulation of international rules, including digital tax and trade, to create conditions for Chinese platforms to compete internationally in the future.

In Chapter 5, Qiyuan Xu raises two important challenges for China's role in global industrial chains: upgrading and security. Industrial chain upgrading must meet the requirements of China's present phase of development, while digital technology and the green economy provide it with roadmaps to the future. Industrial chain security is related more to the ongoing China–US trade conflict and Covid-19 pandemic–related shocks as well as digital technology and the imperative to create a green economy.

The chapter points out that traditional trade and production integration has evolved in the digital age, as globalisation has generated cross-border flows of information in addition to the traditional flows of commodity sales and capital. Massive cross-border flows of information have implications for national security, particularly in relation to dual-use technologies, while the mechanisms of global governance remain in the age of pre-digital globalisation. This is the context in which the chapter discusses China–US conflicts, which are uniquely complex because conflicts in the information sector directly impinge on matters of national security, and international competition to achieve technological primacy will become increasingly prominent and difficult to resolve.

The chapter then discusses the three basic trends in global industrial chain restructuring: diversification, digitisation and the low-carbon imperative. On diversification, the chapter argues that Covid-19 has affected the industrial supply chains of different countries to varying degrees and global supply chains have encountered enormous uncertainty. Adjustments have been made to the structure of the supply chains for medicines, computer chips and other key industries, and the establishment of domestic emergency backup supply chains, the repatriation of key industries, a return to regionalisation as well as the shortening of supply chains have occurred. On digitisation, the chapter argues that China has a strong manufacturing capacity and a complete supporting network, which provide a good foundation for the application of digital technology in manufacturing. However, the digital development of China's industrial chain also faces challenges, including setting up the rules of governance for cybersecurity and cybergovernance systems. Tackling climate change has added constraints to the growth potential of developing economies and, in the context of the trend towards low carbon, carbon tariffs will make an export-oriented development model more difficult to replicate.

In this context, the chapter argues that China's industrial chains are both globally influential and vulnerable. While China possesses a significant export advantage in high-centrality intermediate goods, the chapter identifies several categories of intermediate goods that are the most vulnerable supply chains for China, including electrical machinery and audio and video equipment. China must therefore pay particular attention to this industry's supply chain security. The chapter then identifies a paradox in industrial supply chains: a country cannot have global influence and competitiveness in an industrial supply chain while simultaneously possessing complete autonomy and control over that chain. The chapter provides case studies of nine major economies that provide strong evidence of this paradox, suggesting that China must create positive political relationships with major nations to secure the competitiveness and efficiency of its industries in improving its industrial supply chain security. The chapter then discusses the new trends in China–US technological competition and China's industrial supply chain strategy on outward relocation versus inward relocation and international regional reorganisation.

China's new strategic priority is to effectively expand domestic demand in driving economic growth. In Chapter 6, Wang Wei argues that it is imperative to craft an integrated system for consumption-led domestic demand and to introduce a new growth mechanism for efficient alignment, strong stimulation, accelerated innovation and orderly transformation towards such a system.

The chapter argues that more robust reform measures are needed to unleash potential domestic demand and fuel growth in China in a more stable and sustained manner. Those measures include deepening supply-side structural reform to ensure effective market supply, accelerating the reform of income distribution and optimising social policies to enhance household affordability and consumption levels, improving policies for consumption growth to consolidate the institutional foundation for expanding domestic demand, transforming and upgrading the manufacturing industry to create a virtuous cycle between investment and consumption, scaling up institutional opening of the service industry for mutual reinforcement between domestic and international circulation, fixing weak infrastructure links to better unleash potential domestic demand and enhancing the green consumption system to foster a green and healthy consumption culture.

Reform of the *hukou* ('household registration') system remains an unfinished task in China. In Chapter 7, Kunling Zhang uses the evolution of China's *hukou* system to illustrate institutional change and its interaction with economic dynamics. The chapter argues that the *hukou* system profoundly affects China's economic development and, in turn, the transformation of China's economy has been deeply shaped by the evolution of *hukou*.

The chapter establishes a theoretical framework of endogenous institutional change to analyse the evolution of the *hukou* system. This framework helps to improve the understanding of general institutional change and offers policymakers a better understanding of decision-making processes in dynamic contexts. Building further on the framework, the chapter applies the concept of adaptive efficiency to evaluate the evolution of China's *hukou* system. This provides an alternative approach to institutional efficiency evaluation and bridges the theories of endogenous institutional change and adaptive efficiency.

The chapter finds that the institutionalisation of the rigid *hukou* system was mainly an exogenous change process implemented from the top down, in which central government enforcement played a dominant role and the roles of individual and local governments were largely neglected; and the rigid *hukou* system eventually hindered economic transformation, thereby inducing its own reform. Reform has fundamentally been an endogenous change process, in which spontaneous market forces and the role of local governments have bounced back through a rebalancing of the powers of the state and market and between central and local governments.

The findings demonstrate that *hukou* reform clarified the property rights of the labour force and rural land, promoted the formation of a decentralised decision-making mechanism, strengthened the role of competition in both the labour and the product markets, reduced the transaction costs of labour mobility and maintained a degree of institutional flexibility that rewarded success and eliminated failures in the system.

The chapter concludes that to further reform the *hukou* system and promote its adaptive efficiency, decision-makers should respect the endogenous forces and logic of adaptation in institutional change. The transaction costs of population mobility must be reduced—not just of migration *per se*, but also of the availability of the 'welfare' attached to *hukou*. Fair competition is necessary to eliminate *hukou*-based discrimination in both the labour and the land markets.

The Covid-19 pandemic is having profound impacts on people's wellbeing. In Chapter 8, Li Shi and Zhan Peng assess the impact of the early Covid-19 outbreak on income distribution and poverty in rural China using mixed data sources. Their objectives are to provide a new method to study the impact of the pandemic in different segments of income distribution.

The main results show that the impact of Covid-19 in the first half of 2020 was expected to reduce the per capita disposable income of rural residents by about 7 per cent throughout the year (baseline model), with the lowest income group suffering the most. If the real income growth rate of rural residents in 2020 was like that in 2019, the pandemic could offset all real growth, leaving real income growth in 2020 at approximately 0 per cent. If the pandemic led to a significant drop in wage rates, its impact on rural incomes would be greatly exacerbated. The pandemic increased the incidence of rural income poverty by 0.38 percentage points.

The chapter also finds that the impact of the pandemic on agricultural production and operations was not obvious, but if it had not been controlled in time, more than 70 per cent of rural households would have been hit harder and the problem of returning to poverty could have been more serious. Timely control of the pandemic, an early emphasis on the farming sector in February 2020 and other measures guaranteed the basic living needs of rural families to a certain extent. The policy implications of the findings are that, to avoid expanding the impact of a future pandemic on residents' income and poverty, steps should be taken to prevent the impact lasting too long and increasing in depth. At the same time, restrictions on the normal operation of key economic activities should be reduced as much as possible to prevent the wage rates of vulnerable workers being significantly affected.

Continuing to look at the impact of the Covid-19 pandemic, Dandan Zhang in Chapter 9 investigates the labour market consequences of China's stringent lockdown policies using comprehensive employee tracking data for 2020. The main findings include the pace of resurgence of the Chinese labour market since March 2020. Among workers from 2019 who were surveyed and tracked in 2020, 61 per cent had resumed work in March 2020; by the end of November, the rate of work resumption had risen by almost 30 per cent to reach about 90 per cent. Second, the findings demonstrate that, even though China's lockdowns effectively controlled the spread of Covid-19, they had substantial impacts on the labour market by delaying the pace of work resumption and causing more job losses during the pandemic period.

Third, the research points out that the unemployment effects of lockdowns can be detected in only a relatively short period. At the end of November, the negative and significant effects of pandemic lockdowns on work resumption could no longer be found. Finally, consistent with the existing literature on the economic crisis and mental health, the chapter finds that the inadequate employment due to the pandemic lockdown imposed negative effects on the mental health status of the labour force, especially those falling into unemployment. The chapter concludes by arguing that understanding the broader social and health impacts of different counter-Covid-19 policies is critical for optimal policy design.

China's carbon neutrality commitment provides a strategic opportunity for its new phase of development. Yongsheng Zhang and Xiang Yu in Chapter 10 argue that carbon neutrality not only poses a huge challenge but also provides a strategic opportunity for China to start a new journey of building a moderately prosperous society. The global consensus on and action towards carbon neutrality mark the end of the traditional industrial era and the beginning of a new era of green development. Carbon neutrality will bring transformative changes to China's economy and is expected to create miracles of high-quality development in the next 40 years. However, achieving this target depends on whether China can realise a fundamental shift in its development paradigm.

The chapter explains why China has proposed 'dual carbon' goals, reflecting the shift from being asked to act to wanting to act. This is mainly because, facing ever-increasing environmental problems, the Chinese Government has realised that the traditional development model is unsustainable and reducing carbon emissions is in its own interests. The authors argue that carbon neutrality can be understood as a profound shift in the development paradigm because it will completely reconstruct the economic system and spatial patterns of the traditional industrial era. As the content and mode of development change, the traditional economic system will be reshaped.

The chapter argues that carbon neutrality could facilitate an economic leap forward because a green transition will drive the economy towards a more competitive structure. However, the dual-carbon goals pose big challenges for China's manufacturing transformation, the biggest of which is how to simultaneously achieve peak carbon and carbon neutrality and maintain manufacturing's share in the economy. The dual-carbon goals are expected to bring about a substantial adjustment in relative prices. The green transition will mean a substantial adjustment in the economic structure: the share of the high-carbon economy will decrease and that of the low-carbon economy will increase.

The chapter suggests two major policy directions. The first is promoting the development of the low-carbon economy. The second is addressing transitional justice. Although green transformation represents a strategic opportunity in the long run, many industries will be severely impacted. Fossil fuel industries and dependent regions will be the first to bear the brunt of transition, including coal, oil and some heavy chemical industries, as well as specific employment groups. China must take strong measures to help with the transition and provide vocational training and financial transfers.

In Chapter 11, Haocheng Shang and Fang-Fang Tang examine the mechanisms and development of emissions-trading markets, comparing the European Union and China. After providing a brief history of global emissions-trading markets, the chapter explains how markets are categorised as either voluntary carbon markets or compliance carbon markets, which differ significantly in terms of regulations, market size and other factors.

In the case of the European Union, its emissions-trading scheme (ETS) is a 'cap and trade' scheme, which sets an absolute limit or 'cap' on the total amount of certain greenhouse gases (GHGs) that can be emitted each year by the entities covered by the scheme. This cap is reduced over time so that total emissions fall. Since the scheme's introduction in 2005, emissions have been cut by 42.8 per cent in the main sectors covered. Auctioning is the default method for distributing carbon allowances to companies participating in the EU ETS, which has very strict penalties for noncompliance—a distinct characteristic of emissions-trading markets compared with typical financial markets and consistent with the motivation of managing GHG emissions.

In the case of China, as in the European Union, the development of its carbon-trading market is a gradual process, although from 2000 to 2020, China made huge progress. On 16 July 2021, trading began in China's national emissions-trading market, the China ETS, into which existing regional pilot schemes are gradually transitioning. The China ETS started with 2,162 firms in the power generation sector—a sector that accounts for 4 billion tonnes of GHG emissions annually—meaning China's scheme surpassed the capacity of the EU ETS and became the world's largest. Carbon allowances are priced in renminbi (RMB). On opening day, trading began at RMB48 per tonne and closed at RMB52.80 per tonne, hitting the daily 10 per cent upper limit on price variation.

The chapter identifies two similarities between the EU ETS and that of China: both are large and unified markets and both have strong political motivation to develop. However, how to regulate a large ETS is a new subject for policymakers. The European Union has a strong desire to be a leader on climate change issues and China aims to be an 'ecological civilisation'. Political motivations push the progress of emissions-trading markets. Given the climate crisis, management of GHG emissions and corresponding trading schemes will be an increasingly important subject in international politics.

In Chapter 12, Xiujian Peng, Xunpeng Shi, Shenghao Feng and James Laurenceson examine the impacts on the Australian economy at the national and state levels and by industry of the transition to carbon neutrality in China using the Victoria University Regional Model (VURM) framework. The chapter highlights the importance of understanding the impacts on Australia's interests of climate action at home and abroad. First, the revenue from its world-leading role as a liquefied natural gas (LNG) and coal exporter is being challenged by the transition away from fossil fuels to renewable energy in other parts of the world, especially in its major fossil fuel export markets: China, Japan and South Korea. Second, understanding the impacts can inform Australia's policies to achieve a just energy transition domestically. Under Australia's federal system, a just energy transition will involve supporting vulnerable regional communities that are affected negatively and disproportionately.

Their simulation results show that although China's imports of Australian fossil fuels will fall significantly, the impact of those changes on the national economy will be negligible. However, the mining sector and those states and territories that rely on fossil fuel production will suffer relatively larger effects. The substantial changes in China's energy mix imply significant changes to its fossil fuel imports. China's import demand for coal, crude oil and gas will fall sharply. By 2050, China's imports of coal will be nearly 60 per cent lower, gas will be more than 47 per cent lower and oil imports will be nearly 35 per cent lower than they were in the baseline scenario. By 2060, China's imports of coal and gas will be more than 60 per cent lower and its oil imports will be nearly 50 per cent lower. The results also show that the decreased demand for Australia's coal, LNG and iron ore caused by China's carbon-neutrality action will reduce Australia's terms of trade, leading to negative structural effects on capital, investment and real GDP.

The chapter concludes by noting the mixed effects of China's net-zero transition on Australian industries, with fossil fuel industries losing, while some other industries, especially export-oriented ones, gain. Regions with high coal and LNG industry concentrations, such as the Northern Territory and Queensland, will be disproportionately and negatively affected.

In Chapter 13, Vishesh Argawal, Jane Golley and Tunye Qiu take an analytical approach to examining the extent to which moderate shocks in political relations affected the exports to China's of four of its major trading partners—Australia, India, Japan and the United States—between 2001 and 2020. During this period, China experienced frequent episodes of both political cooperation and political conflict with each of these trading partners.

The chapter reviews literature that investigates the extent to which moderate shocks in political relations affect trade outcomes. The findings can be summarised as: trade strengthens when 'bonds of friendship' (or political cooperation) strengthen, in the short run only (suggesting accidental deviations from a Pareto optimal equilibrium in which there is no long-term relationship) or in both the short and the long runs (suggesting that politics has significant and lasting impacts on trade); trade weakens in times of conflict (in the short and/or the long runs); and there is no evidence of political relations impacting on trade in either of these two ways.

This chapter finds that government shocks had no significant short or long-run effects on any of the four countries' exports over this period. In contrast, evidence of small, positive short-term effects was found following a shock to the military–

political relations index for Australia and the United States, with Australian exports experiencing a long-term positive effect as well. For Japan and India, there were no significant short or long-term coefficients for either of the two political relations indices.

The key conclusion from the chapter is that trade is overwhelmingly undertaken by companies that are principally motivated by economic considerations, such as profit, cost and quality. These considerations reflect cross-country variation in production complementarities and purchasing power. These economic fundamentals create a separation between these actors and the strategists in country capitals preoccupied with geopolitical alignment and could also ensure that trading links are strengthened even as political relations decline.

The precarious US–China relationship is causing many uncertainties globally. In Chapter 14, Wing Thye Woo discusses this important relationship by focusing on three areas of competition between the two countries: economic, geostrategic and technological.

In examining the bilateral relations, the chapter points out that the institutional arrangements that define the three types of competition could become the basis of US–China cooperation to coordinate the supply of global public goods to ensure common global prosperity in a harmonious world that achieves the United Nations' 17 Sustainable Development Goals and the 1.5°C target of the Paris climate treaty.

Realising these goals, according to this chapter, will require China and the United States to share a realistic definition of what constitutes national security in a multipolar world. It is also suggested that the construction of institutional arrangements between the United States and China will address their respective national security concerns without negatively impacting their economic interaction. Furthermore, those institutional arrangements can keep geostrategic and technological competition from causing a downward spiral in economic ties that could end globalisation.

The chapter accordingly makes an important suggestion to enhance EU-style deep regional economic integration, which could be called the Pacific Asia Union (PAU). Such a union would not only be difficult to manipulate to participate in a proxy war, but also would not accept a subservient relationship to any big power. The PAU would be big enough to be a persuasive voice in moderating US–China tensions and to work with multilateral institutions to help develop sensible rules for US–China engagement.

The chapter comes up with some concrete steps that could be taken moving forward. To reverse the downward spiral in US–China relations, Australia and the Association of Southeast Asian Nations (ASEAN) should encourage the Asian-Pacific community to merge the overlapping economic blocs of the Regional Comprehensive Economic

Partnership Agreement, the Comprehensive and Progressive Agreement for Trans-Pacific Partnership and the Indo-Pacific Economic Framework to form the PAU. The second step is for the PAU to work with the United Nations and its agencies to formulate guidelines for US–China relations that would segment their economic, technological and geostrategic competition.

References

Cai, F. 2018. 'How Has the Chinese Economy Capitalized on the Demographic Dividend during the Reform Period?' In R. Garnaut, L. Song and F. Cai (eds), *China's 40 Years of Reform and Development: 1978–2018*, pp. 235–56. Canberra: ANU Press. doi.org/10.22459/CYRD.07.2018.13.

Kuznets, S. 1955. 'Economic Growth and Income Inequality.' *American Economic Review* 65(1): 1–28.

Piketty, T. 2014. *Capital in the Twenty-First Century*. Cambridge, MA: Belknap Press of Harvard University Press.

Piketty, T., L. Yang and G. Zucman. 2019. 'Capital Accumulation, Private Property, and Rising Inequality in China, 1978–2015.' *American Economic Review* 109(7): 2469–96. doi.org/10.1257/aer.20170973.

Ravallion, M. and S. Chen. 2007. 'China's (Uneven) Progress against Poverty.' *Journal of Development Economics* 82(1): 1–42. doi.org/10.1016/j.jdeveco.2005.07.003.

Sicular, T. 2013. 'The Challenge of High Inequality in China.' *Inequality in Focus* 2(2): 1–5. doi.org/10.1017/CBO9781139035057.003.

Song, L. 2022. 'Decarbonizing China's Steel Industry.' In R. Garnaut (ed.), *The Superpower Transformation: Making Australia's Zero-Carbon Future*, pp. 219–39. Melbourne: La Trobe University Press.

Song, L. and Y. Zhou. 2020. 'The COVID-19 Pandemic and Its Impact on the Global Economy: What Does It Take to Turn Crisis into Opportunity?' *China & World Economy* 28(4): 1–25. doi.org/10.1111/cwe.12349.

Tyers, R. and Zhou, Y. 2020. 'US-China Trade Conflict: The Macro Policy Choices,' *The World Economy* 43(9): 2286–2314.

United Nations (UN). 2015. *The Millennium Development Goals Report 2015*. New York, NY: UN.

World Bank. 2009. *Innovative China: New Drivers of Growth*. Washington, DC: The World Bank. Available from: openknowledge.worldbank.org/handle/10986/32351.

Zhou, Y. and L. Song. 2016. 'Income Inequality in China: Causes and Policy Responses.' *China Economic Journal* 9(2): 186–208. doi.org/10.1080/17538963.2016.1168203.

2

China's new development paradigm and future development

Justin Yifu Lin

The year 2021 was the year in which China was to achieve its First Centenary Goal,[1] start the Fourteenth Five-Year Plan and the Long-Term Goal for 2035 and move towards its second centenary goal of the Chinese nation's great rejuvenation. In 2018, General Secretary of the Chinese Communist Party (CCP) Central Committee and President of China Xi Jinping declared the world was facing a great change unseen in a century, and in 2020 he proposed a new development paradigm to serve China's future economic development. In this chapter, I will discuss the following four questions: Why is the world undergoing a great change unseen in a century, and how will this evolve? What is the new development paradigm and how should it be implemented? What is China's future development potential? What reforms are necessary for China to tap into this future potential?

The origin and trends of 'a great change in the world unseen in a century'

'A great change in the world unseen in a century' was a statement made by President Xi Jinping at the Central Foreign Affairs Conference in June 2018. Why is this change taking place? The economy is the answer. We can see this clearly in the changes in the world's economic structure.

---

[1]   The First Centenary Goal was proposed by the Chinese Communist Party at its Fifteenth Congress in 1997, under which, at the 100th anniversary of the founding of the party in 2021, it would lead the government and the people to achieve the goal of building a moderately prosperous society, including the elimination of extreme poverty, which was achieved in 2020.

In 1900, the Eight-Nation Alliance—a coalition of forces from the United Kingdom, the United States, France, Germany, Italy, Russia, Japan and the Austro-Hungarian Empire—invaded Beijing. Their combined gross domestic product (GDP) measured on purchasing power parity (PPP) accounted for 50.4 per cent of the world's GDP (PPP).[2] The Austro-Hungarian Empire collapsed after World War I, divided into several countries, and ceased to be a world power. Later, Canada's economy grew and Canada became the large, industrialised country it is today. By 2000, the GDP of the Group of Eight (G8) countries—comprising the United States, the United Kingdom, France, Germany, Italy, Russia, Japan and Canada—accounted for 47 per cent of global GDP (PPP). After World War II, developing countries in Asia, Africa and Latin America shed their colonial and semicolonial status one after another, gained political independence, and began their pursuit of industrialisation and modernisation. However, in the century from 1900 to 2000, the proportion of the eight major powers in the global economy dropped by only 3.4 percentage points. That is, during the whole twentieth century, international politics and the global economy were dominated by these eight industrialised powers.

By 2018, when President Xi put forward his thesis of 'a great change in the world unseen in 100 years', the G8's share of global GDP had dropped to 34.7 per cent (Feenstra et al. 2015),[3] meaning it had lost the power to lead the world's political and economic affairs. The most obvious signal of this change was the outbreak of the Global Financial Crisis (GFC) in 2008 when the G20, rather than the G8, became the leading international body governing the world's response.

The two countries most affected by this change are the United States and China. In 2000, the United States accounted for 21.9 per cent of global GDP (PPP). In 2014, China surpassed the United States and became the world's largest economy, measured on PPP. The United States' GDP (PPP) now accounts for about 16 per cent of the global total and is lower than that of China. This shows the influence of the United States is declining and that of China is on the rise—a change in the status quo of which US politicians, policy research circles and the intellectual community are all keenly aware. Therefore, to maintain the predominance of the United States, former president Barack Obama put forward his strategy of a 'Pivot to the Asia-Pacific'. After president Donald Trump came to power, he launched a trade and a science and technology war against China for specious reasons, listing Huawei and other Chinese high-tech enterprises on the US trade-restriction Entity List and cutting off supply of key components to those enterprises on the list. He hoped to decouple the United States from China and ally with other countries to restrain China's development and maintain the United States' advantage in science and technology. This policy of restraining China's development and international

---

2   Russia's GDP is assumed to be half that of the former Soviet Union in the dataset (Maddison 2016).

3   By 2014, Russia had been suspended from the G8, and by 2017, it had permanently withdrawn, so that the G8 no longer existed in 2018; the G8 figure is provided for the purpose of demonstration.

influence is supported by both the Democratic and the Republican parties in the United States. It is understood that under President Joe Biden and future presidents US policy towards China will only 'change the soup but not the ingredients' (Chinese idiom for changing a book's cover but not its contents). China is now the world's largest trading country, the largest trading partner of more than 120 countries, and the second-largest trading partner of more than 70 others. This tension between the world's top-two nations could be defined by the so-called Thucydides Trap,[4] ushering in a host of challenges and uncertainties for the world and resulting in 'a great change unseen in a century'.

This great change in the world's economic structure is due to China's dynamic and rapid development since 1978 when it began to reform and open up. Development is a basic right of all countries, as stipulated in the 'Declaration on the Right to Development' unanimously approved by the UN General Assembly in 1986. Because China cannot voluntarily reduce incomes and its levels of development to alleviate the United States' anxiety about losing its predominance, a new stable world may only appear when China's economy becomes twice as big as, and reaches per capita GDP half that of, the United States.

Due to the regional income gap, if China's total per capita GDP reaches half that of the United States, the per capita GDP of its high-income regions—including the greater metropolitan areas of Beijing, Tianjin and Shanghai and the coastal provinces of Shandong, Jiangsu, Zhejiang, Fujian and Guangdong—is likely to be at the same level as that of the United States, with a combined population of more than 400 million people. The economy of this part of China will be the same size as that of the United States. GDP per capita represents the average levels of labour productivity and scientific and technological achievement. By that time, compared with this part of China's economy, the United States will no longer have an advantage in science and technology and there will be no areas in which it can strangle China's development. Meanwhile, China has another 1 billion people living in its central and western regions and their per capita GDP is only about one-third that of the United States. The economy of this part of China is roughly the same size as that of the United States and is still in the catch-up stage. Its economic growth rate will be faster than that of the United States—that is, China's overall economic growth rate will be higher than that of the United States.

Under such circumstances, relations between China and the United States may tend to ease because, first, the United States will no longer have a technological advantage with which to strangle China's development. Second, China's total economy will be

---

4   In the Thucydides Trap, an existing power will feel threatened by a new rising power and will inevitably respond, so that war becomes unavoidable. This theory originated from the study of the ancient Greek historian Thucydides. In the fifth century BCE, Sparta faced the rising power of Athens, with tensions leading to the outbreak of three decades of war that left both states devastated.

twice the size of the United States', and third, China will remain the largest market in the world. Since 2008, China has contributed about 30 per cent to the growth of the world economy and markets every year. This rate is likely to only increase in the future. A basic rule governing trade between two countries is that the smaller economy will generally benefit more than the larger one—that is, the United States stands to benefit in terms of its own employment, development and prosperity through trade with China. For its own benefit, therefore, the United States must maintain good economic and trade relations with China.

The above conclusion is supported by historical experience. In 1900, Japan was a member of the Eight-Nation Alliance. In 2000, Japan was the only country in Asia to enter the G8, making it the leading country of Asia in the twentieth century. However, in 2010, China's GDP, measured by the market exchange rate, surpassed that of Japan, and its influence was on the rise. Japan's right-wingers felt a great sense of loss and created problems including around the contested Diaoyu (Senkaku) Islands, and Sino-Japanese relations were tense. Recently, Sino-Japanese relations have improved. The reason is China's economic scale is already 2.8 times that of Japan; any unhappiness cannot change this fact. If Japan wants to develop its economy, it needs the Chinese market, so relations between the two countries have recently tended towards mutually beneficial cooperation.

In a nutshell, this 'great change unseen in a century' is due to the rise of emerging market economies, especially the rapid development of China, accompanied by changes on the global economic and political maps. A new stable world structure will eventually emerge from China's further development.

The new development paradigm

In May 2020, when President Xi visited members of the Chinese People's Political Consultative Conference National Committee, he proposed that China should 'construct a new development paradigm with domestic circulation as the core element, and domestic and international dual circulation promoting each other'. At the July meeting of the Political Bureau of the CCP Central Committee, the new development paradigm was officially adopted as the strategic orientation for China's future economic development. China is now the world's second-largest economy and the largest trading country, and any change in its strategic positioning will affect not only China itself, but also the world. In the past, the strategic orientation of China's development was to 'make full use of both domestic and international markets and both resources from China and abroad', which was generally regarded at home and abroad as the implementation of an export-oriented strategy. However, the new development paradigm proposes that China will for the first time make domestic circulation the core element—a change that has caused curiosity both domestically and internationally. The following is an analysis of why domestic circulation is the core element of the new development paradigm and whether it is still important to make full use of domestic and international markets and resources.

Domestic circulation as the core element of the new development paradigm

In his strategic positioning of the new development paradigm, President Xi proposed making domestic circulation the core element with short and long-term, deep reform considerations.

In 2020, the world experienced the outbreak of the Covid-19 pandemic. All countries endured impacts that many international economic development institutions and scholars regard as being the worst since the Great Depression in the 1930s. Most countries sustained negative economic growth, reduced household incomes, shrinking demand and sharply reduced investment, which will inevitably affect international trade. The pandemic is likely to linger beyond 2022 or even longer, and the outlook for international trade in the next few years is not optimistic.

China is a big exporting country. When exports are restrained, it needs to rely more on domestic circulation for consumption to maintain economic growth. The United States has adopted policies to restrain China's exports and continues to work to suppress China's high-tech industry. For example, it has banned the sale of Huawei products and listed some Chinese enterprises on its Entity List, restricting their exports. If these enterprises want to continue to develop, more of their products must be consumed domestically in China. This is the short-term reason for China's new position on domestic circulation.

China's move on domestic circulation is determined by the basic law of economics. Although many scholars call China's economic development model export-oriented, the fact is the proportion of exports in China's total GDP was highest in 2006, at only 35.4 per cent. By 2019, this proportion had fallen to 17.4 per cent. In other words, 82.6 per cent of China's GDP in 2019 arose from domestic consumption— data that suggest that China's economy is already dominated by internal circulation.

The declining weight of exports in GDP since 2006 reflects two basic economic laws.

1. The larger the size of a country's economy, the higher will be the proportion of domestic circulation. Modern manufacturing requires a large-scale economy. When a small economy develops a modern manufacturing industry, domestic market capacity is limited, the proportion of domestic absorption is small and most of what is produced must be exported. On the contrary, if a large economy develops modern manufacturing, there will be greater consumption in the domestic market and the proportion of exports will be relatively low. Take

Singapore as an example. In 2019, its proportion of exports to GDP was as high as 104.9 per cent because its domestic market was too small. At the same time, some component parts for export goods were imported from abroad and the finished products were exported. In 2006, China's exports accounted for only 35.4 per cent of the total economy, which was much lower than in Singapore, due to the large size of the Chinese economy.

2. The larger the share of the service industry in the whole economy, the higher will be the proportion of domestic circulation. This is because a large part of the service industry is nontradable. As of 2019, the proportion of exports in the United States and Japan—both large economies—was only 7.6 per cent and 13.4 per cent, respectively, because the service industry proportion in the total economy sat around 80 per cent and 70 per cent, respectively. Therefore, the higher the proportion of a country's service industry in the total economy, the lower will be its proportion of exports. The development level of the service industry is positively related to the economic development and income level of a country.

The proportion of China's exports dropped from 35.4 per cent in 2006 to 17.4 per cent in 2019 because of the massive increase in China's economic size and per capita income that occurred in the intervening years, as well as the rapid expansion of the service industry. In 2006, China's per capita GDP was only US$2,099, increasing to US$10,261 in 2019. In 2006, China's economy accounted for only 5.3 per cent of the world's total, and the service industry accounted for only 41.8 per cent of China's GDP. By 2019, these two figures had risen to 16.4 per cent and 53.6 per cent, respectively. The proportion of China's economy in the world economy has increased threefold, and the service industry's share of the Chinese economy has increased by 11.8 percentage points. These two changes explain the decline in the proportion of exports and the increase in the proportion of domestic circulation.

Looking to the future, China's economy will continue to develop, and its income level will continue to rise. With the increase in income level, the proportion of China's economy in the global economy will increase from 16.4 per cent to 18 per cent, then 20 per cent and then to 25 per cent. The proportion of China's service industry in total GDP will gradually approach 60 per cent, 70 per cent and then 80 per cent from the present 53.6 per cent. With the imposition of these two factors, the proportion of China's exports in the total economy will gradually drop from 17.4 per cent to 15 per cent, 12 per cent and then 10 per cent. In other words, the proportion of domestic circulation in China's GDP will gradually approach 90 per cent from the current 82.6 per cent. Therefore, China's economy is already dominated by domestic circulation and will become even more so in the future.

The Chinese Government's statement of its development paradigm simply confirms the fact that China is a big economy. With continued improvements to China's income level, its economy will become larger and larger, the proportion of the service industry in the total economy will become higher and higher and the proportion of domestic circulation will become ever larger.

It is important to clarify this fact. In the past, many within and outside China considered it to be an export-oriented economy. When the GFC hit in 2008, many foreign scholars attributed it to the global imbalance caused by China's export-oriented development strategy. The United States also unreasonably blamed China for the worsening of its trade deficit (Lin 2013a). All of this was due to widespread misperceptions about the nature of the Chinese economy.

If we mistake the Chinese economy for an export-oriented one, it is natural to expect that China will face economic trouble in the event of Sino-US trade friction or other unexpected crises, such as the impact of Covid-19 on global exports. If, instead, we clarify the fact that domestic circulation has become the core element of China's GDP, both the Chinese people and the world will be better able to recognise the economic reality and understand the laws governing economic development. If, as a large economy, China manages its own affairs well, no matter what happens in the international economy, it will be able to maintain its overall development for the better by relying on domestic circulation.

International circulation remains important

The new development paradigm explicitly highlights domestic circulation as the core element of China's economy. Is it no longer important to make full use of domestic and international markets and resources? In fact, it is just as important as ever.

The new structural economics that I advocate emphasises that, to achieve dynamic economic development, we must make full use of the comparative advantages of various countries and regions (Lin 2013c). The products of industries with comparative advantages should not only circulate in the domestic market, but also enter the international market, to realise economies of scale and accelerate economic growth and capital accumulation.

Measured by the market exchange rate, China's economy is the second largest in the world, accounting for 16.4 per cent of the world's total in 2019, which means 83.6 per cent of the global market remains to be fully relied on to better develop China's industries with comparative advantages.

China does not have comparative advantage in many industries. Many natural resources are in short supply in China and some of its capital and technology-intensive industries remain far behind those of developed countries. In addition, with ongoing economic development and accompanying rises in wage levels, China will continue to lose its comparative advantage in labour-intensive industries.

In this situation, to reduce the cost of economic development, China should make greater use of all kinds of goods, including natural resources, capital and technology, which can be provided by the international market at a lower cost than home production. For industries and products that have no comparative advantages in China, those that can be imported should be imported. The only exceptions should be those few high-tech products that are related to national or economic security and could be strangled by foreign actors.

China should carefully analyse which countries are likely to seek to strangle its development. European countries, Japan and South Korea have comparative advantages in high-tech industries, but they have no ambition to maintain or fight for global hegemony. China is the largest single market in the world. If these countries want to develop their economy well, they must also make full use of domestic and international markets and resources. To better develop their technologies and products with comparative advantages, they are unlikely to cut off their nose to spite their face by banning the export of their products to China. If we think about it carefully, the United States is the only country that has the incentive to sacrifice the opportunities of the Chinese market to maintain its position of global predominance. In the face of China's rapid economic development, its size and influence are getting closer to or even surpassing those of the United States, and Biden and future presidents of the United States are likely to continue Trump's policy of banning exports of sophisticated technologies to China, causing economic decoupling.

Most of the high-tech products for which China has no comparative advantage are available not only in the United States, but also in Europe, Japan and South Korea. As Ren Zhengfei, CEO of Huawei, said, the company should have alternative options for all kinds of high-tech products, but if it can buy them from abroad and more cheaply than producing them itself, it will continue to rely on foreign suppliers. China should do the same. This policy is also beneficial to other countries. It is only in the case of the very few products for which the United States is the sole supplier—and which China cannot import from another international source— that China should seek to produce domestically.

Even as China makes domestic circulation the core element of development, it must simultaneously promote dual domestic and international circulation. In fact, this is also an important component of the new development paradigm. Meanwhile, the better China's economic development, the higher will be its income level and the larger its economy, the more dominant its domestic circulation will become.

The potential of China's future development

The further development of China's economy is necessary for the country to weather this 'great change unseen in a century' and develop significant domestic circulation as the core of its economy. The speed of China's development depends not only on the potential of future economic growth, but also on efforts to tap into this potential.

How should we look at China's future development potential? During the period of reform and opening-up from 1978 to 2020, the average annual growth rate of China's economy was 9.2 per cent. Never in human history had any country or region maintained such a high growth rate for such a long time. The issue of China's future growth receives great attention domestically and internationally. At present, academic and public opinion at home and abroad are generally not optimistic about China's future development potential. There are two reasons for this.

The first reason cited is that China's development in the past 42 years has been abnormally rapid and will inevitably return to normal growth levels. According to Larry Summers, a world-renowned economist, former US Treasury secretary and president of Harvard University, China will fall back to a normal growth rate of 3–3.5 per cent (Pritchett and Summers 2014). Meanwhile, according to the tenth edition of the Penn World Table, China's per capita GDP at the end of 2019 had reached US$14,129 according to the PPP of US dollars in 2017 (Feenstra et al. 2015). Some economists have used this figure to make comparisons with Germany and Japan, finding that the average annual growth rate for Germany was only 2.3 per cent in the 16 years after its per capita GDP reached US$14,120, and Japan's average growth rate was 4.4 per cent in the 16 years after reaching this level. Germany and Japan are famous for their economic development performance. Based on their average growth rates in this period, China's growth potential in the 16 years from 2019 to 2035 should therefore not be high, which sounds reasonable.[5]

The second cited reason is that China's population has begun to age. Facing the same problem, other countries have seen a significant slowdown in their economic growth. It is believed that its ageing population will also inevitably slow China's growth.

The above reasoning seems convincing; however, I disagree with it, due to the many factors that allowed China to achieve an annual growth rate of 9.2 per cent over the past 40 years, the most decisive of which was its ability to make full use of its latecomer advantage in economic development—an advantage that China still, to a large extent, possesses.

---

5   Liu Shijin, *Understanding the 14th Five-Year Plan: Reform Agenda under the New Development Paradigm*, Beijing: CITIC Press, 2020.

For any country or region, economic development and improvement of living standards depend on the continuous improvement of productivity, which requires continuous technological innovation and industrial upgrading. The technologies and industries of developed countries are at the global forefront and their technological innovation and industrial upgrading must naturally rely on their own inventions. Investment in these activities is very large, the risks are very high and the rate of progress is very slow. Historical experience shows that the normal pattern for developed countries over the past hundred or more years is average annual growth of per capita income of 2 per cent, plus a 1–1.5 per cent expansion through population growth, for an overall economic growth rate of 3–3.5 per cent. However, developing countries can use industrial and technological gaps with developed countries to introduce mature technology as the source of their own technological innovation and industrial upgrading. The costs and risks of this method are relatively small. Developing countries taking this route can develop their economies faster than developed countries. After China's reform and opening-up, it became one of 13 developing economies to make use of this advantage, achieving growth rates of 7 per cent or higher for 25 years or more in the process (Commission on Growth and Development 2008).

Therefore, China's future development potential depends not on current income levels, but on the gap between China and developed countries such as the United States.

Again, we take Germany and Japan as examples. Germany's per capita GDP reached US$14,120 in 1971, which was 72.4 per cent of the per capita GDP in the United States at that time. Undoubtedly, Germany was already one of the most developed countries in the world and had exhausted most of its latecomer advantage. To carry out technological innovation and industrial upgrading, Germany needed to rely on its own inventions and its economic growth rate naturally slowed. In 1975, Japan's per capita GDP also reached US$14,120, which was 69.7 per cent of that of the United States at the time. Japan had also become one of the most developed countries in the world, with its technology close to the global forefront. Most of its economic growth also relied on its own inventions, naturally leading to a slowdown of its development.

China's GDP per capita reached US$14,129 in 2019, but this was only 22.6 per cent of that of the United States for the same year. When did the per capita GDP rates of Germany, Japan and South Korea—the three best-performing advanced countries— reach 22.6 per cent of that of the United States? For Germany, it was in 1946, Japan in 1956 and South Korea in 1985. From 1946 to 1962, Germany's average economic growth rate reached 9.4 per cent; from 1956 to 1972, Japan's average economic growth rate was 9.2 per cent; and from 1985 to 2001, the average annual growth rate in South Korea was as high as 9 per cent despite the fact it suffered from the Asian Financial Crisis and the GFC and suffered negative growth in 1998.

China should reach about 9 per cent annual growth over the 16 years from 2019 given the experiences of Germany, Japan and South Korea when relying on the same latecomer advantage.

It is true that countries with ageing populations have slower economic growth, however, these are generally developed countries and their technology has already developed to the global forefront and technological progress has come to depend on their own inventions. The economic growth rate for developed countries is only between 3 and 3.5 per cent, including 2 per cent of per capita income growth and 1–1.5 per cent of population growth, as mentioned above. When an ageing population stops growing, the economic growth rate will drop significantly to about 2 per cent.

Although China's population is also beginning to age, its per capita GDP is only 22.6 per cent of that of the United States. Technological innovation and industrial upgrading can make use of the latecomer advantage and reallocate labour from low value-added to high value-added industries to improve labour productivity. The room for such adjustments is still very large. Therefore, if China can exploit its latecomer advantage, even if the population and labour force do not grow, it can grow faster than ageing developed countries.

In addition, China's retirement age is very low and can be gradually raised, which is conducive to increasing labour supply. Moreover, the most important thing for a labour force is not only quantity, but also quality. As such, China also has the potential to improve its education system to increase the quality of its labour force.

Let us compare the population growth of Germany, Japan and South Korea in the 16 years after their per capita GDP reached 22.6 per cent of US levels and examine the contribution of population factors to their economic growth. The average annual population growth of Germany from 1946 to 1962 was 0.8 per cent, that for Japan from 1956 to 1972 was 1 per cent and for South Korea from 1985 to 2001 it was 0.9 per cent. China's natural rate of population growth was 0.3 per cent in 2019, and it could drop to zero in the future. Therefore, even if we do not consider the possibility of raising the retirement age and improving the quality of labour through education, if China uses its latecomer advantage to develop its economy, when compared with Japan, Germany and South Korea, the impact of population growth on economic growth will be, at most, 1 percentage point. Therefore, if China can make good use of its latecomer advantage, it should have an annual growth rate of 8 per cent to 2035.

Moreover, when compared with Germany, Japan and South Korea in those years, China has an additional advantage for future development. Today, a large part of the new economy comprises internet, mobile communications, new energy and so on, and the research and development (R&D) cycle for these products and technologies is very short, with human capital the main input for their innovation. Given that developed countries began developing their economies at the start of the Industrial Revolution—with capital accumulated over hundreds of years—their per capita financial and material capital is much greater than China's, giving them comparative advantages in traditional capital-intensive industries.

For the new economy with short R&D cycles and human capital as the main input, the importance of financial capital is relatively small. In this domain, China and developed countries are on the same starting line, but China has advantages in human capital compared with many developed countries. Human capital consists of innate intelligence and intelligence acquired through education. Currently, the gap between China and developed countries in education from kindergarten to university and postgraduate studies is not large, while innate intelligence is normally distributed in the same proportion in the population of any country. For the R&D of new technology, what matters is not the proportion of talented individuals in a given country, but the absolute number. China has a population of 1.4 billion people and therefore a potentially large number of such intelligent individuals and, as such, it has an advantage in this new economy, the main input of which is human capital.

At the same time, China possesses the advantage of a large domestic market, which newly developed products and technologies can immediately enter, ensuring their production rapidly reaches economies of scale. If new products and technologies need hardware, China has the most complete set of industries in the world. Therefore, in the new economy, China and developed countries can at least keep abreast of each other—an advantage that Germany, Japan and South Korea did not enjoy when they were at the same development level as China is today.

China's advantage in the new economy is clearly reflected in the number of 'unicorns' (private startups with a value of more than US$1 billion) that are less than 10 years old and have not yet been listed on the market. According to Hurun's unicorn list, in 2019, there were 484 unicorns globally—206 in China and 203 in the United States (Hurun 2021). In 2020, there were 586 unicorns—233 in the United States and 227 in China. China is on a par with the United States in the number of such companies.

Based on its latecomer advantage and the realities of the new economy examined above, China has a potential average annual growth rate of at least 8 per cent until 2035. However, growth potential represents possible future growth based on supply-side technological innovation. In reality, one must also consider the demand side and other factors. For example, how fast a car can drive depends not only on the highest speed in its design, but also on the quality of the road, the weather and the abilities of the driver. To achieve high-quality development in the future, China must work to solve the challenges of environmental deterioration, peak carbon,

carbon neutrality, urban–rural and regional gaps and so on, as well as the problem of technological 'strangling' by US attempts to suppress China's development. China must pursue its own technological inventions, rather than relying on the latecomer advantages of technological importation, adaptation and re-innovation. Considering the above problems, it is entirely possible for China to achieve an average annual growth rate of about 6 per cent in the period 2021–35.

An explicit goal mentioned by President Xi in his proposals for the Fourteenth Five-Year Plan and the 2035 vision was for China's GDP and the income of urban and rural residents to be doubled by 2035 from their 2020 baseline. To achieve this, an economic growth rate of 4.7 per cent per year would be required between 2021 and 2035. If China can achieve a growth rate of about 6 per cent, GDP per capita will cross the threshold of US$12,535 by 2025 and China will become a high-income country. This will be a historic moment for both China and the world because, to date, only 18 per cent of the world's population resides in high-income countries—a proportion that would double if China joined their ranks. With that growth rate, China's per capita GDP should be at US$22,000 or higher by 2035, based on the PPP of 2019 dollars.

By the same token, China has a potential annual growth rate of 6 per cent from 2036 to 2050, according to the latecomer advantage and the beneficial innovation paradigm of the new economy. To achieve high-quality growth, China must also solve its social and economic problems. It cannot develop completely according to its technological potential, but it should be possible to achieve an annual growth rate of about 4 per cent. Based on this calculation, China's per capita GDP will reach half that of the United States by 2049, when the nation will celebrate the centennial of the founding of the People's Republic of China. This will be an important indicator of the great rejuvenation of the Chinese nation. Moreover, as mentioned in the first part of this chapter, the world order will attain a stable new structure on the reaching of this milestone.

Deepening reform and opening-up

How does China turn an annual growth rate of about 6 per cent in 2021–35 and 4 per cent in 2036–50 into reality? The most important thing is for China to recognise its potential, do its own thing well and deepen both reform and opening-up.

According to the new structural economics I advocate, a vital principle for economic development is for nations to make good use of their comparative advantages. To bring comparative advantage into full play, the economy needs a vibrant market to mobilise entrepreneurs' enthusiasm and allocate resources well. The economy also needs a facilitating state to overcome market failures that will inevitably arise from the process of technological innovation and industrial upgrading, to make markets more efficient. In the process of technological innovation and industrial upgrading, it is necessary to provide incentives to first-movers and help them overcome infrastructure bottlenecks. At the same time, China is a country in transition, carrying out its economic reforms in a gradual, dual-track approach. In a manner apparently inconsistent with the proper use of China's comparative advantages, the government has continued to provide protection and subsidies to state-owned enterprises in capital-intensive industries established before the economic reforms. State-owned enterprises that are nonviable but nonetheless necessary for the operation of the national economy, ensuring people's livelihoods or for national security have been provided with continuous protection and subsidies during the transitional period. At the same time, the government implemented new approaches for the new enterprises in labour-intensive industries that are consistent with China's comparative advantages, opening market access to entrepreneurs, attracting foreign investment and setting up industrial parks to facilitate the development of these industries. Relying on these pragmatic approaches, China's economy has achieved stable and rapid development in the past 40 years of transition. But this approach has also left in its wake various interventions and distortions in the market (Lin 2013b).

After more than 40 years of rapid development and capital accumulation, most of the industries that ignored or shunned their comparative advantage in the early stages of reform and opening-up have since moved in line with that advantage. Enterprises previously lacking viability have become viable. The nature of protection and subsidies in the dual-track system has changed from providing charcoal in the snow (that is, assistance) to providing icing on the cake. Therefore, the comprehensive deepening reform proposed by the Third Plenary Session of the Eighteenth Central Committee in 2013 should be implemented. The distortions left by dual-track reform should be eliminated to allow the market to play a decisive role in resource allocation. The role of the government is to help enterprises overcome market failure.

The product market in China has been essentially liberalised, but many structural obstacles in the factor markets remain.

For the financial market, China should improve its services to the real economy. In China's real economy, farmers and micro, small and medium-sized enterprises account for 50 per cent of taxes paid, 60 per cent of GDP and more than 80 per cent of employment. China's financial structure comprises mainly big banks, stockmarkets, corporate bonds and venture capital—arrangements that mainly serve large enterprises. To realise the financial system's function of servicing the real economy, it is necessary for reforms to develop regional small and medium-sized financial institutions that can provide better financial services for farmers and micro, small and medium-sized enterprises, in addition to improving existing financial arrangements.

In terms of improvements in the labour market, China should reform the household registration system and solve the problem of high housing prices by returning to a policy in which houses are used for living in, not speculating on, to facilitate flows of talented workers.

China should implement a policy allowing rural collective land to enter the market to increase the supply of land for industrial, commercial and housing purposes.

In terms of property rights reform, it is necessary to implement the stated policy of consolidation and development of the state-owned economy and encouragement of, support and guidance for the development of the private economy, so that private enterprises will not be subject to access or operation obstacles due to different property rights arrangements in the market.

China has adopted a dual-track system to its opening-up. In the early stage of transition, foreign direct investment was allowed for industries that were deemed consistent with China's comparative advantages, while there were many restrictions on foreign investment for industries that were not. However, given the country's rapid development and accumulation of capital, many industries for which it once possessed no comparative advantage have since gained such advantages. Apart from a few industries related to national security and the operation of the national economy and people's livelihoods, China should expand the policy of opening-up to make full use of international resources. China should expand the scope of pilot free-trade zones, reduce tariffs and cut the negative list of foreign investment. In addition, successful policies in the pilot free-trade zones should be implemented throughout the country.

Internationally, China should more actively promote reform of the World Trade Organization (WTO) and participate in regional economic cooperation agreements; good examples are the recently signed Regional Comprehensive Economic Partnership Agreement (RCEP) and the China–European Union Investment Agreement. In addition, China has expressed its willingness to join the Comprehensive and Progressive Agreement for Trans-Pacific Partnership (CPTPP) and should strive to achieve this goal as soon as possible.

Another advantage of China's deepening reform and further opening-up is that other countries will be able to make better use of China's market and resources. As the largest and fastest-growing market in the world, China can provide other countries with opportunities for development, meaning such countries will not readily join the US blockade of China. If the United States wants to isolate China, it will be the United States that finds itself isolated. Therefore, further opening-up will help resolve the adverse international situation that China is facing.

Conclusion

In the face of the 'great change unseen in a century', China should maintain its determination in the new development paradigm, continue to deepen reform and expand its opening-up and make good use of its development potential. In this way, no matter how uncertain the international situation becomes, China will be able to maintain stability and development by relying on its domestic circulation to realise its great rejuvenation. In so doing, it will also create opportunities for other countries to develop and contribute to the early arrival of a new and stable global structure.

References

Commission on Growth and Development. 2008. *The Growth Report: Strategies for Sustained Growth and Inclusive Development*. Washington, DC: International Bank for Reconstruction and Development & The World Bank On behalf of the Commission on Growth and Development. Available from: openknowledge.worldbank.org/bitstream/handle/10986/6507/449860PUB0Box3101OFFICIAL0USE0ONLY1.pdf.

Feenstra, Robert C., Robert Inklaar and Marcel P. Timmer. 2015. 'The Next Generation of the Penn World Table.' *American Economic Review* 105(10): 3150–82. Available from: www.ggdc.net/pwt. doi.org/10.1257/aer.20130954.

Hurun. 2021. *Global Unicorn Index 2021*. [Online]. Available from: www.hurun.net/en-US/Info/Detail?num=R18H7AJUWBIX.

Lin, Justin Yifu. 2013a. *Against the Consensus: Reflections on the Great Recession*. Cambridge, UK: Cambridge University Press. doi.org/10.1017/CBO9781139855709.

Lin, Justin Yifu. 2013b. 'Demystifying the Chinese Economy.' *The Australian Economic Review* 46(3): 259–68. doi.org/10.1111/j.1467-8462.2013.12035.x.

Lin, Justin Yifu. 2013c. 'New Structural Economics: The Third Wave of Development Thinking.' *Asia Pacific Economic Literature* 27(2): 1–13. doi.org/10.1111/apel.12044.

Liu, Shijin. 2020. *Understanding the 14th Five-Year Plan: Reform Agenda under the New Development Paradigm*. Beijing: CITIC Press.

Maddison, Angus. 2016. *Historical Statistics of the World Economy, 1–2008 AD*. [Online]. Groningen, Netherlands: Maddison Project. Available from: datasource.kapsarc.org/explore/dataset/historical-statistics-of-the-world-economy-1-2008-ad/information/?disjunctive.country_name&disjunctive.indicator_name.

Pritchett, Lant and Lawrence H. Summers. 2014. *Asiaphoria meets regression to the mean*. NBER Working Paper Series No. 20573, October. Cambridge, MA: National Bureau of Economic Research. doi.org/10.3386/w20573.

3

China in the twenty-first century: A national balance sheet perspective

Xiaojing Zhang and Cheng Li

Introduction

In the light of Richard Koo's (2009) pioneering explanation of Japan's decades-long economic stagnation, aggregate balance sheets have attracted increasing attention from both academics and policymakers, especially during periods of financial turmoil. When looking at China, the country's aggregate sectors, especially households, have accumulated considerable wealth, and considerable debt, thanks to the high growth, high savings and financial deepening following the inception of market reforms. This was not the case, however, before the 1980s (see Chow 1993). In this context, a balance sheet perspective has gained even more importance for better understanding the accumulated results of China's economic development over the past four or more decades. It is hard to believe that the structural changes in growth patterns and the associated transformation of economic and financial structures and risk dynamics can be adequately addressed without such a stock-based perspective.

The academic literature on the compilation and analysis of China's national or sectoral balance sheets has largely emerged since the 2008 GFC. Among others (Cao and Ma 2012; Ma et al. 2012; Du 2015), Professor Yang Li and his research team from the Chinese Academy of Social Sciences[1] began working on the topic

---

1   The research team later became the so-called Center for National Balance Sheet (CNBS), led by Professor Xiaojing Zhang from the Chinese Academy of Social Sciences. So far, it is the only institution to release China's national balance sheets regularly.

in 2011, leading to the compilation of annual national and sectoral accounts for 2000–19, which are available from the CEIC database (www.ceicdata.com/en; also see Appendix 3.1). Relying on these data, Professor Li's team has published a series of academic books and articles (Li et al. 2012a, 2012b, 2013, 2015, 2018, 2020; Li and Zhang 2013, 2021; Li 2018) that draw citations from leading international scholars (for example, Sheng 2016; Frecaut 2017; Naughton 2017; Piketty et al. 2019). It is also noteworthy that, at the time of writing, official statistics for China's balance sheet accounts are yet to be released.

In this chapter, we first present the main findings of our recent work on aggregate balance sheets, including wealth accumulation, structural distribution and macrofinancial risks in the first two decades of the twenty-first century. Next, we compare the case of China with that of the United States and other major economies, whose balance sheet data are publicly available. In so doing, we highlight some characteristics of the Chinese economy that are associated with its development stage and other relevant structural features. We conclude with relevant policy issues that are implied by this national balance sheet perspective.

Wealth accumulation

The opening years of the new millennium were nothing short of extraordinary: the internet bubble burst at the turn of the century, the GFC hit in 2008, there have been trade frictions between the United States and China since 2018, and the Covid-19 pandemic erupted in the closing weeks of 2019. Yet, thanks to appropriate policy responses and its 2001 entry into the WTO, China has weathered these crises comparatively well and its economy continues to rapidly expand. China has also continued to make phenomenal progress in accumulating wealth.

Conceptionally, as the net difference between total assets and liabilities, 'net wealth' (or 'net worth' or 'net assets') comprises domestic non-financial assets and net foreign assets. As shown in Figure 3.1, according to our estimation, the former rose from RMB38.4 trillion to RMB661.9 trillion in the period from 2000 to 2019 and accounts for the lion's share of total net wealth (about 98 per cent in 2019). Net foreign assets increased from RMB480 billion to RMB13.6 trillion over the same period. The fact that this position has stayed positive and significant suggests China is playing the role of net provider of savings to the rest of the world.

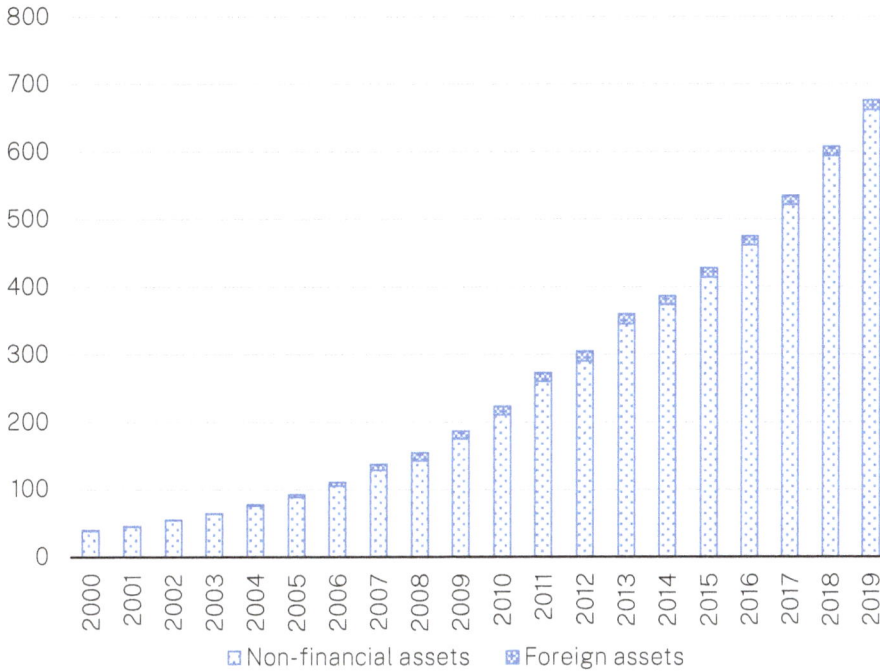

Figure 3.1 China's national wealth accumulation, 2000–19 (RMB trillion)
Source: CNBS (www.nifd.cn/Center/Details/23).

Next, from a dynamic perspective, the annual growth rate of China's net wealth averaged 16.2 per cent over the period 2000–19, which is higher than the average growth rate of nominal GDP during the same period, at 12.8 per cent. In Figure 3.2, we compare China with some major global economies. Two findings can be reported: first, wealth growth volatility shares a similar trend with GDP growth, reflecting a general consistency between stock and flow data. Second, as also shown in Table 3.1, wealth expansion has generally outpaced GDP growth, and this is especially true in the case of China.

China

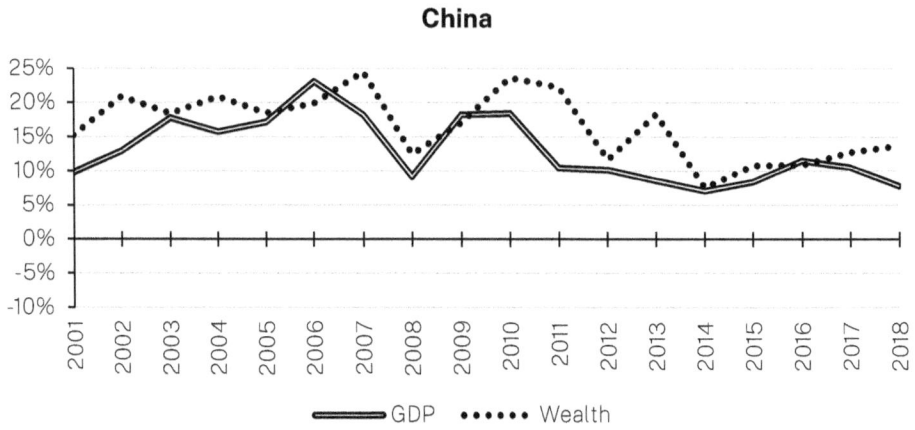

GDP ••••• Wealth

United States

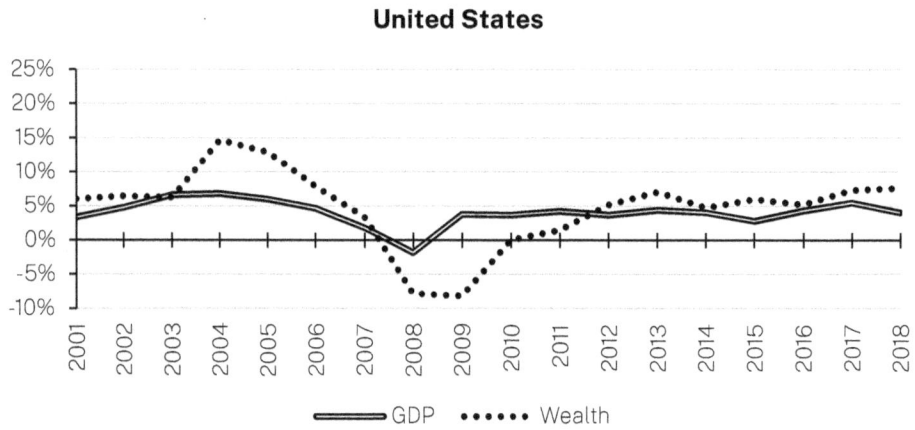

GDP ••••• Wealth

Japan

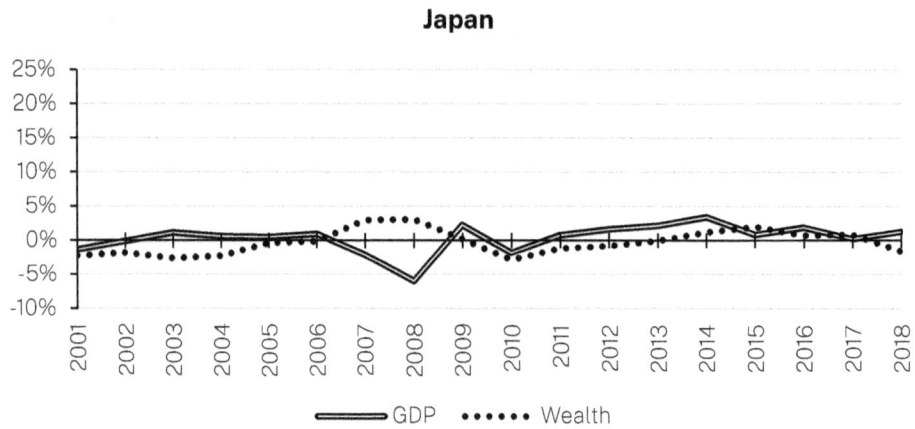

GDP ••••• Wealth

Germany

France

United Kingdom

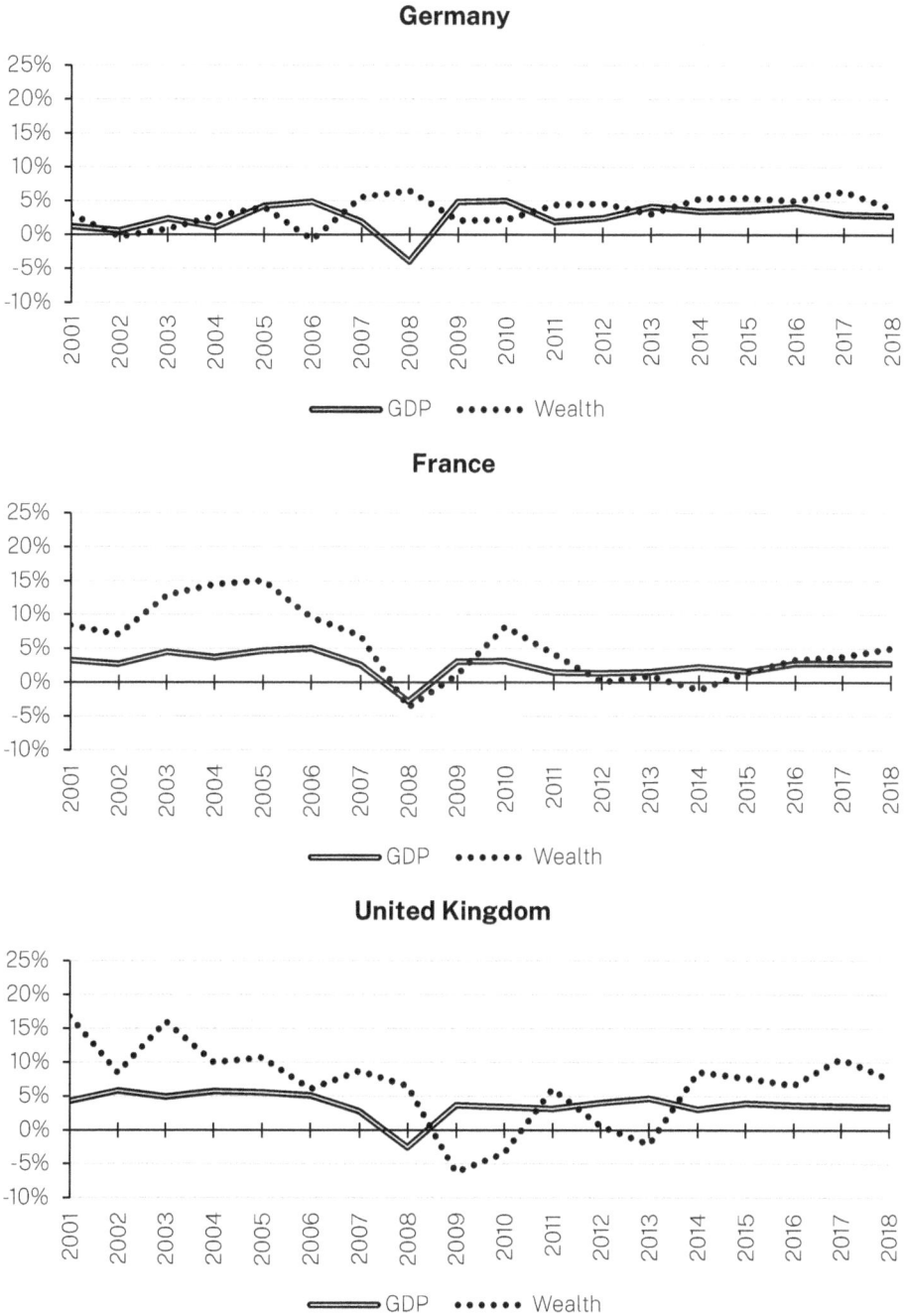

Figure 3.2 Comparison of national wealth growth and GDP growth (annual rate in nominal terms)

Sources: China data from CNBS (www.nifd.cn/Center/Details/23); data for other countries, see Li and Zhang (2021: Appendix 1).

Table 3.1 Comparison of national wealth growth and GDP growth (average for 2001–18)

Indicator (%)	China	United States	Japan	Germany	France	United Kingdom
Wealth growth rate	16.6	4.8	-0.3	3.5	5.4	6.6
GDP growth rate	13.0	4.0	0.3	2.6	2.6	3.8

Sources: China data from CNBS (www.nifd.cn/Center/Details/23); data for other countries, see Li and Zhang (2021: Appendix 1).

China's strong propensity for saving and upward asset revaluation has contributed to the expansion of national wealth. On the one hand, the high savings rate (usually measured as savings in GDP) corresponds to rapid fixed capital formation, thereby leading to continuous incremental growth in non-financial assets. Accordingly, consumption accounts for a relatively small share of income flow. To be more specific, it is well known that precautionary motives, among other factors, have led China to maintain a relatively high savings rate, persisting in the range of 40–50 per cent over a long period, and reaching 44.6 per cent in 2018. By contrast, as shown in Figure 3.3, the United States' gross savings rate has typically been less than half that of China's and was down to 18.6 per cent in 2018. Indeed, most major economies have a savings rate below 30 per cent. Clearly, the savings rate determines the speed of wealth accumulation and if, say, 40 per cent of GDP is saved, nearly 40 per cent of newly produced economic output further serves wealth accumulation through investment in factories, equipment, housing and other structures, and so on.

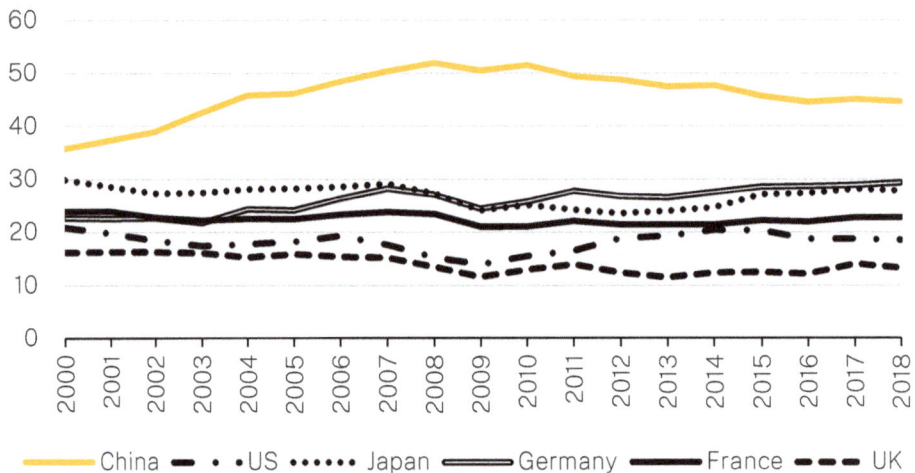

Figure 3.3 Gross savings rate of major economies (per cent)

Source: World Bank World Development Indicators DataBank (databank.worldbank.org/source/world-development-indicators).

The revaluation of assets, including land and housing, serves as another important driver of rapid growth in China's aggregate wealth. However, as presented in Table 3.2, in comparison with capital formation, the effect of revaluation contributed an increasingly diminishing share to wealth growth.

Table 3.2 Decomposition of wealth accumulation in major economies: Capital formation and revaluation (per cent)

Period	Average growth and contribution	China	United States	Japan	Germany	France	United Kingdom
2001–06	Wealth	28.0	10.2	–1.2	1.6	14.8	12.2
	Capital formation	16.4	4.6	3.7	1.0	3.8	6.9
	Revaluation	11.6	5.6	–4.9	0.6	11.0	5.3
2007–12	Wealth	25.3	–0.6	–0.3	3.7	1.7	0.5
	Capital formation	16.5	2.9	3.6	2.2	2.5	4.1
	Revaluation	8.8	–3.5	–4.0	1.6	–0.8	–3.6
2013–18	Wealth	11.5	5.8	0.5	4.8	2.1	8.0
	Capital formation	9.2	3.9	4.0	2.2	2.4	4.9
	Revaluation	2.7	1.9	–3.4	2.7	–0.2	3.0

Source: CNBS (www.nifd.cn/Center/Details/23).

Eventually, by construction, total national net wealth is held by households, general government (or the public sector)[2] and the foreign sector (negligible in size); a sectoral division may also be important for better understanding China's development pattern and structural changes. As shown in Figures 3.4 and 3.5, government wealth increased from RMB8 trillion in 2000 to RMB40 trillion in 2009, then surpassed RMB100 trillion in 2015, before reaching RMB162.8 trillion at the end of the period under consideration. Turning to households, wealth in this sector increased from RMB30.6 trillion in 2000 to RMB100 trillion in 2007, before expanding to RMB512.6 trillion in 2019.

---

2   The 'general government' is defined as the aggregation of central and local governments and nonprofit public institutions (*shi ye dan wei*).

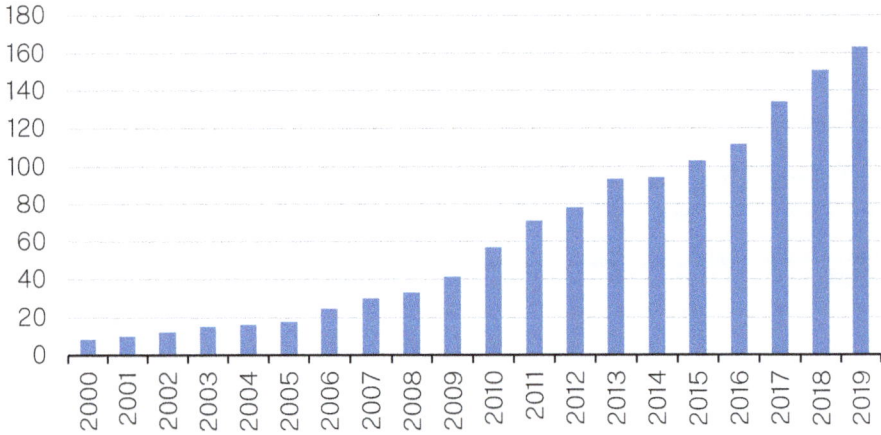

Figure 3.4 Net worth of general government sector, 2000–19 (RMB trillion)
Source: CNBS (www.nifd.cn/Center/Details/23).

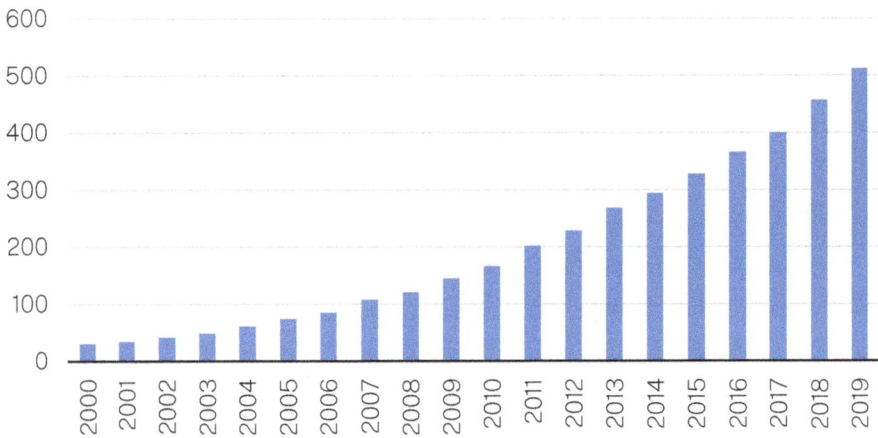

Figure 3.5 Net worth of household sector, 2000–19 (RMB trillion)
Source: CNBS (www.nifd.cn/Center/Details/23).

Wealth comparison: China and other major economies

In a certain sense, wealth, as a cumulative result of income growth, serves as a more representative indicator than income flow (for example, GDP) for measuring and comparing economic size and capacity across countries. Hence, there is a growing body of literature on international competition focusing on this stock indicator. To the best of our knowledge, the earliest attempts at wealth research and estimation, such as William Petty's masterpiece *Political Arithmetic* (Petty 1899), stemmed from the need for reliable indicators of international competitive advantage in the economic, political and even military realms.

Nevertheless, such a perspective is often limited by the availability of data. Given this concern, we next compare China with seven major economies for which the official statistics of national wealth accounts have been released. As shown in Table 3.3, in 2018, China's GDP reached a level 65 per cent of that in the United States, and 80 per cent of its wealth level. Moreover, China's wealth exceeded those of Japan, Germany, France and the United Kingdom combined, while its GDP was only slightly smaller than the sum of these four countries. This indicates that China has made even greater strides in its economic catch-up from a stock perspective than a flow perspective.

Table 3.3 International comparison of national wealth and GDP, to the end of 2018 (US$ billion)

Indicator	United States	China	Japan	Germany
Wealth	110,208.70	88,559.50	29,907.40	23,093.50
GDP	20,611.90	13,394.40	4,844.20	3,845.10
Indicator	France	United Kingdom	Canada	Australia
Wealth	17,825.00	13,287.80	8,637.90	8,375.90
GDP	2,704.40	2,732.30	1,629.90	1,339.20

Note: Corresponding countries' exchange rates are dated at the end of 2018.

Sources: China data from CNBS (www.nifd.cn/Center/Details/23); data for other countries, see Li and Zhang (2021: Appendix 1).

More interestingly, China's catch-up in wealth came later than its catch-up in income/output terms. As can be seen from Figure 3.6, in the first decade of the new century, the ratio of China's GDP to that of the United States was higher than the ratio of China's national wealth to that of the United States. The turning point was reached in the GFC, during which US households' wealth suffered greater losses than their Chinese counterparts.

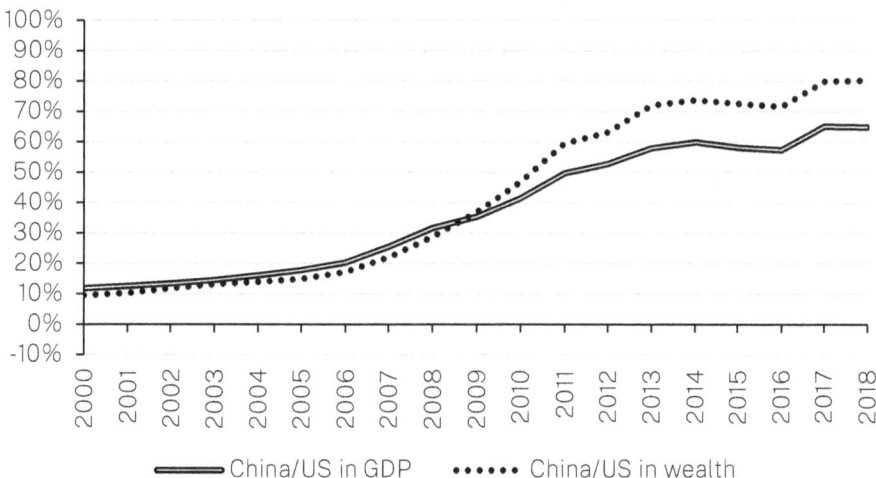

Figure 3.6 China–United States comparison: Flow versus stock
Source: CNBS (www.nifd.cn/Center/Details/23).

It should be stressed, however, that China's wealth catch-up with the United States and other advanced economies has been driven not only by rapid economic growth and high savings, but also by a revaluation effect. As well as the aforementioned factors, when conducting international comparison, it is obvious that asset values are affected by changes in the renminbi exchange rate. In fact, during the period between two major reforms in July 2005 and July 2015, China witnessed a significant decade-long appreciation of the renminbi against the US dollar, which served as a key driver of the rapid increase in the ratio of China's national wealth to that of the United States.

Furthermore, given the different statistical standards of each country's national balance sheet accounts, international comparisons based on these should be conducted with great caution. As far as China and the United States are concerned, any comparison of their relative wealth is beset by the problem of inconsistent approaches in their treatment of non-financial assets, especially land. Specifically, on the US national balance sheet, the items 'land' and 'buildings' held by households, nonprofit institutions and corporations are combined, and thus the values of these two kinds of assets are not separately available. When it comes to the treatment of the financial sector for federal and state governments, the balance sheet contains the value of buildings only, without accounting for the value of the land underlying structures.[3] That is, in the above comparison, US wealth does not include government sector land values, whereas this (primarily the value of state-owned construction land) is included in China's accounts. For a better comparison, if we deduct the value of state-owned construction land (RMB31.5 trillion in 2018, or US$4.6 trillion), China's national wealth in 2018 would shrink to US$84 trillion, with the ratio to US wealth down from 80 per cent to 76 per cent.

For the sake of reference, Table 3.4 shows wealth estimates for China and the United States made by Thomas Piketty's team in the World Inequality Database (wid.world; also see Piketty et al. 2019). According to this alternative data source, China's national wealth had already reached 76 per cent of the level of the United States in 2015, while this ratio was only 25 per cent in 2000 (see Table 3.2). Notably, in addition to estimating the nominal net wealth of each country, Piketty uses a deflator to convert the results into constant-price balance sheets, and the scope of the estimation also deviates from the *System of National Accounts 2008* (UN et al. 2009).

---

3   For the scope and method of compilation of the national balance sheet in the United States, please refer to Bond et al. (2007) and Wasshausen (2011).

Table 3.4 Comparison of net wealth in China and the United States, estimated by the World Inequality Database (€ billion)

	2000	2005	2010	2015
China	15,661.96	25,582.38	41,939.91	65,531.42
United States	61,855.67	76,567.46	66,724.57	86,264.08
China–US ratio	25.3%	33.4%	62.9%	76.0%

Source: World Inequality Database (wid.world).

In summary, although there is no uniform standard for estimating wealth and other stock indicators, China's overall national strength, as measured by wealth, ranks second in the world to the United States and the gap between the two countries has become even narrower than GDP figures would suggest. While the above statement is generally tenable, there are some caveats to any attempts at comparative analysis, not least from the perspective of resource allocation efficiency and future development potential. With the additional consideration of population size, China's wealth data become far less rosy than aggregate indicators would suggest.

The first problem facing China's economy are the so-called 'zombie firms' and implicit local government debts. Due to data availability, this problem—which leads to distorted asset and liability figures—is not fully reflected in the balance sheet. Although some implicit local debts such as financing platform loans are reflected in the corporate sector, other forms of implicit debt are not included. Of course, zombie firms are not unique to China—Organisation for Economic Co-operation and Development (OECD) countries, for instance, also have estimates of zombie companies—but this problem is far more acute in China. If zombie firms and implicit local debts are considered, estimates of China's aggregate wealth will shrink further.

Another problem is related to China's wealth quality. There are various dimensions of assessing wealth quality. For instance, housing properties built in China in the 1950s to 1980s may last only 20 years or so, while those in advanced economies may last for as long as 50 or even 100 years. That is, housing properties in China should have a higher depreciation rate than those in advanced economies. Similar problems exist in the estimation of the value of infrastructure and other kinds of capital stock. Indeed, some argue that the value of China's housing stock is overestimated because depreciation is often not properly considered. Another issue is to do with the liquidity and cashability of wealth. It is widely known that due to its less-developed financial markets, China has limited international pricing power for various commodities and assets, so, in the event of a crisis, China's wealth cashability could be worse than that of the United States and other developed countries. For instance, a great amount of the net foreign wealth held by the Chinese Government is in the form of US Treasury bonds, the cashability of which is to a large extent subject to the coordination of the US Government and its financial system.

The third issue is the efficiency of wealth accumulation. Since wealth/capital stock plays a major role in generating income flows, the higher the wealth-to-income ratio, the less income will be generated from each unit of wealth and the less efficient output will become. As displayed in Figure 3.7, the wealth-to-GDP ratio in China increased from 350 per cent to 613 per cent in the period 2000–18, reflecting a steep fall in wealth accumulation efficiency. Although advanced economies also witnessed rising wealth/income ratios (reflecting falling wealth accumulation efficiency as a common trend), China's ratio seemed to increase the fastest.

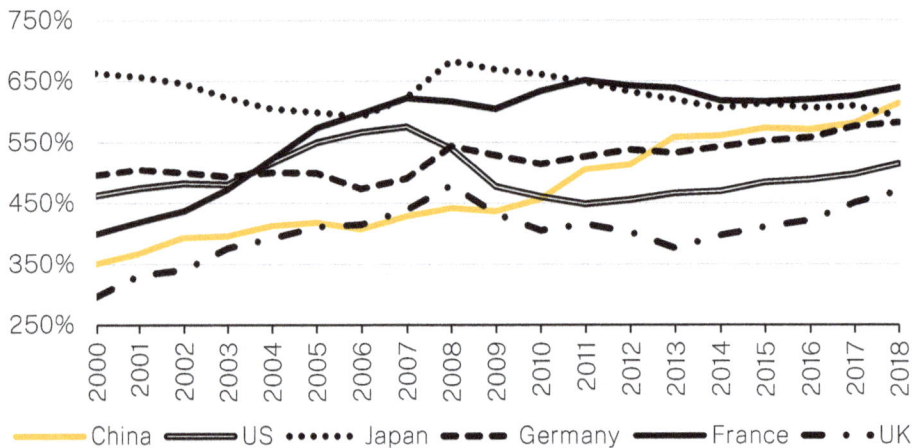

Figure 3.7 International comparison of national wealth/GDP

Sources: China data from CNBS (www.nifd.cn/Center/Details/23); data for other countries, see Li and Zhang (2021: Appendix 1).

Government and household wealth distribution

Government wealth and debt

According to our estimation, shown in Figure 3.8, China's household sector wealth reached RMB512.6 trillion in 2019, accounting for 76 per cent of China's national wealth (RMB675.4 trillion), while government sector wealth reached RMB162.8 trillion, accounting for 24 per cent of the total. From a dynamic perspective, the share of household wealth as a proportion of national wealth increased during the period 2000–05, decreased during 2005–11, before rising again in the years since. However, if we take the decade's average, this share fell slightly from 78.4 per cent of national wealth to 75.2 per cent over the course of first two decades of the new century.

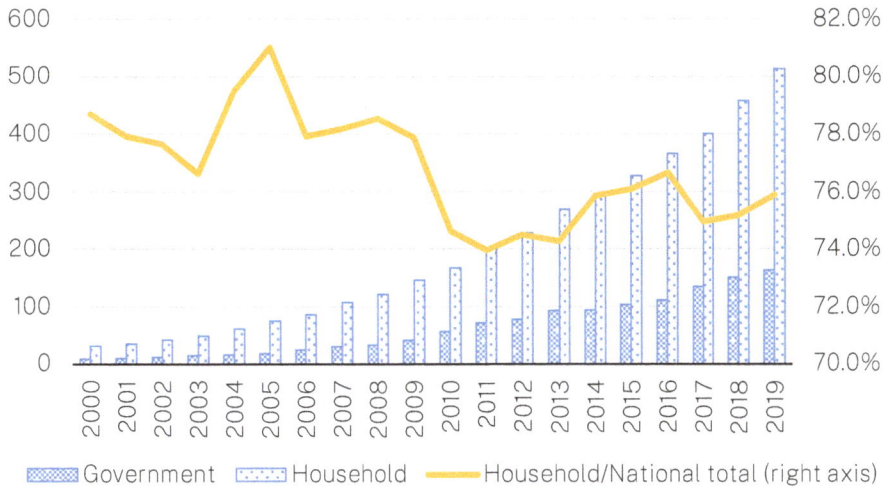

Figure 3.8 Household–government wealth distribution in China, 2000–19
Source: CNBS (www.nifd.cn/Center/Details/23).

It is noteworthy that given international standards, total net wealth is distributed between households and the government sector by a certain proportion. The corporate sector's net assets are initially divided by a certain equity ratio of the household and government sectors and thus, by construction, its net wealth is set to zero.

To better understand China's characteristics and relevant trends, we next provide an international comparison of wealth distribution based on this perspective. First, as can be seen in Figure 3.9, advanced economies witnessed a decline in the net value of government assets after the GFC, the value of which even entered negative territory in the United Kingdom and United States. For China, however, government wealth continued to increase over the same period.

Second, the net assets of the Chinese Government as a share of total national wealth appear to be much larger than those held by the governments of major advanced economies. During the period 2008–18, the net assets held by the Japanese, French and Canadian governments represented only 0–5 per cent of their respective national wealth, while that held by the UK and US governments was represented in negative figures. In 2018, those held by the German Government accounted for a slightly higher share, of 6 per cent, but in sharp contrast, the net wealth of the Chinese Government exceeded 20 per cent of national wealth for most years during the period 2008–18.

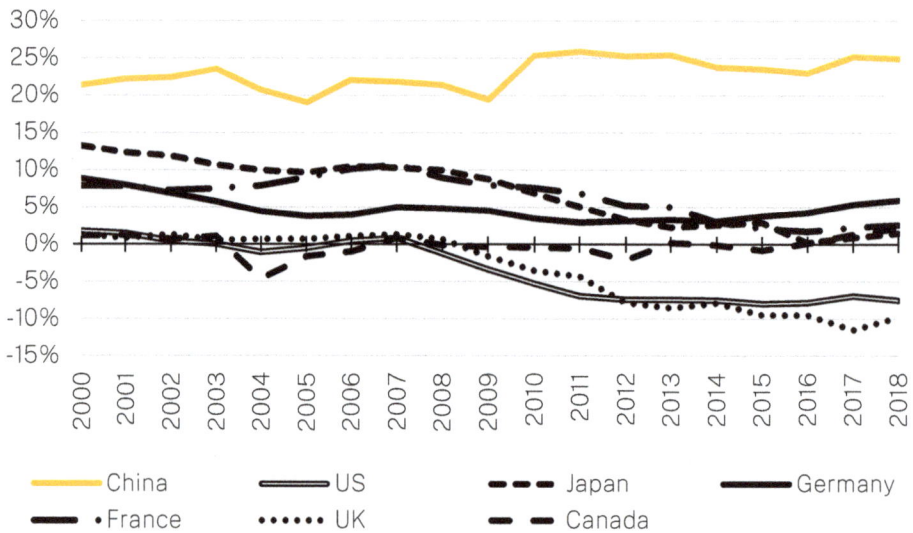

Figure 3.9 Net assets of the government sector as a share of total national wealth

Sources: China data from CNBS (www.nifd.cn/Center/Details/23); data for other countries, see Li and Zhang (2021: Appendix 1).

Adopting a broader perspective, the International Monetary Fund (IMF) has collected the government and public sector balance sheets for 58 economies. It is worth noting that the IMF's data, based on the *Government Finance Statistics* database (IMF 2022),[4] differ from the national balance sheets released by the statistical authorities of the various countries assessed, as well as from our estimation for China. Despite this concern, these data are more comparable across countries due to a consistent statistical framework, and thus can be used as supplementary data for the international comparison of government wealth. Figure 3.10 shows the net assets of the government sector as a share of GDP for the 58 economies, and we also ranked the top-10 economies with the highest share, in addition to Group of Seven (G7) countries.

As the figure shows, China ranks very highly on this indicator and, in fact, only six of the sampled countries had net asset/GDP ratios higher than China's: Norway, Uzbekistan, Kazakhstan, Czech Republic, Russia and Australia. They are either resource-rich countries, with natural resources accounting for a large chunk of domestic assets held by the government, or, like China, countries engaging in market reforms. By contrast, all G7 countries except Canada have negative government net assets.

---

4   See IMF (2014) for more detail.

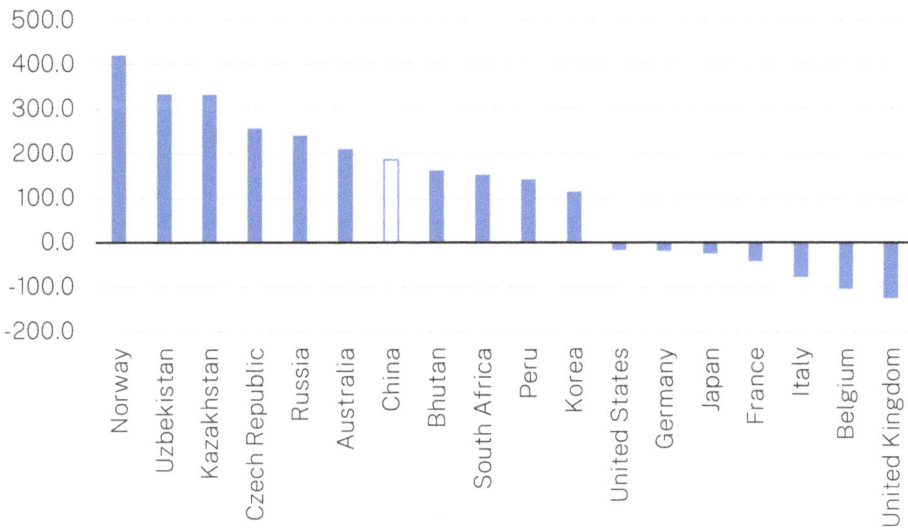

Figure 3.10 Share of government net assets in GDP, 2016 (per cent)
Sources: For China, CNBS (www.nifd.cn/Center/Details/23); for other countries, IMF (2022).

Notably, there are some differences in the international comparisons shown in Figures 3.9 and 3.10—in particular, the net assets of the Japanese and German governments are positive in Figure 3.9 and negative in Figure 3.10. This discrepancy is due to the IMF's harmonisation of the inconsistent statistical standards of various countries. The main difference lies in the treatment of pension funds. The government balance sheets released by the statistical authorities of Japan and Germany do not include pension liabilities, which are included by the IMF, thus causing a sharp decrease in the net assets of both governments and turning them from positive to negative.

In terms of international comparison, China's wealth distribution is skewed in favour of the government sector, for the following reasons: first, the government accounts for a significant share of the primary distribution of national income. For example, in 2018, the gross income of China's government sector in primary distribution reached RMB11.7 trillion, including RMB9.6 trillion from the net production tax. As displayed in Figure 3.11, the latter accounts for about 15 per cent of China's GDP, while this share is only 7 per cent for the United States and less than 13 per cent for other major developed economies. Given the sharp difference in net production tax, the Chinese Government takes a larger share of income after primary distribution, giving rise to long-term wealth accumulation. In contrast to the large share of production tax, China's labour compensation (including remuneration, bonuses and social security contributions paid by employers) represents a smaller share of the primary distribution. As can be seen in Figure 3.12, labour compensation as a share of US GDP has stayed between 60 per cent and 70 per cent, and this figure is generally above 55 per cent for other economies except China, whose labour compensation share of GDP is only about 50 per cent.

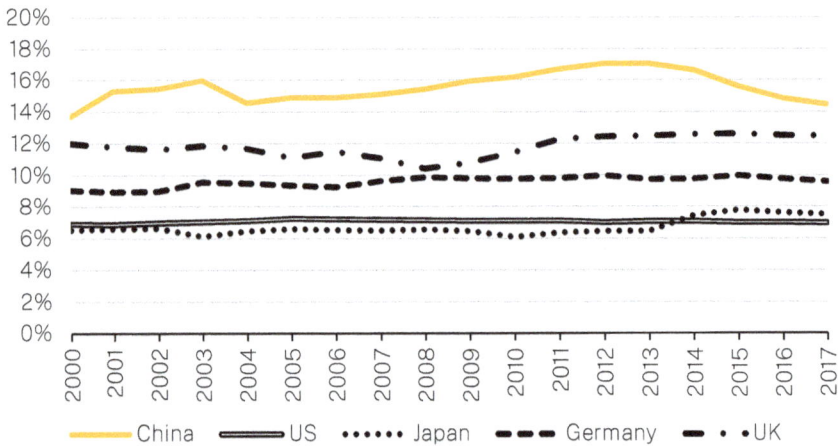

Figure 3.11 Net production tax as a share of GDP in primary distribution
Source: Wind (www.wind.com.cn/en/data.html).

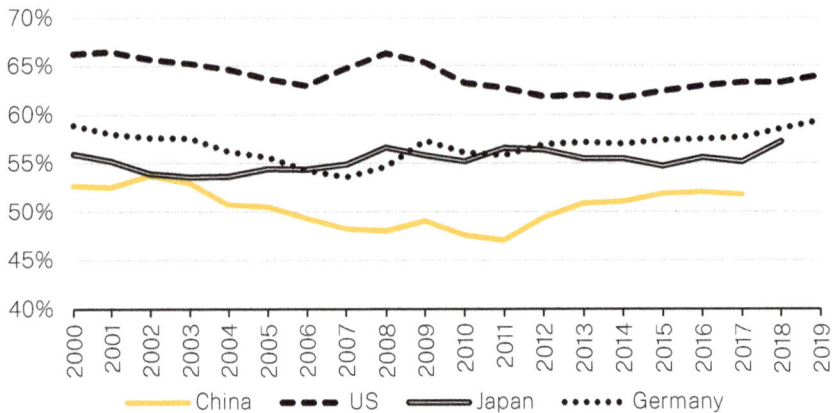

Figure 3.12 Labour compensation as a share of GDP in primary distribution
Source: Wind (www.wind.com.cn/en/data.html).

Second, the debt stock of China's government sector is relatively small. Figure 3.13 shows the size of each country's government debt as recently estimated by the IMF. Among the 15 comparable countries represented, only the Russian and Indonesian governments have leverage ratios—defined as the government debt-to-GDP ratio—smaller than China's, while those of a few advanced economies are far greater than China's. Since the GFC, most major economies witnessed increased leverage of the government sector, whose debts swelled, while China's government debt expansion has continued at a slower pace. However, this characteristic of China's economy could conceal implicit local government debts. Unlike many other countries, in China, an important part of public debt is assumed by state-owned enterprises (SOEs) and local financing platforms. According to our estimation, the balance of Urban Construction Investment Bonds issued by local government financing vehicles soared from RMB300 million in 2007 to RMB8.9 trillion by the end of 2019, and their share in the balance of all non-financial corporate bonds rose from less than 1 per cent to 38 per cent. Amid rising government wealth accumulation (such as the infrastructure stock arising from local government financing vehicles), those government debts through financing vehicles are classified as corporate sector liabilities, thus leading to inflation of government net assets. If these implicit debts are deducted from government assets, the financial leverage of the sector would be much higher.

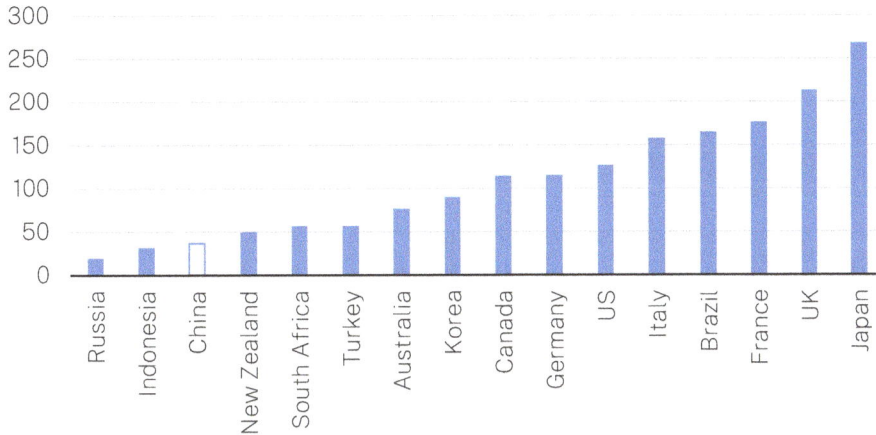

Figure 3.13 Government liabilities as a share of GDP, 2016 (per cent)
Sources: For China, CNBS (www.nifd.cn/Center/Details/23); for other countries, IMF (2022).

Household wealth and debt

We next decompose various factors contributing to wealth accumulation in the household sector. As shown in Table 3.5, the mechanism driving household wealth underwent a major reversal before and after the GFC. After the crisis, non-financial assets (mainly dwellings) contributed a generally smaller share to household wealth accumulation in China, while financial assets, especially net equity, contributed a rising share. In the United States, for instance, non-financial assets contributed an average of 2.1 per cent to household wealth accumulation before the GFC, which turned negative during the recession period and rebounded to 1.8 per cent in recent years but was still sharply below the pre-GFC level. Accordingly, the contribution of financial assets to wealth accumulation in the United States rose from 2.9 per cent to 3.9 per cent. This reversal can be ascribed to the following facts: first, the accumulation of physical assets slowed amid sluggish global economic performance; second, global financial markets, especially stock markets, rebounded swiftly in the post-GFC era, with the stock market indices of most developed countries exceeding pre-GFC levels. The finance-dominated channel of wealth accumulation in the United States and other major developed economies essentially reflects a restructuring of world wealth distribution, and the lack of genuine wealth growth. To a large extent, this is consistent with the argument for 'secular stagnation' facing the global economy in the post-GFC era (Summers 2014).

Table 3.5 Decomposition of contributions to household wealth accumulation: An international comparison, 2018 (per cent)

	United States			China		
	2001–06	2007–12	2013–18	2001–06	2007–12	2013–18
Average household wealth growth	5.8	0.4	5.7	10.7	10.4	8.4
Growth attributed to non-financial assets	2.9	–1.3	1.8	5.8	4.9	4.0
Growth attributed to net financial assets	2.9	1.7	3.9	4.9	5.5	4.3
Including: Net equity	2.2	0.0	2.3	3.3	3.6	2.8
Others	0.7	1.7	1.6	1.6	1.9	1.5

	Japan			Germany		
	2001–06	2007–12	2013–18	2001–06	2007–12	2013–18
Average household wealth growth	–0.8	–0.8	1.5	2.3	2.7	3.7
Growth attributed to non-financial assets	–1.9	–0.5	–0.3	1.1	1.7	2.1
Growth attributed to net financial assets	1.2	–0.3	1.8	1.2	0.9	1.6
Including: Net equity	0.7	–0.7	0.9	0.0	–0.2	0.4
Others	0.5	0.4	0.9	1.2	1.1	1.2

	United Kingdom			France		
	2001–06	2007–12	2013–18	2001–06	2007–12	2013–18
Average household wealth growth	7.0	1.6	1.7	6.1	2.5	5.0
Growth attributed to non-financial assets	6.1	1.2	0.9	5.7	0.7	2.8
Growth attributed to net financial assets	0.9	0.4	0.8	0.4	1.7	2.2
Including: Net equity	0.4	–0.1	0.3	–0.3	0.3	0.5
Others	0.5	0.5	0.5	0.7	1.4	1.7

	Australia			Canada		
	2001–06	2007–12	2013–18	2001–06	2007–12	2013–18
Average household wealth growth	11.21	4.87	7.93	–0.7	4.6	4.7
Growth attributed to non-financial assets	8.98	3.77	6.15	–2.5	3.1	2.5
Growth attributed to net financial assets	2.23	1.10	2.50	1.7	1.6	2.2
Including: Net equity	1.58	–0.09	0.72	1.2	1.1	1.3
Others	0.65	1.19	1.77	0.5	0.5	0.9

Sources: China data from CNBS (www.nifd.cn/Center/Details/23); data for other countries, see Li and Zhang (2021: Appendix 1).

Nevertheless, the characteristics of China's household wealth accumulation differ in many aspects from those of advanced economies. After the GFC, China's financial assets contributed a smaller share to household wealth—down from the pre-crisis 4.9 per cent to 4.3 per cent—and the effect of net equity also slid, from 3.3 per cent to 2.8 per cent. In addition to the economic slowdown in the post-GFC era, two other factors have contributed to the slowing accumulation of China's household financial assets.

First, China's underdeveloped direct financing market—not least the equity financing market—has a limited wealth distribution effect. In the post-GFC era, stock and equity assets have represented a slightly smaller share in the aggregate financial assets of the economy—down from the peak of 37 per cent in 2007 to 29 per cent in 2019. This reduction also has to do with China's mediocre stock market performance compared with that of advanced economies, especially the United States.

Second, the share of stocks and equities held by the household sector decreased after 2013. The hefty stimulus plan launched by China to cope with the effects of the GFC intensified its government-led economic growth model; and, while local government debt swelled, so did the state sector of the economy. As a result, China's government sector has possessed a growing share of net wealth, stocks and equities since 2013. In the meantime, given the diminishing proportion of stock and equity assets held by the country's household sector, the inflating effects of rising equity values have accrued primarily to the government sector.

This wealth distribution structure, which differs markedly from that of advanced economies, is reflective of certain characteristics of the Chinese economy associated with its development stage (government-led economic catch-up) and economic institutions (a public ownership–dominant system). To put it simply, government-led economic catch-up requires more economic resources to be concentrated in the public sector, and the public ownership structure includes numerous SOEs and publicly owned land, all of which has amplified the stock of government-owned assets. In advanced economies, apart from fiscal policies and market regulations, governments generally do not participate in economic activities such as production and investment, while land privatisation and an extremely small share of SOEs also mean that government net assets represent a rather marginal, or even negative, share of GDP in those economies.

Financial risks from the balance sheet perspective

Despite the tremendous wealth accumulated over the past four decades of reform and opening-up in China, many institutional and structural problems and risks have also built up, prompting the central government to make 'preventing and defusing major risks' the top priority of its recent policy agenda, which is summarised as 'three tough battles'.[5] Overall, thanks to roughly three years of concerted effort, China has managed to mitigate certain financial risks, especially preventing a systemic financial crisis. Despite these successes, China's overall macroeconomic risks remain alarming and tend to concentrate in government and other public institutions.

Financial risk mitigation under the policy to reduce and stabilise the leverage ratio

Aggregate financial leveraging constitutes a major source of financial fragility, so the effective reduction and stabilisation of the leverage ratio have mitigated overall financial risks.

First, as shown in Figure 3.14, the financial sector leverage ratio[6] peaked at the end of 2016 before decreasing substantially over the next three years. Whether measured in terms of assets or liabilities, China's financial sector leverage ratio in 2019 had declined approximately to its 2013 levels. In fact, the financial deleveraging policy has led to significant reductions in the off–balance sheet business of banks and the magnitude of shadow banking. According to a report produced by a research team from the China Banking and Insurance Regulatory Commission (Research Team of CBIRC 2020), by the end of 2016, China's shadow banking had reached a massive scale: exceeding RMB90 trillion in the broadest definition of the term, or RMB51 billion in its narrower sense. The rampant growth of shadow banking was effectively curbed with the implementation of a special three-year campaign. By the end of 2019, shadow banking in China, broadly defined, shrank to RMB84.8 trillion— down nearly RMB16 trillion from its record high of RMB100.4 trillion at the end of 2017. The riskiest shadow banking, as narrowly defined, decreased to RMB39.14 trillion—down RMB12 trillion from its record high.

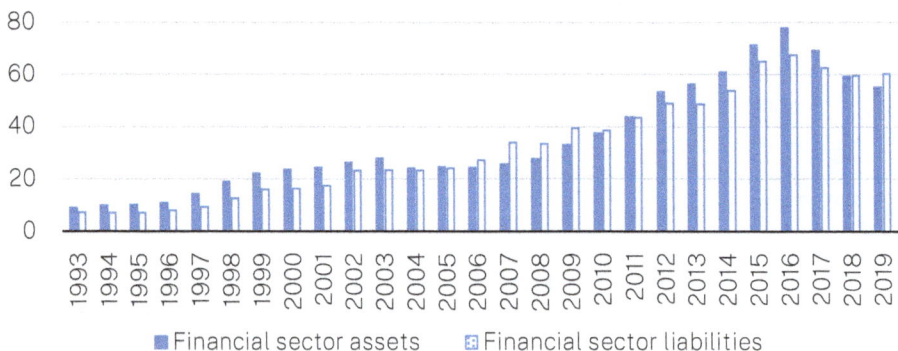

Figure 3.14 Financial sector leverage ratio in China (per cent)
Source: CNBS (www.nifd.cn/Center/Details/23).

---

5   In addition to preventing financial risk, the other two 'battles' are 'reducing poverty' and 'tackling pollution'.
6   The ratio is defined as the assets/liabilities of the financial sector scaled by GDP.

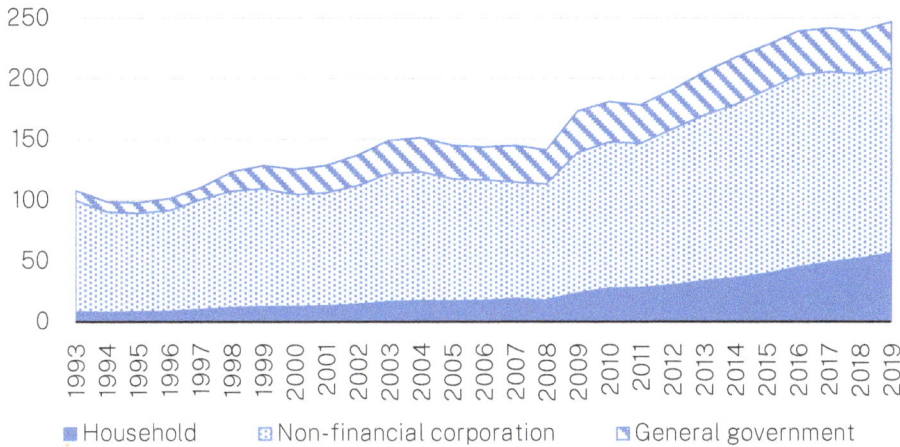

Figure 3.15 Leverage ratio of the real economy sector in China (per cent)
Source: CNBS (www.nifd.cn/Center/Details/23).

Second, as shown in Figure 3.15, the leverage ratio of China's real economic sectors[7] remained relatively stable over the period 2016–18. Notably, great progress was made in deleveraging by the corporate sector. With one of the highest leverage ratios in the world, China's corporate debt has topped the policy agenda of its deleveraging operations and, thanks to various efforts, the leverage ratio of the sector decreased from 160.4 per cent in Q1 2017 to 151 per cent at the end of 2019—down 10.6 percentage points in three years.

China's overall financial risk remains high and is concentrated in the general government sector

Since the peak of the Covid-19 pandemic, China's macro-leverage ratio has increased sharply. By Q3 2020, this ratio reached 270.1 per cent, which was close to the average of the advanced economies and emerging economies combined—namely, 273.1 per cent. However, it is 61.7 percentage points higher than the average ratio for emerging economies (208.4 per cent). It is believed that this once-in-a-century public health crisis has led to a further rise in China's overall financial stress.

Furthermore, despite the impressive deleveraging in non-financial corporations, financial risk has more recently tended to concentrate in the general government sector—a structural change that can be understood from the point of view of assets as well as liabilities.

---

7   The ratio, also referred to as 'macro-leverage ratio', is defined as the total debts of households, general government and the non-financial corporate sector, scaled by GDP.

Yi Gang (2020), governor of the People's Bank of China since 2018, estimated the risk undertaking of China's financial assets, with his analysis grounded on numerous assumptions that are basically consistent with China's national conditions and regulation. For deposits, it is assumed that 90 per cent of the household sector's risk and 80 per cent of deposit risk from other sectors are undertaken by financial institutions and that other risks are shared by households and other corresponding sectors. It is assumed that 70 per cent of loan risks are undertaken by financial institutions. Moreover, it is assumed that the default rate of collateralised and guaranteed loans is 50 per cent—that is, financial institutions and borrowers each assume 50 per cent of the potential financial losses. As far as wealth management and trust are concerned, it is assumed that 80 per cent of the risk is undertaken by financial institutions, given the implicit guarantee. Regarding treasury bonds, local government bonds and central bank bills, they can be deemed as assets free from credit risk for their holders, and the risks of those bonds are solely assumed by the government sector, whereas the risks in other bonds, such as corporate bonds, are assumed by their holders. In addition, currencies, reserve funds, central bank loans and international reserve assets are deemed to be risky assets whose risks should be undertaken by the government sector alone.

Based on the above assumptions made by Yi, we estimated the share of risky assets in total financial assets for each sector in 2018 to be: 9.4 per cent for the household sector, 13.8 per cent for the corporate sector, 17.7 per cent for the government sector, 54.5 per cent for financial institutions and 4.6 per cent for the foreign sector. Financial institutions and the government sector are the top two in terms of their share of risk undertakings. Since most Chinese financial enterprises are state-owned and even private financial institutions are supposed to be backed, at least implicitly, by the government to prevent systemic financial risk, relevant losses must still be covered by the government. Further assuming that 80 per cent of financial institutions are rescued by the government in a crisis, a total of 61.3 per cent of financial asset risks are thus expected to eventually be assumed by the government.[8]

Turning to the liability side, by our calculation with CNBS data, 21.8 per cent of China's total real-economy liabilities in 2018 were owed by households, 63.1 per cent by corporations and 15.1 per cent by the government sector. We assume that most private sector liabilities are undertaken by the private sector while public sector liabilities are primarily undertaken by the government. In view of this, the corporate sector can further be divided into SOEs and non-SOEs. Our estimate shows that the liabilities of the former as a share of total corporate sector liabilities grew from 57 per cent at the beginning of 2015 to 67 per cent by the end of 2018. Following

---

8   Namely, 54.5% × 0.8 + 17.7% = 61.3%.

such data, the public sector (combining SOEs and government) is estimated to have assumed 57.4 per cent of total debt risks in 2018,[9] which is close to the asset-side analysis presented above.

To summarise, whether from an asset-side or liability-side perspective, the broadly defined government sector assumes some 60 per cent of financial risks in China, so it seems reasonable to argue that financial risks have become heavily concentrated in the public sector.

Conclusion and policy implications

In this chapter, we draw on our estimation of China's national balance sheet to show, from an international perspective, the trends and structural changes in the country's wealth accumulation and financial risk dynamics over recent years. Although the work into such a promising line of research should be viewed as somewhat preliminary, the descriptive analysis and international comparison presented here nonetheless have important policy implications.

China's reform since the late 1970s is generally characterised as 'incremental' or gradualist, meaning that new development occurs outside the existing system without upending the old system. Incremental reform was able to achieve 'Pareto improvement'—that is, welfare improvement for all with compatible incentives, which did not produce 'losers' and thus was welcomed by all. However, unlike the incremental reforms of earlier years, today's reforms—which focus on the existing wealth stock—involve adjustments to vested interests, making Pareto improvement hard to achieve. In such circumstances, welfare improvement for some often comes at the expense of a welfare loss for others. With these concerns in mind, the following policy issues can be addressed.

Optimising the allocation of national wealth

As documented above, government wealth accounts for nearly one-quarter of China's national total, which is extremely high by international standards. With these tremendous resources and assets in hand, the government provides important assurances of the country's capacity to cope with various risks and achieving economic resilience and even national security. However, a crucial aspect of incremental reform is to activate these inventory assets and make use of government wealth with more efficiency and higher returns.

---

9   Namely, 63.1% × 0.67 + 15.1% = 57.4%.

In fact, making efficient use of government-controlled public wealth is a global issue and not unique to China. As Detter and Fölster (2015) pointed out in their book *The Public Wealth of Nations*, the public wealth held by governments is staggeringly large, even by conservative estimates, and a 1 per cent increase in the return on public wealth, according to their estimation, would yield an additional US$750 billion in revenue to the state. More professional management of assets held by central governments around the world could easily raise returns on assets by 3.5 per cent, thus incurring additional public revenue of US$2.7 trillion, which exceeds the sum of current global infrastructure projects, including in transportation, energy, water conservancy and telecommunications. It should be noted that their book focuses on commercial assets and excludes non-commercial or non-operating assets such as natural resources and administrative and public institutions.

In the case of China, government-allocated resources encompass not only commercial assets, but also natural resources and assets for social purposes. Thus, the allocation and efficiency of government assets in China appear to be more complex. Some serious challenges need mentioning, including market price distortions (especially regarding production factors and energy), as well as inefficiency and undersupply of public services. Hence, incremental reform should be carried out to substantially reduce direct government allocation of resources and reinforce market-based mechanisms and instruments to improve resource allocation efficiency.

To achieve this goal, China should first create a well-functioning property system for the paid acquisition and use of natural resources. In particular, Chinese law stipulates that an explicit property ownership system and sound management system should be established for natural resources owned by the nation—including land, mineral deposits, water, forests, hills, grassland, wasteland, maritime space, uninhabited islands and mudflats—and give play to the guidance and restrictive effects of spatial planning on the allocation of natural resources; promote market-based allocation of non-traditional natural resources such as radio frequencies; and improve the paid use of natural resources.

Second, the exit mechanism for the state sector from the economy should be improved and the associated layout of state-owned assets/capital should be optimised in favour of market efficiency. To deal with negative externalities, state capital should be concentrated in strategic industries, critical sectors and infrastructure vital to China's national security, economic resilience, sustainable development and people's wellbeing. It is important to properly consider the reasonable proportion of state involvement in the financial sector to maintain control over systemically vital financial institutions and to optimise the equity structure of other institutions based on market principles. Also, SOE reforms should be steadily advanced through new arrangements such as public–private partnerships and mixed-ownership restructuring to improve allocative efficiency.

Third, real estate investment trusts (REITs) are another promising initiative aimed at activating infrastructure and other inventory assets. REITs originated in the United States in the 1960s,[10] and publicly traded REIT pilot programs launched in China focus particularly on infrastructure sectors (Yin 2020). By our estimation, the public infrastructure assets on the government balance sheet amount to RMB9.56 trillion, which does not include commercial municipal public infrastructure with corporate operations or non-municipal public infrastructure that has been invested in and operated across cities and provinces. However, according to various studies (Jin 2016; Hu et al. 2016; Zhu and Zhu 2020), the full scope of infrastructure assets is roughly RMB37–53 trillion. If this huge stockpile of public wealth can be activated through REITs, SOEs and local governments will be provided with a long-term solution to the debt problem.

Fourth, reforming the distribution of aggregate wealth/income in favour of households, especially low and middle-income families, is also key to improving the allocative efficiency of economic resources and the promotion of private consumption. Clearly, such a rearrangement of wealth/income further contributes to achieving 'common prosperity'—a goal that has been recently underscored by China's central authorities. We suggest that a more systematic approach be taken to achieving this: in addition to the SOE reforms presented above, policy efforts should include further reduction of taxes and administrative fees, the institution of fiscal/monetary policies that support small and mid-sized enterprises and reform of rural land and housing systems to facilitate rural households' ability to increase their income through property and assets.

Liability management and 'sustainable' debt accumulation

Turning to the liability side, we focus exclusively on the debts of SOEs and local governments, which represent the lion's share of China's national debt. SOE debts account for 60–70 per cent of non-financial corporate sector debts, and thus constitute a key to reducing and stabilising the overall leverage ratio in the corporate sector. First, a large chunk of SOE debt is based on financing platforms that were explicitly or implicitly guaranteed by the government sector, especially local authorities. Although this is no longer the case under the Budget Law that took effect in 2015, we suggest such debt should be covered in new local debt-swap

---

10   By the end of 2019, the global publicly traded REITs market value exceeded US$2 trillion, with assets including office buildings, department stores, apartment buildings, hotels, warehouses and other commercial facilities, as well as infrastructure such as roads, airports, ports, communication, water, electricity and gas supply, and data centres.

programs. Second, some SOE debts should be restructured through market-oriented debt-for-equity swaps. Third, policy efforts should be advanced to foster the exit of zombie SOEs,[11] thereby making room for the entry of new firms.

In terms of local government debt, more local government bonds should be issued to not only cover the current-year deficits, but also to swap the aforementioned implicit debts (such as those through financing platforms). In addition, government deposits should be put into active use. In fact, by the end of 2019, China's government deposits amounted to RMB33.9 trillion, accounting for 34.4 per cent of the country's GDP in the same year, which is much greater than the shares for many advanced economies.[12] It is believed that making more active and efficient use of such huge government deposits will encourage local government initiatives to reinforce their fiscal capacity and alleviate the shortage of funds.

Putting all this together, China's rapid economic development can be ascribed to its system of 'catching up', in which SOEs, local governments and financial institutions have supported one another, with the central government as guarantor in a role like a 'lender of last resort'. This has the following advantages: all risks are guaranteed by the central government, allowing SOEs, local governments and financial institutions to concentrate on development with fewer scruples about debt stress and risk. It enables massive levels of resources to be mobilised in a short time for high growth (Zhang et al. 2019). On the other hand, this system naturally leads to soft budgetary constraints for SOEs and local governments, and thus constitutes the root cause of China's unchecked credit expansion and resulting high leverage ratio. In the meantime, credit markets are also distorted by the system as financial institutions often have expectations or illusions about implicit guarantees for investment and financing projects with state capital. Because of the latter, the golden rule that 'whoever owns must repay' is broken, giving rise to moral hazards, distorting financial asset pricing and inefficiencies in financial resource allocation. With this in mind, it is important to neutralise the implicit government guarantees in favour of a 'sustainable' debt accumulation path featuring market-based risk pricing. This also requires a mix of policies aimed at restructuring bankrupt SOEs and hardening and enforcing the budgetary discipline of local governments.

Appendix 3.1

---

11 'Zombie enterprises' are those whose income flows cannot cover their debt payments.

12 By comparison, the US Government's deposits stood at US$916 billion, or 5 per cent of US GDP in 2016; Germany's government deposits reached €330.8 billion in 2016, or 11 per cent of GDP; the UK Government's deposits totalled £86.3 billion in 2016, representing 4 per cent of GDP; and Japan's government deposits were ¥80.4 trillion in 2015, or 15 per cent of GDP.

Table A3.1 National balance sheet of China, 2019 (RMB billion)

	Households		Non-financial corporations		Financial institutions		General government		Foreign sector		National total		Total of all sectors##	
	Assets	Liabilities/ net worth	Assets	Liabilities/ net worth	Assets	Liabilities/ net worth	Assets	Liabilities/ net worth	Assets	Liabilities/ net worth	Assets	Liabilities/ net worth	Assets	Liabilities/ net worth
I. Non-financial assets	249,933		341,950		3,421		66,599				661,903		661,903	
1. Fixed assets	249,933		175,121		1,593		20,934				447,581		447,581	
2. Inventory			119,344				934				120,277		120,277	
3. Other non-financial assets			47,485		1,828		44,731				94,045		94,045	
II. Financial assets and liabilities	325,027	62,338	97,266	439,216	437,208	440,629	134,194	37,958	39,425	52,979	993,695	980,141	1,033,120	1,033,120
1. Currency	6,384		666		697	8,286	157		382		7,904	8,286	8,286	8,286
2. Deposits	112,067		62,115		19,894	228,040	33,918		2,977	2,930	227,993	228,040	230,970	230,970
3. Loans	1,420	62,338		118,060	182,195			189	5,784	8,813	183,616	180,587	189,400	189,400
4. Undiscounted bank acceptance bills			3,330	3,330							3,330	3,330	3,330	3,330
5. Insurance	12,969		5,558			18,527			94	94	18,527	18,527	18,622	18,622
6. Interbank loans					11,960	11,960					11,960	11,960	11,960	11,960
7. Reserve funds					23,586	23,586					23,586	23,586	23,586	23,586
8. Bonds	2,734		1,451	23,465	82,716	28,142	858	37,769	3,526	1,909	87,759	89,376	91,285	91,285
9. Shares and equity	170,211		6,115	269,220	33,307	28,776	85,000		6,043	2,680	294,633	297,996	300,676	300,676
10. Securities investment funds	19,242		3,342		48,836	81,075	9,655				81,075	81,075	81,075	81,075

CHINA'S TRANSITION TO A NEW PHASE OF DEVELOPMENT

	Households		Non-financial corporations		Financial institutions		General government		Foreign sector		National total		Total of all sectors‡‡	
11. Central Bank loans					12,237	12,237					12,237	12,237	12,237	12,237
12. Others				4,607			4,607				4,607	4,607	4,607	4,607
13. Direct investment			14,689	20,534					20,534	14,689	14,689	20,534	35,223	35,223
14. Official foreign exchange reserves					21,780				84	21,864	21,780		21,864	21,864
Net worth	512,622							162,835		-13,554		675,457		661,903
Total assets	574,960		439,216		440,629		200,793		39,425		1,655,598		1,695,023	
Liabilities and net worth		574,960		439,216		440,629		200,793		39,425		1,655,598		1,695,023

Source: Li et al. (2020).

References

Bond, C., T. Martin, S. McIntosh, and C. Mead. 2007. 'Integrated Macroeconomic Accounts for the United States.' *Survey of Current Business* 87(11).

Cao, Y. and J. Ma. 2012. 'Investigating National Balance Sheet.' [In Chinese]. *Caijing Magazine* (15).

Chow, G. 1993. 'Capital Formation and Economic Growth in China.' *Quarterly Journal of Economics* 108(3): 809–42. doi.org/10.2307/2118409.

Detter, D. and S. Fölster. 2015. *The Public Wealth of Nations: How Management of Public Assets Can Boost or Bust Economic Growth.* New York, NY: Springer. doi.org/10.1057/9781137519863.

Du, Jinfu (ed.). 2015. *Government Balance Sheet: Theory and Applications in China* [In Chinese]. Beijing: China Financial Publishing House.

Frecaut, O. 2017. 'Systemic Banking Crises: Completing the Enhanced Policy Responses.' *Journal of Financial Regulation and Compliance* 25(4): 381–95. doi.org/10.1108/JFRC-02-2017-0024.

Hu, L., G. Fan and J. Xu. 2016. 'Revised Estimation of China's Infrastructure Capital Stock.' *Economic Research Journal* 51(8): 172–86.

International Monetary Fund (IMF). 2014. *Government Finance Statistics Manual 2014.* Washington, DC: IMF.

International Monetary Fund (IMF). 2022. *Government Finance Statistics Database.* [Online]. Washington, DC: IMF. Available from: data.imf.org/?sk=a0867067-d23c-4ebc-ad23-d3b015045405.

Jin, G. 2016. 'Infrastructure and Non-Infrastructure Capital Stocks in China and their Productivity: a New Estimate.' *Economic Research Journal* 51(5): 41–56.

Koo, R. 2009. *The Holy Grail of Macroeconomics: Lessons from Japan's Great Recession.* Hoboken, NJ: Wiley.

Li, C. 2018. 'China's Household Balance Sheet: Accounting Issues, Wealth Accumulation, and Risk Diagnosis.' *China Economic Review* 51: 97–112. doi.org/10.1016/j.chieco.2018.04.012.

Li, C. and Y. Zhang. 2021. 'How Does Housing Wealth Affect Household Consumption? Evidence from Macro-Data with Special Implications for China.' *China Economic Review* 69(10): 101655. doi.org/10.1016/j.chieco.2021.101655.

Li, Y. and X. Zhang. 2013. *China's Road to Greater Financial Stability: Some Policy Perspectives.* Washington, DC: IMF Press.

Li, Y., X. Zhang, X. Chang and W. Cao. 2015. *National Balance Sheet of China 2015: Leverage Adjustments and Risk Management*. [In Chinese]. Beijing: China Social Sciences Press.

Li, Y., X. Zhang, X. Chang, D. Tang and C. Li. 2012a. 'China's Sovereign Balance Sheet and Its Risk Assessment: Part I.' [In Chinese]. *Economic Research Journal* 47(6): 4–19.

Li, Y., X. Zhang, X. Chang, D. Tang and C. Li. 2012b. 'China's Sovereign Balance Sheet and Its Risk Assessment: Part II.' [In Chinese]. *Economic Research Journal* 47(7): 4–21.

Li, Y., X. Zhang, X. Chang, D. Tang and X. Liu. 2013. *National Balance Sheet of China 2013: Theory, Method, and Risk Assessment*. [In Chinese]. Beijing: China Social Sciences Press.

Li, Y., X. Zhang, X. Chang and Y. Zhang. 2018. *National Balance Sheet of China 2018*. [In Chinese]. Beijing: China Social Sciences Press.

Li, Y., X. Zhang, L. Liu and D. Tang. 2020. *National Balance Sheet of China 2020*. [In Chinese]. Beijing, China Social Science Press.

Ma, Jun, Xiaorong Zhang and Zhiguo Li. 2012. *A Study of China's National Balance Sheet*. [In Chinese]. Beijing: Social Sciences Academic Press.

Naughton, B. 2017. 'Is China Socialist?' *Journal of Economic Perspectives* 31(1): 3–24. doi.org/10.1257/jep.31.1.3.

Petty, W. 1899. *The Economic Writings of Sir William Petty*. Cambridge: The University Press.

Piketty, T., L. Yang and G. Zucman. 2019. 'Capital Accumulation, Private Property, and Rising Inequality in China, 1978–2015.' *American Economic Review* 109(7): 2469–96. doi.org/10.1257/aer.20170973.

Research Team of China Banking and Insurance Regulatory Commission (CBIRC). 2020. 'Report on Shadow Banking in China.' [In Chinese]. *Financial Regulation Research* 107(11): 1–23.

Sheng, A. 2016. *Shadow Banking in China: An Opportunity for Financial Reform*. Hoboken, NJ: Wiley. doi.org/10.1002/9781119266396.

Summers, L. 2014. 'U.S. Economic Prospects: Secular Stagnation, Hysteresis, and the Zero Lower Bound.' *Business Economics* 49(2): 65–73. doi.org/10.1057/be.2014.13.

United Nations, European Commission, International Monetary Fund, Organisation for Economic Co-operation and Development and World Bank. 2009. *System of National Accounts 2008*. New York, NY: United Nations.

Wasshausen, D. 2011. 'Sectoral Balance Sheets for Nonfinancial Assets.' Paper presented in IMF/OECD 'Conference on Strengthening Sectoral Position and Flow Data in the Macroeconomic Accounts,' on February 28-March 2, 2011, Washington DC.

Yi, G. 2020. 'Revisiting China's Financial Asset Structure and Policy Implications.' [In Chinese]. *Economic Research Journal* 55(3): 14–17.

Yin, Y. 2020. 'Several Points on Doing Well the Work of Infrastructure REITs.' [In Chinese]. *China Finance* (23): 12–14.

Zhang, X., X. Liu and J. Wang. 2019. 'Debt Overhang, Risk Accumulation and Institutional Reform: Beyond the Developmental State.' [In Chinese]. *Economic Research Journal* 54(6): 4–21.

Zhu, F. and X. Zhu. 2020. 'Research on the Estimation of China's Infrastructure Net Capital Stock and Fixed Capital Consumption.' [In Chinese]. *The Journal of Quantitative & Technical Economics* 37(6): 70–88.

4

The platform economy in China: Innovation and regulation

Yiping Huang

Introduction

The platform economy refers to the new economic model that relies on network infrastructure such as cloud computing, internet and mobile terminals and uses digital technology such as artificial intelligence (AI), big-data analysis and blockchain to match transactions, transmit content and manage processes (Huang et al. 2022). Platform enterprises are not new, but application of digital technology has enabled digital platforms to break through the limits of traditional platforms in terms of scale, speed and computation, thus gaining unprecedented influence. So far, the more successful platforms are concentrated in the consumer sector, which can be divided into two types by function: transaction facilitation and content transmission. Transaction-enabling platforms aim to deliver transaction information and facilitate settlement of transactions, which can be further subdivided into platforms of e-commerce, payment, car calling, takeaway delivery and so on. Content-transmission platforms, such as social media and short video platforms, transmit information, news, opinions, entertainment, finance, science and technology, and promote content sharing. In the future, as new communication technologies such as 5G, with high throughput and low latency, lead to the establishment of the 'Internet of Everything', the industrial internet could become a new growth area and could give rise to new types of digital platforms.

The development of China's platform economy is not only a product of digital technological progress, but also the result of market-oriented reform. All the top platforms are privately owned. Measured by the number of world-leading platforms in 2019, each with market valuation of more than US$10 billion, China's platform economy is now the second largest in the world, second only to the United States

(CAICT 2021). This is a very impressive achievement considering that China is still a developing country. However, compared with the world's leading platforms, most of China's top platform companies do not possess many technological advantages. They succeeded mainly by learning and applying international cutting-edge digital technologies. However, it is worth noting that, during the first three industrial revolutions, China's technological applications significantly lagged the leading countries. During the current fourth industrial revolution, for the first time in history, Chinese companies have been advancing closely behind the international economic and technological frontiers.

In addition to digital technological breakthroughs and market-oriented reforms, China's unusual success in developing the platform economy is also attributable to four factors. The first is good digital infrastructure, which is largely the result of massive government investment in this area. The penetration rates of both the internet and smartphones in China are quite high, especially compared with other developing countries. These provide the technological basis for digital platforms to connect with huge numbers of users any time and anywhere. The second is the huge population, which makes some digital economic innovations more feasible and efficient. With a very large market, it is relatively easy to promote new digital platform models and easier to realise economies of scale. The third factor is relatively weak protection of individual rights. The downside of this 'weak protection' is widespread improper and illegal collection and analysis of personal data and violation of individuals' privacy. But it does give rise to many vibrant, innovative economic models based on big-data analysis and digital technology application. The fourth factor is segregation from the international market, which protects domestic platforms from international competition and provides space for them to innovate and grow. Of all these factors, the third is already changing and the fourth must change sooner or later. Therefore, maintaining the innovative capability of platform enterprises and ensuring sustainable growth of the platform economy in China are important challenges for both enterprises and the government.

The platform enterprises have already brought about some fundamental changes to the Chinese economy. On the one hand, platform enterprises support innovation, promote growth, improve efficiency and provide jobs. They not only take advantage of their long tails to reach a huge number of users, but also use big-data analysis to achieve accurate marketing and improve transaction efficiency. Today, digital platforms are already an integral part of people's daily lives, substantially reducing the entry barriers for online innovation, entrepreneurship and employment, and greatly contributing to productivity improvement and economic growth. On the other hand, the platform economy is rife with unfair competition that harms consumers. Some platforms use their vast market power to crowd out competitors. Some stifle innovation by means of 'killer' mergers and acquisitions (M&As). Others illegally obtain personal information and use algorithms to impose discriminatory pricing on consumers. More seriously, some platforms adopt practices of disorderly capital expansion, interfering with the market and social order. One important factor behind all these 'irregular' and 'illegal' behaviours is the lack of proper rules.

It is against this backdrop that China's platform economy saw the first year of 'strong regulation' in 2021,[1] after the Politburo of the Chinese Communist Party Central Committee and the annual Central Economic Work Conference, both held in December 2020, called for 'strengthening antimonopoly regulation and preventing disorderly expansion of capital'. The policy document issued by nine government departments led by the National Development and Reform Commission, *Opinions on Promoting Standardised, Healthy, and Sustainable Development of the Platform Economy*, outlined the scope of the 'strong regulations' (NDRC 2021). Intensive regulatory actions began in 2021. In April, China's State Administration for Market Regulation (SAMR) slapped a RMB18.23 billion (US$2.78 billion) fine on Alibaba Group for a monopolistic act of abusing its dominant market position, which was the first and biggest shock to the market. Throughout the rest of that year, a series of new laws and regulatory policies on data protection, antitrust, unfair competition and protection of workers' rights were issued by various regulatory bodies. Chinese President Xi Jinping pointed out that the purpose of the 'strong regulation' was to achieve the goal of 'developing through regulation and regulating through development'. In the Western media, this policy is often described as a 'crackdown'. Although the strong regulation did cause some negative effects from time to time, the true policy intention was to enhance the strengths of the platform economy and to minimise its shortcomings, ultimately making China's platform economy 'stronger, better and bigger'.

Improving the governance system is the basic premise for orderly development of the platform economy, which is currently a vibrant new economic sector without a complete policy framework. Therefore, an important motivation of the 'strong regulation' is to correct those inappropriate behaviours and complete construction of the governance building blocks. These initiatives already play positive roles in facilitating healthy development of the platform economy, but they also create some negative effects: from the beginning of 2021, the platform economy workforce shrank, the professional pride of employees declined, investment decreased by one-quarter and many founders of the leading platforms retired. More importantly, some investors, managers and employees started to wonder about the real policy intention. Weakening of activity and dynamism also contributed to a slowing of overall economic growth during the second half of 2021. It can be normal for extensive regulatory action to lead to temporary weakening of activity. What must

---

1　The term 'strong regulation' is directly translated from Chinese and can also be understood as 'heavy regulation' or 'strict regulation'. It refers to the general process of constructing a comprehensive regulatory framework for the platform economy.

be avoided is policy action causing a sustained downturn in the platform economy due to misunderstanding or improper policy implementation, which would run counter to the original intention of making the platform economy 'stronger, better and bigger'. From early 2022, policymakers began to voice a gradual turn in the 'strong regulation'. The Politburo meeting at the end of July explicitly stated that the 'special governing policy actions' should end and be replaced with routine regulation. However, it is not yet clear exactly what policy changes this will bring.

This chapter attempts a preliminary assessment of the 'strong regulation' policy starting in 2021 and proposes some policy directions for improving the governance of the platform economy. It intends to achieve the above goals by addressing the following questions. What factors contributed to the extraordinary development of China's platform economy during the past two decades? What was the motivation of the 'strong regulation' policy? What is the net impact of this policy on the outlook for the platform economy? And how can regulators do better in fostering orderly and sustainable development of the sector?

The main conclusions of this chapter can be summarised as follows. First, China has developed a large platform economy within a relatively short period, but most domestic platforms do not enjoy technological advantages. Some of the key contributing factors to the success of the platform economy, such as weak protection of individual rights and separation from the international market, are not sustainable in the long run. Therefore, it is important to construct a new governance structure aimed at improving the effectiveness of the market and the competitiveness of the industry. Second, some key characteristics of the platform economy have mixed impacts on economic operation. Economies of scale can improve efficiency but can open the way for the formation of monopoly power. Platforms create many opportunities for 'gig jobs', but these can harm workers' rights and interests if they lack proper social protection schemes. While data analysis reduces information asymmetry for the platforms, it can also exacerbate information opacity for other platform users, such as online businesses and consumers. Third, the original intention of the 'strong regulation' was to achieve orderly and healthy development, but 'campaign-style' regulation and regulatory competition have already caused many problems. It could be worth replacing the 'strong regulation' policy with a normal comprehensive governance system, clarifying policy objectives, improving policy coordination, adopting routine and responsive regulation, creating a data policy framework and adjusting the labour protection system. Fourth, within the broad governance structure, there should be some separation of economic regulation and antitrust policy, with the former maintaining efficient market functions and the latter repairing functions in that market. The perception of 'big being bad' would be harmful for development of the platform economy, as economies of scale are a natural feature of platforms.

In fact, economies of scope could help reconcile economies of scale with sufficient competition. Therefore, the key to preventing monopolies in the platform economy is ensuring the 'contestability' of the market—that is, levelling the entry barriers for potential competitors, which include not just licences but also other sunk costs (Baumol 1982; Furman et al. 2019). Fifth, the National People's Congress should accelerate the enacting of the Digital Economy Law, which could serve as the basic law for the governance of the platform economy, connecting different laws and regulations. It would also be useful to clearly define important concepts such as 'disorderly expansion of capital'. At the same time, China should actively participate in the formulation of international rules, including digital tax and trade, to create conditions for Chinese platforms to participate in international competition in the future.

Economic contribution of digital platforms

There are many platform enterprises in the traditional economy, such as department stores and farmers' markets. However, the platforms discussed in this chapter are digital ones utilising technologies such as the internet, big data, AI, mobile terminals, cloud computing, machine learning and so on. The basic functions of digital platforms are not significantly different from those of the traditional ones, but application of digital technology makes some of the original features much more prominent. Platforms often have a network effect: the more users, the greater is the value of the platform. They also have two-sided (or multisided) market effects: the more buyers (or sellers), the greater is the value of the platform to the sellers (or the buyers) (Rochet and Tirole 2003). These effects exist in all platforms, but they are more striking in digital platforms. In addition, revenue from advertising businesses based on the massive user size and big data could account for significant portions of the digital platforms' total revenue. Therefore, digital platforms sometimes subsidise users, such as with free use of social media services, to expand the user scale and generate more revenue from advertising. This last feature is not common in traditional platforms.

Development of China's platform economy started in the early 1990s. The first internet company, InfoHighWay, was established in 1995, after the country connected to the internet in 1994. Several prominent internet companies, including Netease, Sina, Tencent and Alibaba, were established in the following years. The first well-known leading digital platform, Alibaba's e-commerce platform Taobao, came online in June 2003, which kicked off a period of rapid development in China's platform economy. The rest, as they say, is history (Figure 4.1).

Exploration (1994–97)	Start-off (1998–2007)	Growth (2008–15)	Competition (2016–19)	COVID (2020)
				"Strong regulation" (2021–)
	JD Multimedia, Ant Group (Alipay) 2004			
	Taobao (Alibaba) (2003)			
	Baidu (2000)			
Alibaba (1999)		PinDuoDuo (2015)		
Tencent, Sina (1998)				
Neteast (1997)		ByteDance, Didi (2012)		
Sohu (1996)		LuFax, WeChat (Tencent) (2011)		
InfoHighWay (1995)				
Connected to internet (1994)		Meituan (2010)		

1990	1995	2000	2005	2010	2015	2020

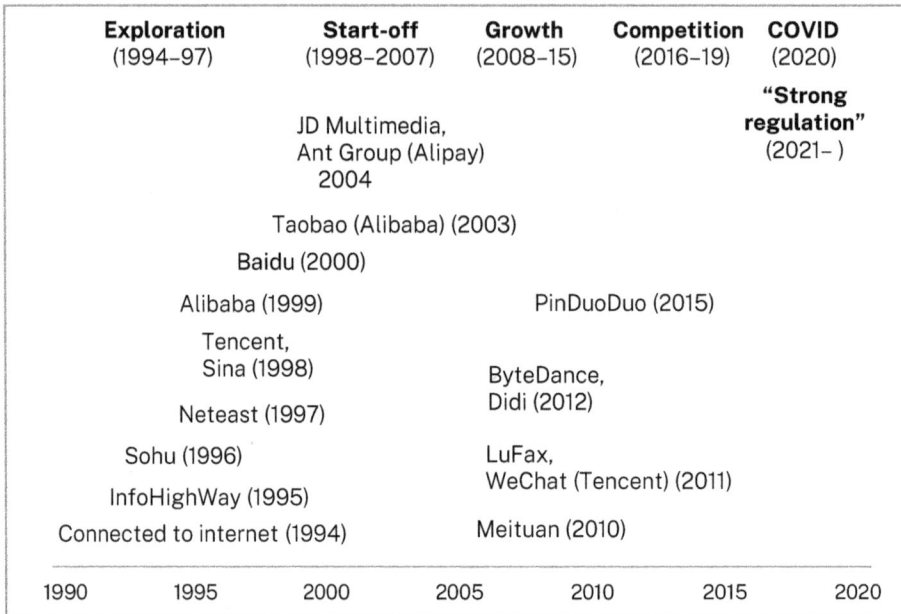

Figure 4.1 Development of China's platform economy
Source: Data compiled by the author.

Economic transformations brought about by digital technology, given its operational characteristics, can be summarised as follows: increasing business scale, increasing operational efficiency, improving the user experience, reducing cost, controlling risk and reducing human-to-human contact. The benefits of these to economic activity are obvious. Activities such as shopping, buying airline tickets, booking hotels, making appointments, communication, teaching, movie watching and many others that once required a lot of back-and-forth movement of people can now be done quickly through mobile terminals. These new businesses not only save time and reach many customers who could not be reached in the past, but also improve operational efficiency. Some activities that were originally difficult to conduct offline can now be done on the platforms. For instance, the entry barriers for opening a store or a company online are much lower, which greatly facilitates innovation and entrepreneurship. There are also a lot of 'flexible' employment opportunities online, absorbing many workers with low education and even those with disabilities. Some platforms can directly connect enterprises and consumers. Through these platforms, enterprises can not only market their products accurately to potential customers but also customise their products according to individual consumers' preferences.

At the macro level, the platform economy was the most important contributor to the growth of China's GDP and total factor productivity (TFP). Between 2001 and 2018, the crudely defined 'digital economy' contributed three-quarters

(74.4 per cent) of China's GDP growth.[2] While TFP growth was weakening during this period, the digital economy played a key role in stabilising the economy by maintaining a consistent positive TFP growth. It is also worth noting that during the past two decades, the largest contribution to economic growth came from capital inputs while the contribution of labour inputs was very small. However, during that period, the contribution of intersectoral labour reallocation to TFP growth was positive, while the contribution of capital allocation was negative. This indicates that the resource allocation function of the labour market is effective, but the capital market does not have the same allocative efficiency. This is worrisome as capital is becoming increasingly important to economic growth, but its allocation remains inefficient. This evidence supports the call for further financial reforms to improve the efficiency of the economy, including the platform economy.

Digital financial inclusion provides an important case study of the innovation of digital platforms. Promoting financial inclusion is a global challenge, the main difficulties of which lie in customer acquisition and risk management. Digital platforms reach many users through the long-tail effect, at nearly zero marginal cost, and provide these users with financial and non-financial services, including mobile payments. In the meantime, these platforms accumulate users' digital footprints to form big data to support financial decision-making. The innovation in both 'access' and 'risk control' provides a possible solution to the financial inclusion challenge, by providing some financial services to small and medium-sized enterprises (SMEs) and low-income households that were difficult for traditional financial institutions to reach. Today, users can enjoy good financial services no matter where they are, as long as they have a smartphone and internet connection. According to Peking University's Digital Financial Inclusion Index, the digital financial inclusion gap between inland and coastal regions substantially narrowed during the period 2011–20. The most successful digital financial inclusion businesses in China—such as mobile payments, big-tech credit online investment and central bank digital currency—are also at the forefront globally. China made a breakthrough in developing financial inclusion during the Thirteenth Five-Year Plan period (2016–20), which was largely attributable to the contribution of digital platforms.

The platform economy has also had a significant impact on economic and financial stability, although the overall impact requires more careful analysis. Two examples are provided here. First, before 2013, both the producer price index (PPI) and the consumer price index (CPI) were highly volatile. The PPI has maintained this high volatility, while the CPI has become a lot more stable. At the same time, the standard deviations of the interprovincial PPI and CPI continued to decline. One possible explanation for the significant increase in CPI stability over the past decade

---

2   Here the digital economy includes three broad industries: the information and communication technology (ICT) producing sector, the ICT intensive-use manufacturing sector and the ICT intensive-use service sector.

is the rapid development of e-commerce and logistics, which led to a high degree of integration among regional markets across the country and a significant increase in their ability to absorb shocks (Chen et al. 2021). Second, the replacement of collateralised assets with big-tech credit using big-data analytics as the primary means of credit risk management could diminish the asset price channel of the 'financial accelerator' generated by collateral lending. In the case of collateral lending, a pro-cyclical (or positive feedback) mechanism between asset prices and credit supply could increase financial instability, as lower asset prices reduce credit supply, which further lowers asset prices. Once data succeed in replacing collateralised assets in credit decisions, this pro-cyclical mechanism is significantly weakened, which could enhance the stability of the financial system (Gambacorta et al. forthcoming).

New challenges of the platform economy

Due to some basic characteristics of digital technology, the emerging platform economy raises many important new challenges. First, economies of scale characteristic of digital platforms can help improve efficiency, but they can also lead to the formation of monopoly power. Economies of scale mean that higher output corresponds to lower average costs, so large enterprises tend to be more efficient and competitive. The so-called long-tail effect shows that, once the platform is established, the marginal cost of expanding the scale of services is basically zero. Therefore, economies of scale of digital platforms make their services available to markets at unprecedented scales. At the same time, this can cause a winner-takes-all situation, because large platforms are much more efficient than small platforms. This means it could become difficult for new competitors to enter the market, effectively allowing incumbent platforms to form monopolies. Therefore, preventing monopolistic behaviour, disruption of market order and harm to the interests of consumers are indeed major challenges.

Second, there could be a conflict of interest between the operational objectives of the digital platforms as enterprises and their regulatory functions as platforms. In a traditional economy, enterprises, the market and the government play the functions of operation, transaction-matching and regulation, respectively. However, the platform enterprise breaks the boundary of the division of labour among these three, as it is a business entity, a trading venue and plays a certain regulatory role. As a regulator, it needs to uphold the principle of fairness and impartiality, but as an enterprise, it must pursue operating profits and obtain returns for investors. It is possible for the platforms to engage in 'self-preferential' practices. For example, some search platforms rank search results according to advertising revenue and some e-commerce platforms open their own online stores to sell best-selling products. These practices are unfair to other online shops and are detrimental to consumers' interests. However, digital platforms have played a positive role in improving social governance, such as e-government, digital government and smart city, around the world. In some countries, there have been instances of platforms interfering in politics, but of course the risk of this is small in China. However, the division of labour and cooperation between a platform and the government in playing the regulatory function has yet to be clarified. For example, how much responsibility should the platforms take for disputes that occur on the platform, and in what way should the government intervene?

Third, digital platform development is a product of innovation, but it can curb innovation at some point. Almost all platform companies are innovative, even though most of the Chinese platform companies do not enjoy global technological advantages. The fact that they started from nothing and grew to global companies in short periods is itself a story of very successful innovation. In addition, platforms often support the innovation and development of small and micro enterprises in various ways, sometimes as incubators. It is worth noting, however, that productivity in the digital economy has seen a significant slowdown in recent years, with its annual contribution to TFP valued at 2.5 (23 per cent of GDP growth over the same period), 1.3 (16 per cent) and 0.71 (13 per cent) percentage points over the periods 2001–07, 2007–12 and 2012–18, respectively. What factors caused this steady deceleration of productivity growth? Was it because Chinese platform companies approached the international technological frontier through continuous catch-up? Or was it because the top platforms used their abundant cash flow to carry out large-scale 'killer' M&As to eliminate potential competitors? Whatever the reason, it is now an urgent task to maintain the platform economy's strong innovation capability.

Fourth, while platform companies provide large numbers of 'gig jobs', they can also cause harm to workers, due to tough working conditions and insufficient social protection. The employment opportunities provided by the platform enterprises are diverse, ranging from translation, consulting and programming, to delivery and maintenance. Many of these jobs have relatively low entry barriers and flexible working hours, which make platform employment quite inclusive, serving as an important complement to formal employment. It is estimated that the total number of takeaway delivery workers nationwide exceeded 7 million, with individual leading platforms directly and indirectly providing tens of millions of jobs. However, the rise of this new labour market has also created some new problems. First, many offline jobs have been affected and the adjustment cost of re-employment is relatively high. While development of the platform economy provides an increase in new jobs, such structural adjustment in employment could still be costly for society. Second, the working conditions of some 'gig workers', especially takeaway delivery workers, are not good, as algorithms make the work increasingly intensive and sometimes dangerous. Finally, there is no good social welfare system for gig workers, many of whom do not have formal employment contracts with the platforms they serve. Therefore, they do not have protection when they experience an accident or unemployment.

Finally, big-data analysis can reduce information asymmetry for the platforms, but it could make information more opaque for other platform users including consumers. Data are the new 'oil' of the digital economy and the central government is proposing to make data a new factor of production, alongside land, labour and capital. The efficacy of big-data analysis has been fully demonstrated in the platform economy, helping platforms to improve operational efficiency, change business models and enhance personalised services. However, there are also many problems with the use of data on platforms. At present, some platforms have irregular or even illegal practices of collecting personal information and 'algorithmic discrimination' and black box algorithms (where the users cannot see the inner workings of the algorithm) are also quite common. Prices for products or services provided by platforms can vary for different users, at different times and in different regions. While there could be good reasons for this, most platform users lack the ability to judge the reasonableness of such dynamic pricing and there is no third-party organisation to oversee this function. Therefore, the basic premise of data as a factor of production should be to establish a suitable governance framework. But since data are a special factor of production, one cannot simply apply the rules of traditional factors such as land and capital in terms of rights, transactions and pricing.

Dilemma of the 'strong regulations'

The 'strong regulations' for the platform economy introduced in 2021 have encountered difficulties in at least two respects. One important purpose of the 'strong regulations' was to establish a complete system of governance for the platform economy. However, simultaneous actions by multiple government departments could cause 'campaign-style' governance that has a big impact on the platform economy. How to balance the long-term goal of constructing a complete regulatory framework with the short-term objective of maintaining healthy development is a major challenge for policymakers. Meanwhile, the platform economy differs from the traditional economy in many ways, which can bring many benefits but also cause many problems. Any regulations should retain the benefits and minimise the problems. However, if the policy is based on the traditional economy, it will not be conducive to healthy development. There are two aspects of the platform governance policy: economic regulation and antitrust provisions. Policy innovations are urgently needed on both fronts and also on coordination between the two.

The United States' antitrust policy is relatively mature, starting with the *Sherman Act* of 1890, which clearly states that joint conspiracy is illegal and attempting to dominate a market is a crime. In 1914, the *Clayton Act* and the *Federal Trade Commission Act* were issued, which, together with the *Sherman Act*, constitute the basic antitrust law in the United States. For a long period, consumer welfare was an important criterion for determining the existence of monopoly power, while consumer prices were an important indicator of consumer welfare. However, this approach makes the current antitrust investigations powerless against the monopolistic behaviour of giant platform enterprises because many platforms not only do not raise prices for consumers, but also lower prices or even provide free services. This, however, does not necessarily mean that consumers are 'subsidised' or that platforms do not exhibit monopolistic behaviour. For instance, platforms do not charge for the use of social media functions, but users do 'pay' by providing data and a market, so the service is not exactly free. This is the background of the rise of the 'New Brandeis' doctrine in recent years, the core proposition of which is 'the curse of big-ness', as some digital platforms not only have a conflict of interest serving as players and referees simultaneously but also often use strategies such as 'predatory pricing' and 'vertical integration' to gain monopoly power (Khan 2017; Wu 2018).

The idea of 'big being bad' might not be suitable for the platform economy. Economies of scale are one of the basic characteristics of digital platforms and the platform economy cannot develop if it is subject to antimonopoly crackdowns when the platforms get bigger. In fact, some of the platform companies in China are very large, but the degree of competition in many sectors—including e-commerce, car-hailing and food delivery—remains quite high. During the past 10 years, the market share of e-commerce businesses changed dramatically, indicating that the platform that previously accounted for a large share did not have a monopoly. So, large scale is not necessarily the same as a monopoly. The key is to watch the 'contestability'—that is, the threshold of entry for potential competitors. Here, barriers to entry include licences and other sunk costs, such as users and data. If the barriers to entry stay low enough, incumbent platforms cannot engage in monopolistic behaviour even if their market share is high. For example, the largest e-commerce platform's share of the national market declined from 92 per cent in 2012 to 42 per cent in 2020, suggesting that this platform did not possess monopoly power in 2012 and that most of its reduced market share was divided between social media platforms, short-form video platforms and other new e-commerce platforms. This phenomenon of new entrants is related to another key feature of the digital platforms: the economies of scope, where the total cost of producing multiple products at the same time is lower than the sum of the costs of producing each product separately. To put it in plain English, once established, the digital platforms may be able to enter other businesses to compete. Economies of scope potentially allow for reconciliation between sufficient competition and economies of scale. Social media platforms can enter the e-commerce field based on their existing users and data, so that even a dominant e-commerce platform cannot enjoy a monopoly dividend. In fact, cross-business operation is very common in China's platform economy, which implies that the antitrust policy might not be the most urgent task and the focus of antitrust enforcement should not be simply on big fines, let alone splitting up large digital platforms. Instead, the policy focus should be on enhancing 'contestability'—that is, lowering the threshold of entry for potential competitors.

In contrast, the task of platform regulation is urgent, especially because of the need to build a complete regulatory system. The important features of the current platform economy regulation are multiple regulators and campaign-style governance, which cause great uncertainty for the platform economy. Previously, few regulators acted to regulate the behaviour of platform enterprises, but once the 'strong regulations' were introduced, all regulatory departments began to compete. Thus, the 'strong regulations' not only involved many departments, but also promulgated more and more new laws, methods and regulations. Many of the 'common' business practices of the past suddenly became problematic, causing 'retroactive' penalties and instability in the sector. The 'strong regulations' have two shortcomings: one is the lack of a unified policy framework, with the relevant laws and regulations not always consistent with one another; the other is the lack of an effective policy coordination mechanism. The latter often leads to what policymakers call short-term enforcement of long-term policy objectives and fragmented implementation of systemic policy strategies. Hence, the purpose of strengthening the governance of the platform economy should be to establish a complete set of regulatory rules and governance tools and eventually transform governance from surprise action to routine regulation.

Many of the platforms' 'irregular' behaviours, such as exclusive agreements and differentiated pricing, were targeted by the 'strong regulations'. These activities must be carefully analysed before taking regulatory action given the characteristics of the platform economy. For instance, if some platforms charge high fees to individual consumers based on asymmetric information and not necessarily on their market power, this activity is more like cheating or fraud than monopolistic behaviour. Again, platforms should be prohibited from relying on their market position to exclude competitors. But if the platforms invest a lot of resources in promoting and marketing their products or services, then exclusive agreements could be reasonable, just like the exclusive agency often seen in medicine. Similarly, whether differential pricing is reasonable depends on market supply, demand and costs, and cannot be broadly identified as discriminatory behaviour. This requires regulatory policies based on rigorous economic analysis, as well as clear procedures to help determine reasonableness.

Reconstructing China's platform economy

The motivation for the 'strong regulations' was to achieve an ideal state of 'regulating through development and developing through regulation'. The goal was not to crack down on the platform economy, which is the most dynamic sector in the Chinese economy. Rather, the authorities intended to make the sector 'stronger, better and bigger'. While it is necessary to construct a comprehensive governance system for this new economic sector, where improper and illegal behaviours are common, the authorities must take care in designing and implementing new policies, including balancing the long-term policy direction with short-term policy impacts. China is already a big player in the global platform economy and new policies should support continued healthy development of this sector. Unfortunately, since the start of the 'strong regulations', momentum in the platform economy has slowed visibly and the gap between the leading Chinese and US platforms has widened significantly. The platform economies of Europe and other regions are also catching up rapidly. If the current downturn is not reversed quickly, China will quickly fall behind. This calls for clarification of the policy goals, construction of a comprehensive governance structure, change in regulatory behaviours and improved policy coordination. In short, the way to build a strong platform economy is through routine and responsive regulation, not campaign-style regulation or regulatory competition. It would be advisable to abandon the term 'strong regulation', which is conducive to political campaign-type policy action.

China must establish a comprehensive governance system for the platform economy. At present, there are many different policies, such as those relating to data protection and antitrust, but there is no coherent framework linking all of them. One way of doing this is to enact the Digital Economy Law to cover all policy and legal issues related to the digital economy. It can provide a systematic legal basis for governance of the platform economy. The objectives of the governance system should be clearly defined to guarantee full competition, support innovation and protect consumer rights. It is also advisable to clearly define the concept of 'disorderly expansion of capital' to avoid 'overkill' by regulation. Implementation of regulatory policy should be on a routine basis, while execution of antitrust policy should be periodical, but both should work towards the same goal: efficient functioning of the market.

There is an urgent need for an effective mechanism for policy coordination for the platform economy. This can be done through clarifying the division of labour and enhanced policy coordination among different regulatory bodies in the short term and by establishing a comprehensive governance organisation for the platform economy in the long term. China's platform economy is regulated by both industry regulators, such as the Ministry of Communications, the People's Bank of China and the Ministry of Industry and Information Technology, and by general regulators such as the SAMR. They are responsible for maintaining market order, antitrust enforcement and data governance rules. One of the main problems in the past was a lack of effective coordination among different policies. All these bodies would regulate digital platforms, causing 'regulatory competition'. In the short term, the State Council could consider establishing a coordination mechanism to work with the various regulatory bodies. In the long term, the authorities could consider setting up a comprehensive regulatory body for the platform economy.

Regulators should take extra care when exercising antitrust enforcement because the platform economy exhibits many new features that differ from those of traditional platforms. This makes some of the conventional ideas of antitrust policy inappropriate in this new area. For instance, free services for platform users do not mean there is no cost for them. Thus, it would be misleading to continue to focus on consumer pricing as an indicator of monopoly behaviour; market share might not be an accurate predictor of monopoly power. The economies of scope make it possible for sufficient competition and economies of scale to coexist; certainly, it would be counterproductive to break up platform companies as size is the source of their efficiency. Therefore, antitrust policy must adopt new thinking, considering the special features of digital technology. One useful concept to keep in mind is 'contestability' of the market. In the Chinese platform economy, competition remains intensive in most subsectors because most leading platforms compete across different subsectors. Therefore, policy priorities should be on maintaining relatively low entry barriers for potential competitors rather than breaking up large platforms or imposing large fines on them.

It is more urgent to correct platforms' behaviour through regulation. The platform economy is full of improper behaviour mainly because there has been a regulatory vacuum. Most of these behaviours are cheating, discrimination or fraud, and have nothing to do with monopolies. It is important to avoid political campaign-style regulations and to opt instead for regulation that is gradual, routine and responsive. This is particularly important for new economic areas like the platform economy, where there is an incomplete policy framework and no mature regulatory practice. Regulation is important, but regulators should allow time and space for the platforms to improve their behaviour. At the same time, it is important to carefully analyse some unique behaviours of the platforms, such as exclusive agreements ('picking one out of two') and dynamic pricing (that is, price discrimination). Not all such practices are monopolistic, discriminatory or illegal. Therefore, formulation and implementation of regulatory policies should be based on rigorous economic analyses.

It is also important to formulate and coordinate data policies and implement algorithmic audits. Again, governance policies for traditional factors such as labour and capital might not be applicable for data. For instance, data is a quasi-public good, with important features such as non-competitiveness and partial exclusivity; the traditional approach of first identifying ownership rights and then trading might not work here. It is recommended that a high-profile data governance committee be established to coordinate data policies, including setting guidelines on the scope of trading of data, algorithm governance and personal information protection and data security; implementing the application, review, issuance, restriction of use and revocation of data licences; promoting algorithm audits; coordinating efforts on personal information protection and data security; and setting up dispute-resolution and coordination mechanisms. It is also recommended that algorithm audits focus on data governance by requiring relevant companies to report on inputs, outputs and result evaluation.

Reference

Baumol, William J. 1982. 'Contestable Markets: An Uprising in the Theory of Industrial Structure.' *American Economic Review* 72(1): 1–15.

Chen, Xinyu, Yiping Huang and Han Qiu. 2021. *Can E-Commerce Markets Enhance Price Stability? Empirical Evidence from Pure Milk Products*. Beijing: Institute of Digital Finance, Peking University.

China Academy of Information and Communication Technology (CAICT). 2021. *White Paper on Digital Economic Development in China*. Beijing: CAICT.

Furman, Jason, Diane Coyle, Amelia Fletcher, Philip Marsden and Derek McAuley. 2019. *Unlocking Digital Competition: Report of the Digital Competition Expert Panel*. London: Digital Competition Expert Panel.

Gambacorta, L., Y. Huang, Z. Li, H. Qiu and S. Chen. Forthcoming. 'Data vs Collateral.' *Review of Finance*.

Huang, Yiping, Feng Deng, Yan Shen and Hao Wang. 2022. *Reconstructing the Platform Economy: Toward Orderly Expansion and Common Prosperity. Report of the Project 'Innovation and Governance of the Platform Economy in China'*. Beijing: National School of Development, Peking University.

Khan, Lina. 2017. 'Amazon's Antitrust Paradox.' *The Yale Law Journal* 126(3): 594–967.

National Development and Reform Commission (NDRC). 2021. *Opinions on Promoting Standardised, Healthy, and Sustainable Development of the Platform Economy*. 24 December. Beijing: NDRC. Available from: www.gov.cn/zhengce/zhengceku/2022-01/20/content_5669431.htm.

Rochet, J.-C. and J. Tirole. 2003. 'Platform Competition in Two-Sided Markets.' *Journal of the European Economic Association* 1(4): 990–1029. doi.org/10.1162/154247603322493212.

Wu, Tim. 2018. *The Curse of Bigness: Antitrust in the New Gilded Age*. New York, NY: Columbia Global Reports. doi.org/10.2307/j.ctv1fx4h9c.

5

Global industrial chain restructuring and China's choice[1]

Qiyuan Xu

The Chinese economy has embarked on a new development phase. While the nation has achieved decisive success in becoming a moderately prosperous society, its development environment is confronting profound and complex changes. In this context, China's industries face two major challenges: industrial chain upgrading and industrial chain security.

Industrial chain upgrading must meet the requirements of China's present phase of development, while digital technology and the green economy provide it with roadmaps to the future. Industrial chain security is related more to the ongoing China–US trade conflict and Covid-19 pandemic–related shocks. To be sure, the logic of the two intersect to a certain degree. In the context of external environmental changes, for example, the China–US conflict has not only caused China to prioritise industrial chain security; it has also made the promotion of industrial chain upgrading even more pressing. Driven by external pressures, China is stressing the need for industrial chain upgrading, even as the issue of security remains the fundamental starting point.

In the absence of Sino-US conflict, the impacts on global supply chains of the pandemic, the digital technology revolution and development of the green economy would have been more neutral and would have largely resulted in conventional survival-of-the-fittest competition between traditional and emerging sectors. But against the background of the trade conflict, the disrupting effects of digital

1 This article was financed by a 2020 research proposal from Finance 40 Forum. This research was undertaken by Xu Qiyuan and Dong Yan. Key members of the research team also included: Zhao Hai, Su Qingyi, Cui Xiaomin, Yao Xi, Yang Panpan, Ma Yingying, Xiong Wan Ting, Dong Weijia, Chen Sichong, Lang Ping, Pan Yuanyuan and Hou Lei.

technology and digital globalisation have led to a deterioration in trust between the two countries. Meanwhile, tackling climate change has become one of the few consensus issues shared by China and the United States, making it more meaningful to the global economy.

In this sense, we regard the China–US conflict as the primary logic behind these dynamics, with the impacts of the pandemic, digital technology and the green economy as three sub-logics. Based on this assumption, this chapter presents seven key conclusions.

In the context of globalisation in the digital age, the China–US conflict is uniquely complex

The existing literature has generally highlighted the fact that the China–US conflict is underpinned by both ideological and 'Thucydides Trap'–like challenges (Allison 2015; Xiao and Xu 2019). Meanwhile, the development of digital technology has blurred the boundaries of dual-use technology (technology used for military and civilian purposes) to such an extent that the China–US conflict has taken on a unique degree of complexity compared with similar historical cases.

Traditional trade and production integration has evolved in the digital age, as globalisation has generated cross-border flows of information in addition to the traditional flows of commodity sales and capital. Massive cross-border flows of information have implications for national security, particularly in relation to dual-use technologies, while the mechanisms of global governance still remain in the age of pre-digital-globalisation.

The encounters and conflicts playing out in the digital sector between China and the United States were never a factor in US–Russia, US–Japan and other conflicts in the past.

Information technology has fostered integration but has ironically led to declining trust between the two countries. This, coupled with the build-up of other complicating factors, such as conflicting ideologies and the Thucydides Trap, have conspired to make China–US relations more complex and vulnerable (Xu and Zhao, 2020). Indeed, it has even relegated trade and investment conflicts to secondary importance. Conflicts in the information sector directly impinging on matters of national security and international competition for top-level technological primacy will become increasingly prominent and difficult to solve. In turn, these could further exacerbate existing contradictions and conflicts in the traditional realms of trade and investment. Both sides should therefore attempt to face conflicts in this sector with greater wisdom and patience.

Three trends in global industrial chain restructuring: Diversification, digitisation and low carbon

Covid-19 has affected the industrial supply chains of different countries to varying degrees and global supply chains have been confronted by enormous uncertainty. In response, multinational corporations (MNCs) have begun to reassess their supply chain management practices—which were formerly concerned primarily with efficiency—turning to consider ways to better balance efficiency and security. Even governments in major nations such as the United States and Japan have begun to reflect on their industrial supply chain policies, emphasising the importance of autonomy and control, with social cost as the ultimate benchmark for industrial configuration. Adjustments have been made to the structure of the supply chains for medicines, computer chips and other key industries, and the establishment of domestic emergency backup supply chains, the repatriation of key industries, a return to regionalisation as well as the shortening of supply chains.

The pandemic will eventually pass but the world will have changed forever. The impact of Covid-19 on political and economic rationales has affected the reconstruction trends of global industrial supply chains. We believe three characteristics will emerge in the development of future global industrial chains.

First, MNCs will enhance industrial supply chain risk-mitigation capabilities by diversifying production (Ma and Cui 2021), which could result in some degree of industrial relocation for China but this differs from simple industry outside moving. In this context, the degree to which China can improve its business environment, ensure the stability and predictability of its supply chains and provide confidence and assurance to global downstream manufacturers will affect its future status in global supply chains.

Second, as the global landscape of factor endowments changes, global industrial supply chains will present knowledge-based, digitisation and capitalisation trends. In this process, the comparative advantage of the global division of labour will be redefined. Although some countries may enjoy a comparative labour cost advantage, many are relative laggards in developing their digital economies and there are bottlenecks in relevant infrastructure. In contrast, China possesses certain advantages and faces certain concerns in the process of industrial chain digitisation and capitalisation.

In terms of advantages, China has a huge market size and relatively fast development of digital infrastructure, which provides conditions for the popularisation and application of digital technology. In addition, compared with the industrial hollowing out in some developed countries, China has a strong manufacturing capacity and a complete supporting network, which also provides a good foundation for the application of digital technology in manufacturing. However, the digital development of China's industrial chain also faces challenges. The rules of governance for cyber security are not yet uniform across countries, China's cyber governance still needs to be improved urgently and adjusted to the new situations, and there are still value conflicts between China and some other countries in this field.

Last, modes of production will become green and low-carbon. This could significantly influence developing countries that are either heavily dependent on energy exports or in the process of industrialisation. Tackling climate change has added constraints on the growth potential of developing economies and, in the context of the trend towards low carbon, carbon tariffs will make an export-oriented development model more difficult to replicate. In March 2019, the European Parliament passed the Carbon Border Adjustment Mechanism. In comparison, in 2008, the US Congress had tried to promote the *Lieberman–Warner Climate Security Act*, which was also related to carbon tariffs. In both cases, exemptions to tariffs were intended to apply only to a few small economies. Such limited exemptions leave larger economies still in the process of industrialisation—such as India, Vietnam and others heavily dependent on high-carbon resource exports—facing substantial challenges for future development. Compared with these developing countries, China has already completed its extensive growth phase and has entered a development phase characterised by intensive growth. In recent years, the embodied carbon emissions of China's exports have started to decline, while its green technology, green industry and green financial markets have all developed rapidly. This will facilitate China's ability to deal with future 'green shocks'.

The current trends towards digitisation and low carbon could become digital and green divides, separating developed and developing countries, with the latter increasingly struggling to catch up with their developed counterparts. For China, such a landscape presents both challenges and opportunities.

China's industrial chains are both globally influential and vulnerable

With reference to Korniyenko et al. (2017), our research shows that China has an advantage in more than 80 per cent of high-centrality export goods, meaning China's supply chains show strong tenacity. According to the UN Industrial Development Organization's industrial classification, China is the only country in the world with industries in the large, medium and small sectors. From 2017 to 2018, global trade included 3,556 intermediate goods according to HS 6-digits level of UN Comtrade database, with China ranked among the top-three export nations globally for 2,247 of these goods by volume. Meanwhile, China exports 858 high-centrality goods (second only to the United States in terms of volume), and it ranked at least third in the world for 693 (of 858) intermediate goods in terms of the size of exports (ranking first in 444 of them in 2017 and 2018).[2] This suggests China possesses a significant export advantage in high-centrality intermediate goods. It also speaks to the significant impact felt by global supply chains during the period before and after February 2020, when China was striving to control the spread of Covid-19, sparking concern around the world. A report released by the United Nations in March 2020 indicated that approximately 20 per cent of global trade of manufactured intermediate goods came from China. If China's intermediate goods exports were to decline by 2 percentage points, the exports of 45 major economies would decrease by approximately US$46 billion, with Europe, the United States, Japan, South Korea and Taiwan (China) most heavily affected.

China has no advantage in 20 per cent of high-centrality export goods. Many of its exports also present 'large import and large export' characteristics, implying that a large quantity of intermediate goods is required during the production process. According to the product-level composite vulnerability index designed by our research team, electrical machinery and audio and video equipment (HS-2:85), mechanical equipment (HS-2:84) and optical medical instruments (HS-2:90) are the three industries with the most vulnerable supply chains in China. In particular, the composite vulnerability index ranking of electrical machinery and audio and video equipment (HS-2:85) is more than three times that of the last two industries; therefore, China needs to pay particular attention to this industry's supply chain security. We have built a system of indices and then classified all 3,285 intermediate goods (according to HS 6-digits level) imported into China in 2017 into four categories based on industrial supply chain vulnerability (Cui et al. 2021).

Category 1 comprises 62 intermediate goods out of 3,285 for which both global export centrality[3] and China's import concentration are high. This category is the most vulnerable to external shocks like the US–China trade war and the global pandemic and is the most challenging for which to implement backup supply chains. Given these risks, this category should be given special assessment and priority. Industrial supply chain security plans should be formulated at the national and industry levels for those goods that possess national security and national development strategy implications.

Category 2 comprises 812 goods for which China's import concentration is lower and supply chain vulnerability is smaller than those in the first category. However, the global export centrality of these products is also higher, hence the potential

---

2   To control the impact the China–US trade war could have on existing trade network relationships, we have designated goods with export centrality in the top 25 per cent between 2017 and 2018 as high-centrality goods.
3   If an intermediate good shows a high global export centrality, it means less countries accounted for a large exports of this goods in the global market.

for future deterioration. China's import concentration is low for this category of goods, imports could easily be diversified and the current volume of imports is typically quite small. However, if the import volume for such goods was to rise significantly over the medium to long term, market concentration would increase and converge with global export centrality. Under such circumstances, goods in this category could be reclassified into Category 1 with the highest vulnerability. For this category of goods, a long-term view should be adopted and industrial supply chain security planning enhanced.

Category 3 comprises 759 goods that display higher import concentration, but lower global export centrality. Further diversification of import sources could be feasible for this category—specifically, the import concentration index of 39.8 per cent for China's high-vulnerability import goods is relatively high, but their global export centrality index is quite low, with electrical machinery and audio and video equipment (HS-2:85), mechanical equipment (HS-2:84) and optical medical instruments (HS-2:90) the usual suspects. China has some room to enhance supply chain diversification for these goods, hence industrial supply chain security remains relatively high for this category.

Category 4 comprises 1,652 intermediate goods with both low global export centrality and low import concentration. The supply chains for this category are the least vulnerable and their positions remain quite stable. The goods in this category represent more than 50 per cent of all imports in the intermediate goods categories and 48.2 per cent of import value.

The paradox of national industrial supply chains and the art of balance

From an industry-level perspective and based on individual country case studies, our research reveals that a paradox exists in industrial supply chains: a country cannot have both global influence and competitiveness in a particular industrial supply chain while simultaneously possessing complete autonomy and control over such a chain.

Our analysis of individual case studies for nine major economies has provided strong evidence of this paradox. Developed economies like the United States, Japan, Germany and other major European nations are established industrial superpowers close to the cutting edge of technological innovation. At the same time, they are also heavily dependent on imported goods and global production networks. We analysed individual countries with the same methodology as the aforementioned China's case, with our research indicating that the more internationally competitive a country's industries were, the more dependent they became on imported intermediate goods trade and the greater was their vulnerability to disruptions in global supply chains.

Take, for example, Japan, South Korea and the United States—countries with strong semiconductor industries, but whose electrical machinery and audio and video equipment (HS-2:85) are also the most heavily reliant on imports. Meanwhile, the mechanical equipment (HS-2:84) of Germany, the United Kingdom, France and Italy are globally competitive, yet their machinery equipment industries also top the rankings in terms of vulnerability. France, for example, is home to Airbus production, but aircraft, spacecraft and their parts and components (HS-2:88) are ranked as the country's third most vulnerable sector to supply chain disruption.

Next, we analysed China's manufacturing data by industry and showed that the industrial supply chain paradox is present in its technologically intensive industries but not in its labour-intensive industries (Yao et al. 2021). In this empirical research, we constructed a set of external reliance indicators for China's manufacturing sector by industry and used UIBE GVC indicators to depict the global position of a particular industry (competitiveness). When controlling for the impact of other variables, we were able to show that for technologically intensive industries, as the position of a particular industry rose in the global value chain, the level of that industry's external reliance also showed a rising trend. It is worth noting that this paradox was found only in technology-intensive industries and not in labour-intensive industries. This could be because supply chains for labour-intensive industries are shorter and circulation within a country can be more readily achieved.

Last, China can learn from the way the United States has achieved a more efficient balance in the face of the industrial supply chain paradox. Our research suggests it managed to achieve security assurances for its industrial supply chains through its political relationships and international alliances. If economic factors were the only consideration, China's global supply chain risk would be lower than that of the United States; however, after taking political relationships and supply interruption capabilities into consideration, China's global supply chain risk rises significantly while risk to the United States remains unchanged. Compared with the United States, China's global supply chain risk is more susceptible to political factors. Based on the US case study, under certain conditions, industrial supply chain security and competitiveness can be obtained. Therefore China, while increasing its industrial supply chain security, must also create positive political relationships with major nations to secure the competitiveness and efficiency of its industries (Su 2021).

China–US tariff exclusion rates could be raised to promote a decrease in bilateral tariffs

During the Trump administration, the United States imposed US$370 billion worth of tariffs on Chinese exports. Given current domestic political conditions, the Biden administration is not in a position to abolish these tariffs. First, since taking office, the Biden administration has issued executive orders to strengthen the *Buy American Act*, and in June 2021, President Joe Biden released his 100-day review of supply chain risks tied to semiconductors, electric vehicle (EV) batteries, rare earths and pharmaceuticals (including active pharmaceutical ingredients). This indicates that the administration's chief international economic policy consideration is to maintain a technological generation gap with China and ensure supply chain security. At a Senate confirmation hearing, the US Trade Representative (USTR), Katherine Tai, expressly stated that the United States was not ready to lift tariffs on China. Second, strong protectionist political demands exist within the United States. Indeed, in a political environment that regards China as a strategic competitor, the two US political parties have reached a consensus that a display of any policy weakness towards China would be pernicious. The relationship between China and the United States has, to some extent, fallen victim to partisan politics. Third, tactically, it is in the Biden administration's interest to save these tariffs for use as potential bargaining chips in its trade negotiations with China. Even free trade advocates within the United States such as former Treasury secretary Hank Paulson and the Business Roundtable who advocate for the cutting of tariffs on China nonetheless believe any such cuts should be used to gain concessions in new rounds of trade negotiations. Katherine Tai has hinted that she supports the above China trade strategy.

Against this backdrop, the possibility of both China and the United States increasing tariff exclusion rates is feasible and realistic.

First, a policy of wideranging tariffs is not the Biden administration's first choice. On coming to power, its first goal was to maintain the technological gap in the United States' favour and ensure supply chain security. It has therefore pursued a 'small yard, high fence' policy on a limited range of trade goods, the more targeted scope of which is meant to limit the negative impact of the tariffs. The administration seems to endorse the assumption that more wideranging tariff measures would entail larger welfare losses for both sides. Nonetheless, tariffs are unlikely to be lifted in the short term. During his election campaign, Joe Biden expressly opposed resolving the China–US trade war by increasing tariffs, but he retracted his statement under political pressure. Various policy orientations since Biden took office suggest that tariff measures are not the policy thrust of the US Government.

Second, the tariff exclusion measures face less internal political pressure. The government has repeatedly stressed it has no intention of 'decoupling' completely from China or engaging in a 'New Cold War'. Meanwhile, the US Government has mentioned explicitly that it will maintain cooperation with China in specific areas against the background of competition with China, and prompt China to play by Western international rules. Under domestic political pressure, however, the

US Government has failed to achieve a breakthrough. Nonetheless, tariff exclusion measures have already been implemented by the USTR and increasing the intensity of these measures could prove less challenging.

Finally, there is enormous room for the United States to increase tariff exclusion rates for China. To date, it imposes tariffs on US$370 billion worth of Chinese exports to the United States, retaining an additional 25 per cent tariff on List 1 (US$34 billion), List 2 (US$16 billion) and List 3 (US$200 billion) goods and an additional 7.5 per cent tariff on List 4 (US$120 billion) goods. Compared with Lists 1 and 2, the exclusion rates for Lists 3 and 4 have fallen significantly (Yao et al. 2020). In the exclusion applications for Lists 1, 2, 3 and 4A, the shares of approved applications are 33.8 per cent, 37.4 per cent, 4.9 per cent and 6.5 per cent, respectively. This is because the goods in Lists 1 and 2, such as automobiles and their parts and instruments, have relatively complicated production technologies and longer supply chains, making it difficult to locate short-term substitutes, so they are therefore being given priority consideration under the USTR exclusion criteria. The goods in Lists 3 and 4—such as leather products, clothing and shoes—have relatively simple production technologies and shorter supply chains. Although their reliance on China is higher in terms of import value and poses greater potential damage to US consumer welfare (Amiti et al. 2020), finding short-term substitutes is relatively easy; hence, their exclusion rates are lower. Over the medium to long term, therefore, the United States will find it easier to expand the scope of exclusions for Lists 3 and 4A.

Finally, the recent sharp rise in inflationary pressures in the US economy puts the Federal Reserve in a dillema. US consumer price index inflation was 9.1 per cent in June 2022 and 8.5 per cent in July. In the first two quarters of 2022, the US economy has entered into a technical recession, which is defined as two consecutive quarters of GDP contraction. Whether the US economy will face the risk of a real recession is still a controversial issue, but inflation is a real pressure for authorities. In addition, a high government debt burden makes it more difficult for the United States to abandon its current loose monetary policy. Given these factors, the Federal Reserve faces a significant dilemma given the inflationary pressures.

A significant increase in the tariff exclusion rate can suppress domestic inflation, this is something the United States should consider. In fact, at their bilateral summit held on 15 June 2021, the United States and the European Union committed to ending the trade war and eliminating tariffs related to the steel and aluminium trade by the end of that year. The bilateral trade involved, however, was worth only US$18 billion—far less than the total in all ongoing trade conflicts between China and the United States, thereby doing little to ease inflationary pressures.

Understanding new trends in China–US technological competition

Adopting a patent-orientated perspective, we conducted a comprehensive evaluation of China's position in global technological competition. By studying Patent Cooperation Treaty (PCT) data from the past two decades, we found four primary characteristics that distinguish China's international patents: 1) they are enormous in quantity especially in recent years, 2) there is a rather low share of core patents, 3) they have shown rapid improvements in the past five years, and 4) they show significant bias towards particular sectors, concentrated in digital communications. A comparison of PCT core patents by industry between China and the United States shows that a significant gap still exists between China and the United States and Japan. This indicates that the United States has overestimated China's technological competitiveness and has taken too many unnecessary measures to contain it. Meanwhile, China should try to view this gap objectively and seek a way to balance the relationship between independent innovation and international technological collaboration, ensuring its active participation in global technological governance.

New drivers of China–US technological competition can be attributed to two factors: the rapid development of new digital technologies and the different philosophy adopted by the Biden administration compared with that under Trump. In the digital space, the United States already regards China as its biggest competitor, and this strategic competition will continue, regardless of which administration is in power. In this regard, the Biden and Trump administrations are in basic agreement.

Nonetheless, the Biden administration differs significantly from its predecessor in its approach to containing China technologically. Specifically, the new administration is more concerned about the negative impact of implementing technology curbs and will likely adjust the Trump-era policies, particularly those that resulted in a lose-lose situation for both countries.

A review of the technology curbs implemented against China during the Trump era shows three areas of negative impact on the United States: first, the excessive controls imposed on China hurt the business interests of US high-tech companies, thereby affecting their R&D investment. Second, excessively rigorous restrictions on US personnel exchanges with China also damaged R&D human capital in specific high-tech sectors in the United States. Third, the United States' position as the centre of international technological collaboration has weakened. US–China technology partnerships have decreased since the inception of the trade war in 2018, but those between China and Europe and China and Japan have increased, partially filling the void left by this downturn. During the Twelfth Five-Year Plan period, the share of China's joint patent applications with Germany, the United Kingdom,

France and Japan was 23.7 per cent—just half that of China–US collaboration. This rose to 38.3 per cent in 2018—equivalent to that of China–US collaboration (Dong and Yao 2021).

Based on these impacts, the Biden administration is focused on how policies on China have negatively affected US technological competitiveness. Hence, the following three areas are expected to feature in its policy framework: 1) an increase in its own R&D investment; 2) targeted curbs based on 'small yard, high fence' characteristics; and 3) leverage alliances and multilateral platforms to create 'alliance groups' targeted at key technology sectors to narrow China's room for diplomatic manoeuvring.

Our forecasts for new trends in China–US technological competition in the Biden era are as follows. First, their technological competition and rivalry in cyberspace will intensify, with an increase in the possibility of parallel systems emerging. As a core area of competition among superpowers, national security has become an extremely generalised concept in geopolitical rivalry. Supply chain and data security have become the current focus of superpower competition. Rising competitiveness has sharply reduced the willingness of nations to collaborate, lowering the effectiveness of multilateral governance mechanisms, and the United States' tough anti-China stance could increase the possibility of the emergence of parallel systems (Lang 2021). However, as both countries remain deeply intertwined in global industrial supply chains, this could be delayed to a large extent.

Our research shows that while the United States has imposed export-control policies on Huawei, the impacts of these sanctions have significantly rebounded on Huawei's US suppliers. Moreover, the financial market's reaction to sanctions against Huawei not only affects suppliers, but also creates a ripple effect throughout industrial supply chains. There was significant contagion effect among industries for at least three of the nine industries in which Huawei's suppliers are involved, affecting 16 of 24 suppliers. The contagion effect could prompt industry associations to try to influence policymaking to counteract such reverse shocks. Meanwhile, the Semiconductor Industry Association of America actively participated to affect a response to the implementation of the policy sanctioning Huawei. Finally, affected US suppliers responded to the sanctions by speeding up their exports to Huawei before they took effect, moving related production lines overseas and putting pressure on the US Government (Chen and Liang 2021).

Second, China–US technological competition will enter an era of comprehensive national power competition based on a model of 'all government and all society'. On the one hand, the information technology revolution has penetrated every aspect of the economy, society, politics and security, and all sectors need to adjust to the new reality. On the other hand, the rise of internet enterprises has led to the sharing of some of the power once belonging to government. The development of both digital industries and cybersecurity requires the cooperation of all parties.

Third, the ongoing contest between China and the United States to shape international rules and discourse power will intensify. In the past two years, European, US and UN organisations have exchanged views about international rules and legal frameworks around cyberspace. New norms in this sector have continued to emerge, and the process of shaping a new system has reached a critical juncture. A contest for power over the universalisation of international norms pertaining to cyberspace will intensify.

China's industrial supply chains: Outward relocation, inward relocation or international regional reorganisation?

In spatial terms, China's industrial supply chains face three possible directions for adjustment: outward relocation, inward relocation and regional reorganisation. However, these are neutral narratives and their outcomes could depend on specific situations—in other words, each could bring favourable and unfavourable outcomes for China.

The unfavourable outcomes for each adjustment direction include the following:

1. Excessive outward relocation of industry could have a hollowing-out effect.
2. The inward relocation caused by excessive policy intervention could lead to a distorted and inefficient allocation of resources.
3. The 'friendly outsourcing' and direct investment backflow policies dominated by the US could lead to a contraction of global production networks towards North America. Other economies in Asia including China, meanwhile, could face more pressure to maintain their position in the global production networks.

More benign outcomes of these adjustments could include the following:

1. Desirable outward relocation of industry is a natural outcome of domestic industrial upgrading and could help to create an international division of labour that is favourable to China, thereby expanding the international influence of its industrial chains.
2. Leveraging the comparative advantages of central and western China, which are less developed compared with the east, and relocating industrial supply chains further inland would improve efficiency and attract more foreign investment.

3. Leveraging China's market and technological advantages to promote regional industrial supply chain consolidation would promote regional economic integration, thereby deepening the integration of the Chinese economy into the East Asian production networks.

In Vietnam, for example, we observed and researched the outward relocation of Chinese industry. It may surprise many to learn that Vietnam became China's third largest export destination in 2020. We sought to break down China's rapidly growing exports to Vietnam and have, to an extent, found answers to several questions about the composition and nature of China's industrial relocation to Vietnam (Yang et al. 2021). Our research reveals two major characteristics of China's exports to Vietnam: first, most are intermediate goods, which are not intended to meet Vietnamese end-user demand; and second, Chinese enterprises' direct investment in and relocation to Vietnam are the key factors underpinning the rise in intermediate goods exports to the country.

China's direct investment in and industrial relocation to Vietnam have fostered closer international production network relationships between the two countries. A portion of China's trade surplus with Europe and the United States has shifted to that with Vietnam and Vietnam's surplus with Europe and the United States. Pressure on China from an excessively concentrated balance of payments imbalance has eased. It is obvious therefore that trade relations between China and Vietnam are more like those that previously prevailed between Japan and China. China has become a key node in the global value chain and Vietnam has the potential to become a secondary node. But, as mentioned at the beginning of this chapter, trends in digitisation and low carbon will present more challenges for Vietnam in the long term.

We make the following recommendations for consolidating domestic industrial supply chains and effectively linking industry in eastern and western China:

1. Local government incentive and restriction mechanisms in central and western China should be improved, market standards and government efficiency enhanced, while working to improve government–enterprise relations.
2. Border provinces in central and western China should actively cooperate on labour with other countries such as Vietnam and Myanmar, both of which have advantages in low labour costs and abundant, young labour forces. Border provinces such as Guangxi and Yunnan should therefore plan to set up labour-intensive industries and enact an economic integration model comprising Chinese industrial supply chains and a Vietnamese or Burmese labour force. By providing language training, tertiary education and other initiatives, these provinces could attract young Vietnamese or Burmese labour to China to learn and work. This would help address China's shortage of young workers and import foreign labour so local industries can remain in China.

The impact on East Asian nations of Europe's pandemic-induced suspension of its automotive industry supply chain has been a revelation in terms of regional supply chain reorganisation: this industry could be suitable for collaboration for East Asia. The automotive industry chain is a typical model of globalised manufacturing. Europe's automotive industry ceased production in March and April 2020 because of Covid-19. China's imports of automotive parts and components faced supply interruptions, while Europe reduced its imports of automotive parts and components from Japan and South Korea. Against this backdrop, the possibility arose for Japanese and South Korean supply to be redirected to meet China's import demand. For Tier 2 and 3 suppliers, the automotive supply chains of Japan and South Korea could be an effective match with China's.

The highly integrated automotive industry serves as an appropriate means for East Asian industrial chain collaboration. In the context of the revolution in new technology and new energy, automotive manufacturing is closely connected to artificial intelligence (AI) and green energy, with East Asian nations such as China, Japan and South Korea each possessing their own advantages. China is one of the leaders in AI and self-driving vehicles, with a comprehensive industry support network and an enormous domestic market. It is therefore expected to play a pivotal role in automotive supply chain collaboration in East Asia. We also note, however, that economic collaboration in East Asia is, to a very large extent, subject to political relations within the region, and therefore faces challenges.

References

Allison, Graham. 2015. 'The Thucydides Trap: Are the US and China Headed for War?' *The Atlantic*, 24 September.

Amiti, Mary, Stephen J. Redding and David E. Weinstein. 2020. 'Who's Paying for the US Tariffs? A Longer-Term Perspective.' *AEA Papers and Proceedings* 110: 541–46. doi.org/10.1257/pandp.20201018.

Chen, Sichong and Liang Qitian. 2021. *Sanctions on Huawei: The loss of US suppliers and its diffusion effect across industry*. Global Development Perspective Working Paper. Beijing: Institute of World Economy and Politics, Chinese Academy of Social Sciences.

Cui, Xiaomin, Xiong Wanting, Yang Panpan and Xu Qiyuan. 2021. *China's industry security: Network analysis on products level*. China's External Economic Environment Working Paper. Beijing: Institute of World Economy and Politics, Chinese Academy of Social Sciences.

Dong, Weijia and Yao Xi. 2021. *The impact of Sino-US conflict on the landscape of China's international technology cooperation*. Global Development Perspective Working Paper. Beijing: Institute of World Economy and Politics, Chinese Academy of Social Sciences.

Korniyenko, Yevgeniya, Magali Pinat and Brian Dew. 2017. *Assessing the fragility of global trade: The impact of localized supply shocks using network analysis.* IMF Working Paper WP/17/30. Washington, DC: International Monetary Fund. doi.org/10.5089/9781475578515.001.

Lang, Ping. 2021. 'How Has the Internet Changed International Relations?' [In Chinese]. *Quarterly Journal of International Politics* 2(June): 90–121.

Ma, Yingying and Cui Xiaomin. 2021. 'Global Industry Chain's Development and Restructuring: The Trend and New Changes.' [In Chinese]. *Globalization* 2 (February): 102–13.

Su, Qingyi. 2021. 'Analysis of Global Supply Chain: Security and Efficiency.' [In Chinese]. *Quarterly Journal of International Politics* 2 (February): 2–33.

Xiao, He and Xu Qiyuan. 2019. 'China and US Relations: From the Perspective of International Order Interaction.' [In Chinese]. *The Chinese Journal of American Studies* 2 (February): 107–29.

Xu, Qiyuan and Zhao Hai. 2020. *Understanding the logic of China–US conflict from the perspective of the three phases of globalization.* Global Development Perspective Policy Brief No. 20.001. Beijing: Institute of World Economy and Politics, Chinese Academy of Social Sciences.

Yang, Panpan, Xu Qiyuan and Zhang Zixu. 2021. *Vietnam as the third largest export destination of China: Why and what it means.* Research Center of International Finance Working Paper. Beijing: Institute of World Economy and Politics, Chinese Academy of Social Sciences.

Yao, Xi, Xu Qiyuan and Zhang Zixu. 2021. *China's external dependence of industry: An assessment based on WIOT.* Global Development Perspective Working Paper. Beijing: Institute of World Economy and Politics, Chinese Academy of Social Sciences.

Yao, Xi, Zhao Hai and Xu Qiyuan. 2020. 'The Impacts on Global Industry Chain of US Tariff Exclusion.' *International Economic Review* 5 (October): 26–42.

6

Challenges and opportunities for China to move towards consumption-led growth

Wang Wei

Domestic demand is the mainstay of an economy's aggregate demand, the fundamental driver of large economies and a cornerstone of a secure, well-managed and resilient economic system.[1] China's new strategic priority is to effectively expand and better meet domestic demand. Over the past decade, China has gradually transformed to a pattern of domestic demand growth largely driven by consumption. In the next decade, China will continue to unlock the potential and build up a cache of trillion-renminbi-scale growth poles to galvanise domestic demand. To that end, it is imperative to craft an integrated system for consumption-led domestic demand with four main features and to introduce a new growth mechanism for efficient alignment, strong stimulation, accelerated innovation and orderly transformation. More robust reform measures are needed to keep unleashing potential domestic demand and fuel growth in China and the world in a more stable and sustained manner.

---

1   A country's domestic demand consists of three components of aggregate demand in the economy: household consumption expenditure, enterprise investment expenditure and government procurement of goods and services. If government procurement is broken down to government consumption and government investment, domestic demand mainly comprises investment demand (enterprise and government investment) and consumption demand (household and government consumption).

Implications of China's strategy to expand domestic demand in the new era

Since 1998, China has implemented three rounds of policy to expand domestic demand. Expansion of domestic demand is high on the policy agenda for macro-control and stable growth to effectively respond to the evolving international economic climate—in particular, shrinking external demand and downward pressure on domestic growth. In contrast to previous stimulus packages, the current episode of domestic demand expansion has been elevated to a long-term 'strategic pillar'. The core of this policy is speeding up the establishment of an integrated system of domestic demand, the essential requirement of which is to 'effectively expand' and 'better meet' domestic demand, which mirrors the transformation of priority from quantity to quality, from unleashing potential to generating new demand and from ad-hoc policy tools to long-term development targets.

The first aspect of this policy is quality over quantity. 'Effectively expanding demand' is about achieving larger quantity, while 'better meeting demand' entails higher quality. Consumption-led growth in domestic demand replaces consumers' appetite for more with cravings for better. On top of quantitative expansion, investment and consumption will also be upgraded in terms of content, channels, means, underlying philosophy and supply–demand alignment, thus creating a solid foundation for China's high-quality development.

Second is the shift from unleashing potential to generating new demand. 'Effectively expanding demand' means unlocking pent-up demand, while 'better meeting demand' means focusing on new markets, services and consumption models created through innovation. Some potential demand is still locked up by bottlenecks in investment and consumption. To remove these bottlenecks, it is imperative to deepen reform and improve the market environment. Better meeting demand is an ongoing process in which greater efforts are made to promote innovation in consumption and guide investment in line with technological progress and change, to cultivate new drivers of consumption growth and to sustainably develop China's enormous domestic market.

The third aspect of this policy is long-term development targets rather than ad-hoc policy tools. Effectively expanding domestic demand also serves the purpose of better meeting demand. Investment and consumption will be prioritised and relations between the market and government policies dynamically adjusted to set up a positive loop in which supply and demand guide and reinforce each other. Effective expansion of domestic demand will help mitigate emerging social tensions in China, gradually make its development more balanced and adequate, and better meet the people's growing needs for a better life.

Consumption-led domestic demand as the main driver of sustained and stable economic development in China

Since the inception of reform and opening in 1978—and particularly over the past 10 years—China's domestic demand has constantly expanded, gaining the advantages of a super-sized domestic market. As this consumption-led development pattern has taken shape, innovation has become an endogenous driver to turbocharge economic growth.

Domestic demand is a leading force to stabilise fundamentals and spur economic growth

In the wake of the 2008 GFC, shrinking global markets and declining external demand have highlighted the growing importance of domestic demand as a pillar of China's economic development. In 2020, China's domestic demand totalled RMB99.9 trillion, representing 97.4 per cent of GDP—up from 92.4 per cent in 2008 (Figure 6.1)—and contributing 7.9 percentage points of annual GDP growth (Figure 6.2). Domestic demand plays a fundamental role in China's stable growth.

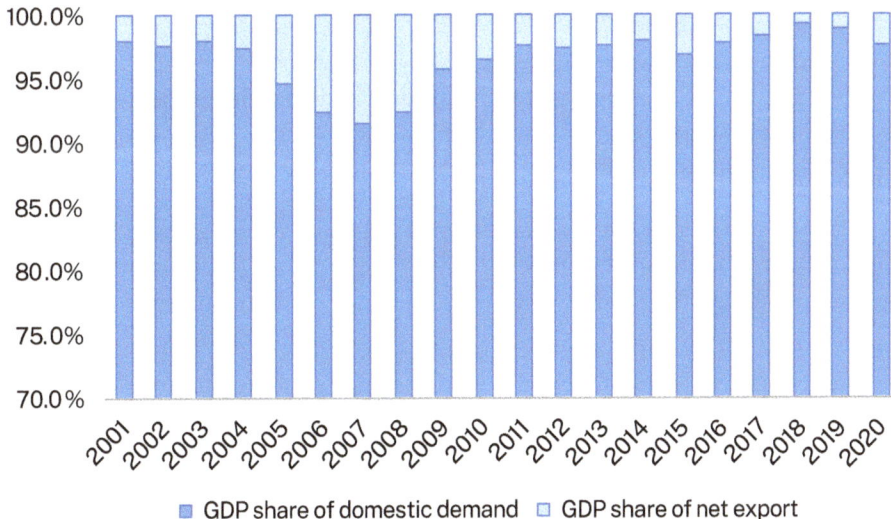

Figure 6.1 China's GDP share of domestic and external demand, 2001–20
Source: NBS.

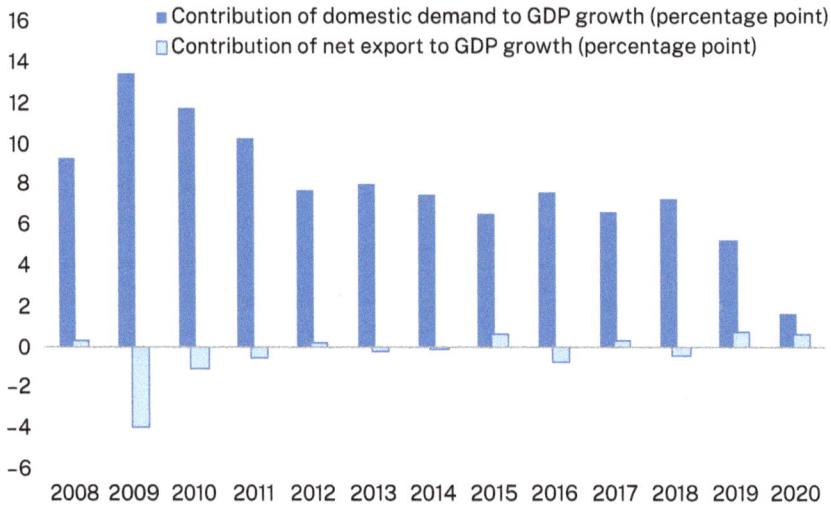

Figure 6.2 Contribution of domestic and external demand to GDP growth
Source: NBS.

The rapid transition from investment-led growth to consumption-led growth of domestic demand

In 2019, consumption and investment contributed 3.5 percentage points and 1.7 percentage points of GDP growth, or 58.6 per cent and 28.9 per cent of the increment, respectively (Figure 6.3). This suggests the emergence of a new growth pattern that is driven more by consumption than investment. The share of household consumption—the absolute mainstay of total final consumption—rose from 21.2 per cent in 1978 to 30.5 per cent in 2020 (Figure 6.4).

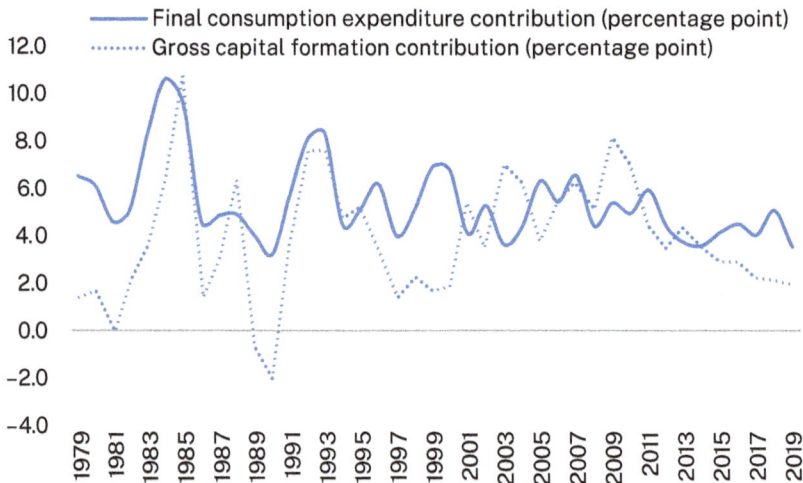

Figure 6.3 Contribution of consumption and investment to GDP growth, 1979–2019
Source: NBS.

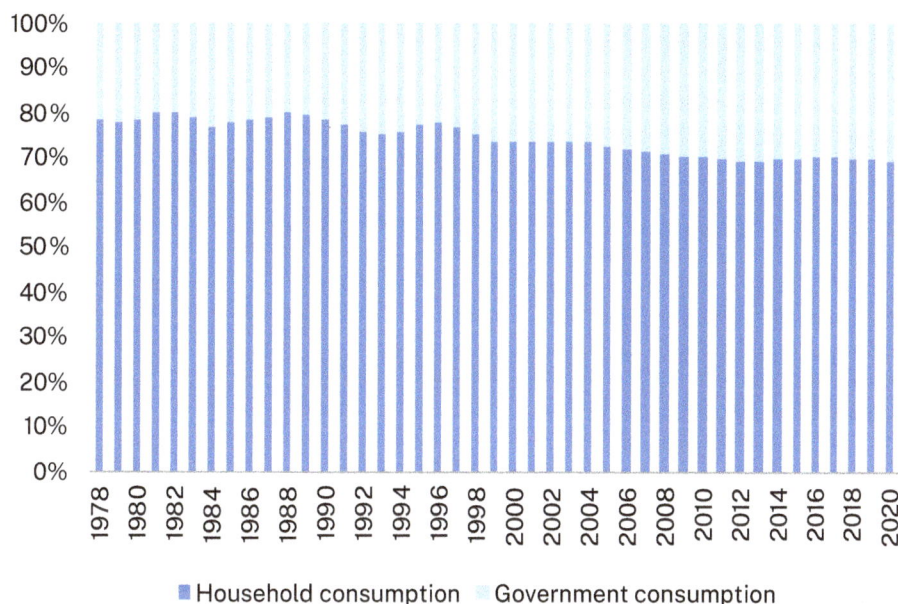

Figure 6.4 Shares of household and government consumption, 1978–2020
Source: NBS.

Rise of new growth drivers, with consumption and innovation moving to the next level

Constant and stable growth and elevated living standards are leading consumption to the next level. With improved quality, growing scale, the clustering effect and increased innovation, consumption is ready to fuel the expansion of domestic demand.

First, consumption has been lifted to a new level. A continuous drop in the Engel coefficient shows that urban and rural household consumption in China have advanced by leaps and bounds. In 2019, China's Engel coefficient dropped to 28.2 per cent, which was 3 percentage points lower than in 2013, moving closer to the tally of developed economies. According to the United Nations standard,[2] Chinese urban and rural residents lead wealthy lives measured by their consumption.

---

2   According to the Food and Agriculture Organization of the United Nations, a coefficient above 60 per cent represents poverty, 50–60 per cent represents a state where daily needs are barely met, 40–50 per cent is a moderately well-off standard of living, 30–40 per cent is a good standard of living, 20–29 per cent is a wealthy life and less than 20 per cent is a very wealthy life. According to these standards, China became a wealthy country from 2017 to 2019.

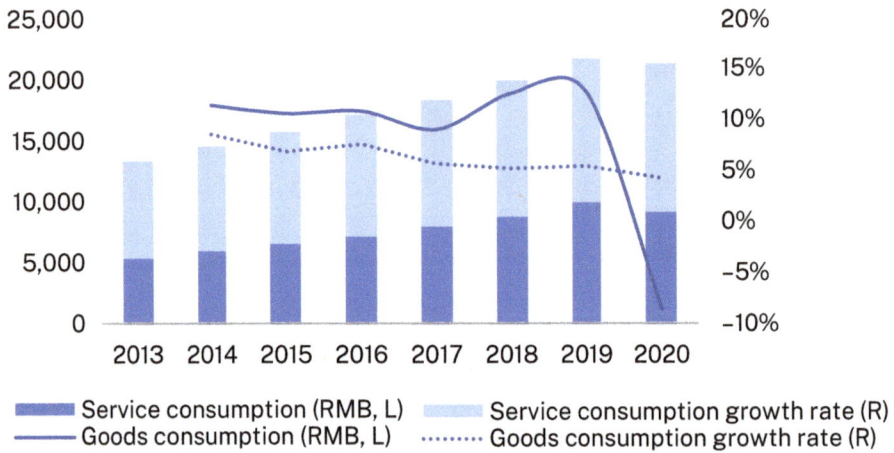

Figure 6.5 Expenditure on goods and service consumption of Chinese citizens, 2013–20
Source: NBS.

Second, consumption is moving to the next level at a faster pace, in a quest for better rather than for more. People's appetites keep growing for consumer goods such as clothing, food, housing and mobility that have cost effectiveness, novel design and recognised branding, triggering a consumption boom for homegrown emerging and legacy brands. In 2021, the share of attention for homegrown brands on internet platforms reached 75 per cent—way above the 25 per cent of offshore brands—making them an important market force for the transformation and upgrading of China's manufacturing industry.

Third, the shift from goods consumption to service consumption has been a main driver of economic restructuring. The share of service consumption to aggregate consumption has increased steadily. From 2013 to 2020, the per capita service consumption expenditure of Chinese residents grew by more than 8 per cent annually—much faster than the growth rate of goods consumption expenditure. The share of service consumption in total consumption expenditure rose from 39.7 per cent in 2013 to 45.9 per cent in 2019—up by 1 percentage point per year (Figure 6.5).

Fourth, China has transformed from a follower to a leader, creating momentum for innovation in consumption. Science and technology have empowered consumption with innovative products, services and models, injecting new impetus for China's consumption growth. China's online retail sales, for example, were worth RMB11.8 trillion in 2020, growing by 27.7 per cent per annum since 2014, which is much faster than the growth rate of retail sales of social consumer goods (Figure 6.6), making China a leading online consumption market.

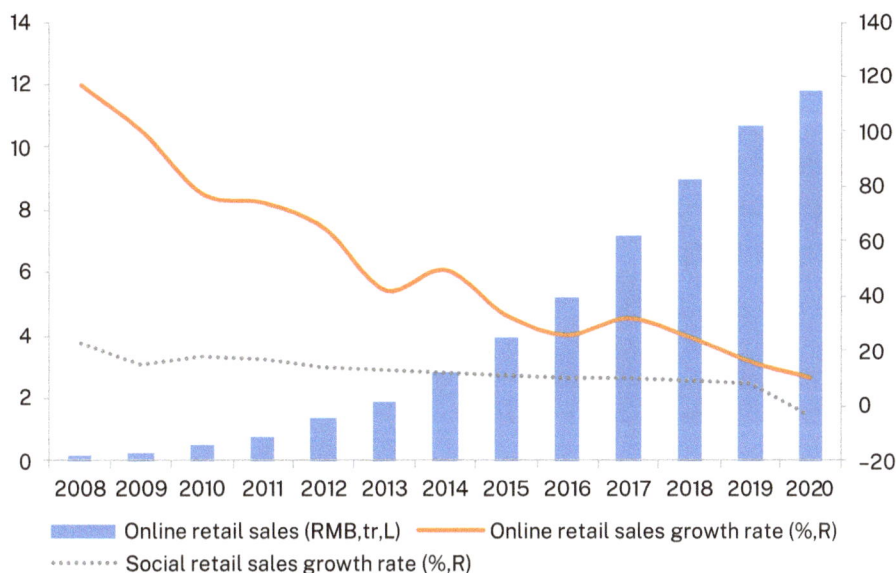

Figure 6.6 China's online retail sales and growth rates, 2008–20

Sources: NBS; Ministry of Commerce.

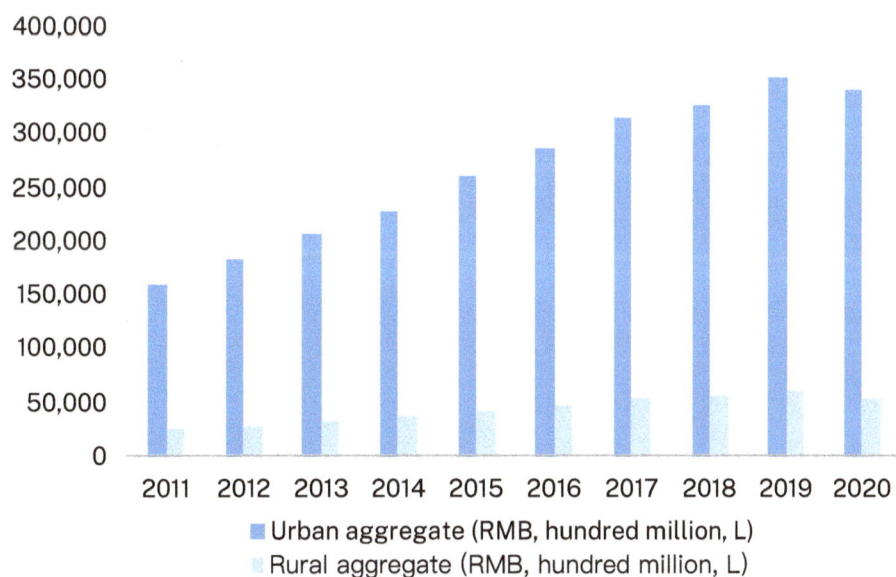

Figure 6.7 Retail sales of consumer goods in urban and rural areas, 2011–20

Source: NBS (various years).

Fifth, the shift from scattered to clustered urbanisation has accelerated the growth of consumption. China's urbanisation rate reached 63 per cent in 2020. Cities claim the lion's share in total consumption. In the early 1990s, urban consumption accounted for more than 50 per cent of China's total retail sales of consumer goods.

That share continued to rise sharply—to 80 per cent in 2010 and 87 per cent in 2020. Cities have become a fountain head of consumption growth and a leading force of development (Figure 6.7).

Optimised investment structure creates foundation for expansion of domestic demand through innovation and upgrading

Over the past 10 years, China's total investment has grown steadily, and 2020 saw RMB52.7 trillion of total fixed asset investment—2.2 times that of 2011 and an increase of 10.4 per cent on average year on year. Infrastructure and the property market remain major magnets for and contributors to investment growth, but new changes have been spotted recently in the investment structure.

First, the service sector is steadily gaining a share of investment to meet emerging needs for services. The distribution of fixed asset investment among primary, secondary and tertiary industries evolved from 2:38:60 in 2011 to 2:29:69 in 2020, leaving the service sector an obvious winner (Figure 6.8).

Second, investment in science and technology has risen rapidly. From 2017 to 2020, the average annual growth rates of investment in high-tech manufacturing and high-tech service industries both exceeded 10 per cent—much faster than that of total fixed asset investment (Figure 6.9).

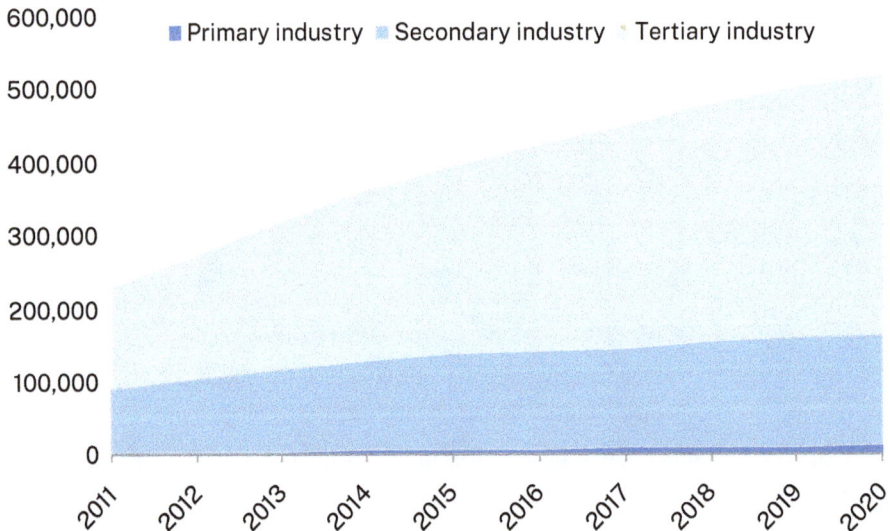

Figure 6.8 Fixed asset investment among three industries (RMB100 million)
Source: NBS.

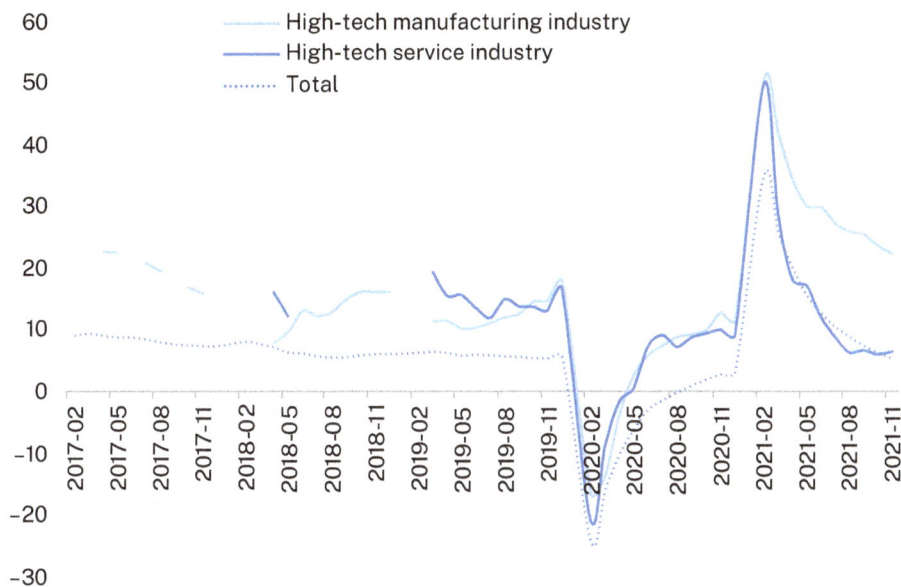

Figure 6.9 Cumulative year-on-year growth rate of completed fixed asset investment (per cent)

Source: Wind.

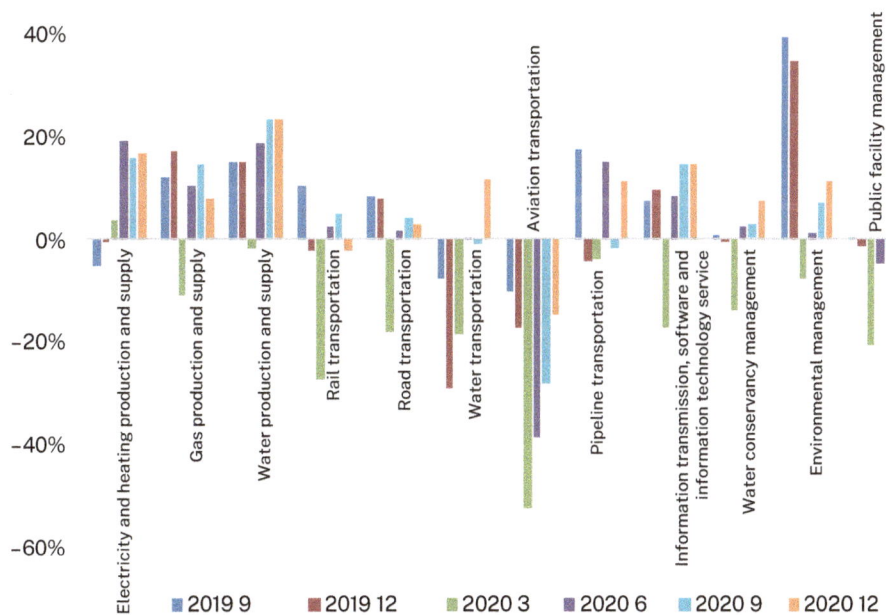

Figure 6.10 Cumulative year-on-year growth rate of infrastructure investment by subsector

Sources: NBS; Tengjing Research.

Third, people's livelihoods have become a priority for infrastructure investment. Infrastructure investment formerly focused on transportation projects, but electricity, heating, water, gas and other services have posted rapid growth in recent years, diverting more investment from other destinations (Figure 6.10).

Fourth, private investment has increased steadily. From 2012 to 2020, private investment in fixed assets (excluding rural households) increased from RMB15.4 trillion to RMB28.9 trillion—up by 8.4 per cent year on year. The share in total fixed asset investment (excluding rural households) varied between 55 per cent and 59 per cent, with an average of 57.1 per cent (Figure 6.11).

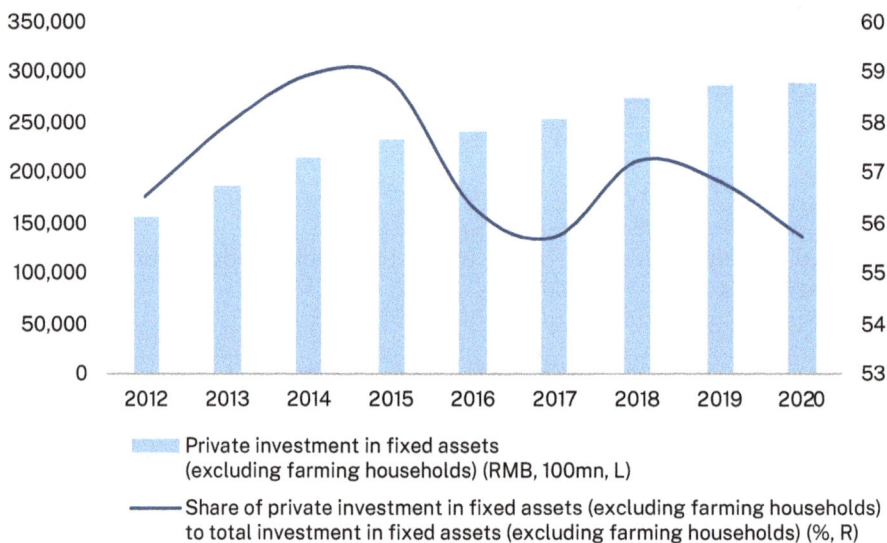

Private investment in fixed assets
(excluding farming households) (RMB, 100mn, L)

Share of private investment in fixed assets (excluding farming households)
to total investment in fixed assets (excluding farming households) (%, R)

Figure 6.11 Amount and share of private investment in fixed assets, 2012–20
Source: NBS.

Strong momentum of and great potential for consumption-led expansion of domestic demand

Consumption-led expansion of domestic demand will unleash huge potential in the coming decade as China catches up with developed economies in consumption and even outperforms them with innovation in consumption.

Great potential to further expand domestic demand with consumption

First, consumption plays an increasingly important role in expanding domestic demand and promises to contribute more to economic growth. According to the experience of developed economies, as per capita GDP grows, the share of final consumption in GDP will take a U-shaped curve, starting to move upward during the advanced stage of industrialisation (Figure 6.12). In recent years, China's consumption to GDP ratio has entered an upward trajectory, reaching 54.3 per cent in 2020—5 percentage points higher than the low recorded in 2010. The contribution of final consumption to GDP growth has remained above 50 per cent for years now. During the Fourteenth Five-Year Plan period (2021–25), China's per capita GDP is expected to grow from 14,000 to 17,000 Geary-Khamis dollars.[3] With reference to the precedents of developed economies with similar per capita GDP, in 2025, China's consumption to GDP ratio could grow to 60 per cent, with RMB90 trillion in final consumption expenditure. Consumption's contribution to GDP growth in the next five years will stay above 60 per cent (Figure 6.13).

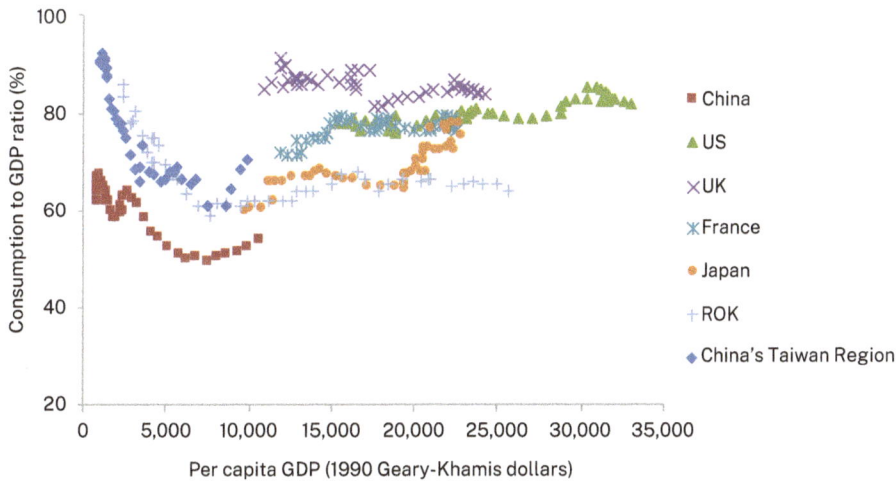

Figure 6.12 Per capita GDP and consumption to GDP ratio
Sources: Development and Research Centre of the State Council; National Institute of Statistics and Economic Studies of France; Groningen Growth and Development Centre; CEIC; Wind.

---

3   The numbers are based on 1990 international Geary-Khamis dollars. The projection is from *Contours of the World Economy 1-2030 AD* by Angus Maddison.

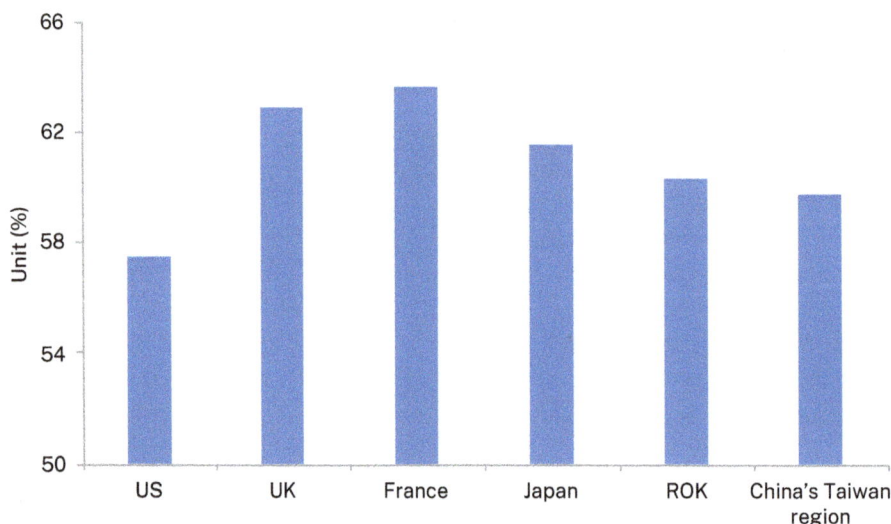

Figure 6.13 Average contribution of consumption to economic growth in developed economies, with per capita GDP from 14,000 to 17,000 Geary-Khamis Dollars

Note: US data are for 1966–76; UK data for 1985–94; France, 1978–89; Japan, 1982–88; South Korea, 1999–2003; Taiwan (China), 1996–2002.

Sources: Development and Research Centre of the State Council; National Institute of Statistics and Economic Studies of France; Groningen Growth and Development Centre; CEIC; Wind.

Second, the immense potential for structural upgrading will make consumption of services a major source of the increase in household consumption. When their per capita GDP reached about 14,000 Geary-Khamis dollars, developed economies had services consumption accounting for 49 per cent of total consumption. When per capita GDP climbed to 17,000 Geary-Khamis dollars, the share of services consumption rose to 53 per cent (Figure 6.14). China's consumption of services constituted 45.9 per cent of total household consumption in 2019, which dropped to 42.6 per cent in 2020 due to the Covid-19 pandemic. It is estimated that by the end of the Fourteenth Five-Year Plan period or at the beginning of the Fifteenth Five-Year Plan period (2026–30), the share will rebound to 50 per cent. More importantly, higher household income and upgraded demand will reshape the structure of service consumption. Across developed economies, the proportion of mobility services generally has remained stable, while those of medical, entertainment and cultural consumption have increased sharply. It is fair to infer that medical services and cultural activities will become engines for service consumption growth in China as well, gaining larger shares of total consumption.

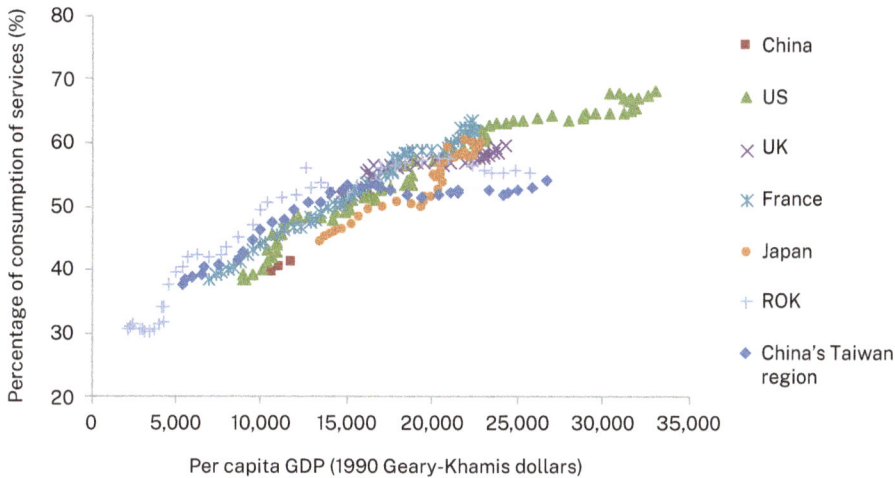

Figure 6.14 Per capita GDP and percentage of consumption of services

Sources: Development and Research Centre of the State Council; National Institute of Statistics and Economic Studies of France; Groningen Growth and Development Centre; CEIC; Wind.

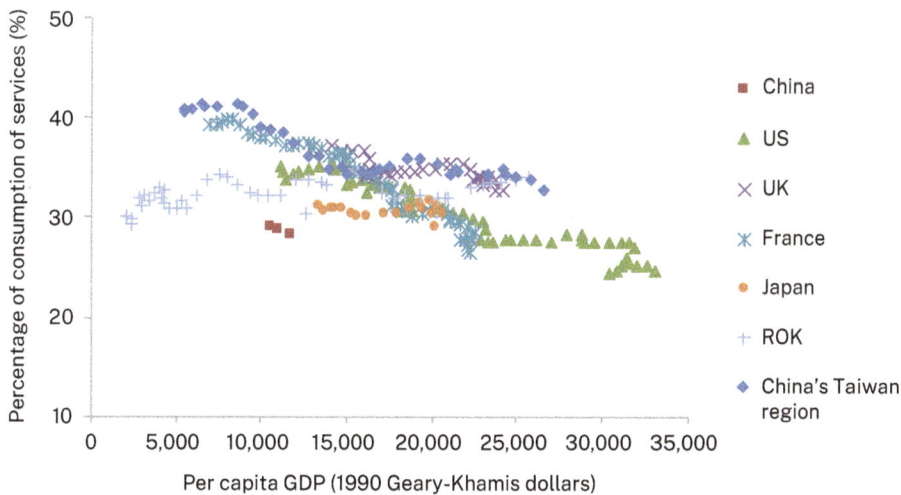

Figure 6.15 Per capita GDP and proportion of durable goods consumption

Sources: Development and Research Centre of the State Council; National Institute of Statistics and Economic Studies of France; Groningen Growth and Development Centre; CEIC; Wind.

Third, as consumption moves to the next level in the quest for better quality, it will unlock the growth potential of durable goods consumption. In general, the share of durable goods in household consumption has declined steadily in developed economies (Figure 6.15). As per capita GDP reaches a higher margin, consumption of durable goods will go through a structural transformation and become more reliant on the trade-up of stock items than on incremental generation. This is particularly true for automobiles, apartments and electrical appliances. To upgrade their living standard, residents prefer to trade up for substitutes with higher quality and more added value. Automobiles are a typical example. Chinese consumers have started to replace old cars with much more expensive new models; however, compared with developed economies, the replacement ratio still lags.

Fourth, evolving consumer preferences suggest an exciting outlook for food consumption. In developed economies, food consumption dropped before stabilising in relation to total consumption expenditure (Figure 6.16), with the distribution of food consumption showing a growing appetite for healthy and high-quality products. In the same vein, Chinese consumers are no longer satisfied with just having enough to eat; they crave something better. With the increase in per capita GDP, consumers prefer nutritious, fresh and reliable-quality food. Healthy diets that ensure nutritional balance will be another driver of consumption upgrading.

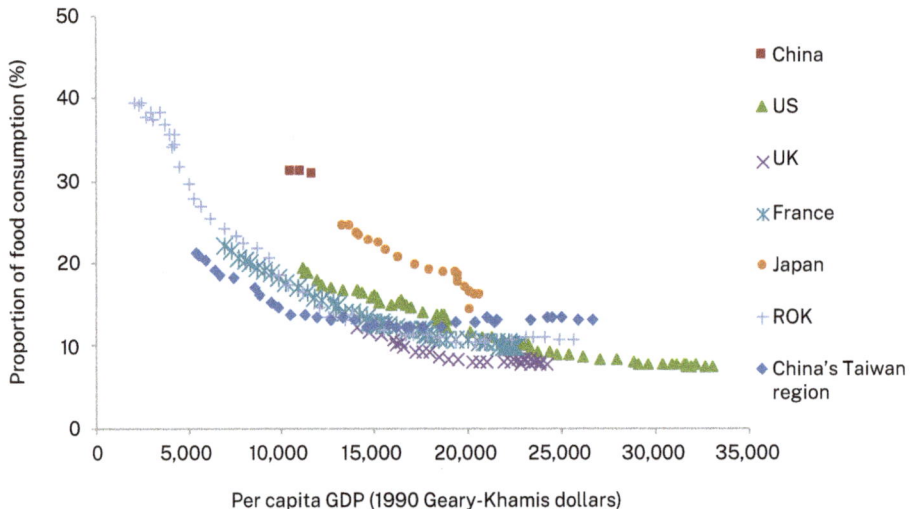

Figure 6.16 Per capita GDP and proportion of food consumption

Sources: Development and Research Centre of the State Council; National Institute of Statistics and Economic Studies of France; Groningen Growth and Development Centre; CEIC; Wind.

Emergence of structural factors that will promote the growth of domestic demand

The next decade will see a series of factors of structural change in China's economic development that will become the main engines of growth in domestic demand, especially consumption growth (Figure 6.17).

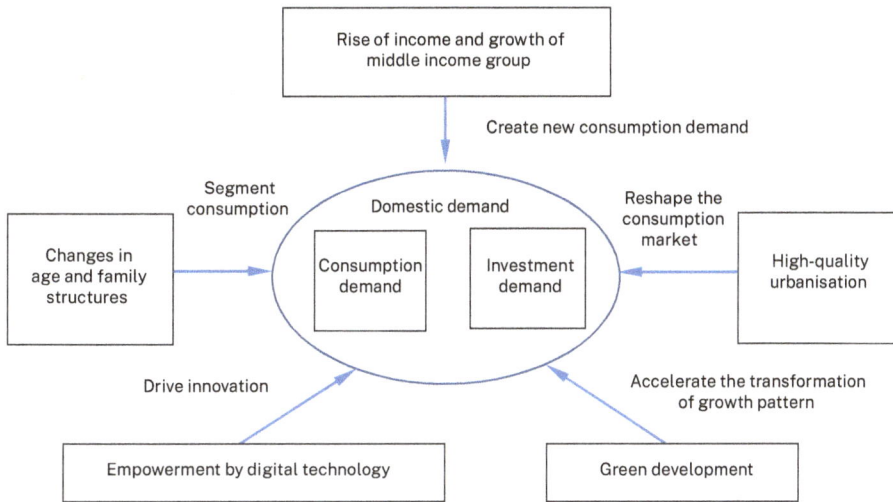

Figure 6.17 Main drivers of China's domestic demand in the next decade
Source: Author's own schema.

First, the growth in and upgrading of consumption will be driven mainly by income growth and the expanding size of the middle-income population. The experience of developed economies indicates that, as the economy approaches the high-income threshold, it will be a critical moment for the growth in national income and the expansion of the middle-income group. For instance, in Japan, South Korea and Taiwan (China), when per capita GDP reached 10,000–17,000 Geary-Khamis dollars, the size of the middle-income group enlarged relatively fast year on year before flattening out (Figure 6.18). The middle-income group has a higher marginal propensity and stronger ability to consume and will pursue high-quality consumption items and new lifestyles. China has the world's largest middle-income population with the greatest potential for expansion. By 2018, China's middle-income group increased to 380 million, or 27 per cent of the national population—up by more than 92 million and 6 percentage points from 2013.[4] It is estimated that, by 2030, the middle-income group will account for 51 per cent of the total population and contribute 79 per cent of household consumption.

---

4   According to a 2018 definition from China's National Bureau of Statistics, families of three within the RMB100,000–500,000 (at 2018 prices) income range are classified as middle-income, those below RMB100,000 are the low-income group and those above RMB500,000 belong to the high-income group. Data in this paragraph are cited from the Chinese Household Income Project (CHIP) conducted by the China Institute for Income Distribution at Beijing Normal University.

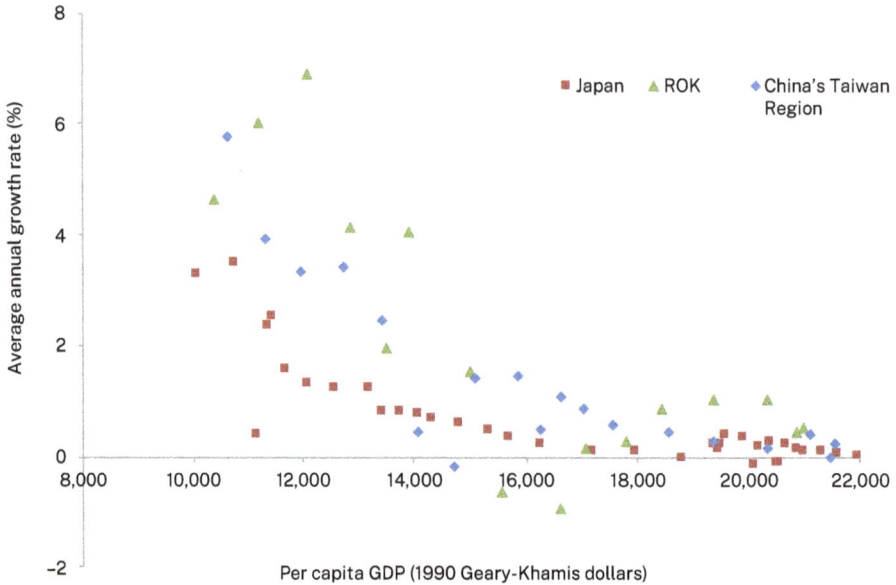

Figure 6.18 Per capita GDP and annual growth of the middle-income group

Sources: Development and Research Centre of the State Council; National Institute of Statistics and Economic Studies of France; Groningen Growth and Development Centre; CEIC; Wind.

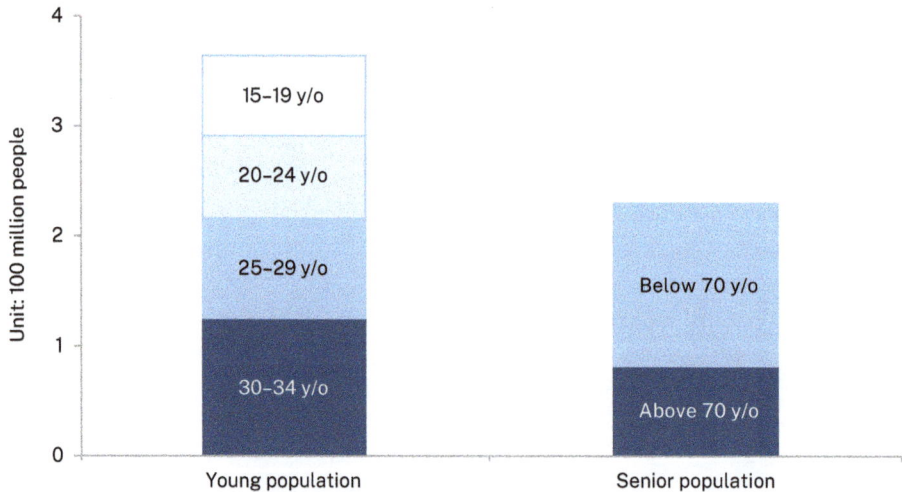

Figure 6.19 China's young and elderly populations, 2020

Source: NBS (2022).

Second, evolving demographics and household structure will further segment consumption. In 2020, the number of Chinese consumers aged 15–34 was 360 million, constituting 25.8 per cent of the total population (Figure 6.19). This group belongs to an era of abundance and the internet. Better educated and always craving the new, they are the most pro-innovation subgroup of consumers.

The consumption market created by Generation Z[5] is projected to reach RMB16 trillion by 2035. Meanwhile, the number of people aged 60 and above exceeded 260 million in 2020, or 18.7 per cent of the total population, while those aged in their sixties made up 55.8 per cent of the total aged population. With adequate time and wealth at their disposal and generally good health, the elderly play an essential role in the growth of consumption. It is predicted that, by 2030, China's 'silver economy' will be worth RMB20 trillion. Moreover, China's housing structure has become increasingly diversified in recent years, with a sharp increase in nuclear families and those with more than one child. This is weakening the function of conventional families and fuelling the demand for social services, thus further segmenting consumption.

Third, high-quality urbanisation will reshape the landscape of consumption growth. China's rate of urbanisation has remained on the fast track recently, but it is still about 20 per cent lower than that of the developed economies. Closing this gap will drive consumption growth and relevant investment. When urbanisation enters a new stage dominated by the rise of city clusters and metropolitan regions, large central cities will become stronger magnets for population and other factors, drawing in consumption markets, lifting those already in large central cities to a higher end and accelerating new consumption modes. These dynamics will recharge consumption in large central cities and turn some into world-class consumption hubs.

Fourth, the penetration of digital technology will empower innovation in consumption. The boom in and in-depth application of digital technology have brought about a constellation of innovations in consumption, redefining how people consume. Take online shopping as an example. With online retail sales exceeding RMB1.8 trillion in 2013, China surpassed the United States as the world's largest online retail market. In 2020, the total rocketed to RMB11.8 trillion. In recent years, particularly since the outbreak of the Covid-19 pandemic, a multitude of business models has thrived, including social and livestream commerce and community group-buying. These online models aggressively embrace innovation, diversify consumption scenarios and create new consumer demands, thus contributing to the growth of domestic demand. It is anticipated that, by 2025, China's online retail sales will reach RMB18.5 trillion—up by 9.5 per cent year on year during the Fourteenth Five-Year Plan period and 3.5 percentage points faster than the growth in total retail sales of consumer goods. Even though the increase of online consumption will replace part of offline consumption, the econometric study results show that every unit of incremental online consumption still creates 0.36 of a unit of total consumption (Wang et al. 2022).[6] This net growth effect is more evident in the central and western regions of the country (Figure 6.20).

---

5   Generation Z refers to people born between 1995 and 2009.
6   Authors' calculations based on official data from provincial and municipal statistics bureaus in China, as well as data provided by Alibaba, which is one of the biggest e-market platforms in China and the world.

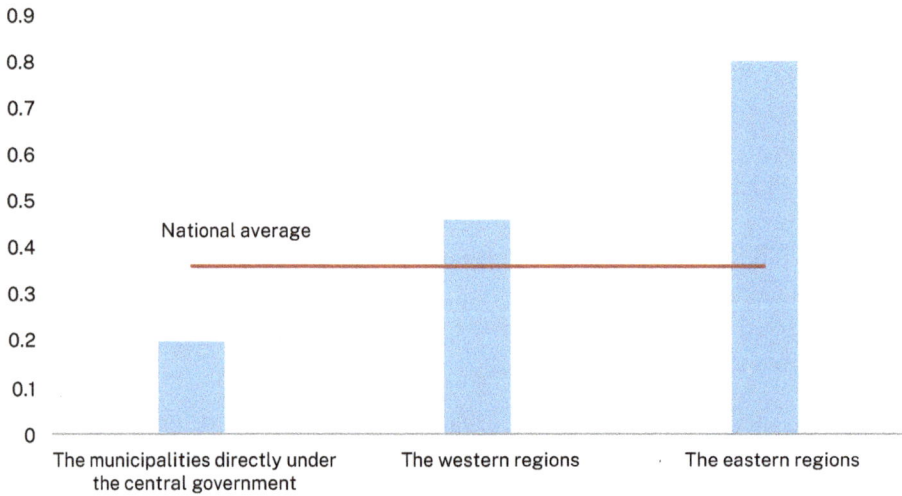

Figure 6.20 Net growth effect of online consumption across regions
Source: The DRC research team.

Fifth, green development will guide an environmentally friendly transformation of consumption. Green and low-carbon growth are inherent in China's socioeconomic development and will remain priorities for the growth of domestic demand and consumption upgrading in the years to come. In 1992, the UN Conference on Environment and Development adopted Agenda 21, urging countries to encourage sustainable consumption. In response to resource and environmental challenges in the wake of overheated growth, developed economies actively promoted green modes of production and lifestyles and advocated reasonable and moderate consumption to achieve sustainable development. They have transformed to green consumption through resource conservation, environmental protection and lower greenhouse gas emissions, helping to reshape domestic demand and safeguard sustainable development.

Consumption upgrading and innovation-driven development will further unleash China's potential demand for investment, particularly in sectors related to services and upgraded goods consumption, such as culture, entertainment, healthcare and nutritious food. Massive investment is needed in transport to enhance connectivity among city clusters and metropolitan areas, new infrastructure to support the digital economy as well as greener transport and energy facilities. Provision of public services such as urban and rural education, aged-care homes and childcare create a yawning demand for investment. Investment potential is also detected in large cities and city clusters for the renovation of shanty towns and the development of public rental housing and trade-up apartments.

A series of trillion-renminbi growth poles will turbocharge domestic demand

In the decade to come, the structural factors mentioned above will create a series of consumption and investment drivers with huge economies of scale, which will translate into prominent growth momentum and spillover effects.

Estimations by the DRC research team show that, by 2025, the five structural factors will nurture 39 domestic demand drivers, including 29 of consumption growth and 10 of investment growth. Among them, 14 consumption poles and four investment poles will command scales in the trillion-renminbi range. These consumption poles will be focused on four engines of residents' demands: quality upgrading, green and healthy transformation, digitisation and service capacity expansion (Figure 6.21).

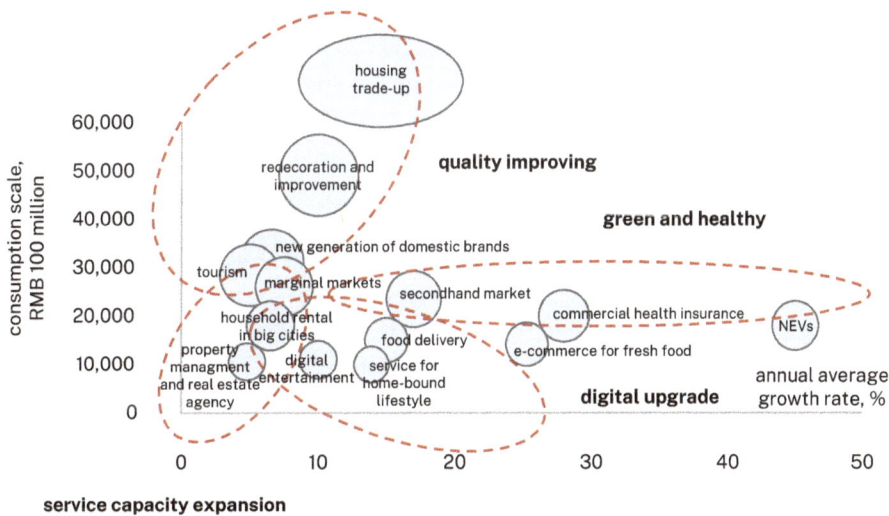

Figure 6.21 Grouping of trillion-renminbi growth poles, 2025
Source: Estimated by the Development Research Centre (DRC) research team.

In terms of quality upgrading, the focus will include housing trade-up, interior decoration and improvements and consumption of emerging domestic brands. With rising household income, urban and rural middle-income groups have a growing demand for better housing, especially larger homes with more bedrooms. Better-quality residential environments and interior decoration are also on their wish list. It is estimated that, by 2025, China will be home to about 160 million urban middle-income households. Assuming they replace their housing every eight years, the average floor space per household is 104.8 square metres and housing prices grow by 5 per cent per annum, the value of demand for housing trade-up will reach RMB22.8 trillion by 2025. If 1.2 per cent of houses are redecorated every year, the total spending will amount to about RMB440 billion annually. In addition, to satisfy consumers' evolving tastes and appetite for high-quality goods, an explosion in domestic brands is taking place in multiple areas with shortening intervals between product releases. Statistics show that, in 2019 alone, emerging domestic brands contributed 44.8 per cent of the sales growth on sampled commercial platforms. Assuming annual growth in total retail sales of consumer goods reaches 7 per cent in 2022–25, online sales contribute 26 per cent of total sales of physical goods and new domestic brands account for 48 per cent of incremental consumption expenditure, the aggregate consumption of these brands will stand at RMB3.1 trillion in 2025.

Green and healthy transformation is most manifest in the consumption of new-energy vehicles (NEVs) and commercial health insurance. Fuelled by peak carbon and carbon-neutrality goals, the market penetration of NEVs in China soared to 13.4 per cent in 2021 and is expected to reach 30 per cent in 2025, with 9 million units in sales volume and RMB1.8 trillion in market size. The ageing population highlights the significance of commercial health insurance to finance the aged care system. Consumption in this regard is forecast to surpass RMB2 trillion in 2025.

Digitisation will see a pivot to online consumption in smaller cities and towns and the use of e-commerce to purchase fresh produce. The consumption potential in smaller cities and towns will continue to be unleashed, with deeper penetration of digital technologies and improvements of digitised distribution systems and commercial infrastructure in rural areas. The Fourteenth Five-Year Plan set an annual growth target of 7.5 per cent for online retail sales in rural areas, which means online consumption in these currently marginal markets will reach RMB2.6 trillion by 2025. Digital transformation in the retail sector is accelerating, fostering new business models like fresh produce 'O2O' (online to offline purchase and delivery services), 'intelligent' wet markets and community group-buying, which are becoming pillars for the upgrading of food consumption. Considering the growth momentum of online retail, in the next five years, retail sales of fresh food will grow by 6 per cent per annum, raising the penetration rate of fresh produce e-commerce to 21 per cent and its total consumption expenditure to RMB1.4 trillion.

For service capacity expansion, the key lies in the provision of rental housing in major cities, real-estate agencies, property management and other housing-related services. Big cities with net population inflows have strong housing demand, especially for rental housing for newly urbanised residents such as migrant workers and college graduates. It is estimated that due to the population growth triggered by urbanisation, by 2025, urban market demand for rental housing will soar to 48.3 million units, or RMB1.8 trillion in market value. According to the Fourteenth Five-Year Plan, consumption of housing-related services such as property management and real estate agencies will grow by 4.8 per cent per annum, reaching RMB1.1 trillion in 2025.

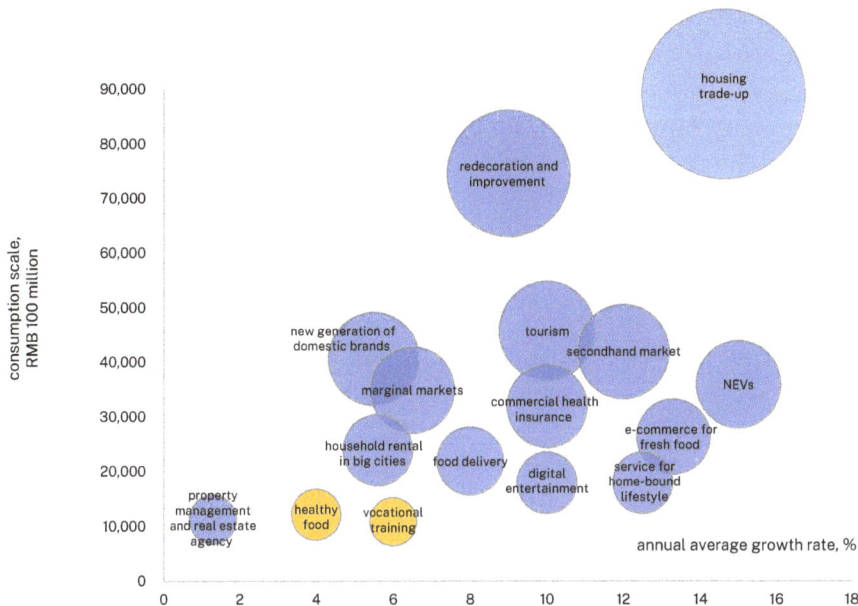

Figure 6.22 Trillion-renminbi growth poles of domestic demand, 2030

Source: Estimated by the Development Research Centre (DRC) research team.

Additionally, consumption expansion will engender four trillion-renminbi investment growth poles: green construction, digital infrastructure, renovation of shanty towns and the recycling industry. Investment in these sectors will reach RMB15 trillion, RMB5.2 trillion, RMB1.8 trillion and RMB1 trillion, respectively, by 2025.

It is expected that during the Fifteenth Five-Year Plan period, these domestic demand growth poles will expand in scale while maintaining their momentum. Meanwhile, the consumption of healthy food and vocational training will join their ranks. By then, consumption growth will benefit from a total of 16 trillion-renminbi poles. Battery swaps and recharging infrastructure will form a new trillion-renminbi growth pole on the investment side, with potential accumulated investment of RMB1.1 trillion (Figure 6.22).

To expand and better meet domestic demand: New requirements for further economic reform and development

Better matching supply and demand

A diagnosis of the supply–demand alignment shows that industrial and consumption upgrading are not synchronised and the manufacturing capacity of high-end products is inadequate. The *Global Competitiveness Report 2019* issued by the World

Economic Forum (WEF 2019) placed China twenty-fourth in the ranking of global innovation capacity and twenty-eighth for comprehensive competitiveness—a stark contrast to its position as the number-one manufacturing powerhouse. The service industry also reports gaps in supply and innovation competence, with the consumer services subsector relatively underdeveloped (Figure 6.23). Challenges include inadequate regulations and standards for education, healthcare, rehabilitation, age-care homes, childcare, culture and entertainment services; shortfalls in infrastructure capacity; lack of professional training and qualifications; and gaps in innovation competence. All these have added to the supply–demand mismatch, making it difficult to meet personalised, stratified and diversified consumer needs.

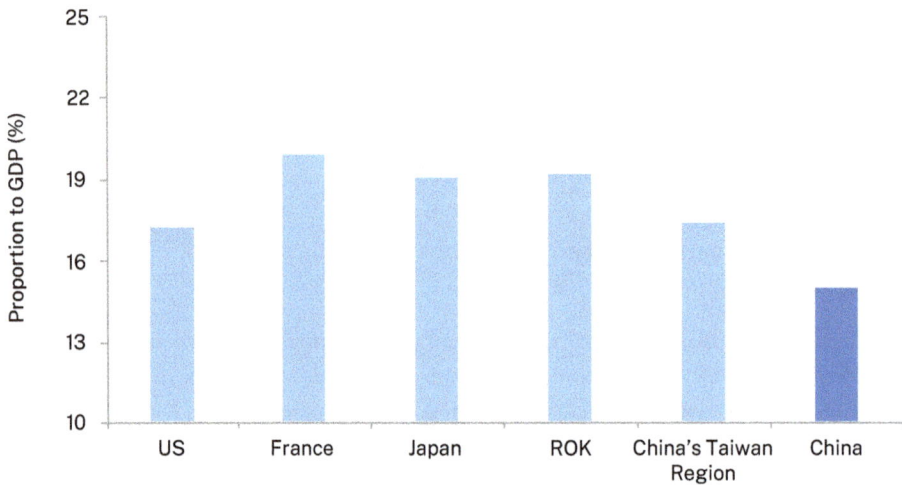

Figure 6.23 Added value of service consumption in relation to GDP: A comparison of China and economies at comparable stage of development

Notes: China's per capita GDP in 2019 was about 13,000 international Geary-Khamis dollars. This graph is based on data for economies at a comparable stage of development.

Sources: Development and Research Centre of the State Council; National Institute of Statistics and Economic Studies of France; Groningen Growth and Development Centre; CEIC; Wind.

A diagnosis of investment–consumption interaction shows that the market is not playing its role in guiding investment. The priorities for investment and consumption upgrading are not fully aligned, leading to low returns on investment and excess capacity in certain areas. For instance, from 2010 to 2017, real estate, transportation, warehousing and postal services claimed more than 50 per cent of total fixed asset investment in the service sector. Yet, the share was much lower for investment related to the improvement of living standards, consumption upgrading, structural reform and industrial restructuring and upgrading (Table 6.1).

Table 6.1 Fixed asset investment in the service sector, 2010–17 (per cent)

Sector	2010	2011	2012	2013	2014	2015	2016	2017
Transportation, warehousing and postal services	19.8	16.6	15.3	14.9	15.1	15.6	15.4	16.3
Information transmission, computer services and software	1.6	1.3	1.3	1.2	1.4	1.7	1.8	1.9
Wholesale and retail	4.0	4.4	4.8	5.1	5.5	6.0	5.2	4.4
Accommodation and catering	2.2	2.3	2.5	2.4	2.2	2.1	1.7	1.6
Finance	0.3	0.4	0.4	0.5	0.5	0.4	0.4	0.3
Real estate	42.7	48.0	48.3	48.1	45.8	42.5	40.8	38.7
Rental and commercial services	1.8	2.0	2.3	2.4	2.8	3.0	3.5	3.5
Scientific research, technology services and geological exploration	0.9	1.0	1.2	1.3	1.5	1.5	1.6	1.6
Irrigation, environmental and public facilities management	16.3	14.4	14.4	15.2	16.1	17.6	19.7	21.7
Residential and other services	0.7	0.8	0.9	0.8	0.8	0.9	0.8	0.7
Education	2.7	2.3	2.2	2.2	2.3	2.4	2.7	2.9
Public health, social security and social welfare	1.4	1.4	1.3	1.3	1.4	1.6	1.8	1.9
Culture, sports and entertainment	1.9	1.9	2.1	2.1	2.2	2.1	2.2	2.3
Public management and social organisation	3.7	3.3	2.9	2.4	2.5	2.5	2.3	2.1

Note: Data updated to 2017.
Source: NBS.

Furthermore, efforts are still needed to balance public and private investment. There is a shortfall of government investment in basic public services[7] and related weak links. Practice should be improved to mobilise and channel private capital and foreign investment to the fill the gap (Figure 6.24).

---

7   The National List of Basic Public Services in the Thirteenth Five-Year Plan encompassed 81 projects in eight areas: public education, employment and business startups, social security, healthcare, social services, housing security, public culture and sports, and services for people with disabilities.

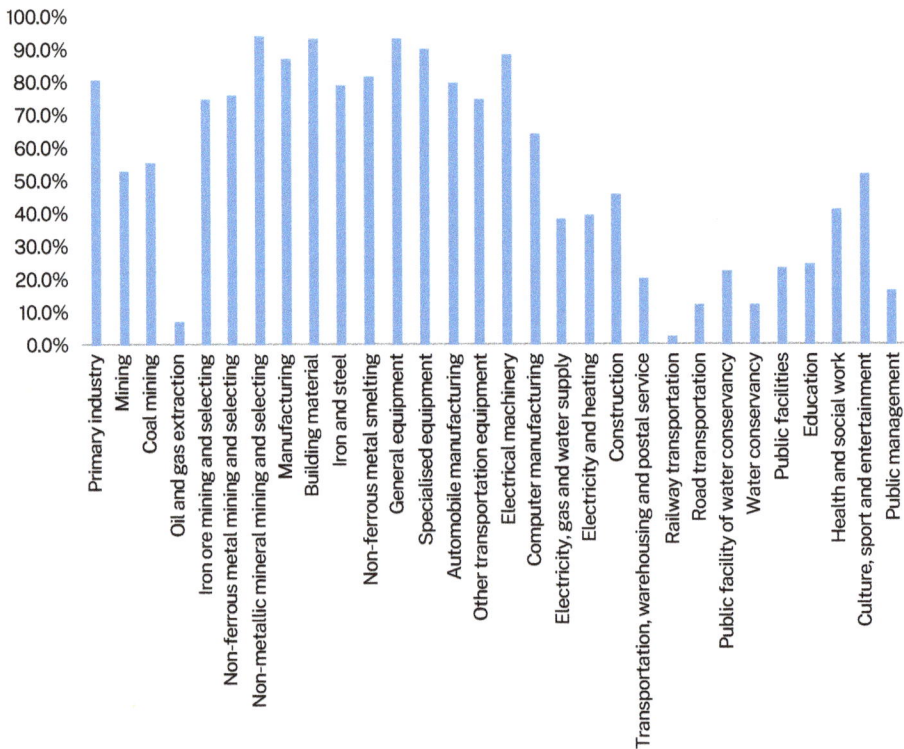

Figure 6.24 Share of private investment by sector, 2017
Source: Wind.

Improving household capability and consumption through optimising income distribution and the social security system

Household income is underrepresented in primary distribution (Table 6.2). In 2020, after modest growth in the previous years, China's Gini coefficient stood at 0.468, in the upper–middle range globally (Figure 6.25).

The middle-income group is a primary driver of consumption growth and innovation. Between 2013 and 2019, the per capita disposable income of this group grew by 8.1 per cent year on year—slower than both the high-income group (8.5 per cent) and the low-income group (9 per cent). In 2018, the middle-income population reached 380 million, which was 27 per cent (Shijin et al. 2021) of the national total; however, their potential has been pent up in comparison with advanced economies.

Table 6.2 Distribution of national income, 2001–09 (per cent)

Year	Primary distribution			Secondary distribution		
	Government	Enterprise	Household	Government	Enterprise	Household
2012	15.6	22.7	61.6	19.5	18.5	62.0
2013	15.2	24.1	60.7	18.9	19.8	61.3
2014	15.2	24.7	60.1	18.9	20.5	60.6
2015	14.9	24.2	60.9	18.5	19.8	61.6
2016	14.5	24.3	61.3	17.9	20.0	62.1
2017	14.0	25.4	60.6	18.0	21.2	60.8
2018	12.8	26.0	61.2	18.7	21.8	59.4
2019	12.7	25.9	61.4	17.8	21.9	60.3

Source: NBS.

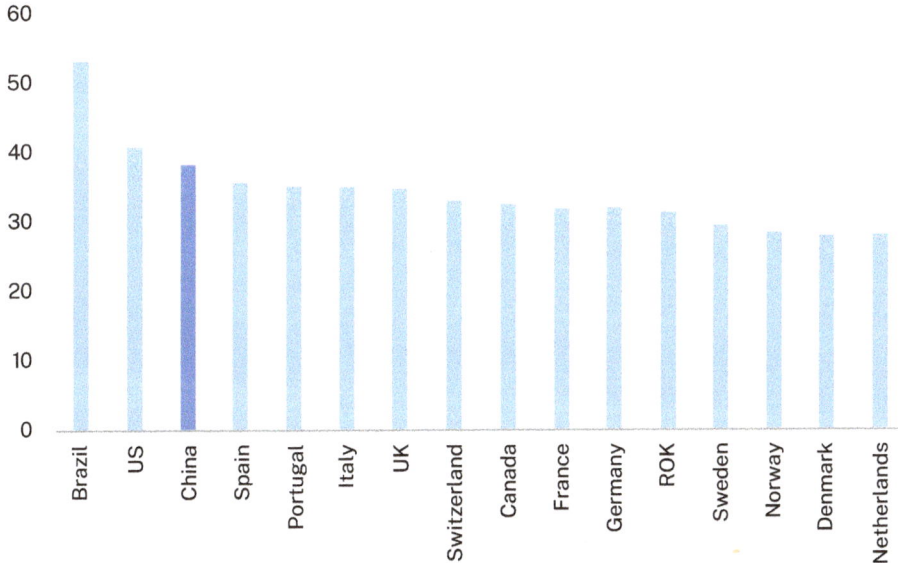

Figure 6.25 A comparison of Gini coefficients, 2016
Source: World Bank.

Great efforts have been made to improve China's social security system. In 2019, employees covered by pension insurance accounted for 41.3 per cent of the total workforce, while those covered by basic medical insurance accounted for 32 per cent, workplace injury insurance 33.3 per cent and unemployment insurance 28 per cent (NBS). More progress is needed to increase the coverage of the safety net.

Transforming and upgrading the distribution system to facilitate economic circulation

Innovation and digital transformation of the distribution system are not occurring fast enough—in particular, the application of modern technology, facilities and equipment is suboptimal at many small and medium-sized distribution enterprises. As a result, they struggle to adapt to the needs of emerging business models, services and scenarios.

The distribution system is not playing a strong role to support the upgrading of the manufacturing industry. China has few modern distribution enterprises that enjoy world-class branding, networks and competitiveness, making it difficult to channel market signals on segmented and rapidly iterating demand to upstream players in a timely and accurate manner.

Chinese cities must strengthen their leading role in consumption innovation. Despite accelerated efforts to innovate and upgrade consumption in recent years, cities are not sophisticated enough to lead and accommodate consumption activities in their commercial zones and central business districts.

Barriers to urban–rural connectivity for consumption and distribution must be removed. Rural areas lag in the development of information and digital infrastructure, the construction of commercial outlets and the availability of e-commerce infrastructure, such as cold-chain, delivery and other supporting services.

Improving the market environment in response to the need for domestic demand innovation

China's institutional environment has yet to be optimised to fuel consumption. Current market access and regulatory policies are not fully adapted to requirements for innovation and development, particularly for new consumption models such as livestream and social commerce, the night-time economy, community group-buying and innovative initiatives for business model convergence, industrial integration, business diversification and hybrid consumption scenarios. In addition, consumer protections must be strengthened.

China must step up its institutional opening to service consumption. In 2020, the openness of many service sectors fell below the Organisation for Economic Co-operation and Development (OECD) average[8] (Figure 6.26). Market access for foreign investment remains restricted in many service sectors, such as healthcare and culture. Insufficient openness limits the options for domestic consumers.

---

8   The Services Trade Restrictiveness Index (STRI) is an objective evaluation index that measures the openness of a country's service industry and an effective analysis tool for benchmarking and simulating policy measures to

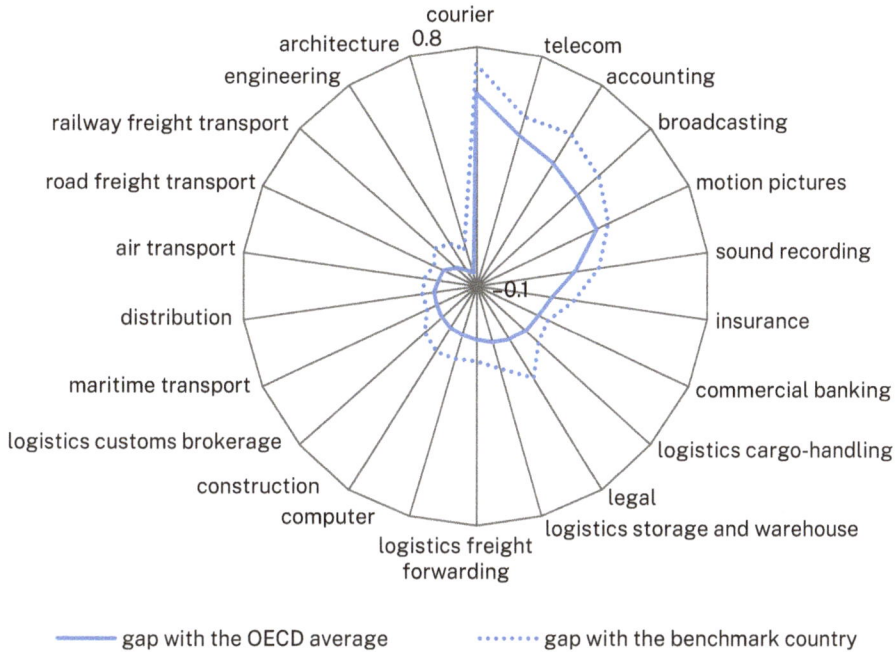

Figure 6.26 International comparison of the openness of China's service sectors

Source: OECD Services Trade Restrictiveness Index database (stats.oecd.org/Index.
aspx?DataSetCode=STRI).

Thoughts on expanding and better meeting domestic demand

Building a consumption-led domestic demand system with four main features

To expand and better meet domestic demand, a complete domestic demand system
is essential. It will boost the role of consumption in piloting domestic demand and
channelling investment, satisfy consumer demand and create new demand through
effective investment, buttress the positive loop between supply and demand, remove
bottlenecks in all domains of the national economy, and create a broad and solid

---

improve a country's service industry openness. The STRI adopts a scale from 0 to 1 in which the smaller the value,
the higher is the degree of openness. These values are calculated based on the most-favoured nation principle
(excluding the effect of preferential trade agreements), integrating input on different territories' laws and regulations
in five dimensions: market access restrictions for foreign investment, personnel mobility restrictions, competition
barriers, regulatory transparency and other discriminatory measures. The STRI covers 22 major service sectors in
38 OECD countries and 10 emerging markets and developing countries including China.

foundation for the growth of domestic demand mainly driven by consumption. To that end, a complete domestic demand system featuring the following four features must be built.

1. It should cover all aspects of demand, including consumption and investment, households and enterprises, goods and services, different regions and rural–urban interaction, the market and the government. In this all-inclusive system, all types of domestic demand can reinforce one another for joint development.

2. It should uphold all life-cycle management. It will oversee the whole life cycle of consumer demand and make corresponding adjustments, regardless of the stage, stratification or type of demand, to incubate and empower diversified consumption at multiple levels and maximise the leading role of consumption in expanding domestic demand.

3. It should integrate all domains of the value chain. With consumption as the powerhouse, a system of domestic demand will integrate production, distribution, circulation and consumption and lift the dynamic equilibrium between supply and demand to the next level, where the two ends grow stronger by reinforcing one another. This virtuous economic cycle will boost the overall performance of the national economy.

4. It should harness all development factors by putting in place a market-based pricing mechanism for all factors of production, committing more investment to human capital, enhancing market functionality for capital and data and enabling emerging factors to better drive domestic demand.

A new mechanism to ensure sustainable growth of domestic demand

To expand and better meet domestic demand in response to people's aspirations for a better life and the country's underlying potential, it is imperative to build a new mechanism that features efficient alignment, strong stimulation, accelerated innovation and orderly transformation. It will navigate consumers' desire for upgrading and boost consumption as the main driver of better and faster sustainable growth of domestic demand.

Efficient alignment aims to create a dynamic mechanism for optimal alignment between investment and consumption, between supply and demand and between the market and policies, to lift the dynamic equilibrium between supply and demand to the next level, where the two ends grow stronger by reinforcing one another. This will scale up the efforts to expand and better meet domestic demand.

Strong stimulation focuses on removing barriers to consumption and investment, establishing a mechanism that combines market incentives and supportive policies to unleash demand, empowering the growth of domestic demand with market forces and a favourable policy environment and steadily speeding up the materialisation of potential demand. Efforts to expand and better meet domestic demand will thus be lifted to the next level.

Accelerated innovation is about seizing opportunities in the new technological revolution, building systems and mechanisms that promote consumption innovation, facilitating innovation in products, services and production, extending the scope of investment and fostering and strengthening new growth engines. This will shift the efforts to expand and better meet domestic demand to a higher gear.

Orderly transformation aims to ensure orderly green transformation of investment and consumption by advancing new philosophies, drafting plans, offering guidance and instituting incentive and restrictive mechanisms. This will lead to a new model for the sustainable development of domestic demand.

Six strategic priorities for expanding and better meeting domestic demand

Innovation will lead to the rise of new drivers of domestic demand. All kinds of market players should be supported for innovation in technology, management and business models, to expand service consumption and fertilise new industries, businesses models and formats. Emphasis should be placed on a greater variety of options with higher quality to be provided by branded vendors. Effective supply of mid-to-high-end goods and services will be stepped up to create and meet the increasingly diversified and segmented demands of all consumer groups.

Digital transformation will provide a lever to lift the dynamic equilibrium between supply and demand to the next level. Digital transformation will move up from the consumer end to the supply end and disseminate from sporadic entry points across the whole value chain. Data, as a new production factor, should be fully leveraged and a rapid response mechanism should be set up to flexibly adjust capacity. High-quality consumption represents an opportunity to enhance supply–demand alignment, which will make the supply system more adaptable and pro-innovation and create the foundation for a digital, smart and green modern distribution system.

The middle-income group will be primary contributors to the sustainable growth of consumption-led domestic demand. Steps should be taken to steadily increase household income, enable equal access to basic public services, optimise government services in employment, increase human capital among low-income groups, guide more skilled workers and migrant workers into the middle-income group and build a strong social safety net for the marginal middle-income population.

Young people will be a focus to galvanise consumption potential. They can set good examples for consumption innovation and take the lead in upgrading and expanding consumption. Innovative and upgraded consumption will bring about an ecosystem based on online–offline integration and coordination. As family size declines, suppliers must acquire both capability and capacity to meet the need for mass consumption and customised convenience.

Large cities will serve as centres of growth poles to pilot and fuel consumption. Measures must be taken to drive high-quality urbanisation, develop city clusters and metropolitan areas, strengthen infrastructure connectivity and boost the economic vibrancy and population carrying-capacity of leading cities, city clusters and other areas with development advantages. It is also necessary to build international consumption hubs and enhance their global influence and capability in resource allocation. Multiple functions of rural consumption will be further explored to build an urban–rural integrated consumption system.

Green development will provide an opportunity to promote a new model of sustainable development for domestic demand. It is important to motivate a green transformation of consumer behaviours, improve the supply capability and quality of green products and services and expedite the development of a green low-carbon consumer market. Moreover, steps should be taken to improve the standards system for green products, reduce the costs of green production and improve the efficiency of resource consumption.

Orientation of future reforms to expand and better meet domestic demand

To achieve China's goal of building an integrated domestic demand system and expanding and better meeting domestic demand, future economic reforms must focus on the following: deepening supply-side structural reform to ensure effective market supply, accelerating the reform of income distribution and optimising social policies to enhance household affordability and consumption levels, improving policies for consumption growth to consolidate the institutional foundation for expanding domestic demand, transforming and upgrading the manufacturing industry to create a virtuous cycle between investment and consumption, scaling up institutional opening of the service industry for mutual reinforcement between domestic and international circulation, fixing weak infrastructure links to better unleash potential domestic demand, enhancing the green consumption system to foster a green and healthy consumption culture, and developing a statistical system that adapts to the requirements of domestic demand development.

References

Lui, Shijin. 2021. *China's Economic Growth Outlook (2021–2030): New Redoubling Strategy*. Beijing: CITIC Press.

National Bureau of Statistics of China (NBS). 2022. *China Statistical Yearbook 2021*. Beijing: China Statistics Press.

National Bureau of Statistics of China (NBS). Various years. *Statistical Communiqué on National Economic and Social Development*. Beijing: China Statistics Press.

Wang, Nian, Su Nuoya and Yu Mingzhe. 2022. *Further Enhance the Leading Role of Online Consumption to Expand Domestic Demand*. Investigation and Study Report No. 278. Beijing: Development Research Centre of the State Council.

Wang Wei. 2021a. *New consumption: A rising powerhouse for the new development pattern*. Background Report at China Development Forum 2021.

Wang Wei. 2021b. 'Committed to Expanding Domestic Demand as A Strategic Pivot for the Sustainable and Stable Development of China's Economy.' *Tsinghua Financial Review* 5: 30–33.

Wang Wei, Deng Yusong et al. 2021. *Housing System and Policies for Major City Clusters*. China Development Press, pp. 11–22.

Wang Wei, Wang Qing, Liu Tao et al. 2017. *A New Chapter of the Service Sector for Consumers: Development Practice and Innovation in Reform*. China Development Press.

Wang Wei, Wang Qing, Liu Tao et al. 2021. *International Consumption Hubs: Theories, Policies and Practices*. China Development Press.

World Economic Forum (WEF). 2019. *Global Competitiveness Report 2019*. Cologny, Switzerland: WEF.

Wang Qing. 2021. 'Orientation of and Thoughts on Developing an Institution to Effectively Expand Domestic Demand.' *The Economic Daily*, February 8.

Wang Qing and Liu, Tao. 2019. 'A Science-Based Perspective to Fundamental Changes in Consumption.' *The Economic Daily*, May 22.

Xingzhou Ren, Wang Wei, Wang Qing et al. *A Research on China's Emerging Consumption Growth Drivers in the New Era*. China Development Press.

Deng Yusong. 2019. *A Study on the Trend and Policies of China's Housing Market (2020–2050)*. Science China Press.

7

China's *hukou* system reform: Endogenous evolution and adaptive efficiency

Kunling Zhang

Introduction

China's National Development and Reform Commission released the implementation scheme for new urbanisation under the Fourteenth Five-Year Plan in late June 2022, proposing to deepen the reform of the *hukou* (household registration) system, making *hukou* a hot topic once again (NDRC 2022). The plan envisages abolishing *hukou* restrictions in cities with a residential urban population of less than 3 million, while for cities with 3–5 million people, *hukou* regulations will be relaxed. In addition, the points system operating in cities with a residential urban population of more than 5 million will be improved to emphasise migrants' local social insurance contributions and length of residence. Although this appears to be a big step forward, the ideas in this round of *hukou* reform are not altogether new, as several previous documents made similar proposals. In recent years, the Chinese Government has indicated its intention to reform the *hukou* system by promoting 'new-type urbanisation',[1] the development of urban–rural integration (State Council 2019a) and establishing a high-standard market system (State Council 2021). At the end of 2019, the central government issued its guidelines on promoting institutional reform of the social mobility of labour and talent, promoting *hukou* reform in the big cities, enlarging the coverage of basic public services and deepening supporting policies (State Council 2019b). These policy ideas were also set out in the Fourteenth Five-Year Plan in early 2021 (Government of the PRC 2021). While these are all

---

1   See NDRC (2020, 2021).

good signs for promoting urbanisation, the government remains circumspect about promoting *hukou* reform in megacities, which are the most favoured destinations for migrants.[2]

If the Regulations on Household Registration released in 1958 are considered the origin, contemporary China's *hukou* system has existed for more than 60 years and undergone drastic changes during the past 40 years of reform. It still has considerable institutional legitimacy, administrative effectiveness and influence on today's China (Zhang et al. 2019). Migrants' access to *hukou*-based welfare is substantially constrained under the regulations, which has seen the system criticised for promoting social stratification (Wu and Treiman 2004), inequality (Afridi et al. 2015), discrimination (Song 2014) and social exclusion (Zhang et al. 2014).

Since the early 2010s, China's rapid economic growth has stalled. Especially after 2012, its GDP growth rate slowed to less than 8 per cent and decreased to less than 7 per cent after 2015 (NBS 2020). Additionally, since 2020, China's economy has been hit hard by the Covid-19 pandemic, making it even more difficult for China to revive its past economic growth glories. The economic slowdown has generated increasing concern that China is confronting the 'middle-income trap'. As an institution that deeply affects labour mobility and residents' welfare, the *hukou* system needs further reform to adapt it to the new economic environment, including the rising costs of labour, weak domestic consumption and social inequality. Although there is consensus on the need for *hukou* system reform, progress has been slow. To explain this apparent contradiction, an in-depth examination of the evolution of the *hukou* system and its interaction with economic transformation is necessary.

China's *hukou* system is a set of government regulations that affects labour mobility and functions as the foundation for residents' rights and resource allocation. The system's institutional attributes make the adoption of an institutional perspective advantageous for studying its evolution. Related studies have produced mixed explanations. Considering the *hukou* system as a formal institutional arrangement, some studies have argued that the key to *hukou* reform is strong advancements of government policies, and that the process should be exogenous and mandatory (for example, Chi and Yang 2003; Peng et al. 2009). Increasingly, however, scholars have realised that exogenous institutional change theories have impediments when attempting to gain a better understanding of institutional dynamics (Aoki 2001, 2007; Greif 2006). Although very few studies have focused on the endogenous forces in *hukou* system reform, some are inspirational. For example, Solinger (1999) holds that under the power of the market, rural migrants and their 'contesting' behaviours in urban areas are a major force of urban institutional change. Young (2013) argues

---

2   According to the Floating Population Dynamic Monitoring surveys, of the rural migrants who want to obtain urban *hukou*, about 68 per cent prefer large cities (Chen and Fan 2016).

that *hukou* system reform is the result of the development of marketisation and internal migration, which forced the government to reform the *hukou* policy to promote economic development.

From the institutional efficiency perspective, an extensive literature has proved that the *hukou* system has played both negative and positive roles in China's economic transformation. On the one hand, many scholars have regarded the *hukou* system as an institutional obstacle that impedes structural transformation (Cai and Wang 2010), population agglomeration (Au and Henderson 2006) and domestic consumption (Song et al. 2010); on the other, the system has been considered a pillar of China's model for rapid industrialisation and development, especially regarding circumvention of the Lewis transition (Wang 2005), maintaining levels of human capital (Fan and Stark 2008) and capital accumulation (Vendryes 2011).

These studies have improved the understanding of the evolution of the *hukou* system; however, they also have their shortcomings. First, scholars have often considered the *hukou* system as exogenously instituted by the government and have overemphasised the role the central government plays in its reform because of its reputation as a 'strong state'. Although a limited number of scholars have realised the role of endogenous forces in *hukou* system reform, theoretical improvement is still necessary to improve the explanation of the institutionalisation and reform of the *hukou* system. Second, studies of the efficiency of the *hukou* system have mostly concentrated on the research framework of neoclassical economics from a static or at best comparative static analysis, and the literature that has used the framework of institutional economics under a dynamic perspective has been limited. This limitation severs the link between institutional change and institutional efficiency, which can hinder proper understanding of institutional change under economic dynamics.

Against this background, this chapter first establishes a theoretical framework of endogenous institutional change to analyse the evolution of the *hukou* system. More broadly, this framework also helps to improve the understanding of general institutional change and offers policymakers a better understanding of decision-making processes in dynamic contexts. Second, it uses the concept of adaptive efficiency to evaluate the evolution of China's *hukou* system. This attempt provides an alternative approach to institutional efficiency evaluation and bridges the theories of endogenous institutional change and adaptive efficiency.

Theoretical framework

Endogenous institutional change

Works on institutional change have considerably advanced the understanding of this topic, but no consensus has been reached (Kingston and Caballero 2009).

Exogenous versus endogenous

North (1990) considers institutions to be the 'rules of the game', which are exogenously imposed. Scholars have tended to treat the state sector as having a central role in initiating and guiding institutional change, because the 'free-rider' problem always exists in the provision of public goods (institutions) (Lin 1989; Nee and Opper 2012). Moreover, the exogenous 'shock' seems necessary to break societies out of suboptimal scenarios caused by the path dependence of specific institutional arrangements (Boettke et al. 2008).

However, this perspective could have an infinite regression problem, such as who enforces the enforcer(s) (Aoki 2001, 2007) or 'who watches the watchman' (Greif 2006: 8). Second, informal institutions are the result of 'unintentional and decentralized patterns of behavior and processes of learning' (Brousseau et al. 2011: 11) that are 'not only slow to change, but also beyond the reach of [the] political elite' (Nee and Opper 2012: 4). Theories of exogenous institutional change cannot be applied to study formal and informal institutional change in the same framework, which dramatically weakens their explanatory power. Third, supporters of exogenous institutional change can oversimplify complex nonlinear aspects of economic systems and overlook the bounded rationality of human behaviour (Chen 1993).

Thus, the idea of institutions-as-rules could be inadequate for defining institutions. It should therefore be complemented by another branch of thought—namely, 'institutions-as-equilibria' (Greif and Kingston 2011), which argues that institutions are the equilibria of the game. Institutions are thus identified as equilibrium patterns of behaviour rather than the rules that induce behaviour (Kingston and Caballero 2009). In this regard, an institutional change can result from a change in shared belief and the behaviour associated with it, which is endogenously generated from a repeated game through the feedback mechanism. A prevailing institution can be undermined when previously shared beliefs no longer allow adequate understanding and prediction of the actions of others (otherwise it will be reinforced; Greif and Laitin 2004; Greif 2006).

Ideas of institutional change are relevant because different theories induce different practical implications. Exogenous institutional change theory tends to overemphasise the role of politics, and the change of its interests and knowledge contribute to institutional change. In this view, one country or organisation could easily change its institutions to promote its development by simply copying some 'good' institutions. However, this has proved practically infeasible according to international experience (Chang 2011). Moreover, the exogenous model regards ordinary individuals as passive 'institution takers' who find challenging a given institution difficult or even impossible. By contrast, endogenous institutional change theories hold that individuals within a given society can contribute to the development of institutions and not just the state sectors, as traditionally assumed. They emphasise that local knowledge, information, thoughts or ideas can affect institutional change because societal development requires creative thinking and innovation, both of which thrive on decentralised decision-making processes (North 1990).

The perspective of endogenous institutional change is increasingly popular because of its powerful explanatory advantages and useful implications. Greif and Laitin (2004) and Greif (2006) investigated institutional change and persistence in the same framework, finding that quasi-parameter shifts were the key condition for institutional self-undermining or self-reinforcing, which led to institutional change or persistence, respectively. The introduction of a quasi-parameter makes their analysis framework more tractable and better able to solve the transformation problem between endogenous and exogenous analysis than other related theories (Aoki 2001, 2007).

Conceptual framework

Quasi-parameter identification is the key to Greif's endogenous institutional change theory. Parameters are often treated as exogenously given in a game. A change in parameter implies a new equilibrium set of the game and hence the possibility for new institutions (institutions-as-equilibria). By contrast, variables are endogenously determined by the game. Variable change does not necessarily induce a new equilibrium; the precise distinction between a parameter and a variable is flexible (Greif and Laitin 2004). For example, technology is usually regarded as exogenously given when studying economic performance in a certain period but as an endogenous variable when studying long-run economic development. Such factors should be treated differently according to different empirical tasks: as parametric when studying institutional self-enforceability, which requires static analysis, but as variables when studying long-run institutional dynamics (Greif 2006). Such parameters are endogenously changed in this manner and with this effect are considered quasi-parameters according to Greif's framework.

An institution can change its self-enforceability and further reinforce or undermine itself through the influences of endogenous quasi-parameter shifts. However, how the change of a quasi-parameter impacts the self-enforcing range of the institution and in what condition the associated behaviours self-enforce in a larger or smaller set of situations remain unsettled in Greif's framework. Although they incorporate a feedback mechanism into their work, a better delineation is necessary regarding the mechanism taking place. Nee and Opper (2012) and DellaPosta et al. (2017) offer sound theoretical contributions that complement the endogenous theory. They hold that an endogenous institutional change starts with random deviation from the former stable institution. Although the deviation could also be intentional (because of the negative feedback caused by quasi-parameter shifts) rather than random, their framework provides a useful complement to Greif's theory in bridging microlevel behaviour and macrolevel institutional change.

They believe the vulnerability of a stable institution depends on the relative benefits of compliance versus deviation. If the benefit gained from a deviation fulfills or outstrips the initial deviator's expectations, risky deviations[3] would reproduce themselves and diffuse in the population through network externalities (Nee and Opper 2012; DellaPosta et al. 2017). This implies that the beliefs and associated behaviours of an existing institution are self-enforcing in a smaller range of situations. The behaviour associated with the institution would not be self-enforcing even in situations in which this previously would have been the case. When more individuals in more situations find it best not to adhere to the existing institution, it will undermine itself by this successful deviation until the 'action group' (usually, the state sector) finally exercises its responsibility to formalise the institutional change, because the cost of enforcing the previous institutions has become too high (Nee and Opper 2012; DellaPosta et al. 2017).

Institutional dynamics rely on the self-enforceability of beliefs and associated behaviours. An institutional change is a change in beliefs, including individual mental structures and collective ideology, and the beliefs undermining processes can lead the associated behaviours to cease being self-enforcing, further leading individuals to act in a manner that does not reproduce the associated beliefs. Endogenous institutional change can be expected when the institutional implications constantly undermine the beliefs and associated behaviours because of quasi-parameter shifts. Conversely, institutional persistence can be expected when the self-enforcing range of the associated behaviours does not decrease. Institutional change endogenously occurs when the self-undermining process reaches a critical juncture, which implies that the cost of institutional enforcement increases to a level at which the action group must adaptively accommodate the existing institution, such that past patterns of behaviour are no longer self-enforcing. Hence, 'institutions can be self-undermining, and the behaviors that they entail can cultivate the seeds of their own demise' (Greif and Laitin 2004: 634). The opposite holds in the case of institutional reinforcement.

The conceptual framework of endogenous institutional change is summarised in Figure 7.1. Given the institutional environment, an existing institution cumulatively induces one or more quasi-parameter shifts through a feedback mechanism. To adjust to the new circumstances, individuals adaptively accommodate their beliefs and associated behaviours based on weighing the relative gains of compliance with or deviation from the existing institutions. Through network externalities, the self-enforceability range of the current institution subsequently changes. After a relatively long period of reinforcing or undermining, endogenous institutional persistence or change can be expected, respectively, when the cost of institutional enforcement reaches a critical level and the action group makes institutional accommodations. The process will then restart again and again.

---

3   Usually, the deviation occurs through informal institutions.

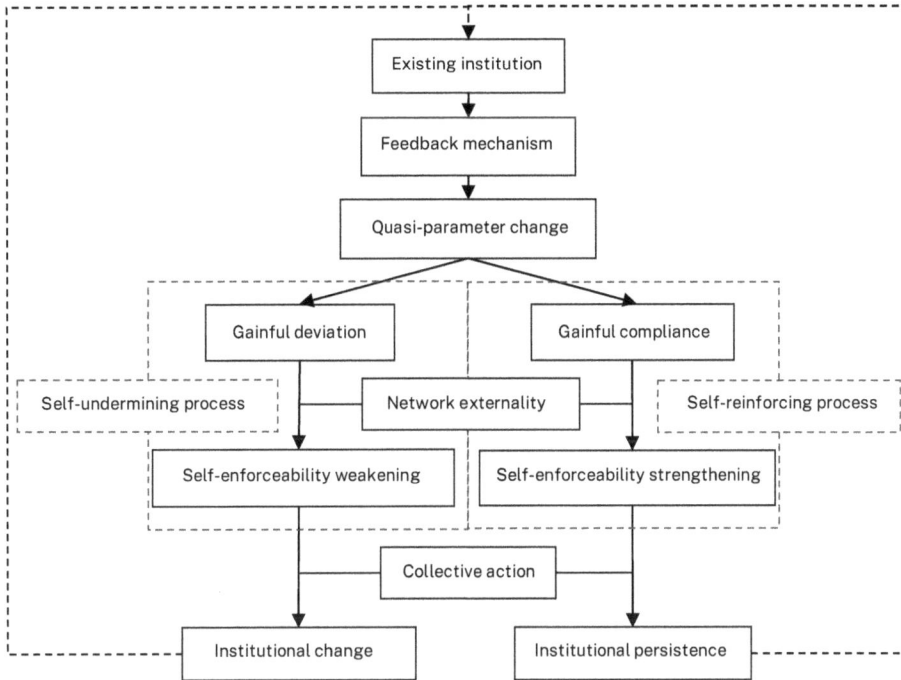

Figure 7.1 Conceptual framework of endogenous institutional change
Source: Author's own schema.

Notably, the processes of institutional change and persistence can be overlapping, and the result is determined by the side that is dominant. This usually leads to the evolution of an institution in a path-dependent manner. Furthermore, endogenous change need not necessarily go through all the processes described; it depends on the nature of the quasi-parameters. When the quasi-parameters can be recognised, anticipated, directly observed, understood or considered by individuals *ex ante*, intentional or designed institutional change can occur. Moreover, institutional change can be generated through endogenous, exogenous or combined ways (Greif and Laitin 2004). What is important is not whether the institutional change is endogenous or exogenous, but whether the institutional change is efficient.

Adaptive efficiency

When an institution has changed or is changing, how can we know whether it is good or bad for economic development? Many criteria have been used to evaluate institutional efficiency, however, most have limitations in their practical applications.

Pareto optimality has often been used to analyse institutional change because it provides a basis on which institutions can be grounded. However, Pareto optimality is a fundamentally short-term static rather than long-term dynamic criterion, which does not fit the idea that an institution and its change exist in uncertain circumstances (Brousseau et al. 2011). Thus, the allocative efficiency criterion, which assumes zero transaction cost and unbounded rationality, could be misleading (North 1990; Ma and Jalil 2008).

Another neoclassical method in institutional efficiency evaluation is cost–benefit analysis, which emphasises that the choice of an institution is based on the comparison of costs and benefits. As Lin (1989: 12) points out, 'given production and transaction costs, one institutional arrangement is more efficient than another whenever it provides more services'. However, the quantity of services an institution provides is not equal to the efficiency of the institution because institutions provide not only services but also, more importantly, incentives.

The emergence of transaction cost theory is revolutionary in institutional economics. Many scholars have used transaction costs in institutional efficiency evaluation (Song and Simpson 2018). However, empirically, transaction cost theory also has limitations (Huang 2017). First, it is challenging to eliminate the technological impact from institutional efficiency evaluation. Second, it is difficult if not impossible to identify the transition costs for a specific institution because of the co-relationship between institutions. Third, we cannot scale the costs of a transaction that does not occur—for example, when the transaction cost is almost infinite in theory, it appears to be close to zero in reality (Zhou 2013).

Adaptive efficiency—first introduced by Marris and Mueller (1980)—as a more critical factor in long-run growth (North 1990, 1994), is a better concept with which to evaluate institutional efficiency dynamics (Brousseau et al. 2011). North (2005: 169) proposes that adaptive efficiency is 'an ongoing condition in which the society continues to modify or create new institutions as problems evolve'. It is 'the ability of some societies to flexibly adjust in the face of the shocks, disturbances, and ubiquitous uncertainty that characterize every society over time and evolve institutions that effectively deal with an altered "reality"' (North 2005: 6), and 'the capacity of the institutions to efficiently evolve over time to better adapt to ever-changing environments (both endogenous and exogenous)' for better economic performance (Song and Simpson 2018: 552). Therefore, to evaluate the efficiency of institutional change, we apply the concept of adaptive efficiency.

Endogenous institutional change theory stresses the roles of the key players such as government officials or private firms and effective government in institutional development. Through the interactions between an institution and ever-changing environmental (quasi-parameter) interactions, the institution adaptively adjusts and endogenously coordinates itself to the environment to generate adaptive efficiency. Adaptive efficiency's fundamental emphasis on institutional experimentation, innovation and creative destruction lends it to the reliable evaluation of endogenous institutional change. The key players and effective governance are centred on and bridge endogenous institutional change and adaptive efficiency. Additionally, an effective government can adaptively react to quasi-parameter shifts and make institutional adjustments that reduce institutional enforcement costs, thereby increasing institutional efficiency.

Thus, it is important to ask: how is adaptive efficiency generated? Using a series of studies by Douglas North, this chapter proposes that there are at least five fundamental principles for evaluating adaptive efficiency:

1. efficiently specified property rights that 'encourage productivity will increase market efficiency' (North 2005: 1)[4]

2. a decentralised decision-making process that 'allows societies to maximize the efforts required to explore alternative ways of solving problems' (North 1990: 81)

3. low transaction costs that facilitate innovation and experimentation-related transactions

4. 'competition in open access orders to address major social problems' (North et al. 2009: 133)

5. institutional flexibility that fosters innovation and experimentation (North 1990, 2005; North et al. 2009).

Each of these five principles is a necessary rather than a sufficient condition for an adaptively efficient institution. For example, even if the decision-making process is decentralised, an institution is not necessarily efficient with a high transaction cost or suppressed competition. Therefore, adaptive efficiency cannot be guaranteed by a simple aggregation of the five factors; rather, they should necessarily work together, and any shortfalls will jeopardise that goal. Moreover, the existence of a capable and credible government is a necessary precondition for such efficiency. Government usually is in the position and has the power to enforce contracts and safeguard fair competition. Especially when it comes to institutional flexibility, a capable, credible and effective government should seek to encourage institutional innovation and experimentation, reward success and eliminate failures. Ideally, the government should try to not do too much, to maintain institutional flexibility, while not doing too little—that is, to be prepared to try, fail, learn and change.

---

4   Here, the use of 'efficient property rights' rather than 'well-specified property rights' is inspired by Hu (2007: 17), who states that 'efficient property rights are the foundation of efficient economic organizations' in summarising North's major arguments about institutions and economic performance. If the property rights system is efficient, whether it is well-specified or ambiguous becomes less important to economic performance in transitional economies—that is, efficient property rights can be de facto property rights, not necessary de jure property rights under consideration of an imperfect institutional environment. This is also part of institutional flexibility.

Empirically, however, measuring adaptive efficiency is a challenging task in institutional economics, and too few quantitative studies of the adaptive efficiency of specific institutions have been conducted. This study believes that coupling—a concept originating in physics that describes a phenomenon in which two or more systems influence each other through various interactions—could be useful. The concept has been introduced to the social sciences because of its useful physics metaphor (Li et al. 2012). Because adaptive efficiency is generated from interactions between an institution and its ever-changing environment, it has theoretical consistency with the concept of coupling, which could provide a possible approach for evaluating adaptive efficiency.

The evolution of China's *hukou* system

The *hukou* system has long been practised in Chinese history, although it was not until the founding of the People's Republic of China (PRC) that its various functions were nationally restored and greatly enhanced.

Exogenous *hukou* system institutionalisation

During the first three years of the PRC (1949–52), the *hukou* system was quite relaxed (Solinger 1999). Enterprises were largely allowed to continue operation in the market and individuals could freely choose their jobs and enjoyed freedom of movement and residence (Cheng and Selden 1994). The government was still attempting to strengthen urban–rural interaction in terms of market transactions. Market mechanisms played a critical role in resource allocation in this period.

To fulfill the dream of national prosperity, the Chinese Government introduced— if not simply copied (Lin et al. 2003)—the economic planning system of the Soviet Union. In 1953, the central government initiated the first Five-Year Plan with a strategy orientated towards the development of heavy industry. To accelerate industrialisation under the conditions of a labour surplus and a capital shortage in a predominantly agrarian society, the government compulsorily allocated resources into and artificially reduced the development costs of heavy industry, including reducing the prices of capital (interest), foreign exchange, energy, raw materials, labour and agricultural products (Lin et al. 2003). Thus, a series of policies and regulations was implemented in both rural and urban areas covering the agricultural and industrial sectors. This led to the gradual emergence of the migration control and resource allocation functions of the *hukou* system (Figure 7.2), which were modelled on the idea of the Soviet internal passport (*propiska*) system (Cheng and Selden 1994).

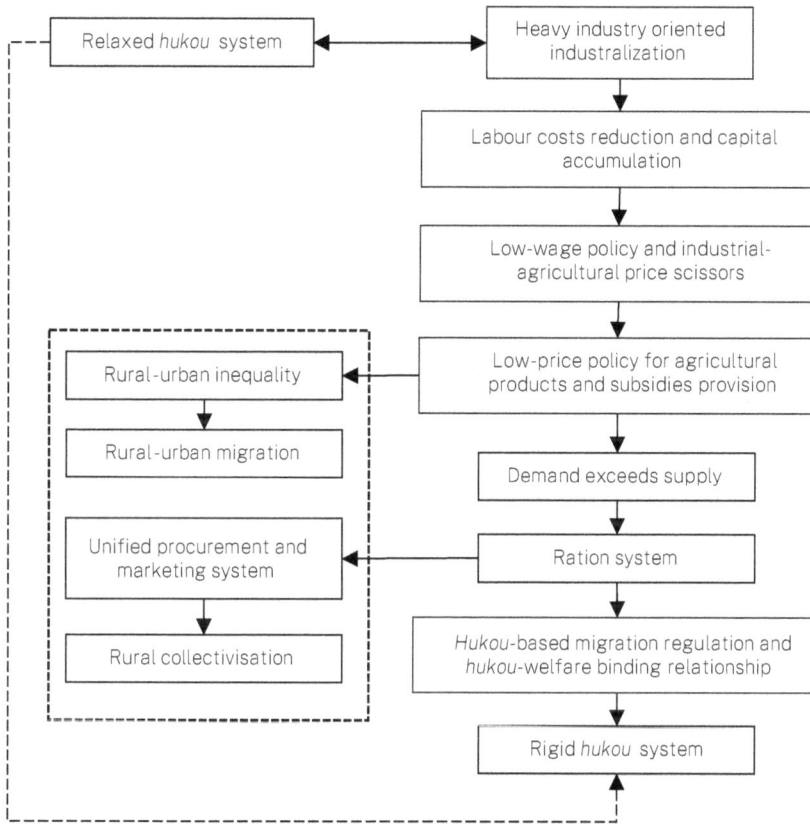

Figure 7.2 Path of institutionalisation of the rigid *hukou* system
Source: Author's own schema.

With these urban-biased rules and regulations established,[5] the institutional incentives implied that moving to urban areas would be the natural benefit maximisation choice for rural residents under the market mechanism. In practice, however, this would induce urban unemployment and put pressure on resource consumption (such as housing, education, public services and food), further jeopardising industrialisation under the planned economy. In response to the negative feedback from all walks of life, including governments and residents, the central government relaxed the *hukou* system and reduced its enforceability. From 1953, the government consecutively issued several documents aimed at preventing farmers from migrating to urban areas. The government also paid a high price in labour and material resources for rural migration control, indicating the high enforcement costs required to maintain the relaxed *hukou* system. Therefore, the

---

5   See Young (2013) for the rights and privileges linked to agricultural *hukou* and non-agricultural *hukou* in pre-reform China.

government increased the pace of its implementation of laws to regulate population mobility. In 1958, it implemented its Regulations on Household Registration in the PRC to strictly regulate population migration and, in 1975, the article on citizens' freedom of residence and movement in the PRC Constitution was abolished.

Although China's development strategy received people's support at the time, the rigid *hukou* system was an exogenously generated institution (Table 7.1). The heavy industry–oriented development strategy did not fit the facts of China's comparative advantage of abundant labour resources (Lin et al. 2003). After this strategy was implemented, the centrally imposed rigid *hukou* system was compulsorily institutionalised to serve the planned economy because the enforcement cost of the relatively relaxed *hukou* system was too high. Thus, the original relaxed *hukou* system was enforced in a smaller range of situations and the institutional arrangement was undermined.

Table 7.1 Exogenous institutionalisation of the *hukou* system

Existing institution	Relaxed *hukou* system
Exogenous shock	Heavy industry–oriented development strategy
Positive or negative feedback	Negative (high level of urban unemployment and overconsumption)
Deviation or compliance	Gainful deviation (farmers persuaded to not move into cities and migrants persuaded to move back to the countryside; migration permission)
Self-enforceability	Decreasing
Government accommodation	Increasingly tightened migration control and the *hukou*–welfare binding relationship
Undermining or reinforcing	Undermining
Institutional change	Rigid *hukou* system

The rigid *hukou* system in the pre-reform era fundamentally affected China's socioeconomic development. Notably, as a de facto agrarian economy, China's agricultural productivity was deeply constrained by the system. In the agricultural sector, as more and more variable factors (labour) are employed with the fixed factors (land), the marginal product falls and the law of diminishing returns applies, thus a low level of agricultural productivity occurs (Sheng and Song 2018). In pre-reform China, the population growth rate was relatively high, especially in rural areas. Under the rigid *hukou* system, the rural population could not freely migrate to urban areas, which increased the labour–land ratio. In addition, suppressed agricultural prices and the commune system deprived farmers of production incentives. All these factors contributed to the relatively low level of agricultural productivity in pre-reform China (Figure 7.3).

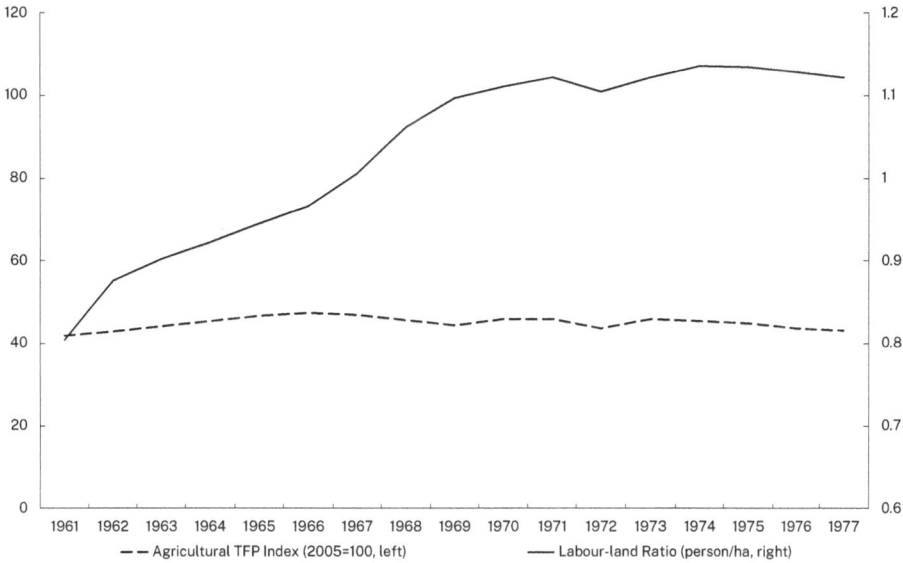

Figure 7.3 Labour–land ratio and agricultural productivity in pre-reform China
Source: USDA (2022).

Endogenous *hukou* system reform

Since the beginning of reforms in 1978, China's *hukou* system has undergone significant adaptations in response to the new realities of de-collectivisation, marketisation, decentralisation and globalisation. To better understand the changes in the system, we look at its two institutional functions.

Population mobility regulation

There are two potential approaches to managing the problem of low agricultural productivity: release the resource-shifting effect or increase production incentives. The former entails reducing the rural labour–land ratio—that is, relaxing the rigid *hukou* system and allowing rural labour to migrate to urban areas. This would release the resource-shifting effect by moving labour from low-productivity sectors to high-productivity sectors, according to the dual-structure theory. However, this is a potentially risky approach because it could cause urban unemployment and overconsumption in an underdeveloped urban economy. The other approach would be to rebuild farmers' production incentives, to which the commune system and price-depression policy were two main obstacles.

Therefore, household responsibility system reform, which began at the bottom through innovations by village famers, was gradually implemented to manage the insufficient incentives of the commune system in the agricultural sector from the late 1970s; this process was characterised as de-collectivisation. Additionally, in

1979, China began to reform its price system to adjust the long-depressed state-controlled prices of agricultural products—a policy that was extended to industrial goods in 1984 (Guo 1992). Consequently, the role of market forces in the economy was enhanced substantially and the role of state forces weakened dramatically. The expanding role of the market and the formation of market price signals have had a pervasive influence on decision-making and resource allocation and noticeable effects on the growth of productivity in the agricultural and industrial sectors.

After the land and price reforms, agricultural productivity was substantially enhanced, which improved the supply of agricultural products, especially grain, and released a lot of surplus rural labour that had been administratively confined to the communes. The surplus rural labour had great incentives to move because of the rural–urban and regional income differences. Moreover, the development of township and village enterprises and the export-led growth strategy in the 1980s generated major demand for unskilled labour. Informally, an increasing number of rural labourers undertook off-farm work and nonstate enterprises recruited rural labour in cities and towns through personal *guanxi* ('kinship or friendship') and *tongxiang* (coming from the same village) networks (Nee and Opper 2012; Young 2013), against the rigid *hukou* system. Institutional deviations started with the movement known as 'leaving the land without leaving the countryside' (*litu bu lixiang*), which broke the rules that fixed farmers to the land in the *hukou* system, and then spread to urban areas. According to the 1982 census, two years before the official *hukou* system reform began, the inconsistency in the population residence–registration numbers was 11.33 million, of whom 6.36 million had not resided in their registration place for more than one year.

In response, in the mid-1980s, the government undertook several reforms to deregulate the *hukou* system—for example, self-supplied food (*zili kouliang*) *hukou* reform[6] and the introduction of a temporary residence permit (*zanzhuzheng*) and national ID card (*shenfenzheng*). After this deregulation, and especially after the 1990s, large numbers of rural surplus labour migrated to urban areas. This considerably reduced the labour–land ratio in rural areas, which further improved agricultural productivity (Figure 7.4), increased farmers' income levels and corrected the labour market mismatch.

---

6   Peasants are allowed to get a type of urban *hukou*, called 'self-supplied food' *hukou*, in small towns when they meet the requirements of either running businesses or being employed in enterprises, and having their own accommodations in towns. They must also self-provide their own food, rather than enjoy food subsidies from the government.

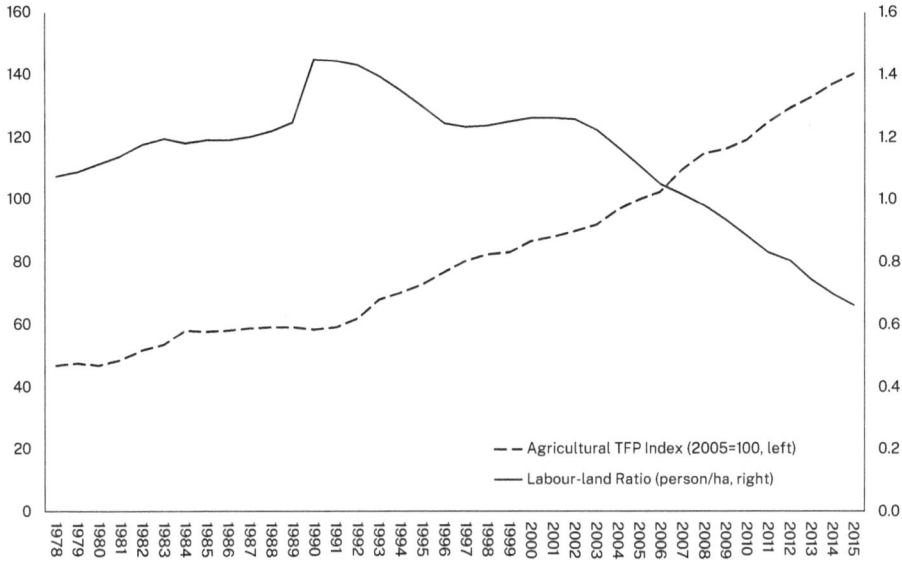

Figure 7.4 Labour–land ratio and agricultural productivity in reform era
Source: USDA (2022).

Table 7.2 shows the endogenous logic of the *hukou* system reform regarding its function of population mobility control.

Table 7.2 Endogenous evolution of the *hukou* system (population mobility)

Existing institution	Rigid *hukou* system
Positive or negative feedback	Negative (low agricultural productivity, high income differences and mismatch of labour supply and demand)
Quasi-parameters	Agricultural productivity, rural–urban and regional income differences and balance of labour supply and demand
Deviation or compliance	Gainful deviation (move to increase farmers' wealth; recruit rural labour at low cost)
Self-enforceability	Decreasing
Government accommodation	'*Zili kouliang*' *hukou* reform, '*zanzhuzheng*' introduction and '*shenfenzheng*' system introduction
Undermining or reinforcing	Undermining
Institutional change	Relatively relaxed *hukou* system

Hukou–welfare binding relationship

More than one quasi-parameter can change spontaneously, which can complicate institutional evolution.

Self-undermining process

Since the early 1980s, China has experienced decentralisation through its implementation of various programs aimed at devolving fiscal and administrative powers to local governments. Further, tax-sharing reform in 1994 specified the corresponding division between the central and local governments regarding financial rights and responsibilities.[7] Because of the binding relationship between *hukou* and welfare, the *hukou* system determines the population base, the size of which determines a local government's budget for public services provision.[8] Local governments had more power to decide *hukou* policies in their administrative jurisdiction (Chan 2009). Additionally, after *hukou* deregulation, population mobility became increasingly common. The booming exchange of information and knowledge gradually promoted the formation of product and labour markets (Solinger 1999). With the deepening of marketisation, local governments found the cost of the *hukou* system was too high and it was increasingly unnecessary to provide financial subsidies for food to urban *hukou* holders. Thus, the government abandoned the ration system and gradually cancelled the grain coupon (*liangpiao*) and other coupons. The link between *hukou* and food rations ended and financial subsidies to maintain urban food security were further decreased. The establishment in 1992 of the goal of creating a socialist market economy further weakened the *hukou*–welfare relationship, including in housing security, employment and social insurance, with these welfare services becoming gradually marketised as commodities and more accessible for migrants in open markets.

In this process, marketisation can be considered a quasi-parameter. The *hukou* reform that deregulated labour mobility control promoted the development of marketisation and marketisation then undermined the *hukou*–welfare relationship (Table 7.3).

Self-reinforcing process

The emergence of what was called the 'migrant workers tide' (*mingong chao*) in the 1990s further promoted *hukou* reform; however, this round of reform was relatively minor. In 2001, China fully reformed the *hukou* regulation in small cities and towns where *hukou* entitled individuals to much less social welfare, which was an easy change to make as it did not put much fiscal pressure on those local governments. In contrast, the *hukou* system in big cities remains potent and intact.

---

7   The rights to tax collection and responsibilities for providing public services.
8   Local fiscal expenditure is based on the registered *hukou* population.

Notably, after the tax-sharing reform that increased the responsibility of local governments, *hukou* became an effective tool for city governments to control local fiscal expenditure and expand fiscal revenue. In the 1980s, many local governments benefited directly by selling urban *hukou* to raise funds for city construction (Chan and Zhang 1999). Subsequently, in local *hukou* reform, especially in big cities, innovations were implemented one after another, including the blue-stamp (*lanyin*) *hukou* reform in the 1990s, the current points system (*jifenzhi*) and the recent 'War for Talent' policy (*rencai zhengduozhan*).[9] However, these reforms unsurprisingly favour the high-skilled migrants who are most likely to benefit the local economy and exclude most low-skilled migrants. To some degree, acquiring *hukou* in these cities has become more difficult than before. In 2014, the central government continued to enforce strict control of population size in megacities through *hukou* reforms (State Council 2014). In recent years, although *hukou* reform has targeted big cities, the government remains cautious about promoting such reform in megacities.

Therefore, the economic benefit from the current *hukou* system means local governments are reluctant to fundamentally change the system, because of the gainful compliance (Table 7.3). In this sense, the *hukou* system is reinforcing. If local governments conduct radical *hukou* reform without the breakdown of the *hukou*–welfare binding relationship, this will jeopardise the local fiscal situation. This is why *hukou* reform in the city of Zhengzhou in the early twenty-first century failed[10] and why most city mayors are opposed to *hukou* reform, according to an official survey in 2012 (Zhou 2012).

Table 7.3 Endogenous evolution of the *hukou* system (resource allocation)

Existing institution	Relaxed migration control and tight *hukou*–welfare relationship	
Quasi-parameters	Marketisation; decentralisation	
Positive or negative feedback	Negative (high cost of providing subsidies to urban *hukou* holders)	Positive (protecting vested interests of insiders and attracting talent and investment for local economic development)
Deviation or compliance	Gainful deviation (detach some welfare from the *hukou* system)	Gainful compliance (maintain the *hukou*–welfare binding relationship)
Self-enforceability	Decreasing	Increasing
Government accommodation	Abolition of the unified procurement and marketing system and phasing out of ration system	Blue-stamp *hukou* reform, the points system reform and the War for Talent
Undermining or reinforcing	Undermining	Reinforcing
Institutional persistence	Comprehensive *hukou* system	

9   Since the first half of 2018, many big cities have begun to introduce a series of preferential *hukou* conversion policies to compete for talent to enhance their economic vitality.
10   In the early 2000s, Zhengzhou, the capital of Henan Province, implemented radical reform to grant *hukou* to qualified migrants, but the change was soon withdrawn.

In summary, the evolution of institutional change is intertwined with institutional undermining and institutional reinforcing during the given period. Ultimately, institutional change or persistence relies on the relative power of that undermining and reinforcing, which can partially explain the persistence of the *hukou* system in modern China.

Adaptive efficiency of the evolution of the *hukou* system

Adaptive efficiency comparison of the evolution of China's *hukou* system

Table 7.4 provides a summary of the adaptive efficiency comparison of the *hukou* system in the pre-reform and reform eras, according to the aforementioned five elements.

Table 7.4 Adaptive efficiency of the *hukou* system in the pre-reform and reform eras

	Pre-reform era	Reform era
Property right	Not well-specified	Relatively effective in terms of property rights of labour and rural land
Decision-making process	Centralised	Decentralised
Transaction cost	Considerably high	Low in labour mobility but relatively high in *hukou*-based land transactions and welfare accessibility
Competition	Suppressed	Boosted
Innovation and experimentation	Low level	Relatively high level

In the pre-reform era, labourers did not fully own the property rights of labour. First, they had no right to freely choose their occupation. Second, the property rights of 'welfare' (including rural land and urban welfare) were separated between rural and urban residents by the *hukou* system. *Hukou* system reform returned the property rights of labour from the state to individuals. The property rights of *hukou*-based welfare also experienced significant reform. The rights to access *hukou*-based urban welfare were still owned by residents with local *hukou*, but the range of urban welfare was substantially reduced under marketisation. The ownership of rural land was still collective, but rights of usage, income and transfers were gradually specified to individual rural *hukou* holders.

Under the pre-reform centralised decision-making system, individual decision-making rights were suppressed, the type of *hukou* determined the types of job available to the holders and the government controlled decisions about rural–urban migration. After the reform, migrants started to make their own migration decisions based on market information. *Hukou* became a less important factor in migration and occupation decision-making. Moreover, local governments worked actively in *hukou* management, which promoted reform of the system. The decentralised decision-making processes at the individual, household, enterprise and local government levels allow the economy to maximise the efforts required to explore alternative means to improve institutional efficiency.

Beginning in the 1950s, the implementation of *hukou* regulations that controlled internal migration substantially increased the transaction cost of labour mobility. *Hukou* reform dramatically reduced these costs in two ways. First, rural *hukou* holders could migrate to and work in urban areas much more easily than they could in the pre-reform era. Second, the development of both the product and the labour markets weakened the *hukou*–welfare relationship, which also contributed to the reduction in the transaction costs of labour mobility.

The labour and product markets existed to a very limited extent in pre-reform China, and competition was considerably suppressed under the planned economy. First, product market competition was distorted by the unified procurement and marketing system and the price scissors between the agricultural and non-agricultural sectors. Second, urban and rural labour were allocated into non-agricultural and agricultural sectors, respectively, according to their *hukou* type, which considerably suppressed intersectoral labour competition. The *hukou* reform that facilitated labour mobility brought marketised competition to the product and labour markets. Labour mobility expanded the scale of the product market and increased the supply level on both the product and the labour sides, which further facilitated *hukou*–welfare decoupling. Lifetime employment for urban *hukou* holders was eliminated and employment policy shifted in a more market-oriented direction.

The pre-reform centralised *hukou* system provided no conditions for innovation and experimentation that could eliminate the failed institutional elements. The decentralisation in the reform era at the individual and government levels contributed to the improvement of the kind of institutional flexibility that could reward successes and eliminate failures in the *hukou* system. For example, Zhengzhou's failed case in the early 2000s can also be identified as an adaptive *hukou* system reform in which a local government trialled various methods of reform to identify which choices would be successful or which could be eliminated.

However, additional improvements are still necessary, especially in terms of *hukou*-based rural land and urban welfare. Reform efforts should reduce the cost of rural land transactions and welfare accessibility.

Measurement of adaptive efficiency of the evolution of the *hukou* system

To better understand the concept of adaptive efficiency, I divide the term into two parts: adaptation and efficiency. Adaptation is generated from the process of interaction between an institution and its environment, which can be captured by the concept of coupling (Li et al. 2012). I assume that a situation in which an institution and the environment coordinate well with each other means the institution is well-adapted to the environment. The higher the degree of coordination, the higher is the degree of adaptation. To make it more tractable, I further assume the term of efficiency is an economic concept, which emphasises economic development efficiency.

Method and variables

Based on what has been specified and the coupling model in the literature (see Li et al. 2012), this chapter proposes an adaptive efficiency evaluation method. X_t represents an institutional arrangement in time t and Y_t represents the economic development level in time t. First, to eliminate the influence of magnitude, X_t and Y_t are standardised values using Equation 7.1, in which X'_t and Y'_t are the original values of the two indicators; X'_{max} and Y'_{max} are the maximums.

Equation 7.1

$$\begin{cases} X_t = \dfrac{X'_t}{X'_{max}} \\ Y_t = \dfrac{Y'_t}{Y'_{max}} \end{cases}$$

Second, AD in Equation 7.2 is the adaptation degree of an institution to the economic environment. The author assumes that the smaller the statistical dispersion between X_t and Y_t, the higher is its adaptiveness.

Equation 7.2

$$AD = \left\{ \frac{X_t \cdot Y_t}{\left(\frac{X_t + Y_t}{2}\right)^2} \right\}^2$$

Third, AE, which represents the level of adaptive efficiency of an institution, is calculated using Equation 7.3.

Equation 7.3

$$AE = \sqrt{AD \cdot \left(\frac{X_t + Y_t}{2}\right)}$$

I use GDP per capita (at 1952 constant price) and the *hukou*-based urban population rate (HUPR) to represent the economic development and the *hukou* system, respectively. The data were collected from the National Bureau of Statistics of China and the *Almanac of China's Population* for various years. The indictor of HUPR is used to represent the *hukou* system for two reasons.[11] First, it can capture the migration control function of the system: the higher the rate, the more restrictive is the regulation on population mobility in the urban area, and vice versa. Second, this indicator reflects the degree of rural–urban division in urban areas: the lower the rate, the larger is the rural–urban division in the urban area. This division is also the division of welfare received by holders of different types of *hukou*. The lower the rate, the larger is the relative number of rural *hukou* holders who cannot access urban welfare. HUPR is calculated based on Equation 7.4.

Equation 7.4

$$HUPR = \frac{Hukou - Based\ Urban\ Population}{Total\ Residential\ Urban\ Population}$$

Results

In Figure 7.5, the degree of adaptation and the adaptive efficiency of the *hukou* system in pre-reform China are substantially low. Although the *hukou* system was created to adapt to the planned economy, it was not well-adapted to economic development because the system did not fit the facts of China's comparative advantage of a labour surplus. Thus, its institutional efficiency was considerably constrained. After the reform in the late 1970s, and especially the *hukou* reform in the 1980s, the degree of adaptation and adaptive efficiency of the system began to increase, and increased still further after the early 1990s, possibly because of the '*mingongchao*' *hukou* reform that opened up small cities and towns and local *hukou* system innovations. Massive labour mobility and proper *hukou* reform were well-adapted to the requirements of economic development in the context of China's integration into the global market.

---

11   This indicator could be imperfect and not capture the complexity of the system but it does capture some of its essential elements, including inequality in welfare accessibility.

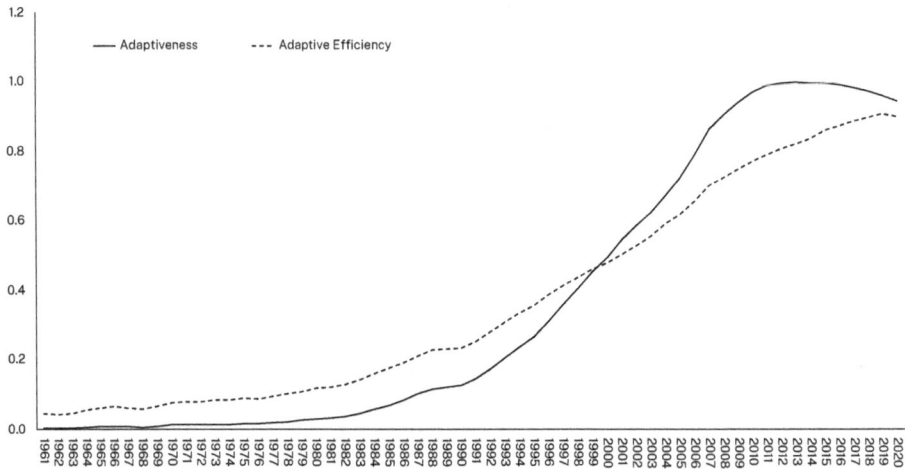

Figure 7.5 Adaptive efficiency of China's *hukou* system, 1961–2020
Source: Author's own calculation.

However, since 2008, the adaptiveness and adaptive efficiency of the *hukou* system have displayed a marginally decreasing trend. The adaptiveness of the system eventually began to decline (a trend that continues today), indicating that the system is having difficulties adapting to the new economic environment, including an ageing population, weak domestic consumption and rising social inequality. The adaptive efficiency of the system is still increasing, but its growth rate exhibits a downward trend. The decreasing adaptiveness of the system is dragging down its adaptive efficiency. This suggests that China's *hukou* system reforms and the current *hukou* system do have adaptive efficiency, but the system is also facing difficulties. Since the GFC in 2008, *hukou* system reform in China has not been well addressed to fulfill the demand for further economic development. For example, the crisis exposed China's over-reliance on international markets and insufficient domestic demand. The *hukou* system is one of the most important barriers to increasing domestic demand (Dreger et al. 2015; Song et al. 2010)—a problem that has not been well addressed by reforms. The *hukou* system is also one of the most critical factors in China's spatial and social inequality and impedes the country's further economic transition. It now faces even more difficulties, especially with the increase in labour costs and China's transformation to the 'New Normal' stage of economic development.

Summary and policy implications

Understanding institutional change is a critical task in the study of economic dynamics, especially for a transitional economy. This chapter uses the evolution of China's *hukou* system as a case study to illustrate institutional change and its interaction with economic dynamics. The findings draw a seemingly tautological but profound conclusion: the *hukou* system significantly affects China's economic development and, in turn, the transformation of China's economy has deeply shaped the evolution of the *hukou* system.

First, based on a theoretical framework of endogenous institutional change, the different ways of the evolution of the *hukou* system in the pre-reform and reform eras are analysed, from which two conclusions are proposed: 1) the institutionalisation of the rigid *hukou* system was mainly an exogenous change process implemented from the top down, in which central government enforcement played a dominant role and the roles of individual and local governments were largely neglected; and 2) the rigid *hukou* system eventually hindered economic transformation, thereby inducing its own reform. Reform has fundamentally been an endogenous change process, in which spontaneous market forces and the role of local governments have bounced back through a rebalancing of the powers of the state and market and between central and local governments. However, institutional undermining and reinforcing processes are intertwined, which complicates *hukou* system reform. The *hukou*–welfare binding relationship, set against the backdrop of decentralisation, has slowed the reform of the system.

Second, based on the theory of adaptive efficiency, five elements are investigated to articulate how the exogenous institutionalisation of the *hukou* system constrained its adaptive efficiency and how the endogenous reform generated adaptive efficiency. The findings demonstrate that the reform of the system clarified the property rights of the labour force and rural land, promoted the formation of a decentralised decision-making mechanism, strengthened the role of competition in both the labour and the product markets, reduced the transaction costs of labour mobility and maintained a degree of institutional flexibility that rewarded success and eliminated failures in the system. All these aspects have played critical roles in improving the adaptive efficiency of the *hukou* system. Empirically, the results show that the adaptive efficiency of the system in the reform era is much higher than that in the pre-reform era but has had a marginally decreasing trend since 2008. This finding suggests that China's *hukou* system reforms and the current *hukou* system do have adaptive efficiency, but the system is facing difficulties.

To further reform the *hukou* system and promote its adaptive efficiency, decision-makers should respect the endogenous forces and the logic of adaptation in institutional change. The transaction costs of population mobility must be reduced—not just the transaction costs of migration *per se*, but also the availability of the 'welfare' attached to the *hukou* system. Fair competition is necessary to eliminate *hukou*-based discrimination in both the labour and the land markets. Furthermore, the safeguard of institutional flexibility is conducive to fostering institutional innovation and eliminating institutional failure. In this regard, giving local governments some autonomy and leaving sufficient room for competition and innovation are necessary to improve the institutional efficiency of the system.

References

Afridi, F., S.X. Li and Y. Ren. 2015. 'Social Identity and Inequality: The Impact of China's Hukou System.' *Journal of Public Economics* 123: 17–29. doi.org/10.1016/j.jpubeco. 2014.12.011.

Aoki, M. 2001. *Toward a Comparative Institutional Analysis*. Cambridge, MA: MIT Press. doi.org/10.7551/mitpress/6867.001.0001.

Aoki, M. 2007. 'Endogenizing Institutions and Institutional Changes.' *Journal of Institutional Economics* 3(1): 1–31. doi.org/10.1017/S1744137406000531.

Au, C.C. and J.V. Henderson. 2006. 'How Migration Restrictions Limit Agglomeration and Productivity in China.' *Journal of Development Economics* 80(2): 350–88. doi.org/ 10.1016/j.jdeveco.2005.04.002.

Boettke, P.J., C.J. Coyne and P.T. Leeson. 2008. 'Institutional Stickiness and the New Development Economics.' *American Journal of Economics and Sociology* 67(2): 331–58. doi.org/10.1111/j.1536-7150.2008.00573.x.

Brousseau, E., P. Garrouste and E. Raynaud. 2011. 'Institutional Changes: Alternative Theories and Consequences for Institutional Design.' *Journal of Economic Behavior and Organization* 79(1-2): 3–19. doi.org/10.1016/j.jebo.2011.01.024.

Cai, F. 2011. 'Hukou System Reform and Unification of Rural–Urban Social Welfare.' *China & World Economy* 19(3): 33–48. doi.org/10.1111/j.1749-124X.2011.01241.x.

Cai, F. and M. Wang. 2010. 'Growth and Structural Changes in Employment in Transition China.' *Journal of Comparative Economics* 38(1): 71–81. doi.org/10.1016/j.jce.2009. 10.006.

Chan, K.W. 2009. 'The Chinese Hukou System at 50.' *Eurasian Geography and Economics* 50(2): 197-221. doi.org/10.2747/1539-7216.50.2.197.

Chan, K.W. and L. Zhang. 1999. 'The Hukou System and Rural–Urban Migration in China: Processes and Changes.' *The China Quarterly* 160: 818–55. doi.org/10.1017/ S0305741000001351.

Chang, H.J. 2011. 'Institutions and Economic Development: Theory, Policy and History.' *Journal of Institutional Economics* 7(4): 473–98. doi.org/10.1017/S1744137410000378.

Chen, C. and Fan, C.C. 2016. 'China's *Hukou* Puzzle: Why Don't Rural Migrants Want Urban *Hukou*?', *China Review* 16(3): 9–39.

Chen, P. 1993. 'China's Challenge to Economic Orthodoxy: Asian Reform as an Evolutionary, Self-Organizing Process.' *China Economic Review* 4(2): 137–42. doi.org/10.1016/1043-951X(93)90014-Q.

Cheng, T. and M. Selden. 1994. 'The Origins and Social Consequences of China's Hukou System.' *The China Quarterly* 139: 644–68. doi.org/10.1017/S0305741000043083.

Chi, J. and J. Yang. 2003. 'An Analysis of the Supply and Demand of the Changes in China's Hukou System: An Explanation from the Perspective of Rural Economic Reform.' [In Chinese]. *Reform of Economic System* 3: 70–73.

DellaPosta, D., V. Nee and S. Opper. 2017. 'Endogenous Dynamics of Institutional Change.' *Rationality and Society* 29(1): 5–48. doi.org/10.1177/1043463116633147.

Dreger, C., Wang, T., and Zhang, Y. 2015. 'Understanding Chinese Consumption: The Impact of *Hukou*', *Development and Change* 46(6): 1331–44.

Fan, C.S. and O. Stark. 2008. 'Rural-to-Urban Migration, Human Capital, and Agglomeration.' *Journal of Economic Behavior and Organization* 68(1): 234–47. doi.org/10.1016/j.jebo.2008.04.003.

Government of the People's Republic of China (PRC). 2021. 'The 14th Five-Year Plan for National Economic and Social Development of the People's Republic of China and Outline of the Vision for 2035.' [In Chinese]. *Xinhua News Agency*, [Beijing], 12 March. Available from: www.gov.cn/xinwen/2021-03/13/content_5592681.htm.

Greif, A. 2006. *Institutions and the Path to the Modern Economy: Lessons from Medieval Trade*. New York, NY: Cambridge University Press. doi.org/10.1017/CBO9780511791307.

Greif, A. and C. Kingston. 2011. 'Institutions: Rules or Equilibria?' In N. Schofield and G. Caballero (eds), *Political Economy of Institutions, Democracy and Voting*, pp. 13–43. Berlin: Springer. doi.org/10.1007/978-3-642-19519-8_2.

Greif, A. and D.D. Laitin. 2004. 'A Theory of Endogenous Institutional Change.' *American Political Science Review* 98(4): 633–52. doi.org/10.1017/S0003055404041395.

Guo, J.J. 1992. *Price Reform in China, 1979–86*. London: Palgrave Macmillan. doi.org/10.1007/978-1-349-11681-2.

Hu, B. 2007. *Informal Institutions and Rural Development in China*. London: Routledge. doi.org/10.4324/9780203947449.

Huang, S. 2017. 'The Origin and Present Situation of Institutional Economics.' [In Chinese]. *Reform* 1: 132–44.

Kingston, C. and G. Caballero. 2009. 'Comparing Theories of Institutional Change.' *Journal of Institutional Economics* 5(2): 151–80. doi.org/10.1017/S1744137409001283.

Li, Y., Y. Li, Y. Zhou, Y. Shi and X. Zhu. 2012. 'Investigation of a Coupling Model of Coordination between Urbanization and the Environment.' *Journal of Environmental Management* 98: 127–33. doi.org/10.1016/j.jenvman.2011.12.025.

Lin, J.Y. 1989. 'An Economic Theory of Institutional Change: Induced and Imposed Change.' *Cato Journal* 9(1): 1–33.

Lin, J.Y., F. Cai and Z. Li. 2003. *The China Miracle: Development Strategy and Economic Reform*. Hong Kong: Chinese University Press. doi.org/10.2307/j.ctv1fj84hd.

Ma, Y. and A. Jalil. 2008. 'Financial Development, Economic Growth and Adaptive Efficiency: A Comparison between China and Pakistan.' *China & World Economy* 16(6): 97–111. doi.org/10.1111/j.1749-124X.2008.00140.x.

Marris, R. and D.C. Mueller. 1980. 'The Corporation, Competition, and the Invisible Hand.' *Journal of Economic Literature* 18(1): 32–63.

National Bureau of Statistics of China (NBS). 2020. *China Statistical Yearbook 2019*. Beijing: China Statistics Press.

National Development and Reform Commission (NDRC). 2020. *Key Tasks for New-Type Urbanisation Construction and Urban–Rural Integration Development in 2020*. Development and Reform Planning [2020] No. 532, 3 April. Beijing: NDRC. Available from: www.gov.cn/zhengce/zhengceku/2020-04/09/content_5500696.htm.

National Development and Reform Commission (NDRC). 2021. *Key Tasks for New Urbanisation and Urban–Rural Integration Development in 2021*. [In Chinese]. Development and Reform Planning [2021] No. 493, 8 April. Beijing: NDRC. Available from: www.gov.cn/zhengce/zhengceku/2021-04/13/content_5599332.htm.

National Development and Reform Commission (NDRC). 2022. *The 14th Five-Year Plan for the Implementation of New Urbanisation*. [In Chinese]. Plan [2022] No. 960, 21 June. Beijing: NDRC. Available from: www.gov.cn/zhengce/zhengceku/2022-07/12/content_5700632.htm.

Nee, V. and S. Opper. 2012. *Capitalism from Below: Markets and Institutional Change in China*. Cambridge, MA: Harvard University Press. doi.org/10.4159/harvard.9780674065390.

North, D.C. 1990. *Institutions, Institutional Change and Economic Performance*. New York, NY: Cambridge University Press. doi.org/10.1017/CBO9780511808678.

North, D.C. 1994. 'Economic Performance through Time.' *The American Economic Review* 84(3): 359–68.

North, D.C. 2005. *Understanding the Process of Economic Change*. Princeton, NJ: Princeton University Press.

North, D.C., J.J. Wallis and B.R. Weingast. 2009. *Violence and Social Orders: A Conceptual Framework for Interpreting Recorded Human History*. New York, NY: Cambridge University Press. doi.org/10.1017/CBO9780511575839.

Peng, X., D. Zhao and X. Guo. 2009. 'The Reform of China's Household Registration System: A Political Economics View.' [In Chinese]. *Fudan Journal (Social Sciences)* 3: 1–11.

Sheng, Y. and L. Song. 2018. 'Agricultural Production and Food Consumption in China: A Long-Term Projection.' *China Economic Review* 53: 15–29. doi.org/10.1016/j.chieco. 2018.08.006.

Solinger, D.J. 1999. *Contesting Citizenship in Urban China: Peasant Migrants, the State, and the Logic of the Market*. Berkeley, CA: University of California Press.

Song, L., W. Jiang and Y. Zhang. 2010. 'Urbanization of Migrant Workers and Expansion of Domestic Demand.' *Social Sciences in China* 31(3): 194–216. doi.org/10.1080/0252 9203.2010.503080.

Song, L. and C. Simpson. 2018. 'Linking "Adaptive Efficiency" with the Basic Market Functions: A New Analytical Perspective for Institution and Policy Analysis.' *Asia and the Pacific Policy Studies* 5(3): 544–57. doi.org/10.1002/app5.249.

Song, Y. 2014. 'What Should Economists Know about the Current Chinese Hukou System?' *China Economic Review* 29: 200–12. doi.org/10.1016/j.chieco.2014.04.012.

State Council. 2014. *Opinions of the State Council on Further Promoting the Reform of the Household Registration System*. National Law [2014] No. 25, 30 July. Beijing: State Council of the People's Republic of China. Available from: www.gov.cn/zhengce/content/2014-07/ 30/content_8944.htm.

State Council. 2019a. 'Opinions of the Central Committee of the Communist Party of China and the State Council on Establishing and Improving the Institutional Mechanism and Policy System for Urban-Rural Integrated Development.' [In Chinese]. *Xinhua News Agency*, [Beijing], 5 May. Available from: www.gov.cn/zhengce/2019-05/05/content_ 5388880.htm.

State Council. 2019b. 'The General Office of the Central Committee of the Communist Party of China and the General Office of the State Council Issued the "Opinions on Promoting the Reform of the System and Mechanism of Labour and Talent Social Mobility".' [In Chinese]. *Xinhua News Agency*, [Beijing], 25 December. Available from: www.gov.cn/zhengce/2019-12/25/content_5463978.htm.

State Council. 2021. 'The General Office of the CPC Central Committee and the General Office of the State Council Issued the Action Plan for Building a High-Standard Market System.' [In Chinese]. *Xinhua News Agency*, [Beijing], 31 January. Available from: www. gov.cn/zhengce/2021-01/31/content_5583936.htm.

United States Department of Agriculture (USDA). 2022. *International Agricultural Productivity*. [Online]. Washington, DC: Economic Research Service, USDA. Available from: www.ers.usda.gov/data-products/international-agricultural-productivity/.

Vendryes, T. 2011. 'Migration Constraints and Development: Hukou and Capital Accumulation in China.' *China Economic Review* 22(4): 669–92. doi.org/10.1016/ j.chieco.2011.08.006.

Wang, F.L. 2005. *Organizing through Division and Exclusion: China's Hukou System*. Stanford, CA: Stanford University Press. doi.org/10.1515/9780804767484.

Wu, X. and D.J. Treiman. 2004. 'The Household Registration System and Social Stratification in China: 1955–1996.' *Demography* 41(2): 363–84. doi.org/10.1353/dem.2004.0010.

Young, J. 2013. *China's Hukou System: Markets, Migrants, and Institutional Change.* New York, NY: Palgrave Macmillan. doi.org/10.1057/9781137277312_2.

Zhang, K., C. Chen, J. Ding and Z. Zhang. 2019. 'China's Hukou System Reform and City Economic Growth: From the Aspect of Rural–Urban Migration.' *China Agricultural Economic Review* 12(1): 140–57. doi.org/10.1108/CAER-03-2019-0057.

Zhang, M., C.J. Zhu and C. Nyland. 2014. 'The Institution of Hukou-Based Social Exclusion: A Unique Institution Reshaping the Characteristics of Contemporary Urban China.' *International Journal of Urban and Regional Research* 38(4): 1437–57. doi.org/10.1111/j.1468-2427.2012.01185.x.

Zhou, B. 2013. 'Adaptive Efficiency: The Deficiency of North's Theory and the Reconsideration.' [In Chinese]. *Research of Institutional Economics* 3: 204–25.

Zhou, K. 2012. 'Why Do Mayors around the World Oppose Household Registration Reform?' *Sohu Finance*, [Beijing], 20 August. Available from: business.sohu.com/s2012/weiguan48/.

8

Changes in income inequality and poverty early in the Covid-19 pandemic: Findings from a mixed data analysis

Li Shi and Zhan Peng

Introduction

This chapter focuses on the impact of Covid-19 on income inequality and poverty in China during the first half of 2020. In early 2020, a new type of coronavirus named Covid-19 was discovered in Wuhan. The outbreak spread across the country and around the world and was particularly severe in Hubei Province, which began to implement 'first-level response' measures for public health incidents on 24 January 2020, with other provinces subsequently following. Social activities were severely restricted, as were normal production activities and consumer demand for a certain period in various regions of China. In March, as the regional outbreaks were controlled to a certain extent, restrictions began to ease. At the end of April 2020, Wuhan lifted its blockade, thus concluding the first round of the pandemic in China.

Using mixed data sources, this chapter proposes a new method to assess the impact of the pandemic while providing some empirical analysis of its effects on income distribution and poverty in the early stages of the pandemic. This study does not analyse the pandemic's impact after June 2020, for two reasons. First, between June 2020 and the outbreak in Shanghai in January 2022, China's pandemic situation was not very serious and the impact on income distribution and poverty was not as large as that in early 2020. Second, since January 2022, new variants of Covid-19 have continued to emerge and China is facing more severe challenges. However, we lack higher-quality data to accurately assess this situation.

The Covid-19 pandemic has had a clear impact on economic activity. During periods of pandemic prevention and control, most economic activities were interrupted. Measures such as community and traffic controls caused a sharp drop in consumer demand, with the greatest impact on consumer enterprises. Most rural migrant workers were forced to delay or give up returning to cities or urban areas for work. Companies with weak capital chains faced bankruptcy (Internet Finance Laboratory et al. 2020; Zhu et al. 2020; Liu et al. 2020; Wang 2020). There were fewer jobs and lower employment income. With China's strong prevention and control measures and policies for the timely resumption of work and production, the economic impact of the pandemic began to gradually subside in March (Xu et al. 2020). While the pandemic was largely under control nationally, some areas such as north-eastern China and Beijing suffered from small-scale outbreaks. At the end of June 2020, the negative impacts of the pandemic had not spread on a large scale. By this time, large amounts of fragmented data had been generated, allowing us to understand the impact of the pandemic from different perspectives. One of the tasks of this study was to integrate the fragmented information to obtain quantitative estimates of the impacts of the pandemic on income distribution and poverty.

Many studies have examined the economic impacts of the Covid-19 pandemic from different perspectives. With China's economic problems as the background, these studies can be divided into three categories: those in the first category qualitatively analysed the possible economic consequences of the pandemic, helping governments at all levels with appropriate decision-making or other scholars to conduct further research (Chen et al. 2020). The second category studied the impact of the spread of the pandemic on population mobility and the economies of different regions based on big data on population migration from websites such as Baidu and AutoNavi (Qiu et al. 2020; Fang et al. 2020; Chinazzi et al. 2020). The third category evaluated or simulated the real impacts of the pandemic by combining various macro or microlevel data.

The third category of research was the most useful for our study, and can be further divided into four subcategories.

Interpretations in the first subcategory were based solely on macrolevel data, including comprehensive interpretations by Xu et al. (2020) and interpretations of specific issues published on the website of China's National Bureau of Statistics (NBS).

In the second, the impact path of the pandemic on the macroeconomy and the financial risk-transmission mechanism during the pandemic were studied based on input–output and general equilibrium models (Liu et al. 2020; Yang et al. 2020; Zhang et al. 2020; Wang and Wu 2021). Alternatively, the impact of the pandemic on international industrial divisions was studied from the perspective of global value chains (Liu 2020; Meng 2020). Furthermore, micro-simulation analysis was conducted based on micro-household survey data to calculate the impact of the pandemic on the scale of migrant workers' remittances (Zhang et al. 2021).

In the third, the pandemic was observed in terms of capital needs, operating conditions and employee status of small and medium-sized enterprises (SMEs) according to survey data of those enterprises. The most influential corporate surveys were the research report of the Peking University Institute of Digital Finance and Research Institute of Ant Group (2020), based on Ant Financial's big data, and a research report based on data from millions of medium and micro-enterprises analysed by a joint research group from Tsinghua University's Graduate School of People's Bank of China (Internet Finance Laboratory et al. 2020). The survey sample size of these two reports was large, the research methods were standardised and the results were credible. Other studies were also based on many enterprise surveys, the results of which are of great reference value (Meituan Research Institute 2020; Zhang and Dai 2020; Zhu et al. 2020).

In the fourth subcategory, the impact of the pandemic on income or consumption was studied based on microsurvey data. A representative example is Liu et al. (2022), who estimated the impact of the pandemic on per capita consumption based on household survey data from the NBS. Wang et al. (2021) conducted three rounds of interviews with informants from 726 villages in seven provinces and found that 31 per cent of rural workers who had jobs in 2019 did not work by late April 2020. Liang et al. (2022) studied the impact of the pandemic on the income and employment of graduates of vocational and technical schools using survey data from January and July 2020.

Owing to data limitations, most existing studies have observed the impact of the pandemic on a certain group or field and lack an assessment of the country's overall income distribution and poverty status. Therefore, this study collects the macro-data available from June 2020 based on nationally representative micro-data, fully integrates different data sources and conducts a comprehensive assessment of the impact of the pandemic on rural income distribution and poverty.

The identification strategy

Basic logic: How the pandemic affected rural household income

The impact of the pandemic on household income is a chain process, as explained in the flowchart in Figure 8.1. From a socioeconomic perspective alone, China's response to the pandemic was manifested as temporary restrictions on economic and residents' activities, including controls on traffic, community and business activity and public places. Hubei Province and Wuhan City began implementing 'first-level' public health response measures on 24 January 2020, subsequently followed by other regions. Consequently, activities across China were severely restricted from this date. Production activities were constrained, consumer demand dropped sharply and economic activities and residents' lives were almost entirely paused.

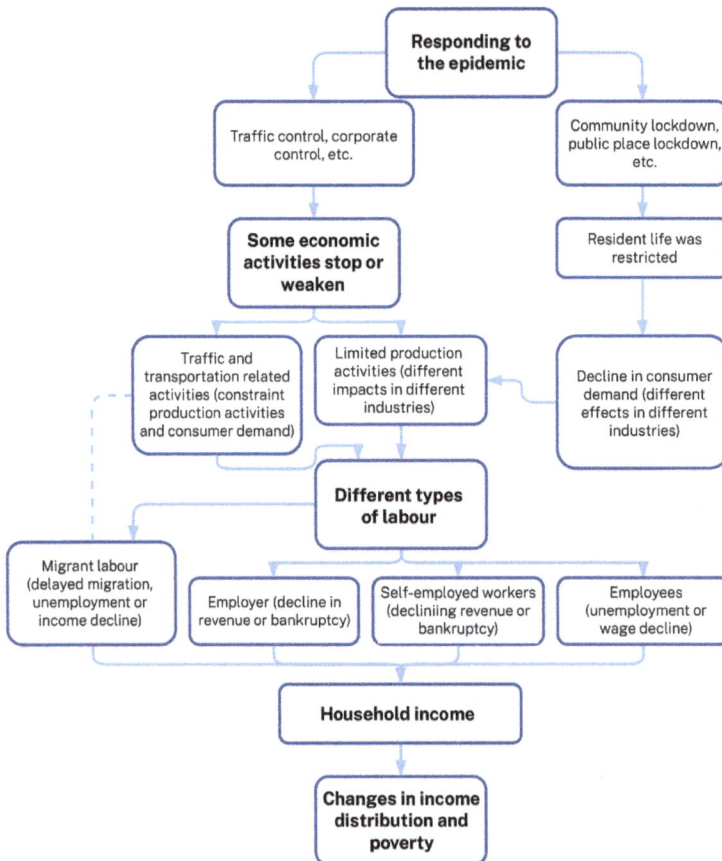

Figure 8.1 The impact mechanism of pandemic controls on income distribution and poverty (schematic diagram)

Source: Authors' own schema.

Three stages of the impact of the pandemic on economic activity

Based on the changes in the pandemic situation, we can divide its impact on economic activities into three stages.

The first stage was the beginning of controls, which coincided with the start of the Spring Festival holiday in China. At this time, most enterprises were closed or were preparing to close as planned and most of the labour force had returned or was preparing to return to their hometowns. The initial stage of pandemic control was manifested in these two aspects. First, consumer demand was greatly suppressed and consumption-related transportation, services, catering and entertainment industries were greatly affected. For example, almost all entertainment activities and all restaurants and retail business activities stopped. Some operating activities relying on the Spring Festival holiday had to be cancelled, resulting in a significant drop in annual revenue—for example, Spring Festival tourism-related flower markets and other tourist activities. If the main economic income of enterprises or self-employed households relied on holiday demand, they suffered great losses. Second, travel was restricted, affecting the transportation of goods during the Spring Festival, thereby affecting the production activities of the corresponding enterprises. For example, the products of many enterprises in Wuhan were difficult to deliver and the upstream supply chain was almost cut off. These impacts were more serious in the key areas for the early stages of the pandemic, such as Hubei and Wenzhou City in Zhejiang Province.

The second stage occurred during the middle to the end of the Spring Festival holiday and extended for more than a month afterwards. In the past, the end of the Spring Festival holiday was accompanied by the recovery of economic activities. However, pandemic controls caused most companies to close for long periods, local labour could not resume work and temporarily unemployed people could not look for new jobs. The migrant labour force that had gone home for the holiday could not return to their urban workplaces in time, meaning pandemic controls began to impact the income of rural households. Approximately a month later, the pandemic in various regions of the country was gradually brought under control, the emergency response level in each region was lowered, and the resumption of work and production was conducted in an orderly manner. This gradually decreased the impact of the second phase.

The influence of the third stage came mainly from overseas. The spread of the pandemic to South Korea, Japan, Europe, the United States and other regions hindered international trade, beginning in late March and early April 2020. As the pandemic was not effectively controlled globally, the risk of a new wave of disease being imported rose and China took corresponding control measures. Domestic and foreign trade–related industries were significantly affected for long periods.

This study focuses on low-income groups and the impacts of the first two stages of the pandemic. The externally generated impacts of the third stage depended on many complex factors, which were limited by data and are not covered in this chapter. In contrast, in 2020, the pandemic within China was brought under control quickly, and economic indicators in March and April showed gradual recovery and the economic situation did not change much (Xu et al. 2020). Based on the simulation analysis of household survey data, this study focuses on the first two stages of the pandemic and their impacts.

What were the affects on economic activity?

We explain the impact mechanism from three perspectives: transportation-related activities, production activities and consumer demand. The immediate impact on travel restrictions was that transportation-related industries were severely affected, as were related industries including logistics and postal services. According to news reports at the time, China Post, a state-owned enterprise (SOE), was not greatly affected and SF Express, a private enterprise, continued to operate. However, other civilian express delivery services and some commercial logistics activities were suspended or their activities were significantly reduced. This further affected downstream production activities and consumer demand relying on these industries.

The restriction of transportation activities further affected production activities in two main ways: travel controls restricted the movement of employees, making it difficult for enterprises to start work, and led to the weakening of industrial chain–related activities, with upstream products not delivered on time and resumption of work delayed; and pandemic controls prohibited large-scale gatherings of people, resulting in companies being forced to suspend or delay resumption of work. The results for enterprises in different industries varied, depending on their position in the industrial chain and final demands. The impact on technology-intensive enterprises was generally smaller than on labour-intensive enterprises. Companies relying on logistics were significantly affected. Small and micro enterprises with relatively little cash flow were less able to deal with sudden income risks and the decline in their net income for the year was larger. According to NBS data, the value added of the manufacturing industry in January–February 2020 fell by 15.7 per cent year-on-year, which was the largest decline among the three announced industrial categories.

To balance pandemic controls and economic development, governments at all levels began to roll out policies promoting the resumption of work and production in early February (see, for example, MoF and STA 2020). After the pandemic was contained in Zhejiang, Guangdong and other areas heavily reliant on migrant workers, chartered planes were sent to pick up these workers so they could return to work in mid-February (see, for example, HRSS 2020; Xuwei 2020). These measures increased the work resumption rate of enterprises above a designated size and allowed them to recover faster. According to regional data, the resumption rate of enterprises above the designated size in many regions exceeded 80 per cent in mid to late February (21 Data Journalism Lab 2020). However, SMEs were slow to resume work, with only 30 per cent resuming by 25 February.[1]

The recovery process for household consumption differed across industries, with households of those employed in catering, retail and residential services rebounding relatively quickly as the pandemic restrictions were lifted. These industries and economic activities are characterised by the fact that operating income does not differ significantly from month to month and short-term shocks do not have long-term effects. However, some special business activities can only be conducted at specific times, such as tourism relying on holidays, short-term housing rental and related economic activities, meaning they experienced a greater impact. Insufficient cash flow could have long-term consequences, leading to bankruptcy or persistent poverty.

However, it should also be noted that although pandemic controls led to a substantial decline in physical business activities, some types of economic activities were not greatly affected, including those relying on the internet such as online gaming, online media and some community services. Employees with fixed or long-term contracts, especially those in large and medium-sized SOEs, government agencies and institutions are generally paid on a fixed basis. These units have a relatively strong ability to deal with short-term risks and are generally unlikely to suffer capital flow disruptions due to short-term shocks, meaning wage payments are unaffected in the short term. Rural residents who were self-sufficient in production were relatively protected, as was the leasing industry for long-term rental services, for whom a temporary reduction in the flow of people did not have a significant impact on operating income.

The Chinese Government considered the potential impact of the pandemic on economic activity in early February 2020 and continuously introduced policy measures to support the survival of enterprises—for example, by increasing subsidies and loans to small and micro-enterprises, reducing value-added taxes and reducing social security contributions. In some regions, enterprise employees were uniformly arranged to return to work. These measures effectively addressed insufficient cash flow, ensured enterprises could resume work quickly and protected them from bankruptcy and layoffs. The impact of the pandemic at the enterprise level was weakened and, ultimately, the impact on residents' income and poverty was reduced.

---

1   The transcript of the press conference about the State Council's joint prevention and control mechanism on 25 February 2020 said: 'According to the monitoring of 2.4 million small and medium-sized enterprises using cloud platforms and e-commerce platforms, the work resumption rate of small and medium-sized enterprises across the country is currently only about 30%.' www.gov.cn/xinwen/gwylflkjz30/index.htm.

Labour related to economic activity

In terms of income, the effects varied according to employment groups. We classified labour into five groups: wage-earning workers, non-agricultural business activities (business owners), self-employed workers, migrant workers and renters.

The wage-earning workforce (or 'employees') was heterogeneous and not all employees were affected significantly. There are two types of employees: those on fixed, long-term or short-term contracts and those with no contract or paid by work volume (or hours worked). Regarding the former, if the companies for which they worked were large and could deal with short-term risks, they did not suffer the short-term impacts of the pandemic. For the latter, the impact of the pandemic was more significant. One less month of work reduced annual income by a certain percentage. This study focuses on the magnitude and likelihood of the latter group's decline in income.

Non-agricultural businesses were hit because their activities were suppressed, as a consequence of which operating income in 2020 declined, operating costs increased and net income decreased. The impact of the pandemic varied greatly among different industries, types of enterprises and regions, with the profits of different types of business activity impacted to varying degrees. The duration of the pandemic's effect on production activities and consumer demand also varied.

Self-employed individuals were vulnerable to shocks under community-control measures, although some of those who used the internet to conduct business saw only a small impact and some even experienced an increase in income. Self-employed workers whose business services were not connected to the internet suffered a greater impact, including grocery and convenience stores and residential service activities that could not be conducted online.

Among the labour categories, 'migrant workers' mainly refers to self-employed workers and employees who do not work in the location of their household registration. Because the work location is not their home location, migrant workers were affected more by travel restrictions than the local labour force and the pandemic had a greater impact on their return to work. Another consequence of restricted population movements was a drop in demand for rental housing, bringing long-term impacts for households whose main source of income was from rentals. However, it should be noted that we mainly considered family income as the starting point and here we specifically refer to non-operating rental behaviour. Business rental behaviour was summarised in the previously mentioned business activities of self-employed labour. Whether the pandemic had a significant impact on non-operating rental demand depended on the length of the lockdown. If the lockdown was short, the effect was small.

Declines in household income

As the income of the labour force fell, household income and consumption changed. In the income distribution measured by household per capita income, there were differences in the labour force composition of low- and high-income households. We were particularly concerned with households near the poverty line.

How to identify the setting of the simulation model

The simulation model aims to determine the economic activity objects affected by the pandemic in the micro-data and infer the impact of the pandemic on different economic activity objects. Owing to the large heterogeneity of the pandemic's impact on them, it is necessary to distinguish between different regions and industries. Some impacts occurred where residents live and some where they are employed. Thus, the area category includes the locations of current residence and of work. Based on this consideration, the model in this study sets the following key indicators:

- X1: Economic activity categories and corresponding groups and symbols:
    - P1: Wage-earners. Among those with wage income greater than zero, those with fixed and long-term contracts and those employed in SOEs, government agencies and institutions are excluded.
    - P2: Primary industry operator. Among those whose net operating income from primary industry is not zero, those who are employed by SOEs, in government agencies and institutions and those who are self-employed are excluded.
    - P3: Secondary industry operators. Among those whose net income from secondary industry operations is not zero, those employed by SOEs, in government agencies and institutions and those who are self-employed are excluded.
    - P4: Tertiary industry operators. Among those whose net income from tertiary industry is not zero, those employed by SOEs, in government agencies and institutions and those who are self-employed are excluded.
    - P5: Self-employed. Net operating income is not zero.
    - P6: Housing rental personnel whose net rental income is not zero.
    - P7: Migrant workers whose remittance income is not zero. The corresponding population here is not a migrant labour force. In the rural household survey, some migrant workers were not recorded as family members. Retaining the identification of 'labour' could underestimate the impact of migrant work on rural households.
- X2_1: Region of current residence: Code for the province of current residence.
- X2_2: Workplace and region, determined by the workplace and its provincial code in the questionnaire data.
- X3: Industry classification of employment activity in the questionnaire.

P1, P2, P3, P6 and P7 were classified not by industry but only by region.

P4 and P5 were determined according to the industry of employed persons in the questionnaire. For those not identified as service industries, the magnitude of the impact was assumed to be the national average.

- X4_S0: Impact of the pandemic (baseline scenario). For the seven types of economic activity groups, the impact of the pandemic was assumed to be as given below:
  - P1: 1) Wage rate. The pandemic could have led to a reduction in wage rates, however, the baseline scenario assumes that wage rates remained unchanged. 2) Working time: The pandemic could have led to a decrease in working hours. In the benchmark scenario, the impact of the pandemic on working hours is extrapolated from the time of worksite-level relief. See section three for a detailed explanation.
  - P2: According to existing information, the impact of the pandemic on agricultural production activities was small and the baseline model was set to remain unchanged.
  - P3: There were different impacts in different regions, inferred from the percentage of total profit decline from February to April, as announced by the NBS in the cumulative value and year-on-year growth rates of total profits from January to April, which must be converted into total profits and year-on-year growth rates for February, March and April. We then estimate the proportion of the impact of the pandemic on the total profits of the industrial sector. See section three for a detailed explanation.
  - P4: Different impacts in different industries and regions, inferred from relevant data from the survey reports of SMEs.
  - P5: Different impacts in different industries and regions. The average impact in different regions comes from the survey report obtained by Peking University based on Alipay big data, and the proportional relationship between different industries is inferred from the survey report of Tsinghua University's Graduate School of People's Bank of China based on the data of millions of small, medium and micro-enterprises. Section three provides further details.
  - P6: We did not have reliable data to reflect the specifics of the rental market. According to the performance of various industries, the pandemic had a greater impact on the tourism industry, with the operating income of tourist hotels dropping significantly. The corresponding changes are reflected in P4. The main target of 'rental housing income' at the household level was non-operating rental behaviour, and most of the targets were ordinary tenants or homestays. According to the fourth economic census announcement, there were only 26,000 homestay employees, accounting for less than 1 per cent

of the total. The rental behaviour of ordinary tenants was mostly long-term. Owing to the relatively timely control of the pandemic in China, long-term rentals in most areas were not significantly affected. Therefore, the reference model setting in P6 did not change.

- – P7: Proportion of labour time reduction. From Baidu's migration big data, we inferred the probability distribution of the number of days migrant labourers in each province delayed returning to urban work and then inferred the delay for each family going out to work. The rate of decline of the wage rate was assumed to be constant.

- • X4_S1: Scenario A affected by the pandemic and the impact of wage rates. The wage rates for P1 and P7 were reduced by 5 per cent from the baseline scenario.

- • X4_S2: Scenario B affected by the pandemic and the impact of falling rental demand. The baseline scenario assumed a random 10 per cent drop in net rental income.

Data

The household income information in this chapter is obtained from the 2018 China Household Income Survey (CHIP2018), which contains detailed information on sources of income, expenditure, labour and employment and identifies the main economic activity objects in the context of the pandemic. Based on the real growth rate of rural per capita disposable income from 2018 to 2020, this chapter extrapolates income and consumption from 2018 to 2020 as a situation without the impact of the pandemic. The real income growth rate for 2018–20 is taken from the 2019 statistical bulletin (NBS 2019) and it is assumed that the income growth rate in 2019–20 without the impact of the pandemic is the same as that in 2018–19. To distinguish as much as possible the differences in the income growth rates of different income groups, households are divided into five groups according to their per capita disposable income, and the real growth rates are projected to 2020 (see Table 8.1).

To estimate the impact of the pandemic, we divided the impact into two dimensions: first, the length of impact; second, the depth of impact over a given period. The starting time is based on the closure of Wuhan on 23 January 2020. The end time is the date regions announced the end of the level-one response. The depth of the impact on different people in different regions varied greatly. We distinguished the following groups: first, according to daily population migration data from Baidu,[2] we estimated the probability distribution of days of delayed return to work for migrant workers in typical provinces. Second, according to the economic data of

---

2   Available from: qianxi.baidu.com/.

enterprises above a designated size from the NBS, we estimated the overall impact of the pandemic on large-scale enterprises. Third, according to the Daokou Economic Recovery Index of Tsinghua University's Graduate School of People's Bank of China (Internet Finance Laboratory et al. 2020), we estimated the impact of the pandemic on micro, small and medium-sized enterprises in various regions. Fourth, according to the research report of the Peking University Institute of Digital Finance and the Research Institute of Ant Group (2020), based on Ant Group's Alipay data, the impact of the pandemic on self-employed workers was obtained.[3]

Table 8.1 Per capita disposable income of rural residents in 2018–19

	2018	2019	Nominal growth rate (%)	Real growth rate (%)	Estimated CPI	Estimated real growth rate for 2018–20 (%)
Per capita disposable income	14,617	16,021	9.60	6.20	1.032	12.78
Groups						
Lowest	6,440	7,380	14.60	11.04		23.30
Lower	14,361	15,777	9.86	6.45		13.32
Middle	23,189	25,035	7.96	4.61		9.44
Higher	36,471	39,230	7.56	4.23		8.63
Highest	70,640	76,401	8.16	4.80		9.83

Source: Per capita disposable income, per capita disposable income of the five groups, nominal growth rate and real growth rate are from NBS (2018, 2019). Other figures based on the authors' calculations.

The impact of the pandemic on income distribution and poverty in rural China

Impact of the pandemic on the income of rural residents

Overall impact on per capita income

The NBS announced that the per capita disposable income of rural households in the first quarter of 2020 was RMB4,641, representing a year-on-year decrease of 4.7 per cent. Considering the income growth rate in the first quarter of 2019 was 6.9 per cent,[4] the pandemic likely caused the income growth rate of rural residents to drop by 11.6 per cent in the first quarter of 2020. The pandemic situation improved in the next three quarters and its impact on the annual income of rural areas was

---

3   Because of space limitations, we did not introduce the process to estimate the impact of the pandemic. Readers can contact the authors for detailed information.
4   Data from the National Bureau of Statistics website, available from: www.stats.gov.cn/english/.

less than 10 per cent. According to the model in this chapter, the pandemic reduced rural households' per capita disposable income by 7 per cent throughout the year (see Table 8.3). This showed that if the growth rate of rural income maintained the 2019 growth rate (6.2 per cent) in the absence of the pandemic, and the government did not add any income compensation measures during the pandemic, the real revenue growth of rural residents' income for the entire year would be –0.8 per cent (equal to 6.2 per cent minus 7.0 per cent). Considering the economic recovery and the government's policy objectives of comprehensively eradicating rural poverty, the income growth rate of rural residents in the next three quarters was likely to be higher than the past trend. Thus, it is likely that the final observed real revenue growth rate for 2020 is greater than zero.[5] The final value depends on economic recovery in the next three quarters and the strength of the government's revenue compensation policy.

The impact on different income groups and sources of income

The lowest income group suffered the most, with total disposable income falling by –8.8 per cent, followed by –7.6 per cent for the middle and upper-income groups. The highest-income group accounted for only –6.6 per cent. The proportion of change in different income sources also varied widely among income groups. The net business income of those in tertiary industry had the highest decline in the lowest income group, reaching –20.6 per cent. None of the other income groups fell below –6 per cent. We set different parameters for non-farm business activities in different regions and industries in the model. Thus, the results show that the industries most vulnerable to the impact of the pandemic were most likely to employ those in the lowest income group. The income of employees who migrated for work also fell the most in the lowest income group, below –8 per cent.

The largest percentage decline in income from home-based work, wage income and net operating income from secondary industry was about –7 per cent. The net operating income of secondary industry declined the most in the highest income group. The income level of families engaged in secondary industry business activities was generally relatively high.

Impact of falling wage rates and falling rental income

In the baseline model, we assume constant wage rates for employees and rental income for households. If these two indicators change, the results of the pandemic's impact on income distribution will change slightly. Among these, the change in wage rates had the greatest impact.

---

5   In April 2020, the International Monetary Fund released its *World Economic Outlook* (IMF 2020a), which predicted that China's real economic growth rate in 2020 would be 1.2 per cent. In its June update, the IMF (2020b) corrected China's economic growth rate to 1 per cent—the only positive rate among all economies. These two predictions are consistent with the rural residents' income growth rate estimated in this chapter.

Assuming the wage rate drops by 5 per cent (Table 8.4), under the multiplier effect of the decrease in working hours, wage income drops by 13.8 per cent, and the return income of employees who work outside the home drops by 10.6 per cent. These two numbers are more than 3 percentage points higher than those of the baseline model. Owing to changes in wage rates, the impact of the pandemic on the per capita disposable income of all rural households expanded significantly, from –7.0 per cent to –8.8 per cent. An important reason for this is that the proportions of workers who received wage income and the families who received income sent back by employees working outside the home were very high.

If the net income from rental housing is assumed to drop by 10 per cent (Table 8.5), the proportion of the impact of the pandemic on the per capita disposable income of households does not change much (only 0.1 percentage point). The main reason is that the proportion of households receiving net rental income was not high (less than 3 per cent). The share of net rental housing income in total rural household income was only 0.6 per cent.

Table 8.2 Income composition without the impact of the pandemic in 2020 (per cent)

Income sources (per capita)	All	Lowest	Lower	Middle	Higher	Highest
Disposable income	17,196	4,371	10,002	13,984	19,464	38,151
Wage income	7,297	2,304	4,055	6,371	9,451	14,302
Business income	5,766	532	3,014	4,220	5,624	15,435
Primary industry	3,601	677	2,379	3,224	3,609	8,114
Secondary industry	320	-251	56	69	295	1,432
Tertiary industry	1,844	106	578	928	1,720	5,889
Property income	516	143	242	259	465	1,471
Net rental income	113	15	31	54	98	369
Net transfer income	3,617	1,392	2,692	3,134	3,924	6,944
Remittance income	1,757	841	1,524	1,730	1,856	2,833

Sources: Estimated to the 2020 level based on relevant data from the CHIP2018 and NBS (2019). The specific calculation method can be found in the text.

Table 8.3 Relative impact of the pandemic on revenue sources, benchmark model (per cent)

Income sources (per capita)	All	Lowest	Lower	Middle	Higher	Highest
Disposable income	-7.0	-8.8	-6.7	-7.2	-7.6	-6.6
Wage income	-10.5	-11.2	-11.4	-11.3	-11.2	-9.4
Business income	-5.5	-11.3	-3.4	-3.6	-5.0	-6.4
Primary industry	0.0	0.0	0.0	0.0	0.0	0.0
Secondary industry	-7.0	\	-3.7	-2.4	-2.7	-6.9
Tertiary industry	-5.1	-20.6	-6.0	-4.3	-4.1	-5.1

Income sources (per capita)	All	Lowest	Lower	Middle	Higher	Highest
Property income	0.0	0.0	0.0	0.0	0.0	0.0
Net rental income	0.0	0.0	0.0	0.0	0.0	0.0
Net transfer income	-3.5	-4.9	-4.1	-4.3	-3.5	-2.7
Remittance income	-7.2	-8.1	-7.3	-7.7	-7.4	-6.5

Sources: Estimated to the 2020 level based on relevant data from the CHIP2018 and NBS (2019). The specific calculation method can be found in the text.

Table 8.4 Relative impact of the pandemic on income sources, benchmark model + wage rate decline by 5 per cent (per cent)

Income sources (per capita)	All	Lowest	Lower	Middle	Higher	Highest
Disposable income	-8.8	-11.5	-8.7	-9.2	-9.6	-7.9
Wage income	-13.8	-14.8	-14.9	-14.8	-14.7	-12.3
Business income	-5.5	-11.3	-3.4	-3.6	-5.0	-6.4
Primary industry	0.0	0.0	0.0	0.0	0.0	0.0
Secondary industry	-7.0	\	-3.7	-2.4	-2.7	-6.9
Tertiary industry	-5.1	-20.6	-6.0	-4.3	-4.1	-5.1
Property income	0.0	0.0	0.0	0.0	0.0	0.0
Net rental income	0.0	0.0	0.0	0.0	0.0	0.0
Net transfer income	-5.1	-7.2	-6.1	-6.2	-5.1	-3.9
Remittance income	-10.6	-12.0	-10.7	-11.3	-10.8	-9.5

Sources: Estimated to the 2020 level based on relevant data from the CHIP2018 and NBS (2019). The specific calculation method can be found in the text.

Table 8.5 Relative impact of the pandemic on income sources, benchmark model + 10 per cent decrease in net rental income (per cent)

Income sources (per capita)	All	Lowest	Lower	Middle	Higher	Highest
Disposable income	-7.1	-8.9	-6.8	-7.2	-7.6	-6.7
Wage income	-10.5	-11.2	-11.4	-11.3	-11.2	-9.4
Business income	-5.5	-11.3	-3.4	-3.6	-5.0	-6.4
Primary industry	0.0	0.0	0.0	0.0	0.0	0.0
Secondary industry	-7.0	\	-3.7	-2.4	-2.7	-6.9
Tertiary industry	-5.1	-20.6	-6.0	-4.3	-4.1	-5.1
Property income	-2.2	-1.1	-1.3	-2.1	-2.1	-2.5
Net rental income	-10.0	-10.0	-10.0	-10.0	-10.0	-10.0
Net transfer income	-3.5	-4.9	-4.1	-4.3	-3.5	-2.7
Remittance income	-7.2	-8.1	-7.3	-7.7	-7.4	-6.5

Sources: Estimated to the 2020 level based on relevant data from the CHIP2018 and NBS (2019). The specific calculation method can be found in the text.

Further observation of the impact of the pandemic on income distribution

Figure 8.2 illustrates the impact of the pandemic on the incidence of poverty and different income segments. The black curve of the first graph on the left is the observed income distribution and the folded line on the left is the income distribution after the impact of the pandemic (sorted by the income distribution before the impact). The abscissa is the amount of income, the ordinate is the cumulative probability density and the economic meaning is the position of the family in the income distribution after sorting based on income from small to large; –0 is the lowest income and 1 is the highest income. The vertical line on the left is the NBS's absolute poverty standard, which is RMB2,995 per person per annum (green vertical line); the vertical line on the right is the absolute poverty standard doubled (purple vertical line). Their intersection points with the income distribution are the corresponding income poverty incidence rates; the lower horizontal line is the income poverty incidence rate calculated according to the NBS standard and the upper horizontal line is the poverty incidence rate calculated according to the poverty standard doubled. The pandemic affected every income segment. Even families in the high-income group could have fallen into poverty because of the pandemic, but the proportion of these was not very high. The middle and right graphs in Figure 8.2 are further explanations of this result.

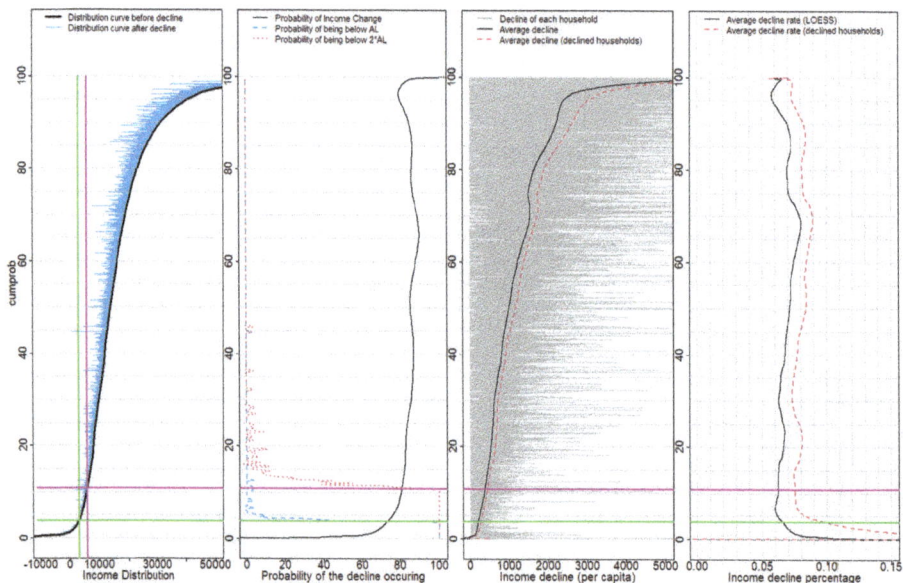

Figure 8.2 The impact of the pandemic on the incidence of poverty

Notes: Estimates for 2020; please refer to the data description section for details. This is the result of a one-time simulation and not the average level of all simulations. Because the simulation model considers random processes, some of the characteristics of the curve could be slightly different from those Tables 8.3, 8.4 and 8.5 in the previous subsection. However, their basic characteristics are the same. The results are from the baseline model.

Source: Authors' own simulations.

There are three curves in the middle-left graph: the probability of a change in income, the probability of falling into absolute poverty after a change in income and the probability of falling below the absolute poverty line doubled after a change in income. All three curves are estimates fitted using a nonparametric method, local regression models (LOESS), to represent the average characteristics of each income segment. Two characteristics were observed in this study: first, the probability of non-poor households being hit by the pandemic was very high; second, the probability of these households then falling into poverty was generally low, and only a very small number of non-poor households had a probability of falling into poverty exceeding 5 per cent, which declined rapidly after being above the poverty threshold. Thus, the proportion of people falling into poverty after being affected by the pandemic was not very high.

Why was the probability of returning to poverty low for most of the population? Households near the poverty line suffered a small drop in income after being affected by the pandemic (see the graph on the right in the centre of Figure 8.2 for details). Three curves show the decline in income for each household, the average decline for all families across different income segments and the average decline for families with changes in income. Two results emerge: first, the decline in the high-income segment was larger; second, the average decline in the bottom 20 per cent of households was about RMB500 and the average decline exceeded RMB2,000 in the top 20 per cent of households. Because the income of low-income households was not significantly reduced after the shock, the probability of their income being lower than the absolute poverty standard after the shock was not very high.

However, when the poverty standard was high (for example, the poverty standard was set at twice the official level), the impact of the pandemic on income was relatively large. There are two main reasons: first, the probability density of income distribution was higher near the median—that is, the closer the per capita income of a family was to the median, the more families were covered by income changes; second, for high-income families suffering from the pandemic, the amount of income decline was relatively high. The latter feature can be observed in the third plot of Figure 8.2.

The black curve in Figure 8.3 is the percentage decline in the per capita disposable income of all households after the decline in income of a specific economic activity object. The red dotted line represents the percentage of households with declining per capita disposable income. The former reflects the impact on the overall income distribution after a specific economic activity was affected by the pandemic. The latter reflects the difference in the degree of influence of specific economic activities on different households. The ordinate represents different quantiles, reflecting the difference between low-income and high-income families.

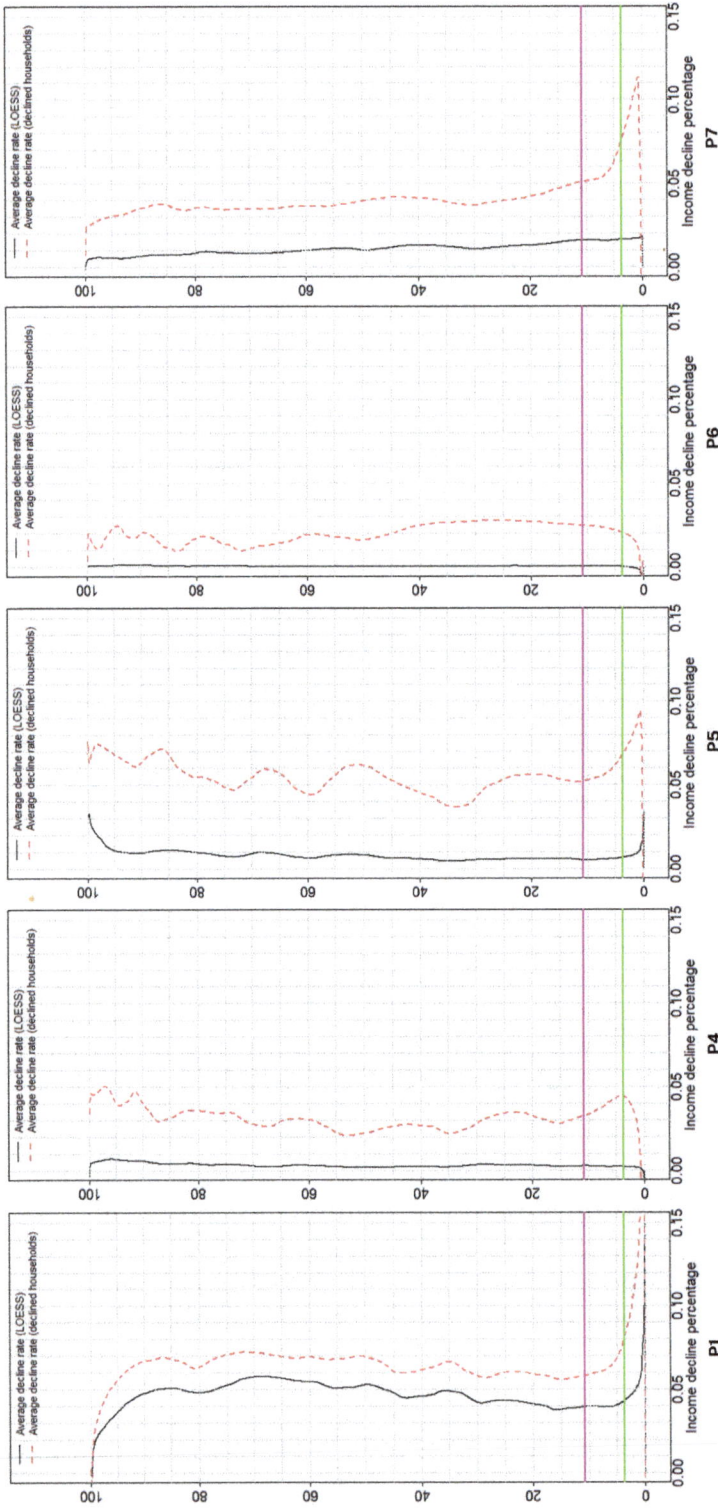

Figure 8.3 The relative proportion of the impact of the pandemic on different economic activity objects

Notes: Estimated for 2020; please refer to the data description section for details. This is the result of a one-time simulation and not the average level of all simulations. Because the simulation model considers random processes, some of the characteristics of the curve could be slightly different from those in Tables 8.3, 8.4, and 8.5 in the previous subsection; however, their basic characteristics are the same. The results of P1, P4 and P5 are from the baseline model. The results of P6 are from Scenario B (X4_S2). The results of P7 are from Scenario A (X4_S1).

Source: Authors' own simulations.

The graph shows that wage income (P1) without fixed or long-term contracts experienced the greatest impact and mainly affected those in absolute poverty. For the non-poor population, the impact on middle and upper-income groups was relatively large. The impact on remittance income (P7) was also large, and the impact experienced by the poor was significantly higher than that of the non-poor group. This shows that temporary wage labour and migrant work are of great significance to poor families.

Both net business income and rental housing income have little effect on income distribution, and the black curves for P4, P5 and P6 are all close to zero. Business activities had a greater impact on middle and high incomes and relatively little impact on low incomes. The impact of net rental housing income was relatively large in the low and middle-income groups, and the red dotted line of P6 had a slightly higher proportion in the low and middle-income groups. This shows that the importance of net rental housing income in low and middle-income households is relatively high. If the pandemic was not effectively controlled to limit the impact on the long-term demand for residential rental housing, households in the low and middle-income groups that mainly rely on rental housing income could suffer a greater impact.

The pandemic in the first half of 2020 had little impact on the incidence of poverty under the absolute poverty standard

Table 8.6 reports the impact of the pandemic on per capita income and poverty. The impact of the pandemic is summarised as follows: first, according to the national poverty standard, the pandemic increased the incidence of income poverty by 0.38 percentage points. Considering the randomness of the impact, Figure 8.4 illustrates the probability distribution of the magnitude of the impact on the absolute poverty incidence. If the real distribution of different economic activity objects in the income distribution is considered, the impact of the pandemic on the incidence of absolute poverty is likely to be between 0.3 and 0.45, which is not large. Second, the pandemic has widened the income gap; the income Gini coefficient has expanded by 0.44 percentage points, while the Theil index has expanded by 0.0032. Third, when the poverty standard is higher (for example, the level is doubled), more families return to poverty because of the pandemic. Under the doubled poverty standard, the proportion of households below this level increased by 1.71 percentage points.

Table 8.6 The impact of the pandemic on poverty and income distribution

	Poverty rate (%)						Gini	Theil
	Absolute poverty standard	Absolute poverty standard doubled	Absolute poverty standard tripled	50% of median income	Average income (RMB)	Median income (RMB)		
Statistical indicators in different states								
No change	3.73	10.83	25.28	14.30	17,196	13,889	0.3892	0.2494
Reduced by 50%	3.84	11.60	26.91	14.30	16,590	13,418	0.3908	0.2501
Reduced by 100%	4.10	12.54	28.69	14.49	15,984	12,921	0.3936	0.2526
Impact of the pandemic								
Reduced by 50%	0.11	0.77	1.63	0.00	−606	−472	0.0016	0.0007
SD	(0.03)	(0.05)	(0.07)	(0.07)	(4)	(16)	(0.0001)	(0.0004)
Reduced by 100%	0.38	1.71	3.42	0.20	−1,212	−969	0.0044	0.0032
SD	(0.04)	(0.08)	(0.1)	(0.11)	(8)	(24)	(0.0003)	(0.0007)

Source: Authors' own calculations.

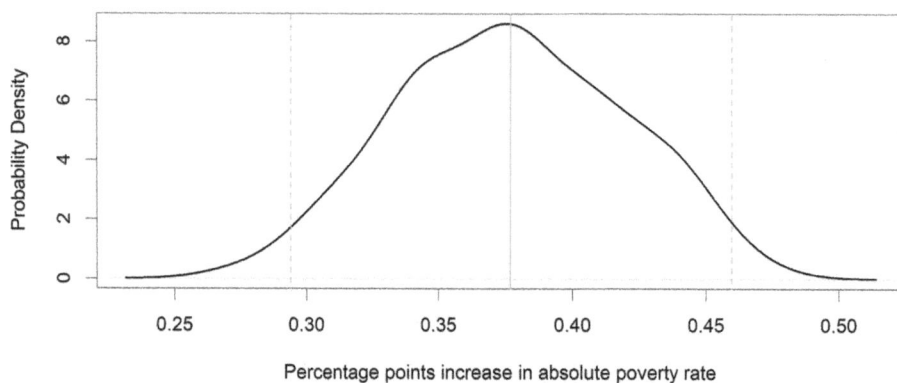

Percentage points increase in absolute poverty rate

Figure 8.4 The impact of the pandemic on the incidence of rural income poverty, absolute poverty standards

Source: Authors' own simulations.

Further discussion: Which groups of people are more likely to return to poverty due to the pandemic?

People with different sources of income are distributed in different parts of the rural income distribution. After each group was affected by the pandemic, there were differences in the increase in rural poverty. These differences can help identify the groups to be targeted with support policies. Table 8.7 reports the percentage point increase in the incidence of poverty among rural residents across China after a decline in the percentage of income for a group of people. The third column of Table 8.7 specifically reports the situation for rural residents in the central region, which suffered the most severe Covid-19 outbreak. The overall results were threefold.

First, when a single group's income decline rate was not high (for example, within 30 per cent), the incidence of rural poverty did not increase significantly. However, when the rate of decline exceeded 50 per cent, the incidence of rural poverty rose sharply. This reveals that, in the short term, the pandemic did not have a serious impact on the incidence of rural poverty. However, if the pandemic is not effectively controlled, the proportion of the population impoverished as a result will be very high.

Second, when a single income drops by approximately 10 per cent, for those in agricultural production and the operational labour force (P2), employees without fixed or long-term contracts (P1), self-employed workers (P5) and those receiving income from remittances (P7), there is a relatively large impact on the incidence of poverty. Owing to the seasonal nature of agricultural production and operational activities, the impact of the pandemic in early 2020 was small. Greater attention must be given to employees without fixed or long-term contracts (P1), self-employed workers (P5) and migrant workers (P7).

Third, employees without fixed or long-term contracts (P1), migrant workers (P7) and self-employed workers (P5) in the central region were more likely to return to poverty because of the pandemic when they experienced income shocks. An obvious problem is that these three categories are prevalent among low-income groups. In addition, the pandemic situation in the central region was more serious than elsewhere and the proportion of people returning to poverty here was significantly higher than in other regions.

Table 8.7 Increase in incidence rate of absolute poverty among rural residents nationwide when the income of a single group of people falls

	Income decline percentage											
	Absolute poverty rate (rural)				Relative poverty rate (rural)				Absolute poverty rate (central region)			
	1%	10%	30%	100%	1%	10%	30%	100%	1%	10%	30%	100%
All income source decline												
All	0.02	0.44	1.83	63.18	-0.04	0.13	0.33	26.68	0.03	0.49	2.01	66.45
Single income source decline												
P1	0.01	0.13	0.54	17.87	-0.07	-0.07	0.31	12.98	0.03	0.15	0.77	19.24
P2	0.00	0.09	0.36	7.70	0.02	0.08	0.63	8.20	0.00	0.07	0.39	4.26
P3	0.00	0.00	0.02	0.17	0.00	0.02	0.03	0.09	0.00	0.00	0.00	0.08
P4	0.00	0.00	0.04	0.92	0.00	-0.02	0.10	1.16	0.00	0.00	0.00	0.96
P5	0.00	0.05	0.19	3.00	0.00	-0.06	0.19	2.86	0.00	0.04	0.18	3.04
P6	0.00	0.00	0.00	0.06	-0.01	-0.04	0.01	0.01	0.00	0.00	0.00	0.06
P7	0.01	0.05	0.24	4.25	-0.02	0.15	0.70	5.93	0.00	0.04	0.33	6.04

Note: P1–P7 are in accordance with the seven categories of economic activity objects introduced in section two.

Source: Authors' own calculations.

Conclusion and discussion

Based on data from the CHIP2018 and third-party information from multiple sources, this chapter examines poverty and the distribution of low-income groups in rural China, estimates the impact of the pandemic on major economic activity objects and comprehensively analyses the impact of the pandemic on the income distribution and poverty status of rural residents. The results showed that the impact of Covid-19 in the first half of 2020 was expected to reduce the per capita disposable income of rural residents by about 7 per cent throughout the year (baseline model), with the lowest income group suffering the most. If the real income growth rate of rural residents in 2020 was like that in 2019, the pandemic could offset all real growth, leaving real income growth in 2020 at approximately 0 per cent. If the pandemic led to a significant drop in wage rates, its impact on rural incomes would be greatly exacerbated.

According to the current official poverty standard, the pandemic increased the incidence of rural income poverty by 0.38 percentage points. To understand this result, we should focus on two aspects. First, the position of the current poverty standard in the income distribution is relatively low and the proportion of the population near the poverty standard is small, so it seems the impact was not significant. If the poverty standard was doubled, the pandemic increased the incidence of income poverty by 1.7 percentage points. Second, the 2020 pandemic was quickly and effectively controlled without amplifying its negative impacts. If the pandemic had lasted longer, the return-to-poverty rate would have been higher and the marginal impact on poverty would have increased substantially.

This chapter distinguishes seven categories of main objects of economic activity. The wage-earning labour force (P1) without fixed or long-term contracts was the most affected by the pandemic, followed by the population that received income from migrant workers. Most rural household income sources include agricultural business income (including that from self-production). The impact of the pandemic on agricultural production and operations was not obvious, but if it had not been controlled in time, more than 70 per cent of rural households would have been hit harder by the pandemic, and the problem of returning to poverty could have been more serious. Timely control of the pandemic, an early emphasis on the farming sector in February 2020 and other measures guaranteed the basic living needs of rural families to a certain extent (Xinhua 2020).

The results of this chapter have two implications. First, to avoid expanding the impact of a similar future pandemic on residents' income and poverty, steps should be taken to prevent the impact lasting too long and increasing in depth. Simultaneously, restrictions or limits on the normal operation of key economic activities should be reduced as much as possible to prevent the wage rates of vulnerable labour being significantly affected. At the time of writing this chapter, the Chinese Government had brought the pandemic under control in a timely manner, which prevented it from having a more serious impact. Second, the scale of low-income groups in China is still relatively large and the income sources of many labourers are fragile. In the context of building a moderately prosperous society and eradicating absolute poverty, future tasks should include alleviating relative poverty, raising the income level of low-income people and enhancing the level of social security and the equalisation of public services.

Owing to the limited information collected thus far, this study mainly focused on the short-term impact of Covid-19. Whether infectious diseases have long-term effects remains an important question. After the first wave of the pandemic in China, it continued to spread in other countries and, by 13 July 2022, Covid-19 had caused 552,993,566 infections and 6,349,952 deaths worldwide (WHO 2022). New variants of the virus are constantly evolving and strains with strong rates of transmission (such as BA.4 and BA.5) are gradually replacing the original strains with weaker transmission (WHO 2022). Prevention and control of the pandemic are becoming increasingly difficult. Since 2021, with the enhanced transmissibility of new variants, the risk of China importing a new wave of the pandemic has increased. China has always implemented a dynamic zero-Covid policy whenever there is an outbreak (even when there is only one case) and strict closure and control measures are implemented. This containment policy has been facing increasing challenges as multipoint distribution becomes more common. This could have a growing impact on income distribution and poverty.

References

21 Data Journalism Lab. 2020. 'The Latest Version of the National Map of Resumption of Work Is Here! The Resumption Rate of Enterprises in 6 Provinces Including Guangdong Has Exceeded 80%, and Another 100% City Has Appeared!' *21st Century Business Herald*, 25 February. Available from: mp.weixin.qq.com/s/7nSbi-60nV97V16Ix_17ig.

Chen, Zhigang, Yue Zhan, Yumei Zhang and Shenggen Fan. 2020. 'Impact of COVID-19 on Global Food Security and Countermeasures.' [In Chinese]. *China Rural Economy* (5): 2–12.

Chinazzi, Matteo, Jessica T. Davis, Marco Ajelli, Gioannini Corrado, Maria Litvinova, Stefano Merler, Ana Pastore Y. Piontti, Kunpeng Mu, Luca Rossi, Kaiyuan Sun, Cécile Viboud, Xinyue Xiong, Hongjie Yu, M. Elizabeth Halloran, Ira M. Longini, jr, and Alessandro Vespignani. 2020. 'The Effect of Travel Restrictions on the Spread of the 2019 Novel Coronavirus (COVID-19) Outbreak.' *Science* 368(6489): 395–400. doi.org/10.1126/science.aba9757.

Department of Human Resources and Social Security (HRSS). 2020. '160 Migrant Workers Take Chartered Flights to Zhejiang Province: Various Measures of the Provincial Department of Human Resources and Social Security to Promote Safe Employment of Migrant Workers.' Media release, 24 February. Changchun, China: Jilin Provincial Department of Human Resources and Social Security. Available from: hrss.jl.gov.cn/zqbmzyq/zccs/202002/t20200224_6859340.html.

Fang, Hanming, Long Wang and Yang Yang. 2020. *Human mobility restrictions and the spread of the novel coronavirus (2019-NCOV) in China*. NBER Working Paper No. 26906. Cambridge, MA: National Bureau of Economic Research. doi.org/10.3386/w26906.

International Monetary Fund (IMF). 2020a. *World Economic Outlook, April 2020: The Great Lockdown*. Washington, DC: IMF. Available from: www.imf.org/en/Publications/WEO/Issues/2020/04/14/weo-april-2020.

International Monetary Fund (IMF). 2020b. 'A Crisis Like No Other: An Uncertain Recovery.' *World Economic Outlook Update*, June. Washington, DC: IMF. Available from: www.imf.org/en/Publications/WEO/Issues/2020/06/24/WEOUpdateJune2020.

Internet Finance Laboratory, Industrial Finance Research Center, Smart Finance Research Center and Beijing Daokou Jinke Technology Company Limited. 2020. *Economic Recovery of Small, Medium, and Micro Enterprises under the Pandemic: Analysis Based on the Operational Data of Millions of Small, Medium and Micro Enterprises*. [In Chinese]. Beijing: Graduate School of People's Bank of China, Tsinghua University.

Liang, Xiao, Scott Rozelle and Hongmei Yi. 2022. 'The Impact of COVID-19 on Employment and Income of Vocational Graduates in China: Evidence from Surveys in January and July 2020.' *China Economic Review* 75. doi.org/10.1016/j.chieco.2022.101832.

Liu, Hongbo, Jianliang Di and Ran Wang. 2022. 'Research on the Impact of COVID-19 on Residents' Consumption.' [In Chinese]. *Statistical Research* 39(5): 38–48.

Liu, Shijin, Yang Han and Dawei Wang. 2020. 'Analysis of the Impact Path of the New Coronavirus Pandemic Based on the Input–Output Structure and Countermeasures.' [In Chinese]. *Journal of Management World* 36(5): 1–12.

Liu, Zhibiao. 2020. 'The New Trend of Economic Globalization and the Reconstruction of Global Industrial Chain Clusters under the New Coronavirus Pandemic.' [In Chinese]. *Jiangsu Social Sciences*: 1–8.

Meituan Research Institute. 2020. *Looking at the Resumption of Work and Consumption Recovery in My Country's Catering Industry during the Pandemic from 15,265 Questionnaires*. [In Chinese]. March. Beijing: Meituan Research Institute.

Meng, Qi. 2020. 'The Impact of the Global Public Health Crisis on China's Participation in Global Value Chains.' [In Chinese]. *Finance & Economics* (5): 77–91.

Ministry of Finance (MoF) and State Taxation Administration (STA). 2020. 'Announcement on Tax Policies to Support the Prevention and Control of the Novel Coronavirus Pneumonia Epidemic.' Announcement No. 8, 8 March. Beijing: Government of the People's Republic of China. Available from: www.chinalawandpractice.com/2020/03/08/ministry-of-finance-and-state-administration-of-taxation-announcement-on-tax-policies-to-support-the-prevention-and-control-of-the-novel-coronavirus-pneumonia-epidemic/?slreturn=20220905012758.

National Bureau of Statistics of China (NBS). 2018. *Statistical Bulletin on National Economic and Social Development.* Beijing: China Statistics Press.

National Bureau of Statistics of China (NBS). 2019. *Statistical Bulletin on National Economic and Social Development.* Beijing: China Statistics Press. Available from: www.stats.gov.cn/tjsj/zxfb/202002/t20200228_1728913.html.

Peking University Institute of Digital Finance and Research Institute of Ant Group. 2020. *Calculation of the Total Number of Self-Employed Households in China and Assessment of the Impact of the New Coronavirus Pandemic: Also on the Value of Financial Technology in 'Stabilizing the Economy'.* [In Chinese]. Beijing: Peking University.

Qiu, Yun, Xi Chen and Wei Shi. 2020. 'Impacts of Social and Economic Factors on the Transmission of Coronavirus Disease 2019 (COVID-19) in China.' *Journal of Population Economics* 33(4): 1127–72. doi.org/10.1007/s00148-020-00778-2.

Wang, Feng and Min Wu. 2021. 'The Impacts of COVID-19 on China's Economy and Energy in the Context of Trade Protectionism.' *International Journal of Environmental Research and Public Health* 18(23): 12768. doi.org/10.3390/ijerph182312768.

Wang, Huan, Markus Zhang, Robin Li, Oliver Zhong, Hannah Johnstone, Huan Zhou, Hao Xue, Sean Sylvia, Matthew Boswell, Prashant Loyalka and Scott Rozelle. 2021. 'Tracking the Effects of COVID-19 in Rural China over Time.' *International Journal for Equity in Health* 20(35). doi.org/10.1186/s12939-020-01369-z.

Wang, Nalin. 2020. 'Research on the Impact of the New Coronavirus Pandemic on Migrant Workers in Hunan.' [In Chinese]. *Rural Economy and Science-Technology* 31(9): 274–76.

World Health Organization (WHO). 2022. 'Weekly Epidemiological Update on COVID-19: 13 July 2022.' *Emergency Situational Updates*, Edition 100. Geneva: WHO. Available from: www.who.int/publications/m/item/weekly-epidemiological-update-on-covid-19---13-july-2022.

Xinhua. 2020. 'Xi Jinping Presided Over the Meeting of the Political Bureau of the CPC Central Committee, Studied the Prevention and Control of the New Crown Pneumonia Epidemic, and Arranged the Overall Planning of Epidemic Prevention and Control and Economic and Social Development.' *Xinhua News Agency*, 21 February. Available from: www.gov.cn/xinwen/2020-02/21/content_5481871.htm.

Xu, Xianchun, Zihao Chang and Ya Tang. 2020. 'A Look at the Impact of the New Coronavirus Pandemic on China's Economy based on Statistics.' [In Chinese]. *Economic Perspectives* 5: 41–51.

Xuwei, Pei. 2020. 'Our City Uses Civil Aviation Charter Flights to Transport 157 Migrant Workers to Guangdong to Return to Work.' *Sohu*, 28 February. Available from: www. sohu.com/a/376468180_120207504.

Yang, Zihui, Yutian Chen and Pingmiao Zhang. 2020. 'Macroeconomic Shock, Financial Risk Transmission and Governance Response under Major Public Emergencies.' [In Chinese]. *Journal of Management World* 36(5): 13–35.

Zhang, Xiaobo and Ruochen Dai. 2020. '60% of Companies' Cash Flow Can't Last for 3 Months: Peking University Investigates What Small, Medium and Micro Enterprises Need Most.' [In Chinese]. Press release. Beijing: China Enterprise Innovation and Entrepreneurship Survey Project Alliance (ESIEC), National Development Institute of Peking University and School of Economics of Central University of Finance and Economics.

Zhang, Yumei, Xinshen Diao, Kevin Z. Chen, Sherman Robinson and Shenggen Fan. 2020. 'Impact of COVID-19 on China's Macroeconomy and Agri-Food System: An Economy-Wide Multiplier Model Analysis.' *China Agricultural Economic Review* 12(3): 387–407. doi.org/10.1108/CAER-04-2020-0063.

Zhang, Yumei, Yue Zhan, Xinshen Diao, Kevin Z. Chen and Sherman Robinson. 2021. 'The Impacts of COVID-19 on Migrants, Remittances, and Poverty in China: A Microsimulation Analysis.' *China & World Economy* 29(6): 4–33. doi.org/10.1111/cwe.12392.

Zhu, Wuxiang, Ping Zhang, Pengfei Li and Ziyang Wang. 2020. 'The Dilemma of Small, Medium and Micro Enterprises and the Improvement of Policy Efficiency under the Shock of the Pandemic: Analysis Based on Two National Questionnaire Surveys.' [In Chinese]. *Journal of Management World* 36(4): 13–26.

9

The impact of Covid lockdowns on China's labour market outcomes in 2020: Evidence based on an employee tracking survey

Dandan Zhang

Introduction

Since its initial outbreak in Wuhan, China, in January 2020, Covid-19 has gripped the world. By the end of 2020, the pandemic had affected 218 countries and caused more than 1.7 million deaths worldwide (WHO 2020). Faced with this unprecedented public health crisis, countries across the world adopted various measures aimed at preventing the spread, ranging from governments imposing draconian rules to restrict human mobility to governments reluctant to adopt any serious preventative measures and explicitly resorting to a strategy of herd immunity. To be effective, policies must be based not only on social preferences and government capacity, but also on an accurate understanding of the costs and benefits of different measures to counter Covid-19. However, relatively little is known about the broader impacts of these policies.

When evaluating the welfare implications of public health policies, two crucial components to consider are their health benefits and economic costs. Multiple studies have shown that strict social distancing and human mobility restrictions can effectively control the spread of Covid-19 and thus save lives. However, it remains unknown how such interventions affect individual welfare in the labour market.

Therefore, it is of great scientific and policy relevance to assess whether Covid-19 countermeasures have brought about a crisis in the labour market and additional health losses due to unemployment or poverty.

Existing studies have reached a consensus that the spread of Covid-19 resulted in a considerable slowdown of economic activity. Particularly in 2020, there was a prevailing sense of pessimism and uncertainty globally. According to a World Bank forecast in June 2020, the global economy was projected to contract by about 5 per cent that year (World Bank 2020). The International Labour Organization (ILO 2020) estimated that 400 million workers globally would fall into unemployment during the second quarter of 2020. The OECD (2020) projected that unemployment rates for its member countries would reach double digits. At the end of 2020, many countries confronted a second wave of Covid-19, which meant stricter lockdowns. The prolonged emergency has cast a shadow over economic recovery globally.

By the end of 2020, China was far ahead of most other countries in its economic recovery. As the country where the pandemic began, China adopted the most stringent epidemic prevention and control policies, which effectively contained the spread of the virus and brought significant health benefits (Qiu et al. 2020; Fang et al. 2020; Tian et al. 2020; Chinazzi et al. 2020; Lai et al. 2020; Hsiang et al. 2020; Chen et al. 2020; He et al. 2020; Qi et al. 2020).

Yet, China has also experienced economic fallout due to the pandemic. In early February 2020, tens of millions of migrant workers, back in their home villages for the Chinese New Year, could not return to cities to resume work because of lockdowns. In addition, efforts to limit interpersonal contact throughout the country caused declines in consumption. Shortages of and a decline in demand for labour resulted in disruptions to production. Many firms were forced to shut and wait for the pandemic to recede.

Some studies have shown that the work resumption rate was extremely low in February 2020 (Li et al. 2020; Zhu et al. 2020; Yi et al. 2020) and that the self-employed suffered considerable losses (Wang et al. 2020b). China's National Bureau of Statistics reported that, in February 2020, the national unemployment rate was 6.2 per cent—the highest level since January 2018. Existing studies of China have highlighted these employment shocks at the height of the pandemic lockdowns, yet few evaluate how long it will take for the Chinese economy to recover fully and how quickly its labour market will return to normal.

To fill this knowledge gap, I use tracking data for incumbent workers at the end of 2019 to investigate four issues. First, I describe the resurgent pace of the Chinese labour market. Second, I analyse whether China's lockdown policies—the world's most restrictive—deferred the return to work of workers. Third, I conduct heterogeneity analysis among different kinds of workers to gauge the most vulnerable groups in the Chinese labour market. Fourth, I explore whether job losses during lockdowns harmed the mental health of the newly unemployed. By addressing these issues, I can clarify the costs and benefits of China's strict prevention and control policies from a broader perspective. The results will help policymakers around the world design effective measures to mitigate the Covid-19-induced slowdown.

The core of my empirical analysis uses comprehensive tracking records drawn from Chinese WeChat users, about 6,000 of whom, employed at the end of 2019, were randomly selected and tracked throughout 2020. This employee dataset includes detailed information on work status, including workload (ratio of current hours worked to hours worked in 2019), hours worked, unemployment duration and earnings, which allow us to examine the lockdowns' impacts on various labour market outcomes. I also measured subjects' mental health at each survey point, allowing us to link changes in work status to variations in mental health. In the second wave of the survey (on 15 June), I asked the date the individual resumed work, which allowed me to construct a daily panel dataset for work status at the individual level. In the analysis, I will use both the three-wave pooled cross-sectional data and the panel data (during the period 3 February to 15 June 2020) to analyse the impact of lockdowns on work resumption, as well as on the mental health of the Chinese labour force.

Each city's lockdown information was collected from news media and government announcements (see Figure 9.1). There were two types of lockdowns in China in early 2020: city lockdown, which restricted mobility between cities, and community lockdown, which was defined as restrictions on mobility within a city. At the start of 2020, the time lag between city lockdowns and community lockdowns was typically one to two weeks, with lockdowns gradually spreading to different cities and prefectures between 23 January and 20 February. The lockdown data (at the prefectural level) can be matched with the employee datasets and form a daily individual-level panel dataset between 3 February and 15 June 2020, which is the period largely overlapping with the first wave of Covid-19 outbreaks in China.

I begin my analysis by describing the dynamic changes in work status both for China as a whole and for different groups of workers. I find that the rate of work resumption increased from 63.1 per cent in early March to 84.2 per cent in mid-June and climbed to 89.7 per cent by the end of November, while the unemployment rate fell from 11 per cent in mid-June to 4.4 per cent in November. The numbers show a V-shaped pattern in the Chinese labour market.

I then quantify the impacts of lockdowns on the labour market outcomes by employing a difference-in-differences (DiD) approach using the daily individual-level panel data. DiD allows us to compare the changes in work status between the locked-down cities (treatment group) and the non-locked-down cities (control group) before and after the enforcement of lockdown policies. Next, I shift to the cross-sectional data for a different survey time to estimate the cumulative effect of lockdowns on work resumption by regressing the individual work status in June or November on the number of lockdown days. The estimation results show that city lockdowns were negatively associated with the probability of work resumption, with the presence of a lockdown policy reducing the likelihood of returning to work by 13.2 percentage points. While the cross-sectional analysis detected this adverse impact in the short run, the negative effect was no longer detectable in November.

I then shift my focus to the mental health impacts of inadequate employment caused by pandemic lockdowns. By using the three-wave pooled cross-sectional data, the estimation results based on the fixed-effect model show that job losses due to lockdowns in general worsened the mental health status of the Chinese labour force, especially the unemployed. This adverse impact reached its worst level in June but was insignificant in November, suggesting optimistic expectations for employment recovery on the part of Chinese workers who were experiencing unemployment near the end of 2020.

This chapter makes several contributions to the Covid-19 literature. First, it contributes to the debate on lockdown policies and their consequences on the labour market. Due to data limitations, few existing studies have been able carry out a causal analysis of the effect of pandemic lockdowns on employment. This study uses up-to-date employee tracking data to address this issue and verifies that there is indeed a negative impact of lockdown policies on work resumption, highlighting the economic costs of public health policies. Second, the study contributes to the debate about the effects of job losses during an economic recession on the mental health of the labour force. Consistent with existing research by Clark and Oswald (1994), Winkelmann and Winkelmann (1998), Kassenboehmer and Haisken-DeNew (2009) and Gili et al. (2013), I find that inadequate employment does harm one's mental health. However, I reveal that these negative impacts diminish with the resurgent pace of the economy, implying that the short-term economic fallout was associated with immediate psychological shocks to discouraged workers, but no *ex-post* effect can be detected once the economy recovered. Third, the data used in this study are not only newly collected individual-level data but also the only tracking data available for China during the Covid-19 pandemic in 2020. This allows us to understand, for the first time, who bears most of the burden of pandemic lockdowns and who are the most vulnerable members of the Chinese labour market.

The remainder of the chapter is organised as follows. Section two provides a literature review on the lockdowns' impacts on public and mental health, the economy and the labour market. Section three discusses the data and presents summary statistics for the sample. Section four discusses the empirical framework to estimate the lockdown effect on employment and the employment effect on mental health. Section five presents results and section six concludes.

Literature review

Disease-control measures and physical health

Even though the stringency of disease-control measures has varied across different countries during the pandemic, the literature has reached a consensus that public health measures can indeed contain the spread of the virus. Early research focused mainly on China, where the virus first broke out. Qiu et al. (2020) find China's lockdown policies effectively reduced Covid-19 infections, avoiding roughly 14 million infections and 560,000 deaths. Fang et al. (2020) estimate the lockdown policy in Wuhan reduced infections outside that city by 64.8 per cent. Tian et al. (2020) conclude that the Wuhan lockdown delayed infections outside the city by 2.91 days, and those cities that enacted control measures had significantly fewer confirmed cases than their counterparts. Using simulation methods, Chinazzi et al. (2020) demonstrate that the lockdown in Wuhan slowed the spread of Covid-19 in China by three to five days and decreased exported cases by 80 per cent. Similarly, Lai et al. (2020) indicate that, without the virus-control measures, there would have been 67 times the number of confirmed cases in China. Based on data from China, South Korea, Italy, Iran, France and the United States, Hsiang et al. (2020) reveal that pandemic prevention and control measures have worked in most countries, except the United States, where they failed to work as expected.

Another strand of literature examines the effects of anti-contagion policies during the pandemic on the mortality rates from other diseases. Both Chen et al. (2020) and He et al. (2020) find that the improvement in air quality due to lockdowns benefited patients with non-infectious diseases such as cardiovascular disease. Using the daily death data from the Chinese Center for Disease Control and Prevention, Qi et al. (2020) conclude that lockdown policies significantly reduced non-Covid deaths outside Wuhan, especially death due to cardiovascular disease, accidental injury and pneumonia-related diseases. These health consequences of lockdowns fall on the benefits side of the ledger. We now turn to the costs.

Economic crisis, labour market outcomes and mental health

The economic costs of the Covid-19 pandemic have been impossible to ignore. In the United States, 14 million workers lost their jobs between February and May 2020 (Borjas and Cassidy, 2020). Globally, Coibion et al. (2020) reveal that 200 million workers were jobless in April 2020—far exceeding the negative shock of the 2008 GFC on the labour market. In India, which enforced a stringent lockdown policy, individuals' incomes contracted by 57 per cent and working hours were reduced by 73 per cent (Lee et al. 2020). Even though South Korea did not adopt lockdown policies during the pandemic, Aum et al. (2020a) found that every 0.1 per cent increase in confirmed cases reduced the employed labour force by 2–3 per cent. Moreover, Aum et al. (2020b) examined the costs and benefits of different pandemic-control measures and concluded that 'targeting on the most vulnerable group' was the cheapest and most efficient approach.

Moreover, an increasing number of studies have focused on mental health during lockdowns, concluding that mental health status has worsened, especially for women, young people, immigrants and undocumented workers. Wang et al. (2020a) conducted an online survey in China and found that levels of anxiety, depression and stress increased significantly during the lockdown, with women and young people suffering most severely. Using a sample of 1,074 Chinese individuals, Ahmed et al. (2020) revealed that most interviewees from Hubei Province, of which Wuhan is the capital, suffered increased levels of anxiety and depression compared with before the lockdown, and that people aged 21–40 experienced a worse mental health status. Using Google search statistics, Brodeur et al. (2020) found that people in the United States and Europe searched for keywords such as 'boring', 'loneliness', 'anxiety' and 'sorrow' more frequently than usual during the lockdown period. Gualano et al. (2020), Rossi et al. (2020) and Aragona et al. (2020) all showed that, during the lockdown in Italy, people tended to suffer from higher anxiety and depression levels, worse sleep quality and more insomnia symptoms. Pieh et al. (2020) found that the general levels of depression and anxiety among Austrians increased by five and three times, respectively, compared with the pre-Covid-19 period, and people also reported lower levels of quality of life and happiness. Kumar et al. (2020) and Nanda (2020) found that migrant workers experienced worse mental health during lockdown, mainly because of lost social security due to unemployment. Holmes et al. (2020) argued that social distancing increased the incidence of suicide attempts and self-harm behaviours, with unemployment, income shock and poverty exacerbating the effect.

Data and summary statistics

Data

Survey data

In 2020, I conducted online surveys and experiments among the Chinese labour force, using the Tencent Thinktank Online Platform. The baseline survey was conducted in early March, when I surveyed a random sample drawn from the more than 100,000 registered WeChat users on the platform. The sample was restricted to those aged between 16 and 65 and employed at the end of 2019—that is, incumbent workers (the information was based on WeChat big-data analysis). I approached more than 10,000 randomly selected WeChat users on the platform to take part in the study, of whom 5,866 completed their questionnaires—that is, a survey response rate of 56.8 per cent. I further restricted the sample to the 5,674 subjects who answered within a reasonable time and for whom all relevant information was available. In mid-June 2020, all 5,674 subjects were revisited with the first tracking survey. Due to attrition (7.5 per cent) and missed reporting for some key variables, the sample size was further reduced to 5,027 people. The second tracking survey was implemented at the end of November, with 4,539 subjects successfully tracked (representing a 5 per cent attrition rate).

In the baseline survey (Mar-2020), about half the subjects were randomly selected to participate in the online experiments. During the second tracking survey (Nov-2020), the remaining half was invited to participate in the same experiments.[1] The game samples for the baseline survey and the second tracking survey were 1,897 and 1,646 people, respectively.

There are more than 1.2 billion Tencent WeChat users in China, accounting for 86 per cent of the population, which guarantees adequate geographical representativeness for the survey data. The baseline sample includes participants from 325 cities or prefectures in 31 provinces, which is 97.3 per cent of all 334 prefectures in China. However, as this was an online survey with participants drawn from active WeChat users, the survey sample could be biased towards those who are more attached to the internet. Compared with the industrial and spatial distributions of Chinese urban employees from the 2019 *China Statistical Yearbook*, the baseline sample featured disproportionately greater representation of residents of large cities (such as Beijing, Shanghai and Guangzhou) and those employed in the information technology industry. To make the survey sample nationally representative, I use a 10 per cent microsample from China's 1% National Population Sample Survey from 2015 to construct sampling weights by interacting six groups of individual characteristics: residential province, industry, gender, age, education and *hukou* (household registration). The provincial and industry distributions before and after weighting are presented in Appendix Table 9.1 with a comparison with the corresponding distributions based on the 1% National Population Sample Survey in 2015. I also performed the Wilcoxon signed-rank test to confirm that the distributions of the survey sample were consistent with those of the 1% National Population Sample Survey from 2015. I weighted the sample throughout the analysis when drawing conclusions at the national level.

---

1   Following the standard experimental literature, three experiments were conducted: altruism, risk and time preference. This information is not used in these data.

Lockdown data

Information on local government lockdowns was collected for each city from news media and government announcements. Most cities' lockdown policies were issued directly by the city-level government, while a few were promulgated by provincial governments. There were two types of lockdown: city lockdowns, which restricted mobility between different cities, and community lockdowns, which were mobility restrictions within a city. At the early stage of the outbreak, to prevent the virus from spreading beyond Hubei Province, city lockdowns were adopted in Wuhan and neighbouring cities. The purpose was to restrict people at the epicentre of the outbreak from travelling to other cities. Later, as more cases were identified in other cities, community lockdowns were implemented to further control the spread of Covid-19 within cities. The time lag between city lockdowns and community lockdowns was typically one to two weeks. The evolution of the number of cities that launched lockdown policies is presented in Figure 9.1. In Appendix Table 9.5, I provide a complete list of cities that adopted different lockdown policies at different times. In China, the lockdowns gradually spread to different regions between 23 January and 20 February 2020. By the end of February, 246 of China's 334 cities/ prefectures had implemented lockdown policies. For the city samples covered by the online survey (325 cities), 19 cities (5.8 per cent) launched complete or partial city lockdowns at some time, with an average duration of 39.6 days. Ninety-one cities (28 per cent) implemented complete or partial city lockdowns, as well as setting up checkpoints at the main entry points. Moreover, 240 cities (73.8 per cent) enforced community lockdowns at some point.

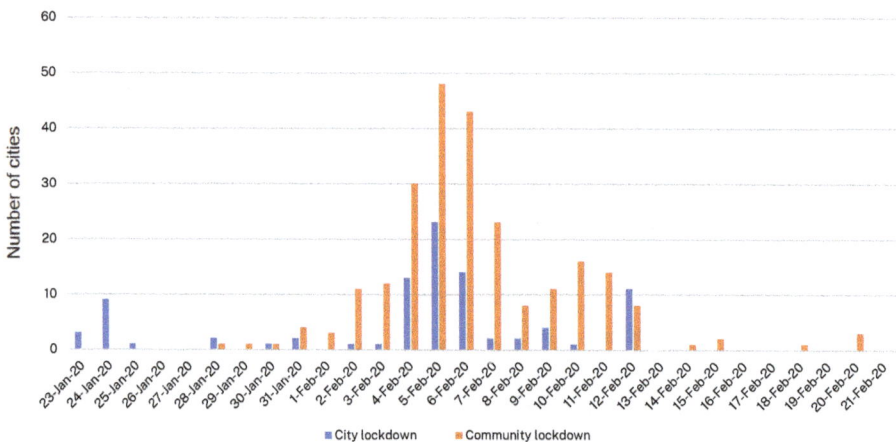

Figure 9.1 Distribution of lockdown dates for cities covered by the employee tracking survey

Summary statistics

The summary statistics of (unweighted) individual characteristics for the 5,674 baseline samples are reported in Column (1) of Table 9.1. As is shown, 50.7 per cent of the baseline sample were male, the average age was 34 years, the average level of schooling was 14.5 years, 53.8 per cent had a college degree or above, 66.2 per cent were married, 69.5 per cent had at least one child, 61.4 per cent were registered with an urban *hukou*, 25.2 per cent were rural migrant workers, 32.5 per cent worked in the private sector, 12.4 per cent were self-employed and the average monthly salary was RMB6,280 in 2019. Columns (2) and (3) report the differences in characteristics between each of the Jun-2020 and Nov-2020 tracking samples and the baseline sample. Further, *t*-tests were performed to gauge whether the tracking samples were randomly selected. As displayed, no systematic differences were found between the tracking samples and the baseline sample, suggesting attrition was not influenced by any of the wide range of individual characteristics measured.

Table 9.1 Sample comparision across three survey waves

	Baseline (Mar-2020)	t-test (Jun-2020– Mar-2020)	t-test (Nov-2020– Mar-2020)
Demographic characteristics			
Male (%)	50.67	−0.36	−1.10
Age (years)	34.29	0.24	0.32
	(8.22)	(8.21)	(8.19)
Years of schooling (years)	14.53	0.01	0.03
	(2.31)	(2.28)	(2.29)
Education level (%)			
Illiterate or primary school	0.65	0.01	−0.01
Junior high	7.01	−0.31	−0.18
Senior high	18.06	0.10	−0.48
College	25.50	0.28	0.12
Postgraduate and above	48.77	−0.07	0.56
Married (%)	66.21	0.68	0.53
Have at least one child (%)	63.31	−0.63	−0.20
Urban *hukou* (%)	61.40	0.15	0.73
Rural migrant (%)	19.49	−0.41	−0.27
Average monthly salary in 2019 (RMB)	6,735.45	12.07	27.51
	(7,066.23)	(7,081.52)	(7,018.61)

	Baseline (Mar-2020)	t-test (Jun-2020– Mar-2020)	t-test (Nov-2020– Mar-2020)
Ownership (%)	**6.36**	**0.02**	**–0.19**
	9.43	–0.14	–0.49
	10.58	–0.58	–0.69
	5.96	0.22	0.30
	32.47	0.05	0.27
	18.67	0.13	0.23
	16.53	0.28	0.59
Occupation (%)			
High-level officer or manager	10.19	0.08	–0.19
Professional or technical personnel	26.00	–0.26	–0.24
Clerk	15.02	–0.34	–0.69
Commercial staff	9.69	0.21	0.37
Service staff	17.43	0.08	0.11
Production or transportation worker	9.31	–0.20	–0.10
Self-employed	8.69	0.37	0.60
Agriculture, forestry, animal husbandry or fishery worker	1.59	0.15	0.20
Other	2.10	–0.09	–0.06
No. of individuals	5,674		

Notes: All the numbers in this table are unweighted. Standard deviations are reported below the means. Sample sizes for the second wave (5,027) and the third wave (4,539) are less than the baseline survey (5,674) due to attrition. t-tests are performed for first or second tracking samples and the baseline sample in Columns (2) and (3), respectively. All t-tests are based on the information collected in the baseline survey.

Table 9.2 Dynamic changes in key variables, November 2019 to November 2020

	Nov-2019	Mar-2020	Jun-2020	Nov-2020
Employment				
At work (%)	100	63.06	84.22	89.69
Work intensity (% of 2019)	100	51.63	80.2	-
Hours worked per week	-	27.36	41.50	43.47
		(22.00)	(17.94)	(18.32)
Work status (%)				
Work at workplace	100	44.12	75.45	-
Work at home	0	18.95	8.76	-
Not returned to work	0	29.44	4.73	-
Unemployed	0	7.50	11.05	4.40

	Nov-2019	Mar-2020	Jun-2020	Nov-2020
Mental health				
Mental health (ranging from 0 to 36)	-	24.09	23.86	25.30
		(6.61)	(7.15)	(6.68)
Monthly earnings				
Monthly earnings in the past month	6,278.59	4,043.01	5,130.38	5,867.07
	(7,066.23)	(8,972.31)	(10,155.52)	(5,850.42)
Percentage of average monthly earnings for 2019	100	64.39	81.71	85.18
Covid-19 perceptions				
Self-reported probability of being infected with Covid-19 (%)	-	9.70	9.53	1.38
		(0.18)	(0.17)	(0.02)
No. of individuals	5,674	5,674	5,027	4,539

Notes: Standard deviations in parentheses. Information about work status was collected in a different way in the third wave. The corresponding information is collected in the line with the standardised employment measure. The method of calculating the unemployed rate for November 2020 is described in Appendix Table 9.2.

Table 9.2 shows dynamic patterns for the welfare of the Chinese labour force, including work resumption, income shocks and changes in mental health status, over three survey waves in 2020 and their initial outcomes in November 2019. The rate of work resumption for all 2019 incumbent workers was as low as 63.1 per cent in March 2020, indicating that more than one-third of the labour force was unable to work by then. The work resumption rate reached 84.3 per cent in the middle of June and, by the end of November, it had risen to 89.7 per cent. These results show a V-shaped pattern for the resurgent pace of work resumption in the Chinese labour market.

In the middle of June, 11 per cent of the labour force self-reported as unemployed. According to the standard unemployment measure (which was only available for the third wave), the unemployment rate for 2019 incumbent workers was 4.4 per cent in November 2020.[2] Moreover, considering the attrition issue, I employed a different method for calculating the unemployment rates based on the baseline sample (5,674 observations) by assuming that subjects lost to attrition who were unemployed in previous waves would also be unemployed in the third wave if they could have been tracked. This gives us a range of estimates for unemployment rates of 2.6–7.6 per cent in November 2020. The detailed calculations are included in Appendix Table 9.2. Regardless of how the unemployment rates are computed, one

2   The National Bureau of Statistics of China (NBS) defines unemployment as the 'working aged labour force who are currently not employed but are actively looking for jobs and are capable of working in two weeks if they get a job offer'. In the third wave of the survey in November, I first asked questions specifically designed to calculate the unemployment rate in a manner consistent with the definition provided by the NBS.

can easily conclude that the unemployment situation reached its highest level in June and declined considerably thereafter. Appendix Table 9.3 shows that, according to the transit matrix of work status across waves, the unemployed labour force was reduced sharply from Jun-2020 to Nov-2020. Up to 5.7 per cent of unemployed workers found a job in the second half of 2020 and only about 2 per cent became newly unemployed.

Yet, 4.4 per cent of 2019 incumbent workers were still suffering from unemployment at the end of 2020. Note that, if unemployment rates among new labour market entrants (mainly college graduates in July) were considered, the unemployment rate would be even higher. This descriptive analysis highlights the fact that unemployment issues in China during the pandemic period should not be neglected.

Among unemployed workers, 78 per cent were female and 83 per cent were part of a married couple with a dependent child or children. This suggests that married couples with children, especially working mothers, bore a greater burden from the pandemic-related employment shocks, likely due to the closure of schools and childcare institutions during lockdowns. Moreover, the unemployment rate among rural migrant workers was 5.3 per cent in November 2020—much higher than the total unemployment rate (4.4 per cent). Further, migrant workers accounted for 29 per cent of the total unemployed labour force, which implies they were more vulnerable in terms of work resumption. In addition, most of the unemployed workers had a low level of education (below junior high) and were clustered in industries such as manufacturing, retail and wholesale.

The average number of days spent unemployed was 211, with more than half of study participants (51 per cent) falling into unemployment for more than half a year. In November 2020, the major sources of income support for unemployed workers took the form of family transfers (47.5 per cent) and reliance on personal savings (38.1 per cent), while only 9 per cent could rely on social security protection. Among social security sources, 8 per cent came from unemployment insurance and the remaining 1 per cent came from the minimum living standard security system.

Methodology and model specifications

The effect of lockdowns on labour market outcomes

I employ a DiD model to identify the impact of counter-Covid-19 measures on the pace of returning to work. First, in the baseline regression, the relative change in the probability of an individual resuming work between the treated and control cities is estimated using the following model (Equation 9.1).

Equation 9.1

$$work_{ijt} = \alpha = \beta lockdown\_policy_{jt} + \gamma COVID - 19_{jt} + \delta_i + \lambda_t + \varepsilon_{itj}$$

In Equation 9.1, $work_{ijt}$ is a dummy variable, equal to 1 if individual i in city j on date t has returned to work, and zero otherwise; $lockdown_{jt}$ is a dummy variable indicating whether a city or community lockdown was in place in city j on date t. The lockdown dummy takes the value of 1 if either a city lockdown or a community lockdown was in place, and zero otherwise. Thus, the coefficient β measures the average effect of lockdown policies. To separately estimate the effect of mobility restrictions across cities (city lockdown) and mobility restrictions within a city (community lockdown), I also include both dummies in Equation 9.1. $COVID - 19_{jt}$ is the logged number of total confirmed Covid-19 patients for city j on date t, which is used to control the time-variant disease spread. λ_i are city fixed effects and π_t indicate date fixed effects. ε_{itj} is the error term.

The city fixed effects, λ_j, which are city-specific dummy variables, can control for time-invariant confounders specific to each city. For example, the city's geographical conditions, short-term industrial and economic structure, income and natural endowments can be controlled by introducing the city fixed effects. The date fixed effects, π_j, are dummy variables that account for shocks that are common to all cities on a given day, such as national holidays and macroeconomic conditions. Because both location and time fixed effects are included in the regression, the coefficient β estimates the difference in the probability of work resumption between the treated (locked-down) and the control cities before and after the enforcement of the lockdown policy. I also add a set of time-variant individual control variables in the regressions to check the robustness of the results.

So far, I have focused on the effect of lockdown policies on whether individual workers resumed work, which is the extensive margin of labour market behaviours. To gauge the effect of lockdown policies on the intensive margin of labour market behaviours, such as workload and hours worked, I conduct the following model using the cross-sectional data in June and November 2020 (Equation 9.2).

Equation 9.2

$$Y_{ijp}^{\tau} = \theta + \gamma lockdown\_days_j + Y_{ijp}^{\tau-1} + \eta X_i + \omega COVID - 19_j + \rho_p + \varepsilon_{ijp}$$

In Equation 9.2, Y_{ijp}^{τ} denotes either the work intensity or the hours worked for individual i in city j of province p. τ denotes the survey wave—that is, June or November 2020. The workload is measured by the percentage workload at the survey time τ relative to the same time in 2019. The hours worked are the total hours worked for the week of survey time τ. The key independent variable is $lockdown\_days_j$, which indicates the number of days of city lockdown implemented in city j. X_i is a set of characteristics that could affect an individual's labour market performance, including gender, age, years of schooling, marital status, number of children, *hukou* categories, and so on. To capture the pandemic effect, I include $COVID - 19_j$ in the model, which is measured as log (1 + total confirmed cases) at the survey time τ; ρ_p are province fixed effects, which are used to control for heterogeneity at the provincial level.

As for Equation 9.2, there could be concern that some unobserved factors at the city level are related to the length of lockdowns and correlate with the workers' labour market performance. To deal with the potential omitted variable problems, I control for the lagged dependent variable—that is, $Y_{ijp}^{\tau-1}$—in Equation 9.2 to tease out the time-invariant city-level unobserved factors.

The effect of work status on mental health

I move on to examine whether job loss can cause mental health problems. Presumably, job loss can affect workers' mental health through the following three channels: first, by exerting a direct effect on mental health; second, by causing a deterioration of an individual's existing mental health problem by reducing his/her salary. Both channels suggest a negative effect from job loss on the mental health status of previously employed workers. Third, during the pandemic, going out to work could increase one's risk of Covid-19 infection and thereby cause mental distress. This channel suggests that job loss could somehow improve mental health by lowering the risk of infection in the workplace. The net effect of job loss on the mental health of employed workers depends on the magnitude of the negative and positive effects.

By adopting all three waves of survey data, I construct a fixed-effect (FE) model to analyse whether the change in work status can cause mental health problems. Compared with the single time-point cross-sectional data, the FE model allows us to tease out individual time-invariant heterogeneity and to some extent allows us to infer causality. The FE models are specified in Equations 9.3a and 9.3b.

Equation 9.3a

$$MH_{ij,m} = \alpha + \beta_1 unemployment_{i,m}$$
$$+ \beta_2\, not\_return\_to\_work_{i,m}$$
$$+ \gamma COVID - 19_{j,m} + \delta_i + \lambda_m + \varepsilon_{ij,m}$$

Equation 9.3b

$$MH_{ij,m} = \alpha + \beta_1 unemployment_{i,m}$$
$$+ \beta_2\, not\_return\_to\_work_{i,m}$$
$$+ \gamma COVID - 19_{j,m} + \eta_1 inc_{i,m-1}$$
$$+ \eta_2 infection\_risk_{i,m} + \delta_i + \lambda_m + \varepsilon_{ij,m}$$

In these equations, $MH_{ij,m}$ is the standard mental health measurement;[3] the key independent variable is whether one is unemployed ($unemployment_{i,m}$) and not yet returned to work (or on vacation) ($not\_return\_to\_work_{i,m}$). To capture the pandemic effect, I include $COVID - 19_{i,m}$ in the model, which is measured as log (1 + total confirmed cases) in the survey month m.[4] δ_i are individual fixed effects and λ_m are survey wave dummies, which measure the time trends of mental health status for the base group (being employed at the end of 2019).

Income ($inc_{i,m} - 1$, log [1 + monthly salary in previous month]/1,000) and self-assessed risk of being infected with Covid-19 ($infection\_risk_{i,m}$) are incorporated in Equation 9.3b to control for the channel through which work status could affect mental health status.

β_1 measures the change in the level of mental health for those who fall into unemployment relative to those who maintain their work status. β_2 captures the difference in the relative change of mental health status between those who had not yet returned to work (or were on vacation) and those who remained in the same work status.

The advantage of the FE model is that it can deal with the endogeneity caused by time-invariant unobserved factors. However, there could be some time-variant unobserved factors that are correlated with one's work status and mental health status at the same time, such as some macro-level demand shocks. Nevertheless, the analysis is based on a very limited period (three to five months). Ignorance of the time-variant factors with spatial heterogeneity in the short run may not cause any biased estimation.

Estimation results for lockdown policies

Impacts of city and community lockdowns on work resumption

I first examine whether the implementation of lockdown policies was associated with a lower probability of returning to work during the Covid-19 pandemic. Table 9.3 summarises the panel regression results by fitting the DiD model (Equation 9.1).

---

3   The General Health Questionnaire (GHQ-12) comprises 12 standardised questions, each of which provides four options from which the respondent can choose. The scores are 0, 1, 2 and 3, with a total possible score of 0–36 points. In GHQ-12, the higher the score, the worse is the mental health status. However, in this chapter, I transform the scores to make the results more intuitive: the higher the score, the better is the mental health status.
4   Lockdown policies at the city or community level are not controlled in this model, because lockdown policies were in effect nationally at the end of February and there was no policy change from March to November. Thus, the time-invariant factors can be eliminated from the models by adding individual fixed effects in the three-wave panel data.

In Column (1), we find a city lockdown is significantly associated with a reduced likelihood of work resumption (in the first half of 2020). After a city implemented complete or partial lockdown (that is, mobility was restricted between cities), the probability of work resumption decreased by 13.2 percentage points compared with the control group.

Table 9.3 Effects of city/community lockdown on work resumption: Panel analysis for 3 February to 15 June

Dependent variable	Work resumption			
	(1)	**(2)**	**(3)**	**(4)**
City lockdown (complete lockdown/partial lockdown)	−0.132***	−0.132***		
	(0.037)	(0.037)		
City lockdown (complete lockdown/partial lockdown/checkpoints)			−0.070**	−0.072**
			(0.032)	(0.033)
Community lockdown		−0.012		0.010
		(0.017)		(0.019)
Log (1 + confirmed cases of Covid-19)	−0.006	−0.006	−0.004	−0.005
	(0.006)	(0.006)	(0.006)	(0.006)
City lockdown + community lockdown (F-test)		−0.144***		−0.062*
Individual fixed effect	Yes	Yes	Yes	Yes
Date fixed effect	Yes	Yes	Yes	Yes
Observations	673,618			
No. of individuals	5,027			
R2	0.681	0.681	0.681	0.681

* significant at 10 per cent

** significant at 5 per cent

*** significant at 1 per cent

Notes: Columns (1)–(4) are estimated using a daily panel dataset for work resumption (that is, return to work). Standard errors clustered at the city level are in parentheses.

In Columns (2) to (4), I further examine whether different lockdown measures have different impacts on work resumption. In Column (2), I include both city and community lockdowns simultaneously in the regression. The inclusion of the community lockdown dummy (its coefficient is statistically insignificant) leaves the size and the level of statistical significance for the city lockdown largely unchanged. In Columns (3) and (4), I redefine the city lockdown to treat the setting up of checkpoints at the main city entrances as the city lockdown, in addition to the complete/partial lockdowns, and repeat the exercises in Columns (1) and (2). As shown in Columns (3) and (4) of Table 9.3, the estimated coefficients for the city lockdown become smaller in magnitude (−7 percentage points) and their levels of statistical significance are reduced to 5 per cent. The comparison of the results based on different model specifications in Table 9.3 suggests the most stringent Covid-19 control and prevention policies were the ones that harmed the labour market and deferred the progress of work resumption.

The estimation results based on the cross-sectional data (Equation 9.2) for the impact of the length of city lockdown—that is, the estimation with the number of lockdown days—are shown in Table 9.4. I estimate model specifications for three different outcomes: work resumption, work intensity and hours worked. Columns (1)–(3) and (4)–(5) are estimation results based on the second and third waves, respectively. As shown in Column (1) of Table 9.4, I find that a longer period of city lockdown was negatively associated with work resumption. A 10-day increase in a city lockdown reduced the rate of work resumption in the middle of June by 1.4 percentage points. But this negative impact was observed only in the short term, with such a negative effect undetectable by the end of November 2020 (see Column [4]), showing that city lockdowns only imposed negative effects for a relatively short period. In Column (2), I estimate the effect of city lockdowns on work intensity. There, the coefficient for the length of city lockdown is negative and statistically significant. An additional 10 days of city lockdown was associated with a 1.9 per cent reduction in the workload percentage (compared with the same period in 2019). As for hours worked (in Columns [3] and [5]), the Tobit estimation results are negative but insignificant overall for both June and November 2020. This could indicate that the impact of lockdowns was absorbed by hours worked in March, having no further impact on later variations in working hours.

Table 9.4 Effects of lockdown days on work status: Cross-sectional analysis

Dependent variable	Jun-2020			Nov-2020	
	LPM: Work resumption	LPM: Work intensity	Tobit: Hours worked	LPM: Work resumption	Tobit: Hours worked
	(1)	(2)	(3)	(4)	(5)
Number of days for city lockdown/10	−0.014**	−1.926**	−0.680	0.002	−0.117
	(0.006)	(0.801)	(0.440)	(0.005)	(0.323)
L. Working at home	−0.045***			−0.078***	
	(0.012)			(0.022)	
L. Haven't returned to work	−0.140***			−0.224***	
	(0.015)			(0.037)	
L. Unemployed	−0.451***			−0.315***	
	(0.035)			(0.027)	
L. Work intensity		0.242***			
		(0.014)			
L. Hours worked			0.272***		0.417***
			(0.015)		(0.021)

Dependent variable	Jun-2020			Nov-2020	
	LPM: Work resumption	LPM: Work intensity	Tobit: Hours worked	LPM: Work resumption	Tobit: Hours worked
	(1)	(2)	(3)	(4)	(5)
Individual controls	Yes	Yes	Yes	Yes	Yes
Industry/occupation/province fixed effect	Yes	Yes	Yes	Yes	Yes
No. of observations	5,027	5,027	5,027	4,539	4,539
R2/pseudo R2	0.174	0.183	0.019	0.155	0.031

* significant at 10 per cent

** significant at 5 per cent

*** significant at 1 per cent

Notes: Columns (1), (2) and (4) are estimated based on the linear probability model (LPM). Columns (3) and (6) are estimated by the Tobit model left-censored at zero. All model specifications in this table have controlled Log (1 + confirmed cases of Covid-19). 'Work resumption' in Column (1) means those who are working in the workplace or at home, while in Column (4) it means those who had a paid job in the past week. 'Work intensity' in Column (2) is defined as the percentage of current workload compared with that at the same time in 2019. 'Hours worked' denotes total working hours in the past week (= daily hours worked * working days in a week). Individual control variables include gender, age and its square, years of schooling, marital status, number of children and *hukou*. Standard errors clustered at the city level are in parentheses.

Event study

The underlying assumption for the DiD estimator is that locked-down and control cities would display parallel trends in the employment situation in the absence of the event. Even if the results show an increase in unemployment and a decline in working hours for the treatment cities after the lockdown, the results could be driven not by lockdown policies, but by systematic differences in the treatment and control cities, such as some macro-demand shocks. Therefore, I examined the trends in the employment situation for both groups before the lockdown and investigated whether the two groups were indeed comparable. Since the launch dates for the lockdowns were clustered largely in February 2020 and my analysis could only start from 3 February 2020, the pre-treatment period was not long enough to test the parallel trends before lockdowns were implemented. Nevertheless, I was still able to study the lifting of a lockdown and test whether the parallel trend assumption holds before the lifting of the lockdown. I conducted an event study and fit Equation 9.4.

Equation 9.4

$$work_{ijt} = \alpha + \sum_{k=m, k \neq -1}^{M} \beta_k \cdot D_{jt,k} + \gamma COVID - 19_{jt} + \delta_i + \lambda_t + \varepsilon_{ijt}$$

In Equation 9.4, $D_{jt,k}$ is a set of dummy variables indicating whether city j has lifted its lockdown on date t. The dummy for $k = -1$ is omitted in Equation 9.4 so that the post-lockdown-lifting effects are relative to the day before the lockdown was lifted in the city. The parameter of interest, β_k, estimates the effect of lifting the lockdown k days after the policy was abolished. I included leads of the treatment dummy in the equation, testing whether the treatment affected employment levels before the lockdown was lifted. Intuitively, the coefficient β_k measures the difference in the employment status between cities in which the lockdown was lifted and cities in which the lockdown remained in effect in period k relative to the difference one day before the lockdown was lifted. If a lockdown reduces employment, β_k would be positive when $k \geq 0$ (that is, lockdown was lifted). If the pre-treatment trends are parallel, β_k would be close to zero when $k < -1$.

In Figure 9.2, there were no observable systematic differences in the trends of work resumption between the two groups one day before the lockdown was lifted—that is, the estimated coefficients for the lead terms ($k < -1$) are close to zero and statistically insignificant. This finding implies that the parallel trend assumption is likely to hold in my setting. In comparison, the trends break after the lockdowns were lifted—that is, the lagged terms ($k \geq 0$) become positive and statistically significant. In addition, I observed that the difference becomes larger as more lags are included, suggesting a cumulative effect on employment when a lockdown was lifted.

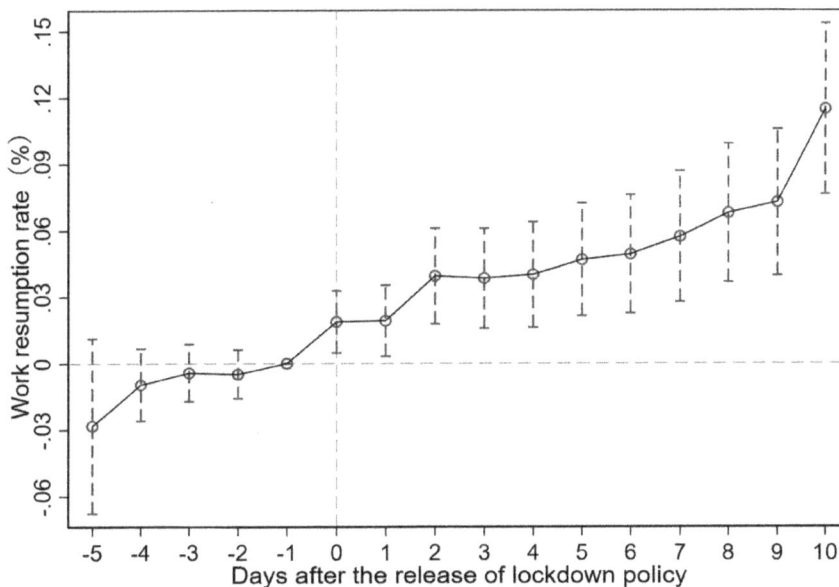

Figure 9.2 Event study: Tests for parallel trends assumption

Notes: This figure summarises the results using the event-study approach (Equation 9.4). I include leads and lags of the lockdown dummy in the regressions. The dummy variable indicating one day before the lockdown policies being lifted is omitted from the regressions. The estimated coefficients and their 95 per cent confidence intervals are plotted. The vertical lines refer to the reference week.

Heterogeneity

In Figure 9.3, I present the heterogeneous impacts of city lockdowns on work resumption based on Equation 9.1. Appendix Table 9.4 shows the corresponding estimation results. Here, I report findings on work resumption and explore the following dimensions: aged under 30, rural migrant worker, having a child under 18 years of age, self-employed and various industry categories. I interacted the city lockdown indicator separately with each of the heterogeneity dimensions in the regression (in Appendix Table 9.4) and then plotted the predicted impacts and their 95 per cent confidence intervals in Figure 9.2. I observed significant heterogeneities with respect to age group, rural migrant status, industry and those who had children aged under six and between six and 18 years. Specifically, the unemployment effect of city lockdowns was greater for rural migrant workers, employed workers aged under 30, wage-earners (not self-employed), those employed in the manufacturing, retail and wholesale industries, and for working parents with a child aged under 18 years. As a side note, I also examined many other dimensions of heterogeneity, including gender, marital status, education level and an index of feasibility of remote work. However, I did not observe strong heterogeneities along these dimensions and thus do not report them in this chapter.

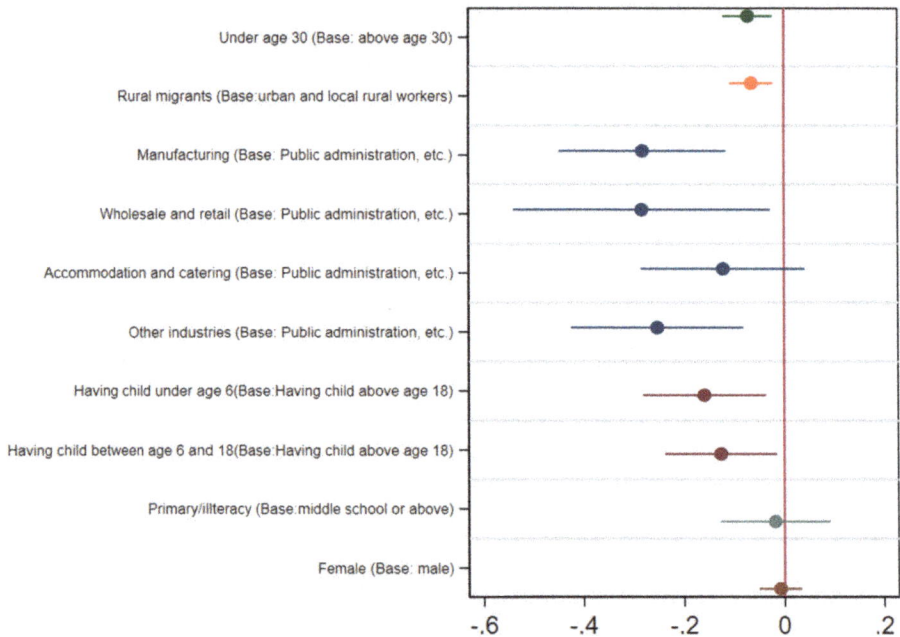

Figure 9.3 Heterogeneous analysis for various groups of workers

Notes: The numbers presented in this figure are based on the estimates from Appendix Table 9.4. Each row in the figure represents the coefficients of the interaction term between city lockdown and various group indicators. The dot and line represent the point estimates and 95 per cent confidence interval, respectively.

Source: Author's calculations based on the estimates from Appendix Table 9.4.

Estimation results for mental health

Impacts of work status on mental health

Having verified that city lockdowns imposed negative effects on work resumption, I examined whether a delay in work resumption or falling into unemployment during the lockdown period was negatively associated with one's mental health status (Equations 9.3a and 9.3b). The corresponding regression results are reported in Table 9.5.

Column (1) of Table 9.5 shows that being unemployed was negatively associated, with a coefficient of –1.92, with one's mental health status. Having not yet returned to work also worsened the level of individual mental health, albeit with a lower magnitude than falling into unemployment (–0.98). Both coefficients were negative and significant at the 1 per cent level, implying that a more unfavourable work status imposed adverse impacts on the mental health of individuals. In Columns (2)–(4), I estimated the direct effect of job loss on mental health by including the channels discussed above as additional explanatory variables in the regression, alongside the variables for work status. I started by including the income shock in Column (2). Once the income shock (1 + salary) was included, the magnitudes of the effects of unemployment/not returning to work were reduced. Next, I added the probability of infection to the income shock. The coefficient on 'probability of being infected with Covid-19' was negative and significant at the 1 per cent level, implying that going to work could increase the probability of being infected with Covid-19. Thus, the inclusion of the variable of 'infection risk' enlarges the magnitude of coefficients for both unemployment and not returning to work, while the direct effects of work status remained negative and statistically significant at the 1 per cent level. In Column (4), to gauge how the adverse impact on mental health potentially changed over time, I further included the interaction terms between the dummies of each survey wave and work status. The results suggest that the adverse effects on mental health of job losses tended to fade over time, with no negative effect detectable in November 2020.

Table 9.5 Effects of work resumption on mental health

	Mental health			
	(1)	**(2)**	**(3)**	**(4)**
Unemployed	–1.920***	–1.594***	–1.609***	–1.519***
	(0.297)	(0.309)	(0.308)	(0.449)
Not returned to work	–0.977***	–0.871***	–0.926***	–0.670***
	(0.182)	(0.185)	(0.186)	(0.212)
Log (1+ salary)		0.412***	0.399***	0.542***
		(0.117)	(0.117)	(0.125)
Probability of being infected with Covid-19			–0.019***	–0.019***
			(0.004)	(0.004)
Unemployment*Wave II				–0.932*
				(0.489)
Not returned to work*Wave II				–0.734
				(0.452)
Unemployment*Wave III				1.429**
				(0.607)
Not returned to work*Wave III				–0.699
				(0.507)
Log (1 + confirmed cases)	0.023	0.015	0.011	0.014
	(0.045)	(0.045)	(0.045)	(0.045)
Wave II	–0.205	–0.231	–0.223	–0.125
	(0.216)	(0.217)	(0.216)	(0.217)
Wave III	0.534**	0.465**	0.288	0.237
	(0.218)	(0.220)	(0.223)	(0.225)
Individual controls	Yes	Yes	Yes	Yes
Individual fixed effect	Yes	Yes	Yes	Yes
R2	0.020	0.022	0.025	0.028
No. of observations				15,240

* significant at 10 per cent

** significant at 5 per cent

*** significant at 1 per cent

Notes: Estimation results are based on all samples in three waves (5,674 samples in the baseline, 5,027 in the second wave and 4,539 in the third wave). The base group is the employed group, which refers to workers who worked at a workplace or at home in March and June and workers employed in November. Individual controls include marital status, years of schooling and number of children. Standard errors clustered at the city level are in parentheses.

Conclusion

When Covid-19 spread across the globe, there was large variation in the public responses to mitigate its impacts: some countries immediately adopted harsh counter-virus measures while others delayed the launch of such policies. I investigated the labour market consequences of China's lockdown policies—an example of a prompt and stringent response to the Covid-19 outbreak—using comprehensive employee tracking data from 2020. Here, I discuss several important implications of the findings.

First, the pace of resurgence in the Chinese labour market since March 2020 has been revealed in the study. Among incumbent workers from 2019 who were surveyed and tracked in 2020, 61 per cent resumed work in March 2020; by the end of November, the rate of work resumption had risen by almost 30 per cent to reach about 90 per cent. The unemployment rate reached its highest level (11 per cent) in the middle of 2020 and then declined to 4.4 per cent by the end of November.

Second, my findings demonstrate that, even though China's lockdowns effectively controlled the spread of Covid-19, they had substantial impacts on the labour market by delaying the pace of work resumption and causing additional job losses during the pandemic period. I found that such policies reduced the likelihood of work resumption by 13.2 percentage points. This was indeed a substantial impact. If the whole nation had launched the most stringent lockdown policies, the total job losses might have reached 102.3 million during the pandemic.

Third, this research indicates that the unemployment effects of the lockdowns were only detectable in the relative short term: by the end of November, the negative and significant effects of pandemic lockdowns on work resumption could no longer be found.

Finally, consistent with the existing literature on economic crises and mental health, I found that the inadequate employment caused by pandemic lockdowns imposed negative effects on the mental health of the labour force, especially for those falling into unemployment. However, I found that, in line with the short-term nature of the lockdown effect on work resumption, these adverse mental health impacts were most severe in the middle of 2020 and became insignificant by November. This could indicate that a sense of optimism eventually came to prevail in the Chinese economy.

Understanding the broader social and health impacts of different counter-Covid-19 policies is critical for optimal policy design. This chapter provides the first empirical evidence that strict city and community lockdowns significantly decreased the welfare of the Chinese labour force, at least in the short term. Policymakers in other countries should take these effects into account when designing their strategies to combat Covid-19. Future research is needed to better understand the welfare implications of different strategies for handling the Covid-19 pandemic in both the short and the long terms.

References

Ahmed, A., M. Aqeel, N. Aslam. 2020. *COVID-19 health crisis and prevalence of anxiety among individuals of various age groups: A qualitative study. J. Ment. Health Train Educ. Pract.* www. researchgate.net/publication/346420352_COVID-19_health_crisis_and_prevalence_ of_anxiety_among_individuals_of_various_age_groups_a_qualitative_study.

Aragona, M., A. Barbato, A. Cavani, G. Costanzo and C. Mirisola. 2020. 'Negative Impacts of COVID-19 Lockdown on Mental Health Service Access and Follow-Up Adherence for Immigrants and Individuals in Socio-Economic Difficulties.' *Public Health* 186: 52–56. doi.org/10.1016/j.puhe.2020.06.055.

Aum, S., S.Y.T. Lee and Y. Shin. 2020a. *COVID-19 doesn't need lockdowns to destroy jobs: The effect of local outbreaks in Korea.* NBER Working Paper No. 27264. Cambridge, MA: National Bureau of Economic Research. doi.org/10.3386/w27264.

Aum, S., S.Y.T. Lee and Y. Shin. 2020b. *Inequality of fear and self-quarantines: Is there a trade-off between GDP and public health?* NBER Working Paper No. 27100. Cambridge, MA: National Bureau of Economic Research. doi.org/10.3386/w27100.

Borjas, G.J. & H. Cassidy. 2020. *The adverse effect of the COVID-19 labor market shock on immigrant employment.* NBER Working Paper No. 27243. Cambridge, MA: National Bureau of Economic Research. doi.org/10.3386/w27243.

Brodeur, A., A.E. Clark, S. Fleche and N. Powdthavee. 2020. 'Assessing the Impact of the Coronavirus Lockdown on Unhappiness, Loneliness, and Boredom Using Google Trends.' *arXiv*: 2004.12129.

Clark, A.E. and A.J. Oswald. 1994. 'Unhappiness and Unemployment.' *The Economic Journal* 104(424): 648–59. doi.org/10.2307/2234639.

Coibion, O., Y. Gorodnichenko and W. Michael. 2020. *Labor markets during the COVID-19 crisis: A preliminary view.* NBER Working Paper No. 27017. Cambridge, MA: National Bureau of Economic Research. doi.org/10.3386/w27017.

Fang, H., L. Wang and Y. Yang. 2020. *Human mobility restrictions and the spread of the novel coronavirus (2019-ncov) in China.* NBER Working Paper No. 26906. Cambridge, MA: National Bureau of Economic Research. doi.org/10.3386/w26906.

Gili, M., M. Roca, S. Basu, M. McKee and D. Stuckler. 2013. 'The Mental Health Risks of Economic Crisis in Spain: Evidence from Primary Care Centres, 2006 and 2010.' *The European Journal of Public Health* 23(1): 103–8. doi.org/10.1093/eurpub/cks035.

Gualano, M.R., G. Lo Moro, G. Voglino, F. Bert and R. Siliquini. 2020. 'Effects of COVID-19 Lockdown on Mental Health and Sleep Disturbances in Italy.' *International Journal of Environmental Research and Public Health* 17(13): 4779. doi.org/10.3390/ijerph17134779.

Havers, F.P., C. Reed, T. Lim, J.M. Montgomery, J.D. Klena, A.J. Hall, A.M. Fry, D.L. Cannon, C.-F. Chiang, A. Gibbons, I. Krapiunaya, M. Morales-Betoulle, K. Roguski, M.A.U. Rasheed, B. Freeman, S. Lester, L. Mills, D.S. Carroll, S.M. Owen, J.A. Johnson, V. Semenova, C. Blackmore, D. Blog, S.J. Chai, A. Dunn, J. Hand, S. Jain, S. Lingdquist, R. Lynfield, S. Pritchard, T. Sokol, L. Sosa, G. Turabelidze, S.M. Watkins, J. Wiesman, R.W. Williams, S. Yendell, J. Schiffer and N.J. Thornburg. 2020. 'Seroprevalence of Antibodies to SARS-CoV-2 in 10 Sites in the United States.' *JAMA Internal Medicine* 180(12): 1576–86. doi.org/10.1001/jamainternmed.2020.4130.

He, G., Y. Pan and T. Tanaka. 2020. 'The Short-Term Impacts of COVID-19 Lockdown on Urban Air Pollution in China.' *Nature Sustainability* 3: 1005–11. doi.org/10.1038/s41893-020-0581-y.

Holmes, E.A., R.C. O'Connor, V.H. Perry, I. Tracey, S. Wessely, L. Arseneault, C. Ballard, H. Christensen, R. Cohen Silver, I. Everall, T. Ford, A. John, T. Kabir, K. King, I. Madan, S. Michie, A.K. Przybvlski, R. Shafran, A. Sweeney, C.M. Worthman, L. Yardley, K. Cowan, C. Cope, M. Hotopf and E. Bullmore. 2020. 'Multidisciplinary Research Priorities for the COVID-19 Pandemic: A Call for Action for Mental Health Science.' *The Lancet Psychiatry* 7(6): 547–60. doi.org/10.1016/S2215-0366(20)30168-1.

Hsiang, S., D. Allen, S. Annan-Phan, K. Bell, I. Bolliger, T. Chong, H. Druckenmiller, L.Y. Huang, A. Hultgren, E. Krasovich, P. Lau, J. Lee, E. Rolf, J. Tseng and T. Wu. 2020. 'The Effect of Large-Scale Anti-Contagion Policies on the COVID-19 Pandemic.' *Nature* 584(7820): 262–67. doi.org/10.1038/s41586-020-2404-8.

International Labour Organization (ILO). 2020. 'Updated Estimates and Analysis.' *ILO Monitor: Covid-19 and the World of Work.* 5th edn. Geneva, ILO. Available from: www.ilo.org/wcmsp5/groups/public/---dgreports/---dcomm/documents/briefingnote/wcms_749399.pdf.

Kassenboehmer, S.C. and J.P. Haisken-DeNew. 2009. 'You're Fired! The Causal Negative Effect of Entry Unemployment on Life Satisfaction.' *The Economic Journal* 119(536): 448–62. doi.org/10.1111/j.1468-0297.2008.02246.x.

Kumar, N., H. Udah, S. Singh, A. Wilson. 2021. 'Indian Migrant Workers' Experience during the COVID-19 Pandemic Nationwide Lockdown.' *Journal of Asian and African Studies.* www.researchgate.net/publication/344397445_INDIAN_MIGRANT_WORKERS_DURING_THE_COVID-19_PANDEMIC.

Lai, S., N.W. Ruktanonchai, L. Zhou, O. Prosper, W. Luo, J.R. Floyd, A. Wesolowski, M. Santillana, C. Zhang, X. Du, H. Yu and A.J. Tatem. 2020. 'Effect of Non-Pharmaceutical Interventions to Contain COVID-19 in China.' *Nature* 585: 410–13. doi.org/10.1038/s41586-020-2293-x.

Lee, K., H. Sahai, P. Baylis and M. Greenstone. 2020. *Job loss and behavioral change: The unprecedented effects of the India lockdown in Delhi.* Becker Friedman Institute for Research in Economics Working Paper No. 2020-65. Chicago, IL: University of Chicago. doi.org/10.2139/ssrn.3601979.

Li, H., Q. Jin and W. Li. 2020. 'Small, Medium and Micro Private Enterprises under the Impact of the Epidemic: Difficulties, Countermeasures and Hope.' [In Chinese]. *The Paper*. Available from: www.thepaper.cn/newsDetail_forward_6042453.

Nanda, J. 2020. 'Circular Migration and COVID-19.' Available from: papers.ssrn.com/sol3/papers.cfm?abstract_id=%203683410. doi.org/10.2139/ssrn.3683410.

Organisation for Economic Co-operation and Development (OECD). 2020. *Turning Hope into Reality*. OECD Economic Outlook, December. Paris: OECD Publishing. Available from: oecd.org/economic-outlook/December-2020/.

Pieh, C., S. Budimir and T. Probst. 2020. 'The Effect of Age, Gender, Income, Work, and Physical Activity on Mental Health during Coronavirus Disease (COVID-19) Lockdown in Austria.' *Journal of Psychosomatic Research* 136: 110186. doi.org/10.1016/j.jpsychores.2020.110186.

Pollán, M., B. Pérez-Gómez, R. Pastor-Barriuso, J. Oteo, M.A. Hernán, M. Pérez-Olmeda, J.L. Sanmartín, A. Fernández-Garcia, I. Cruz, N. Fernández de Larrea, M. Molina, F. Rodríguez-Cabrera, M. Martín, P. Merino-Amador, J.L. Paniagua, J.F. Muñoz-Montalvo, F. Blanco, R. Yotti and ENE-COVID Study Group. 2020. 'A Nationwide, Population-Based Seroepidemiological Study.' *The Lancet* 396(10250): 535–44. doi.org/10.1016/S0140-6736(20)31483-5.

Qi, J., D. Zhang, X. Zhang, P. Yin, J. Liu, Y. Pan, T. Takana, P. Xie, Z. Wang, S. Liu, G.F. Gao, G. He and M. Zhou. 2020. 'Do Lockdowns Bring about Additional Mortality Benefits or Costs? Evidence Based on Death Records from 300 Million Chinese People.' *medRxiv*. Available from: www.medrxiv.org/content/10.1101/2020.08.28.20183699v2. doi.org/10.1101/2020.08.28.20183699.

Qiu, Y., X. Chen and W. Shi. 2020. 'Impacts of Social and Economic Factors on the Transmission of Coronavirus Disease 2019 (COVID-19) in China.' *Journal of Population Economics* 33: 1127–72. doi.org/10.1007/s00148-020-00778-2.

Rossi, R., V. Socci, D. Talevi, S. Mensi, C. Niolu, F. Pacitti, A. Di Marco, A. Rossi, A. Siracusano and G. Di Lorenzo. 2020. 'COVID-19 Pandemic and Lockdown Measures Impact on Mental Health among the General Population in Italy.' *Frontiers in Psychiatry* 11: 790. doi.org/10.3389/fpsyt.2020.00790.

Tian, H., Y. Liu, Y. Li, C.H. Wu, B. Chen, M.U.G. Kraemer, B. Li, J. Cai, B. Xu, Q. Yang, B. Wang, P. Yang, Y. Cui, Y. Song, P. Zheng, Q. Wang, O.N. Bjornstad, R. Yang, B.T. Grengfell, O.G. Pybus and C. Dye. 2020. 'An Investigation of Transmission Control Measures during the First 50 Days of the Covid-19 Epidemic in China.' *Science* 368(6491): 638–42. doi.org/10.1126/science.abb6105.

Wang, C., R. Pan, X. Wan, Y. Tan, L. Xu, C.S. Ho and R.C. Ho. 2020a. 'Immediate Psychological Responses and Associated Factors during the Initial Stage of the 2019 Coronavirus Disease (COVID-19) Epidemic among the General Population in China.' *International Journal of Environmental Research and Public Health* 17(5): 1729. doi.org/10.3390/ijerph17051729.

Wang, J., F. Guo and Y. Li. 2020b. *Quantitative Estimation of the Impact of the New Crown Pneumonia Epidemic on Self-Employed Businesses: On the Value of Digital Finance in Mitigating the Impact*. [In Chinese]. Beijing: Institute of Digital Finance, Peking University. Available from: idf.pku.edu.cn/bqzt/xw/501534.htm.

Winkelmann, L. and R. Winkelmann. 1998. 'Why Are the Unemployed So Unhappy? Evidence from Panel Data.' *Economica* 65(257): 1–15. doi.org/10.1111/1468-0335.00111.

World Bank. 2020. *Global Economic Prospects, June 2020*. Washington, DC: World Bank. Available from: openknowledge.worldbank.org/handle/10986/33748.

World Health Organization (WHO). 2020. *Coronavirus Disease (COVID-19) Dashboard*. [Online]. Geneva: WHO. Available from: www.who.int/emergencies/diseases/novel-coronavirus-2019.

Xi, J. 2020. 'Communiqué of the Fifth Plenary Session of the Nineteenth Central Committee of the Communist Party of China.' [In Chinese]. *Xinhuanet*, 29 October. Available from: www.xinhuanet.com/2020-10/29/c_1126674147.htm.

Yi, H., Y. Yuan and H. Liang. 2020. *Quantitatively Tracking the Progress of National Resumption of Work after the Epidemic: Detailed Explanation of CICC Daily Starting Index*. [In Chinese]. Beijing: China International Capital Corporation. Available from: research.cicc.com/frontend/recommend/detail?id=1042.

Zhu, W., P. Zhang, P. Li and Z. Wang. 2020. 'The Plight of Small, Medium and Micro Enterprises and the Improvement of Policy Efficiency under the Impact of the Epidemic: Based on the Analysis of Two National Questionnaire Surveys.' [In Chinese]. *Management World* 6: 5–7.

Appendix

Table A9.1 Sample distribution

	Survey sample		1% National Population Sample Survey, 2015
	Unweighted	Weighted	
Industry distribution (%)			
Agriculture, forestry, fishing, mining and quarrying	4.41	9.96	15.34
Manufacturing	16.13	31.72	22.58
Electricity, gas, steam and water supply	3.28	1.07	1.28
Construction	6.64	6.76	7.66
Wholesale and retail trade	9.71	16.42	17.56
Transportation and storage	4.72	3.48	5.08
Accommodation and food service activities	4.21	2.82	5.27
Information and communication	9.45	2.57	1.50
Financial and insurance	4.23	2.24	2.10
Real estate	2.27	0.77	1.68
Professional, scientific and technical	2.22	0.58	0.88
Education	7.17	5.89	4.30
Human health and social work	4.42	2.66	2.62
Arts, entertainment and recreation	3.67	0.89	0.85
Public administration and defence	6.71	5.99	5.29
Other services	10.75	6.17	6.02
Province (%)			
Beijing	5.01	1.54	2.40
Tianjin	1.23	0.82	1.65
Hebei	5.50	6.05	4.91
Shanxi	2.80	2.38	2.59
Neimenggu Autonomous Region	1.50	1.03	1.97
Liaoning	3.12	3.40	3.84
Jilin	1.39	1.04	1.94
Heilongjiang	1.69	1.96	2.87
Shanghai	3.51	1.42	2.74
Jiangsu	5.78	8.32	6.84
Zhejiang	5.76	4.79	4.68
Anhui	2.77	3.27	4.00
Fujian	3.33	2.01	3.12
Jiangxi	1.85	1.94	2.96

	Survey sample		1% National Population Sample Survey, 2015
	Unweighted	Weighted	
Shandong	6.10	9.47	7.24
Henan	5.30	8.35	5.71
Hubei	4.48	8.90	4.30
Hunan	4.35	6.28	4.48
Guangdong	15.79	11.92	9.60
Guangxi Zhuang Autonomous Region	3.21	3.19	2.90
Hainan	0.55	0.12	0.65
Chongqing	1.89	1.32	2.36
Sichuan	5.22	4.57	5.15
Guizhou	1.27	0.66	1.90
Yunnan	1.43	1.95	2.64
Xizang Autonomous Region	0.09	0.04	0.12
Shanxi	2.61	1.63	2.63
Gansu	1.02	0.75	1.48
Qinghai	0.11	0.03	0.37
Ningxia Autonomous Region	0.55	0.10	0.48
Xinjiang Uyghur Autonomous Region	0.81	0.73	1.45
No. of observations		5,674	990,486

Table A9.2 Calculating unemployment rate for the third wave

	Definition	Number	Unemployment rate
Observations in each wave			
u-Obs in baseline survey		5,674	
v-Obs in the second wave		5,027	-
w-Obs in the third wave		4,539	-
Numbers used to calculate number of unemployed workers			
a-Number of unemployed workers in the third wave	Unemployed AND actively seeking job AND could return to work in two weeks	69	-
b-Number of discouraged workers in the third wave	Have fallen into unemployment in June AND currently is not actively seeking jobs in November	77	-

	Definition	Number	Unemployment rate
c-Number of workers who unexpectedly withdrew from labour market during Jun-2020 and Nov-2020	Employed in June AND currently unemployed, including those who are retired or taking care of family members in November	67	-
d-Number of untraceable obs in the third wave who were unemployed in Jun-2020		54	-
e-Number of untraceable obs in the second wave who were unemployed in Mar-2020		58	-
f-Number of untraceable obs in the third wave who were unemployed/had not resumed work in Jun-2020		71	-
g-Number of untraceable obs in the second wave who were unemployed/had not resumed work in Mar-2020		217	
Unemployment rate calculation			
Unemployment rate I (%)	= (a + b)/(w–c)	3.26	4.37
Unemployment rate II (%): assume untraceable samples are unemployed if and only if the untraceable ones are unemployed in the last wave	= (a + b + d + e)/(u–c)	4.60	7.41
Unemployment rate III (%): assume untraceable samples are unemployed if and only if the untraceable ones are unemployed/waiting to return to work in the last wave AND also assume those who quit the labour market are unemployed	= (a + b + f + g + c)/u	8.83	11.77
Unemployment rate IV (%): assume untraceable samples in June are unemployed if and only if they are unemployed in the second wave (March) AND assume untraceable samples in November are unemployed if and only if they are unemployed/waiting to return to work in the second wave (June)	= (a + b + f + e)/(u–c)	4.90	7.62

Note: The calculations for unemployed rates are weighted by the sample weight.

Table A9.3 Transition matrix for work status

Panel A: June–November 2020			
	Work status in Jun-2020 (%)		
Work status in Nov-2020 (%)	**Work**	**Not return to work**	**Unemployment**
Work	71.26	3.41	5.72
Not return to work (on vacation)	2.66	0.31	0.71
Unemployment	1.23	0.77	2.15
Out of labour market	1.41	0.00	0.00
Attrition	7.66	0.24	2.47

Panel B: March–June 2020			
	Work status in Mar-2020 (%)		
Work status in Jun-2020 (%)	**Work**	**Not return to work**	**Unemployment**
Work	52.99	19.80	2.20
Not return to work	0.92	2.93	0.37
Unemployment	2.88	3.72	3.25
Attrition	6.278	2.988	1.685

Notes: All numbers are weighted by the sample weight. The sample sizes for the baseline, the second and the third waves are 5,674, 5,027 and 4,539, respectively. 'Out of labour market' indicates those who had jobs in June 2020 but did not participate in the labour market in November 2020 for personal reasons. Attrition here includes both untraceable samples and those with incomplete or unreliable information.

Table A9.4 Heterogeneous analysis for various groups of workers: Panel analysis for 3 February to 15 June

Dependent variable	Work resumption					
	(1)	**(2)**	**(3)**	**(4)**	**(5)**	**(6)**
City lockdown	−0.132***	−0.100***	−0.119***	0.109	0.076	0.009
	(0.037)	(0.035)	(0.039)	(0.085)	(0.052)	(0.049)
City lockdown *Under age 30		−0.073**				
		(0.030)				
City lockdown *Rural migrant			−0.065**			
			(0.026)			
City lockdown *Manufacturing				−0.283***		
				(0.101)		
City lockdown *Wholesale and retail				−0.284*		
				(0.155)		
City lockdown *Accommodation and catering				−0.122		
				(0.099)		

Dependent variable	Work resumption					
	(1)	(2)	(3)	(4)	(5)	(6)
City lockdown *Other industries				−0.254**		
				(0.104)		
City lockdown *Wage-earner					−0.234***	
					(0.045)	
City lockdown *Has child aged under 6						−0.159**
						(0.074)
City lockdown *Has child aged between 6 and 18						−0.127*
						(0.068)
Individual fixed effect	Yes	Yes	Yes	Yes	Yes	Yes
Date fixed effect	Yes	Yes	Yes	Yes	Yes	Yes
No. of observations					673,618	440,994
No. of individuals					5,027	3,291
R2	0.681	0.681	0.681	0.682	0.682	0.679

* significant at 10 per cent
** significant at 5 per cent
*** significant at 1 per cent

Notes: Columns (1)–(7) are estimated using a daily panel dataset for work resumption (that is, return to work). Base groups for heterogeneous analysis in each column are listed as follows: Column (2), above age 30; Column (3), urban or rural local worker; Column (4), works in industry other than manufacturing, wholesale and retail, accommodation and catering; Column (5), self-employed; Column (6), worker with child aged over 18, conditional on having at least one child. Standard errors clustered at the city level are in parentheses.

Table A9.5 Lockdown status of Chinese cities

Panel A					
City name	City lockdown start date	Community lockdown start date	City name	City lockdown start date	Community lockdown start date
Huanggang	23/1/2020	1/2/2020	Wuhai	12/2/2020	28/1/2020
Ezhou	23/1/2020	4/2/2020	Lüliang		29/1/2020
Wuhan	23/1/2020	10/2/2020	Ganzhou	6/2/2020	30/1/2020
Xianning	24/1/2020	5/2/2020	Wuzhong		31/1/2020
Yichang	24/1/2020	10/2/2020	Sanmenxia		31/1/2020
Jingmen	24/1/2020	10/2/2020	Yinchuan	31/1/2020	31/1/2020
Shiyan	24/1/2020	10/2/2020	Xinyang	6/2/2020	31/1/2020
Enshi	24/1/2020	10/2/2020	Lishui		1/2/2020
Jingzhou	24/1/2020	10/2/2020	Anshun	5/2/2020	1/2/2020
Xiaogan	24/1/2020	10/2/2020	South-east Guizhou		2/2/2020

Panel A					
City name	City lockdown start date	Community lockdown start date	City name	City lockdown start date	Community lockdown start date
Huangshi	24/1/2020	11/2/2020	Xinzhou		2/2/2020
Qinhuangdao	25/1/2020	8/2/2020	Jinhua		2/2/2020
Tangshan	28/1/2020	6/2/2020	Liupanshui		2/2/2020
Xiangyang	28/1/2020	10/2/2020	Guiyang		2/2/2020
Dongying	30/1/2020	10/2/2020	Yulin		2/2/2020
Chongqing	31/1/2020	8/2/2020	Wenzhou	2/2/2020	2/2/2020
Jining	3/2/2020	7/2/2020	Fangchenggang	8/2/2020	2/2/2020
Ningbo	4/2/2020	5/2/2020	Bayannur	12/2/2020	2/2/2020
Zaozhuang	4/2/2020	12/2/2020	Hohhot	12/2/2020	2/2/2020
Panjin	5/2/2020	6/2/2020	Xilin Gol League	12/2/2020	2/2/2020
Fuxin	5/2/2020	6/2/2020	Zunyi		3/2/2020
Dalian	5/2/2020	6/2/2020	Guigang		3/2/2020
Fushun	5/2/2020	6/2/2020	Jincheng		3/2/2020
Chaoyang	5/2/2020	6/2/2020	Huai'an		3/2/2020
Jinzhou	5/2/2020	6/2/2020	Binzhou		3/2/2020
Tieling	5/2/2020	6/2/2020	Taizhou		3/2/2020
Shenyang	5/2/2020	6/2/2020	South-west Guizhou		3/2/2020
Yangzhou	5/2/2020	6/2/2020	Zhoushan		3/2/2020
Dandong	5/2/2020	6/2/2020	Fuzhou	6/2/2020	3/2/2020
Liaoyang	5/2/2020	6/2/2020	Wuxi	9/2/2020	3/2/2020
Shuangyashan		4/2/2020	Ulanqab	12/2/2020	3/2/2020
Zigong		4/2/2020	Erdos	12/2/2020	3/2/2020
Zhenjiang		4/2/2020	Lu'an		5/2/2020
Anshan		4/2/2020	Maoming		5/2/2020
Lianyungang		4/2/2020	Huaihua		5/2/2020
Wuhu		4/2/2020	Ganzi		5/2/2020
Songyuan		4/2/2020	Liuzhou		5/2/2020
Huainan		4/2/2020	Suqian		5/2/2020
South Guizhou		4/2/2020	Kaifengw		5/2/2020
Tongren		4/2/2020	Meizhou		5/2/2020
Bengbu		4/2/2020	Pingdingshan		5/2/2020
Nanyang		4/2/2020	Nanchong		5/2/2020
Xi'an		4/2/2020	Quzhou		5/2/2020
Wenshan		4/2/2020	Lijiang		5/2/2020
Dezhou		4/2/2020	Heihe		5/2/2020

Panel A

City name	City lockdown start date	Community lockdown start date	City name	City lockdown start date	Community lockdown start date
Fuzhou	4/2/2020	4/2/2020	Suizhou		5/2/2020
Hangzhou	4/2/2020	4/2/2020	Fuyang		5/2/2020
Harbin	4/2/2020	4/2/2020	Weifang		5/2/2020
Zhumadian	4/2/2020	4/2/2020	Huzhou		5/2/2020
Nantong	4/2/2020	4/2/2020	Zhuhai		5/2/2020
Changzhou	4/2/2020	4/2/2020	Hengshui		5/2/2020
Zhengzhou	4/2/2020	4/2/2020	Guilin		5/2/2020
Linyi	4/2/2020	4/2/2020	Meishan		5/2/2020
Jingdezhen	4/2/2020	4/2/2020	Daxinganling		5/2/2020
Nanjing	4/2/2020	4/2/2020	Yichun		5/2/2020
Xuzhou	4/2/2020	4/2/2020	Quanzhou		5/2/2020
Jiujiang	6/2/2020	4/2/2020	Liaocheng		5/2/2020
Yingtan	6/2/2020	4/2/2020	Zhoukou		5/2/2020
Huaibei	9/2/2020	4/2/2020	Daqing		5/2/2020
Bijie		5/2/2020	Jiaxing		5/2/2020
Hechi		5/2/2020	Yancheng		5/2/2020
Haikou		5/2/2020	Sanya		5/2/2020
Wuzhou		5/2/2020	Zhaoqing		5/2/2020
Chengde		5/2/2020	Luzhou		5/2/2020

Panel B: Summary

Statistics for lockdown policies	No.	%
City lockdown (complete lockdown/partial lockdown)	19	5.8
City lockdown (complete lockdown/partial lockdown/checkpoints)	91	28.0
Community lockdown	240	73.8
Number of city lockdown days (complete lockdown/partial lockdown)	39.63	
	(SD)	(17.63)
Total number of cities	325	100.0

10

The strategy and pathway towards China's carbon neutrality[1]

Yongsheng Zhang and Xiang Yu

On 22 September 2020, Chinese President Xi Jinping announced at the Seventy-Fifth UN General Assembly China's aim to reach peak carbon dioxide emissions by 2030 and achieve carbon neutrality before 2060. This commitment reflects China's responsibility as a major country, and is a major strategic opportunity for it to start comprehensively building a modern socialist country. As President Xi told the General Assembly, green transformation requires a revolution in the models of production and consumption, and brings enormous challenges.

Why China proposed 'dual carbon' goals

China's goal of carbon neutrality is not intended as a tool for use in climate negotiations, but rather demonstrates its responsibility as a major country. It is a strategic choice for China as it enters a new stage of development and is the result of profound changes in its conception of development since the Eighteenth National Congress of the Chinese Communist Party (CCP) (Zhang et al. 2021).

The shift from being asked to act to wanting to act

In terms of addressing climate change, China has already shifted from being pressured by others to cut emissions to taking a proactive approach of its own. In the early days of tackling climate change, China's primary focus was on domestic environmental issues and it did not pay enough attention to global

---

1   This report is based on series of speeches by Yongsheng Zhang (Zhang, 2021a,b,c,d,e,f), and was originally published as Zhang and Yu (2021).

climate change. The popular development concept was that reducing emissions would affect economic growth, which was considered the highest priority. Although environmental protection has been a basic national policy since 1983, due to the conflict between environmental protection and economic development under the traditional model of industrialisation, rapid economic development has caused severe environmental problems.

Facing ever-increasing environmental problems, the Chinese Government realised the traditional development model was unsustainable and that reducing carbon emissions would be in its own interests. Since the Eighteenth National Congress of the CCP, there has been a profound change and the concept of the 'ecological civilisation' has been elevated to an unprecedented level. China has continuously improved its environmental understanding and actions, introduced strict environmental policies and proposed goals for achieving peak carbon before 2030 and carbon neutrality before 2060.

China's ambitions and responsibilities for addressing climate change

China's carbon-neutrality goal demonstrates its ambition as well as responsibility as a major country to address climate change. It reflects China's new development concept and confidence and shows it is moving from learning from Western countries towards being a leader in the global community.

President Xi delivered an important speech at the 2015 Paris Climate Summit, noting the mutual benefits between economic growth and an effective response to climate change, and a win-win cooperation among all countries rather than 'zero-sum game'.

China's climate ambitions reflect the policy consistency of its internal and external approaches: from the internal concept of development to external action, and from its domestic actions to its international action on climate change.

Carbon neutrality as a profound shift in the development paradigm

The process of achieving global carbon neutrality

More than 140 countries have committed to achieving carbon neutrality, signalling a profound shift in the development paradigm globally. The carbon emissions of these countries account for about 75 per cent of the world's total, about 60 per cent of the world's population and about 75 per cent of total economic volume.

More importantly, some 70 per cent of these countries are developing countries (eciu.net/netzerotracker). According to the traditional development model, carbon emissions are expected to peak and then decline, showing an inverted-U-shaped curve. The commitment to carbon neutrality of so many developing countries and their determination to drive economic growth through a low-carbon model can be seen as a subversive change to traditional development theory—an epoch-making change (Zhang 2021).

In past discussions about development, emphasis was placed on efficiency improvement, industrial upgrading and the so-called 'smile curve'. It is true that a country can upgrade to the top of the industrial chain and reduce its production-side carbon emissions by transferring high-emitting industries to other developing countries or regions. However, its consumption-side emissions will not be so much reduced because of the need to import products with high embedded emissions. This kind of industrial upgrading has little substantial benefit for the global response to climate change and emissions reduction. 'Green transformation' under the ecological civilisation concept refers to the transformation of the content and mode of development.

Back to the original aspiration of development

When material wealth reaches a certain level, the content and mode of growth shall change. If a new growth model does not appear, however, economic growth must rely on material consumerism or over consumption. Therefore, a considerable part of so-called modern economic activity is, in the Keynesian sense, like continually digging trenches and filling them back in, which means high GDP growth does not lead to improved wellbeing. Modern economic activity follows a model of high growth and low wellbeing with heavy environmental costs. If this model is not radically changed, the problem of unsustainability cannot be solved simply by improving efficiency (Zhang 2021a).

The original aspiration of economic development was to improve wellbeing, helping people live a better life. What is a good life? People have not only material needs, but also many non-material needs—needs that must be met through a different development concept. As well as tangible material resources, there are intangible resources such as knowledge, a healthy environment and culture. Green transformation is a systematic transformation of previous concepts of development, resources, production and consumption, business models and policies.

Needs consists of market needs and non-market needs. GDP is a measurement of market-oriented growth content. Therefore, if growth targets are weighted too heavily towards GDP, economic development will inevitably enter an overly materialised state and a large number of non-material needs cannot be met. Such growth will not only affect people's wellbeing, but also cause massive environmental problems.

The global consensus on and actions towards achieving carbon neutrality will completely reconstruct the economic system and spatial patterns of the traditional industrial era. As the content and mode of development change, the traditional economic system will be reshaped. Whether it is industrial concepts such as industry and services, or spatial concepts such as cities and villages, great changes will take place—changes that will be accelerated by the rise of the internet. There will also be profound changes in the development content and modes of energy, transportation, construction and agriculture (Zhang 2021).

Mechanisms for achieving carbon neutrality

Carbon neutrality will facilitate an economic leap

China's 2060 carbon-neutrality goal shows the political resolve of the country's top leaders and has created strong market expectations. Whether it is the industries likely to be most impacted, emerging green industries, governments or enterprises—all have high expectations for carbon neutrality. The formation of market expectations is very important, because with stable expectations, people will take concerted action, and many expectations will be self-fulfilling, although it is impossible to accurately predict what specific technologies will emerge between now and 2060 and the exact pathway towards carbon neutrality (Zhang 2021).

A green transition would drive the economy towards a more competitive structure. For example, the change from the fossil energy to a new energy structure, from fossil fuel vehicles to electric vehicles, will make China's economy more competitive. After the Eighteenth National Congress of CPC, China abandoned the traditional idea of allowing pollution first and treatment later, and no longer worried that protecting the environment would affect economic growth. During the Fourteenth Five-Year Plan period, China's economy has maintained a relatively high growth rate and environmental quality has been greatly improved. Protecting the environment can improve people's wellbeing—something that cannot be measured by the market. These improvements may not be reflected in terms of GDP but they are felt by residents as intangible improvements in wellbeing (Zhang 2021).

Carbon neutrality and the beginning of a new journey

The global consensus on and action towards carbon neutrality mark the end of the traditional industrial era and the beginning of a new era of green development. This historic change coincides with China beginning on a journey towards building a modern socialist country. For China, this is a historic opportunity. In the past, when the Chinese talked about realising modernisation, they were mostly talking about catching up with Western countries. However, the new standard of modernisation, in which humans and nature coexist in harmony, is something the West has not achieved yet. For example, developed countries have high carbon emissions and poor performance on the UN Sustainable Development Goals. This means China could narrow the gap with developed countries in the competition for a green transition.

In the new era of green development, China has advantages in many industries, including photovoltaics, wind energy, electric vehicles, robotics, 5G and internet technology, high-speed rail and ultra-high-voltage energy transmission. China now has 372 million cars on its roads, with annual car sales of about 25 million. There is a huge growth opportunity in switching these to electric vehicles. What is more important is the change in lifestyle this will generate (Zhang 2021).

Just as it was difficult to imagine 40 years ago the tremendous changes reform and opening-up would bring, China is likely to create a new green development miracle between now and reaching carbon neutrality in 2060. Over the past 40 years, China has learnt much from the experiences of Western economic and industrial development, but this model is unsustainable. In the next 40 years, China will embark on a new journey of sustainable and green development. If the Industrial Revolution was the West's major contribution to the world, the green development revolution could provide China with an opportunity to make new and major contributions to the world (Zhang 2021).

The 'dual carbon' goals and challenges for China's manufacturing transformation

The proportion of fossil fuel energy in China is as high as 85 per cent and industry is responsible for about 70 per cent of carbon emissions; therefore, the most direct challenge to achieving the country's dual carbon goals will be the transformation of energy and industry. According to the 'Working Guidance' for peak carbon emissions and carbon neutrality issued by the CPC Central Committee and the State Council on 22 September 2021, the proportion of non–fossil fuel energy consumption will reach about 20 per cent by 2025 and 25 per cent by 2030, and the total installed capacity of wind and solar power generation will reach more than 1.2 billion kilowatts. By 2060, the proportion of non–fossil fuel energy consumption will exceed 80 per cent. There has been much research and scenario analysis of China's energy transition. In this chapter, we will focus on China's dual carbon goals and its manufacturing industry (Zhang 2021).

The biggest challenge to China's manufacturing industry is how to simultaneously achieve the dual goals of peak carbon and carbon neutrality, maintain manufacturing's share in the economy as the government set and GDP growth. In 2020, the manufacturing industry accounted for 27 per cent of Chinese GDP; GDP will double in 2035, from RMB100 trillion in 2020 to about RMB200 trillion. If manufacturing's share in the economy is kept stable and peak carbon is achieved by 2030 (the industrial peak would occur earlier), the GDP of the newly added RMB27 trillion manufacturing industry in the future will almost see zero carbon emissions in 2035. This is an enormous challenge. At present, industrial carbon emissions (including energy sector) account for 70 per cent of China's total, and come mainly from six high-energy-consuming industries. If direct, indirect and processing emissions are included, the emissions from these industries are about 80 per cent of the total industrial carbon emissions. Achieving the above three goals will largely depend on the transformation of the manufacturing industry. Manufacturing cannot develop in the way as it has in the past; it must greatly increase the value added of products.

Will carbon neutrality increase the cost of manufacturing in China? In terms of overall costs, the green transition will bring reductions across the whole society. Costs here include external, hidden, long-term and opportunity costs and lost wellbeing—costs not previously reflected in commodity prices. Under the traditional development model, companies appeared to have lower costs and higher efficiency, but once the above costs are considered, the traditional model produces a high-cost economy. The green transition is largely about 'recalculating the ledger' by factoring in all costs. As a result, many concepts will have to be redefined and the policy implications will be significant. Since 2010, China has been the world's largest manufacturer—the world's factory—but it bore the environmental costs, maintaining the competitiveness of its manufacturing industry at the expense of the environment and people's wellbeing.

If carbon emissions are included in costs, will this reduce the relative competitiveness of China's manufacturing industry globally? In general, no, because it is not just China that is now working towards carbon neutrality; it is being implemented globally. The overall competitiveness of China's manufacturing industry will not decline due to the dual carbon goals, but certain industries and products will be affected. However, in other emerging fields, such as solar and wind energy and smart electric vehicles, the dual carbon goals will greatly enhance the global competitiveness of Chinese manufacturing.

The dual carbon goals are expected to bring about a substantial adjustment in relative prices. The green transition will mean a substantial adjustment in the economic structure, the share of the high-carbon economy will decrease and that of the low-carbon economy will increase. This adjustment will be achieved through changes in the relative prices of high-carbon and low-carbon products: the price of the former will rise, while that of the latter will fall. This is the process of re-optimising the allocation of resources across the whole society. It can be expected that the costs of producing, and prices for, high-carbon industrial products will continue to increase in the future, while demand will decrease. At the same time, the prices of products in emerging green industries, such as new energy and smart electric vehicles, are falling sharply, and the cost of new energy will be very low in the future (Zhang 2021).

Incorporating the 'dual carbon' goals into the ecological civilisation plan

On 15 March 2021, President Xi presided over the ninth meeting of the Central Finance and Economics Committee, emphasising the need to incorporate peak carbon and carbon neutrality into the overall planning for China's ecological civilisation. Many people understand carbon neutrality as simply an issue of replacing fossil fuel energy with new energy and do not realise that carbon neutrality will require a comprehensive and profound transformation of modes of production and lifestyles. Only by integrating it into the overall planning for the ecological civilisation will the goal of carbon neutrality be achieved (Zhang 2021).

Why should carbon neutrality be incorporated into ecological civilisation planning?

If carbon neutrality is not incorporated into planning for the ecological civilisation, it will be difficult to achieve. The prerequisite for carbon neutrality is the replacement of fossil fuels with new energy, but this requires a systemic shift. For example, the transformation of energy must involve the government's systems of environmental supervision, pricing, carbon emissions trading and green technology innovation, its business model, electrification of energy users, financial, fiscal and taxation systems, and performance assessment. It also involves other areas such as transport systems. The exclusion of any one of these could make the transformation impossible.

If carbon neutrality is not incorporated into ecological civilisation planning, mistakes could be made in the promotion of carbon neutrality. What we really need to solve is the traditional, unsustainable development model, which leads to climate change, high resource consumption, biodiversity loss and environmental pollution. Climate change is only one aspect of unsustainable development and addressing it must also facilitate the solution of other problems of unsustainability. Without incorporation into planning for the ecological civilisation, carbon neutrality will not necessarily promote the solution of other issues of unsustainability and it could even exacerbate the problems. In addition to the climate system, the collapse of any one of the subsystems such as biodiversity, the environment and resources could lead to the collapse of the global ecological system.

Pollution control and carbon reduction must be mutually reinforcing

Although the transition to new energy will greatly reduce carbon emissions, the production of the infrastructure and equipment required for it will entail extensive resource consumption and potentially cause its own environmental damage. At present, people pay more attention to the carbon emissions of new energy generation itself, ignoring the rapid development of new related industries that will bring about a substantial increase in demand for critical minerals and other resources. According to a report of the International Energy Agency (IEA 2021), the demand for minerals in photovoltaic power generation is about five times that for gas power generation to produce the same amount of electricity; the demand for minerals to produce an electric vehicle is six times that for conventional cars. Achieving the global 2050 net-zero carbon emissions target will increase total mineral demand sixfold. Therefore, solving climate change will reduce consumption of some resources and address some environmental problems—for example, reducing the burning of coal will also improve air quality—but it will increase consumption of other resources and could cause new environmental issues.

So, assuming we have completely shifted to renewable energy, the cost of which is far lower than that of fossil fuel energy, this does not mean the problem of unsustainability is solved, because the use of new energy will also bring significant resource consumption and environmental damage. For example, with lower energy prices, people will use more electric appliances. Even if the production and use of these appliances do not emit carbon dioxide, the production process will consume resources and have other impacts on the environment. The more energy used, the more resource consumption and pollution problems it brings.

The strategy and mechanism for achieving carbon neutrality

To realise its dual carbon goals, China has introduced the '1+N' measures and formulated a detailed timetable and roadmap.

The carbon-neutral strategy

To achieve carbon neutrality, it is important to really understand the substance of carbon neutrality so as to strategically avoid a wrong path. Other issues are of a more technical nature and are relatively easy to solve (Zhang 2021).

One issue is confidence. Since China's industrialisation is not yet complete, some people worry about whether the carbon neutrality goal will hinder this process. Economists usually believe in the power of the market and that if energy resources are depleted, new forms of energy and resources will emerge spontaneously in the market. Achieving carbon neutrality by 2060 is essentially equivalent to assuming global fossil fuel energy will be depleted by 2050 or 2060. In this way, the question before us is how can we create a prosperous world under these conditions? Moreover, the current cost of solar and wind energy is almost the same as the cost of coal-fired electricity, and it will drop sharply in the future. With the support of electric vehicles, internet and 5G technologies and robots, creating a prosperous new world once fossil fuel energy is depleted should be possible.

The second issue is strategic direction. There are two ways to achieve carbon neutrality. One is with low carbon emissions and low neutrality, which mean carbon capture and storage technologies will be used to offset remaining emissions. The other is high carbon emissions and high neutrality, which means we follow business-as-usual development that relies on carbon capture and storage technologies. The fundamental goal of carbon neutrality is achieving sustainable development; carbon reduction is only a part of it. If we only focus on carbon reduction, we will not solve other problems of unsustainability.

The third issue is the window of time in which to achieve carbon neutrality. The logics for carbon peak and carbon neutrality are not the same; carbon neutrality will not necessarily follow peak carbon. We must transform our means of production and lifestyles as required for carbon neutrality to achieve an earlier and lower peak in carbon emissions. Since China is to realise modernisation by 2035, the intervening period is our window of opportunity for achieving green transformation. If this transformation is not achieved in that timeframe, we will be locked into a high-carbon state and the cost of delayed transformation will be much higher.

The fourth issue is the carbon neutrality roadmap. While China should follow the goals of peak carbon by 2030 and carbon neutrality by 2060, the situation will differ between industries and regions, requiring differentiated plans. The roadmap involves many technical issues, including reform of China's energy system, cost–benefit analysis and the slope of the emissions-reduction curve. To achieve carbon neutrality, we should neither follow the traditional path nor proceed blindly (Zhang 2021).

Mechanism for achieving carbon neutrality

Jumping from the traditional development model to the new green model will be like the jump from the old division of labour to a new one, and like jumping from fossil fuel energy to renewables and from conventional vehicles to smart electric vehicles. There are several prerequisites for this transition.

The first is the determination of the government. Chinese leaders have gained insight into historical development trends. At the same time, China's system of government provides institutional guarantees for translating this vision into policies and actions.

The second prerequisite is the new market constraints. Strictly limiting carbon emissions means changing the market constraints on companies, thereby changing their behaviour.

The third prerequisite is to stabilise market expectations, which will guide the behaviour of market players. At present, the market has signalled a clear response: as fossil fuels represent the energy of the past, financing for them is becoming increasingly difficult. New energy and electric vehicles represent the future and there will be a lot of investment into this market. With stable market expectations, there will automatically be favourable conditions for realising carbon neutrality (Zhang 2021).

Two major policy directions

The first policy direction will be promoting the development of the low-carbon economy. The development of new energy and smart electric vehicles will encounter many difficulties, including unstable operations of new energy, issues of internet security, electricity prices and other bottlenecks, which must be solved.

The second policy direction is to pay special attention to transitional justice. Although green transformation represents a strategic opportunity in the long run, many industries will be severely impacted. Fossil fuel industries will be the first to bear the brunt of transition, including coal, oil and some heavy chemical industries and regions, as well as specific employment groups. China must take strong measures to help with the transition and provide vocational training and financial transfers (Zhang 2021).

Conclusion

China's commitment to carbon neutrality provides a strategic opportunity as it steps into a new stage of development. Carbon neutrality not only poses a huge challenge but also provides a strategic opportunity for China to start a new journey towards building a prosperous society. The global consensus on and action towards carbon neutrality mark the end of the traditional industrial era and the beginning of a new era of green development. Carbon neutrality will bring transformative changes to China's economy and it is expected to create a high-quality development miracle in the next 40 years. However, achieving this target depends on whether China can realise a fundamental shift in its development paradigm.

References

International Energy Agency (IEA). 2021. *The Role of Critical Minerals in Clean Energy Transitions*. World Energy Outlook Special Report. Paris: IEA.

Zhang, Yongsheng. 2021a. 'Carbon Neutrality is a Strategic Opportunity for China, and It Is Expected to Open the Next 40-Year Development Miracle.' [In Chinese]. *Sina Finance*, 19 April. Available from: baijiahao.baidu.com/s?id=1697457997 869646643&wfr=spider&for=pc.

Zhang, Yongsheng. 2021b. 'Carbon Neutral Technological Innovation: Urgent Need for New Business Thinking and Business Models.' [In Chinese]. *Sino-Singapore Jingwei*, 28 May. Available from: baijiahao.baidu.com/s?id=16993557998815847129&wfr=spid er&for=pc.

Zhang, Yongsheng. 2021c. 'The Overall Competitiveness of China's Manufacturing Industry Will Not Decline Due to the "Dual Carbon" Goal.' [In Chinese]. *Sino-Singapore Jingwei*, 28 May. Available from: baijiahao.baidu.com/s?id=1700972656 077807508&wfr=spider&for=pc.

Zhang, Yongsheng. 2021d. '2060 Carbon Neutrality, Creating a Green and Prosperous New World.' [In Chinese]. *Sohu*, 31 May. Available from: www.sohu. com/a/469558899_100042088.

Zhang, Yongsheng. 2021e. 'Carbon Neutrality is Not Simply Replacing Fossil Energy with New Energy.' [In Chinese]. *Beijing News*, 15 July. Available from: baijiahao.baidu.com/s? id=1705336029848922139&wfr=spider&for=pc.

Zhang, Yongsheng. 2021f. 'Carbon Neutrality: Strategic Opportunities for China's Development.' In He Yongjian and Jing Chunmei (eds), *China Carbon Neutralization Progress Report*. Beijing: Social Sciences Literature Press.

Zhang, Yongsheng, Chao Qingchen, Chen Ying, et al. 2021. 'China's Carbon Neutrality Will Lead Global Climate Governance and Green Transition.' *International Economic Review* (3): 9–26.

Zhang, Yongsheng and Yu, Xiang. 2021. 'The Strategy and Pathway towards Carbon Neutrality in China.' In Xie Fuzhan (ed.), *Analysis and Forecast of China's Economic Situation* (2022). Social Sciences Document Press.

11

The mechanisms and development of emissions-trading markets: A comparison of the European Union and China

Haocheng Shang and Fang-Fang Tang

The history and structure of emissions-trading markets

Brief history of global emissions-trading markets

In the 1960s, Crocker (1966) and Dales (1968) proposed the idea of pollution rights trading, allowing emissions rights to be exchanged as normal goods. The United States was the first country to practise this idea to solve the problem of pollution emissions. The US *Clean Air Act Amendments* of 1990 initiated the first large experiment in the use of market-based regulation to control environmental problems with the introduction of a trading program for sulphur dioxide emissions (Burtraw and Fueyo Szambelan 2009). Germany, Australia and the United Kingdom were also pioneers in building emissions-trading schemes (ETSs).

The Kyoto Protocol was open for signing from 16 March 1998 to 15 March 1999 and received 84 signatures by the closing date. Parties with commitments under the protocol (Annex B parties) have accepted targets for limiting or reducing greenhouse gas (GHG) emissions. These targets are expressed as levels of allowed emissions or assigned amounts over the first commitment period (2008–12). The allowed emissions are divided into assigned amount units.

Emissions trading, as set out in Article 17 of the Kyoto Protocol, allows countries that have emissions units to spare—emissions permitted to them but not 'used'—to sell this excess capacity to countries that have exceeded their targets. Thus, a new commodity was created in the form of emissions reductions or removals. Since carbon dioxide is the principal greenhouse gas, people speak simply of trading in carbon. Carbon is now tracked and traded like any other commodity. This is known as the 'carbon market'.

After expiration of the Kyoto Protocol in 2012, emissions-trading markets continued to grow rapidly. By August 2022, there were approximately 32 ETSs implemented or scheduled for implementation globally, covering 38 national jurisdictions (World Bank 2022), with a market value of approximately US$270 billion. Some of the biggest such systems are those in the European Union, North America (the Western Climate Initiative and Regional Greenhouse Gas Initiative) and China. EU emissions allowances ended 2021 above €80 per tonne—more than double their price at the end of 2020. Those surging prices, combined with a modest rise in volume, led to a record high turnover of €760 billion, which was approximately 90 per cent of total global carbon credits turnover in 2021. Table 11.1 shows the major events in global emissions-trading markets.

There was no unified global emissions-trading market until 2022, but existing ETS markets developed and connected. Although major developing economies have set their goals for carbon neutrality, the progress made with their ETSs has not been significant. As the highest-emitting country, China has provided a well-designed agenda and become a pioneer in and leader of emissions-trading markets. More details about the EU ETS will be provided later in the chapter.

Table 11.1 Main events in global emissions-trading markets

Year	Major event
1998	Kyoto Protocol signed Emissions Reduction Market System (Chicago area, USA)
2002	UK Emissions Trading Scheme
2003	Chicago Climate Exchange (Voluntary) (USA) NSW Greenhouse Gas Abatement Scheme (Australia)
2005	Kyoto Protocol enters into force EU ETS Norway ETS Japan Voluntary ETS
2007	Norway, Iceland and Liechtenstein join EU ETS Western Climate Initiative (California, USA, and Quebec, Canada)
2008	Switzerland ETS (CH-ETS) New Zealand ETS
2009	Regional Greenhouse Gas Initiative (RGGI) (USA)
2010	Tokyo ETS (Japan)

Year	Major event
2011	Saitama Target Setting Emission Trading Scheme (Japan)
2012	India Performance, Implementation and Trading Mechanism (IND PAT) São Paulo ETS announced (Brazil) California ETS (USA)
2013	Quebec ETS (Canada) Kazakhstan ETS Rio de Janeiro ETS announced (Brazil) China ETS I (experimental, five pilots: Beijing, Shanghai, Tianjin, Guangdong and Shenzhen) China ETS I (experimental, two more pilots: Hubei, Chongqing)
2014	South Korea ETS (KETS)
2015	Paris Agreement passed China ETS I (experimental, two more pilots: Sichuan, Fujian)
2016	China ETS (National) announced
2021	China ETS (National) launched

The function of emissions-trading markets

Although there are six recognised GHGs,[1] current emissions-trading markets are referred to as carbon markets. Carbon markets are categorised as either voluntary carbon markets (VCMs) or compliance carbon markets (CCMs), which are significantly different to each other in terms of regulations, market size and other factors (Varsani and Gupta 2022).

VCMs are unregulated markets that enable entities, including individuals, firms and governments, to buy carbon offsets from project developers on a voluntary basis to achieve their carbon compensation and neutralisation. Companies can voluntarily purchase carbon offsets, certified to private standards, as part of their sustainability strategies. The size of VCMs are quite small compared with CCMs. VCMs are also lacking in regulation and transparency requirements. A lack of high-quality carbon offsets (projects with high environmental and social integrity) has held back the growth of this market.

CCMs are also referred to as ETSs, which form the mainstream of global markets. They are market-based mechanisms in which regulators distribute for free or by auction a limited number of carbon-emissions allowances to regulated companies. Each carbon allowance typically allows its owner to emit 1 tonne of GHG (mostly carbon dioxide). Firms that are more advanced in their emissions reductions can sell their unused allowances to other parties to cover their excess emissions. By setting trading rules and requirements, regulators allow the market to optimally decide

---

1   According to the Kyoto Protocol, greenhouse gases include carbon dioxide, methane, nitrous oxide, hydrofluorocarbons (HFCs), perfluorocarbons (PFCs), sulphur hexafluoride and nitrogen trifluoride.

behaviour (buying credits versus reducing emissions), with a lever to gradually reduce the overall supply of emissions allowances. The goal for CCMs is to provide pathways for decarbonisation and internalise externalities from climate change.

Like classical capital markets, an established ETS has a primary and a secondary market. In the primary market, regulators typically distribute for no cost or by auction allowances to regulated entities to comply with their emissions limits. In May 2022, the total number of carbon allowances in circulation was 1,449,214,182, according to the European Commission (EC 2022). Once regulated, companies are allotted an allowance, which they can trade on secondary markets (in line with their emissions requirements) using both spot or derivatives contracts such as futures, options and swaps.

There are various carbon finance products. Table 11.2 presents some examples.

Table 11.2 Major categories of carbon assets

Primary market	Secondary market	Financing market	Supporting Market
Carbon allowance (distribute/auction) CER[2]	Spot trades Futures Index products Theme funds & derivatives	Carbon pledge Carbon repo Carbon deposit	Carbon (or Climate) Insurance

Under the EU ETS, the most popular product is carbon emissions (CE) futures, which have the best liquidity and the largest market share, avoid problems of incomplete information and protect investors from market risks. Figure 11.1 shows the trading process of a CE futures deal.

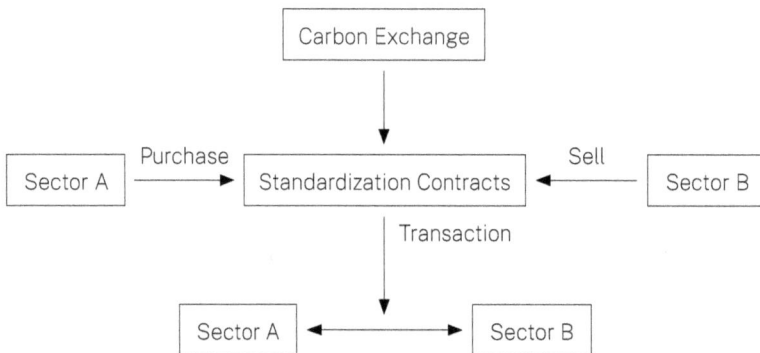

Figure 11.1 A typical carbon emissions futures trading process
Source: Authors' own schema.

---

2   A type of emissions unit issued by the Clean Development Mechanism (CDM) Executive Board for emissions reductions achieved by CDM projects and verified by a Designated Operational Entity under the rules of the Kyoto Protocol.

Evidence from the European Union and China

As a leading example for other markets, the EU ETS is the most mature and functional ETS globally. It began in 2005 and covers about 40 per cent of emissions in the European Union. It is currently the world's largest regional carbon market.

China's emissions passed those of the United States in 2005 and, by 2012, had surpassed the combined contribution of the United States and the European Union (Figure 11.2). To face the challenges of climate change and its responsibilities, China launched its national ETS in 2021, which is now the most progressive among all the developing countries.

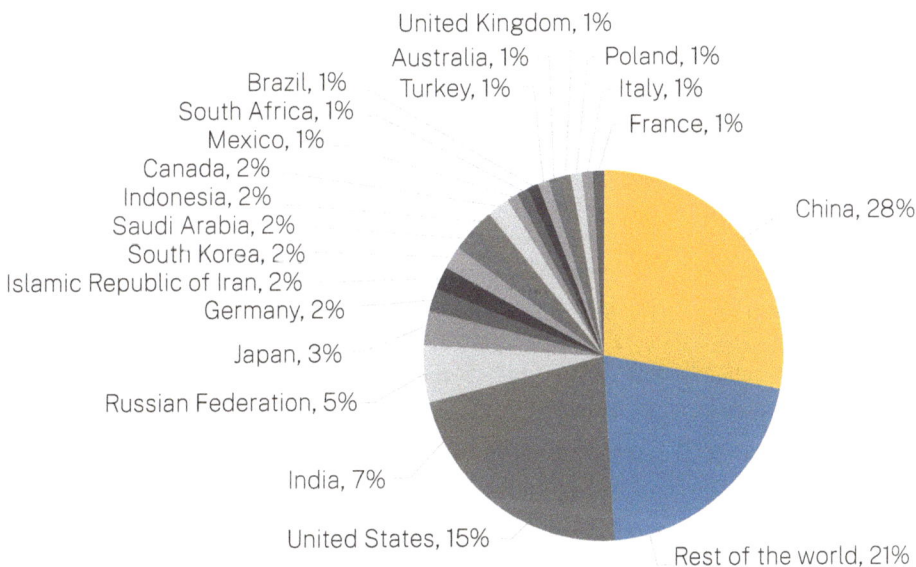

Figure 11.2 Each country's share of carbon dioxide emissions in 2020
Source: UCS (2022).

EU ETS: Playing a leading role

Developing path

The EU ETS is important through its role as the 'cornerstone' of climate change policies for the European Union. It is also a pioneer for other ETSs. In 1997, EU countries promised that in 2012 (the year the Kyoto Protocol expired), their carbon emissions would be 8 per cent lower than in 1990. To make it practical, in June 1998, the European Commission published a report, *Climate Change: Towards an EU Post-Kyoto Strategy,*[3] which aimed to initiate an ETS no later than 2005. On 13 October 2003, the European Parliament passed Directive 2003/87/EC[4] and confirmed the EU ETS would begin in 2005.

The EU ETS is a 'cap and trade' scheme, which sets an absolute limit or 'cap' on the total amount of certain GHGs that can be emitted each year by the entities covered by the scheme. This cap is reduced over time so that total emissions fall. Since the scheme's introduction in 2005, emissions have been cut by 42.8 per cent in the main sectors covered.

The EU ETS passed through three phases from 1 January 2005 to the end of 2021 and is now entering the fourth:

1. 2005–07 (Phase 1): *Learning by doing.* A three-year pilot phase aimed at creating the basic infrastructure for the trading of carbon allowances and establishing a pricing mechanism. In this period, the goal was to detect and analyse potential flaws in the scheme and familiarise members with the rules. The EU ETS set excessive emissions rights quotas in this period in the absence of reliable emissions data.

2. 2008–12 (Phase 2): *Formal period I.* Trade among members was approved to meet their Kyoto Protocol permissions. Using audited emissions data, regulators created an emissions cap for various firms and gradually reduced the carbon allowances supply. Three non-EU countries (Iceland, Norway and Liechtenstein) joined the scheme. The 2008 GFC crushed the global economy and dampened economic activity, with lower demand for carbon allowances driving prices down.

3. 2013–20 (Phase 3): *Formal period II.* In December 2012, the Doha Amendment added new emissions reduction targets for the Second Commitment Period (2012–20) for countries participating in the Kyoto Protocol (UNFCCC n.d.). The EU ETS followed this amendment and set two goals:

   a. Reduce emissions by 21 per cent by 2020 compared with 2005.

   b. Reduce emissions by 43 per cent by 2030 compared with 2005.

   The most recent reduction targets endorsed by the European Parliament and the European Council are:

   a. By 2030: GHG emissions to be at least 55 per cent below 1990 levels under the proposed 'European Green Deal', set in the Climate Law.

   b. By 2050: Carbon neutrality target under the proposed European Green Deal, to be set in the Climate Law.

---

3   *Communication from the Commission to the Council and the European Parliament—Climate Change: Towards an EU Post-Kyoto Strategy,* Document 51998DC0353, available from: eur-lex.europa.eu/legal-content/EN/TXT/?uri=celex%3A51998DC0353.

4   *Decision (EU) 2015/1814 of the European Parliament and of the Council of 6 October 2015 Concerning the Establishment and Operation of a Market Stability Reserve for the Union Greenhouse Gas Emission Trading Scheme and Amending Directive 2003/87/EC (Text with EEA relevance),* Document 32015D1814, available from: eur-lex.europa.eu/legal-content/EN/TXT/?toc=OJ:L:2015:264:TOC&uri=uriserv:OJ.L_.2015.264.01.0001.01.ENG.

Since these goals are more ambitious and challenging, this phase is focused mainly on regulating excess supply, and has seen an increase in carbon prices on the back of reforms such as the following (EC n.d.):

a. 'Backloading': a reform introduced in 2014 with the aim of increasing carbon prices and therefore the incentive to invest in low-carbon technology. For 2014, 2015 and 2016, 400, 300 and 200 million fewer EU ETS allowances (EUAs), respectively, were intended to be auctioned than originally scheduled.

b. Market Stability Reserve: As a long-term solution, the reserve began operating in January 2019. It addresses the current surplus of allowances and improves the system's resilience to major shocks by adjusting the supply of allowances to be auctioned. The 900 million allowances that were backloaded in 2014–16 were transferred to the reserve rather than auctioned in 2019–20.

4. 2021–30 (Phase 4): *Formal period III.* This phase is implementing stricter policy measures to reduce carbon emissions. The allowances supply cap will reduce at a rate of 2.22 per cent every year, compared with 1.74 per cent previously. This phase is also focused on providing two funding mechanisms for low-carbon innovations to help energy-intensive sectors in their transition to a low-carbon economy (Aither 2022):

a. Innovation Fund: Assisting innovative technologies in the industry.

b. Modernisation Fund: Assisting investments in 10 low-income EU member states, to promote a low-carbon economy, enhance energy efficiency and modernise energy systems.

Table 11.3 presents more details about the four periods of the EU ETS.

Table 11.3 Major periods of the EU ETS

	First period	**Second period**	**Third & fourth periods**
Region	All EU members	All EU members plus Iceland, Norway and Liechtenstein	All EU members[5] plus Iceland, Norway and Liechtenstein
Sector	Energy-intensive industries including oil refineries, steelworks and production of iron, aluminium, metals, cement, lime, glass, ceramics, pulp, paper	First period sectors plus commercial aviation	Second period sectors plus petrochemicals, carbon capture and storage, and some chemical industries[6]
Emissions	Carbon dioxide	Carbon dioxide and nitrous oxide (voluntary)	Carbon dioxide, nitrous oxide and perfluorocarbons (PFCs)

---

5 After Brexit, the United Kingdom withdrew from the EU ETS.
6 Ammonia, nitric acid, oxalic acid and glyoxylic acid.

Mechanism and rules

The EU ETS is a cap and trade scheme in which a cap is set on the total emissions of the GHGs covered by the scheme. The cap is reduced over time so total emissions fall. Trading parties receive or buy emissions rights allowances and trade with one another. In 2012, the EU ETS separated the cap into two: the fixed-installation cap and the aviation cap. After each compliance cycle, a member must surrender enough allowances to cover all its emissions or face heavy fines. If a company reduces its emissions, it can keep the remaining allowances to cover its future needs or trade them.

Auctioning is the default method for distributing carbon allowances to companies participating in the EU ETS. However, in the scheme's first two periods, all allowances were allocated for free to members based on their economic conditions because of a lack of reliable emissions data. In phase three, auction became the main method for the power generation industry. For other industries, the transition from free allocation to auctioning is taking place progressively. Some allowances continued to be distributed for free until 2020 and beyond.

A monitoring, reporting and verification (MRV) system is also a key part of the scheme. On 29 January 2004, the European Parliament passed Decision 2004/156/EC[7] and set the MRV rules for phase one. After the experimental period, it implemented Decision 2007/589/EC[8] for phase two. Member countries must submit an emissions report in each compliance cycle. The report, especially the emissions data, must be audited and verified by an accredited MRV sector before 31 March of the subsequent year. Once verified, operators must surrender the equivalent amount of emissions rights allowances by 30 April of that year.

The EU ETS has very strict penalties. In 2005, the noncompliance penalty was set at €40 per unit (of carbon dioxide). The most recent penalty price is €100 per missing allowance (that is, €100 per tonne of excess carbon dioxide emissions), which is much higher than the current trading price. In addition, the trading party must make up the difference in the following year. The penalty is a distinct characteristic of emissions-trading markets compared with typical financial markets and is consistent with motivations of managing GHG emissions.

---

7   2004/156/EC: *Commission Decision of 29 January 2004 Establishing Guidelines for the Monitoring and Reporting of Greenhouse Gas Emissions Pursuant to Directive 2003/87/EC of the European Parliament and of the Council (Text with EEA relevance) (notified under document number C(2004) 130)*, Document 32004D0156, available from: eur-lex.europa.eu/legal-content/EN/TXT/?uri=CELEX%3A32004D0156.

8   2007/589/EC: *Commission Decision of 18 July 2007 Establishing Guidelines for the Monitoring and Reporting of Greenhouse Gas Emissions Pursuant to Directive 2003/87/EC of the European Parliament and of the Council (notified under document number C(2007) 3416) (Text with EEA relevance)*, Document 32007D0589, available from: eur-lex.europa.eu/legal-content/EN/ALL/?uri=CELEX:32007D0589.

In theory, the price of emissions allowances should establish the marginal cost of emissions reductions sufficient to meet the cap set under the EU ETS. However, there has been substantial volatility recently in the price of EU ETS allowances (EUAs), which had remained about €10 per tonne of carbon dioxide emitted during the 10 years before 2017 (Figure 11.3). From 2017, the price started to rise. During the Covid-19 crisis, global economic activity slumped for a period; however, with the extreme expansion of monetary policies, the EUA price jumped rapidly, as with other commodities. The EUA price is now more closely correlated with other global financial market targets (such as petrol prices), performing not only the decarbonisation progress but also macroeconomic changes and policy effects.

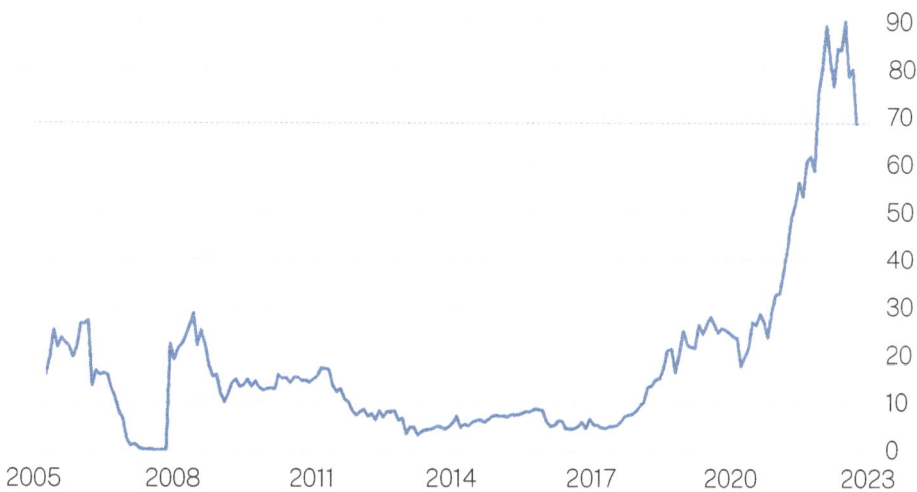

Figure 11.3 EU ETS allowance prices, 2005–22 (€)
Source: Trading Economics (2022).

Summary

The EU ETS is the most established and functional among existing emissions-trading markets. We could learn much from its progress.

First, the establishment of the EU ETS relied on stable political and economic goals, especially the European Union's commitment to addressing climate change. However, the 2022 global energy crisis caused by the war in Ukraine and high inflation in the European Union has placed a drag on the climate agenda. Many European countries have put their strict climate commitments aside to increase the share of coal-fired electricity. It is uncertain whether these actions will impact the EU ETS.

Second, a unified and developed financial system has also been critical to the scheme's success. The carbon allowances and other financial products are priced in euros (€), so all EU members can trade without additional financial burdens.

Third, the EU experience may not transfer easily to other regions—for example, it would be much harder to build a unified Asian trading scheme. The financial systems in Asia (especially in large economies like China and Japan) are not connected and there is no single regional currency, making cross-border trading much more difficult. In addition, the economic conditions, population structure and industry advantages among Asian countries are very different to those in Europe, with widely varying levels of emissions. Countries like India and Vietnam are still undergoing rapid industrialisation and emit a lot of GHGs, while Japan has already entered its post-industrial era. As of August 2022, although there were several domestic emissions-trading markets—in China, Japan and South Korea—there was no plan for a unified regional market in Asia.

The moral and political responsibilities to act on climate change were also an important motivation for the establishment of the EU ETS. Unlike naturally formed financial markets, an ETS is an artificial system, born from concerns about climate change and the goal of net-zero emissions. The European Union wants a sustainable and environmentally friendly economy, and the ETS is a tool for achieving that ambition. From a political perspective, cooperation on combatting the climate crisis is free from most international controversies. The pioneer status of the EU ETS gives the European Union a political tool to leverage other economic issues and enforce its power discourse.

However, not all major countries are willing to accept their responsibilities or have an interest in developing an ETS. As a large emitter, the United States has significant responsibilities and nearly all the advantages for founding a national market: robust financial systems, advanced environmental technologies and potential to provide transparent emissions data. However, on 4 August 2017, the Trump administration delivered an official notice to the United Nations that the United States intended to withdraw from the Paris Agreement as soon as it was legally able to do so. Although the Biden administration re-joined the Paris Agreement and committed to providing leadership on climate change issues, there is still no national ETS in the United States.

Fourth, an additional virtue of the EU ETS is as an example of a mature ETS to encourage global progress and cooperation on establishing such schemes.

In 2014–17, the European Commission cooperated with China on a three-year project to support the design and implementation of emissions trading in China. The project provided technical assistance for capacity-building and supported the seven existing regional pilot systems and the establishment of a national ETS.

In their joint statement on climate change at the European Union – China summit in 2015, the European Union and China agreed to further enhance their bilateral cooperation on carbon markets. Against this background, the European Commission and China's National Development and Reform Commission agreed on a new project for 2017–20, the Platform for Policy Dialogue and Cooperation between EU and China on Emissions Trading. It aimed to provide capacity-building and training to support Chinese authorities in their efforts to implement and develop a nationwide ETS.

The South Korean ETS (KETS), launched in 2015, covers 66 per cent of the country's total GHG emissions. It is the first mandatory ETS among non–Annex I countries under the United Nations Framework Convention on Climate Change (UNFCCC). The European Commission supported South Korea through a technical assistance project focused on building the necessary capacity to implement the KETS.

China's ETS: A rising star

On 22 September 2020, Chinese President Xi Jinping told the UN General Assembly that China would strive to reach its peak carbon dioxide emissions by 2030 and carbon neutrality by 2060, in what is known as the 'dual carbon' goal. As in the European Union, the development of China's carbon-trading market is a gradual, three-step process. From 2000 to 2020, China made huge progress and its national trading scheme began in 2021.

Development path

The founding of China's ETS had three steps:

1. Before 2000: *Doubt and lack of motivation*. The UNFCCC entered into force on 21 March 1994, before the Kyoto Protocol. The framework sets nonbinding limits on GHG emissions for countries and contains no enforcement mechanisms. China took a passive attitude to this framework—the reasons for which are complex, but partly because it had no domestic GHG emissions law in the 1990s. At that time, China was entering into a period of rapid growth and environmental protection was ignored or viewed as an 'unnecessary cost'. The Kyoto Protocol was the turning point for China's attitude. It realised the economic potential of action under the deal, especially donations from other parties, and was eager to join the Clean Development Mechanism (CDM) to adopt new technologies.

2. 2000–10: *Opening the mind*. In 2002, China approved the Kyoto Protocol and joined international CDM discussions. In 2009, then premier Wen Jiabao attended the Copenhagen Climate Change Conference and promised that by 2020, China's carbon dioxide emissions per unit of GDP would decrease by 40–45 per cent from the 2005 level.

3. 2010–: *Huge progress*. After 2010, China tested and initiated domestic emissions-trading markets. Instead of building a unified market directly, China first established ETS pilots in major cities and provinces. In 2011, seven pilots

were approved to start carbon trading in 2013–15. On 9 December 2017, China announced the start of the national ETS and established two emissions data centres, in Beijing and Wuhan, although no real trading occurred until 2021.

On 16 July 2021, trading began in China's national emissions-trading market, the China ETS, into which the existing regional pilots are gradually transitioning. In the short term, the pilots will continue to operate in parallel with the national market, covering the sectors and entities not included in the latter. Over the medium to long term, as more sectors are included in the national ETS, entities already covered by regional systems are expected to be integrated into the national market.

The China ETS started with 2,162 firms in the power generation sector—a sector that accounts for 4 billion tonnes annually of GHG emissions—meaning China's scheme surpassed the capacity of the EU ETS and became the world's largest. Carbon allowances are priced in renminbi (RMB). On opening day, trading began at RMB48 per tonne and closed at RMB52.80 per tonne, hitting the daily 10 per cent upper limit on price variation (Figure 11.4).

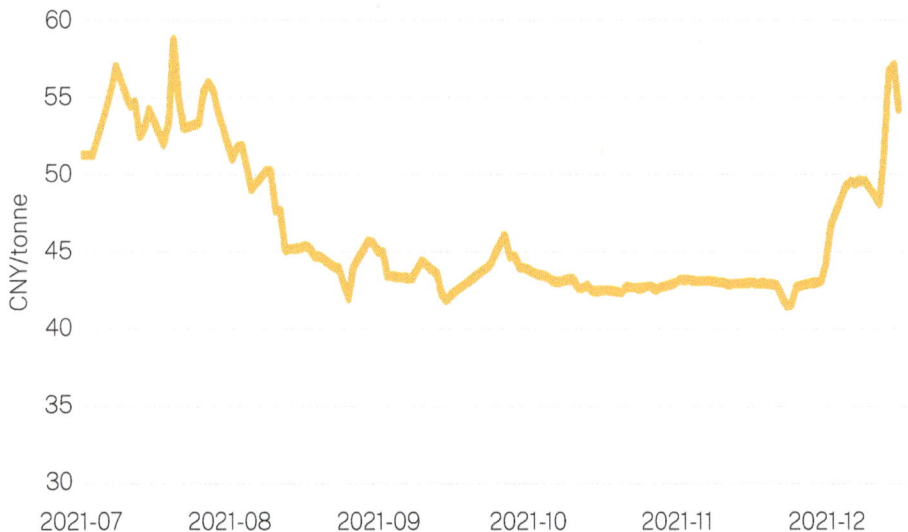

Figure 11.4 China ETS emissions allowance prices in 2021
Source: Slater et al. (2022).

In the year since carbon trading officially began, up to 194 million tonnes of carbon emissions allowances have been traded, with the total trading value approaching RMB8.5 billion (US$1.23 billion), according to the Ministry of Ecology and Environment (MEE). The price of carbon emissions allowances closed at RMB58.24 per tonne on 15 July 2022—up 14 per cent from the first trading day.

The cap for the China ETS is set from the bottom up: the sum of total allowance allocations to all covered entities forms the cap. It is an intensity-based cap, which changes according to production levels. The national ETS was estimated to have a cap of 4,500 metric tonnes of carbon dioxide equivalent per annum for 2019 and 2020. The Draft Interim Regulations published by the MEE in 2021 outlined the possibility of centralised development of a cap and allocation plan, implying the potential for a top-down process for cap-setting in future.

The allowance allocation for the China ETS has two levels (ICAP 2022):

- Free allocation. Benchmarking is used as the main allocation method, with four distinct benchmarks: conventional coal plants below 300 MW, conventional coal plants above 300 MW, unconventional coal and natural gas. Entities received allowances at 70 per cent of their 2018 output multiplied by the corresponding benchmark factor. Allocation was subsequently adjusted to reflect actual generation in 2019 and 2020. A unit load (output) adjustment factor distributed more allowances for entities operating at load rates lower than 85 per cent.

- Auctioning. Allocation currently occurs through free allocation, but the Draft Interim Regulations clarify that auctioning will be introduced and gradually expanded. There is currently no timeline for this.

Transactions in the China ETS have two distinct stages: those taking place from July to September representing a preparation phase, and real trading, from October to mid-December. With covered entities having received their allowances gradually from the MEE over the course of the year, demand picked up in October to mid-December as operators with a shortage began searching for allowances to buy.

The China ETS's MRV system was built and tested during the first compliance cycle. According to the MEE, the first year's compliance rate was 99.5 per cent. Failure to comply with the ETS requirements can result in a penalty of RMB100,000–500,000 for a firm, in addition to having to make up the difference in the following year. This is much lower than the penalties under the EU ETS.

The MEE has indicated that other sectors with high emissions intensity, such as steel, metal, mining and petrochemicals, will be included in the ETS before 2025.

Characteristics

The structure of the China ETS is very similar to the EU ETS. The ETS pilots provided rich lessons and experiences for establishing the national scheme. Operation of the national ETS during the first compliance cycle was stable, but it is still an experimental project compared with the EU ETS. Given China's large share of GHG emissions, it has a long way to go to expand and regulate the scheme.

High level of compliance

Back in 2013, the compliance rate was not ideal and nearly all the pilot schemes experienced delays in compliance—possibly because of the lack of experience among the covered entities; the weak penalties could be another reason. In 2015, most pilots completed their compliance obligations on time. Tables 11.4 and 11.5 present the compliance summaries for 2013 and 2015, respectively.

The first cycle of the national ETS has maintained the pilot schemes' high rates of compliance. We can expect that after a better MRV system and stricter penalties are established, the level of compliance will continue to grow even as more sectors are covered.

Table 11.4 China ETS pilots summary of compliance, 2013

	Compliance due date	Compliance rate	Announcement	Penalty
Shanghai	30 June	100% (191/191)	Rate announced 30 June	n/a
Shenzhen	30 June (extended to 10 July)	99.4% (631/635)	Compliance entity list announced 3 July	n/a
Guangdong	15 July	98.9% (182/184)	Rate announced 15 July; entity list announced 6 August	2 entities
Tianjin	31 May (extended to 25 July)	96.5% (110/114)	Rate announced 28 July; entity list announced 15 August	n/a
Beijing	15 June	97.1% (403/415)	Entity list announced 19 June; rate announced early September	12 entities

Table 11.5 China ETS pilots summary of compliance, 2015

	Expected compliance date	Compliance date	Compliance rate
Shanghai	30 June	30 June	100% (191/191)
Shenzhen	2 June	30 June	99.8% (635/636)
Guangdong	2 June	8 July	100% (186/186)
Tianjin	31 May	1 July	100% (109/109)
Beijing	15 June	15 June	99%

Trading volume grows rapidly, but liquidity is low

Before the establishment of the national ETS, the trading volumes in the pilot schemes were quite small. According to the 2019 annual report of the International Carbon Action Partnership (ICAP), as of 31 December 2018, the accumulated trading volume in all pilot schemes reached 282 million tonnes of carbon dioxide equivalent. Guangdong's scheme—the largest pilot—made up the largest share of trading volume (94.3 million tonnes) and trading value (US$283 million). After the launch of the national ETS, the trading volume has been growing rapidly. The first year's trading volume was 1.94 billion tonnes of carbon dioxide equivalent—nearly eight times the accumulated trading volume of the pilot schemes.

The turnover rate of the China ETS is just 3 per cent, which is much lower than the EU ETS (more than 80 per cent in 2020). It seems that the willingness and motivation to trade in carbon in China have a lot of space to grow.

Progressive coverage scope

During the experimental periods, China expanded the market coverage by adding new sectors to the pilot schemes. For example, in 2016, the Shanghai scheme covered waterway transportation and, in 2015, Beijing's covered some public transportation. The pilot schemes also lowered the inclusion thresholds. The national ETS now includes more than 2,000 power generation entities. The MEE has announced the inclusion of more sectors in coming years, but there is no strict timeline.

Unsatisfying data quality

It must be noted that there is a serious issue with the China ETS—not with the trading scheme itself, but with a more fundamental element: the relevant emissions data.

From the monitoring sample of 2021, 89 of 300 institutions (including 94 national quality test centres) had violated regulations (The Paper 2022). Among these 89, nine were suspected of providing false testing or monitoring reports, another nine had provided test results that were beyond their testing capabilities as certified by their verifying qualification permits, while the others exhibited customary violations such as not separating testing items or not following standard procedure adjustments.

Among the 94 national quality test centres, 29 violated regulations: four were suspected of providing false testing or monitoring reports, while another two had provided test results that were beyond their testing capabilities.

On 14 March 2022, the MEE published details of some typical examples of the manipulation of reports on carbon emissions data. On 22 May 2022, the Supreme People's Procuratorate, the Ministry of Public Security and the MEE issued a legal document titled[9] 'Notice on Law-Violating Crimes of Dangerous Waste Abandoning

---

9   www.spp.gov.cn/xwfbh/wsfbt/202205/t20220506_556243.shtml#1.

and False Reporting of Automatic Monitoring Data on Key Pollution Units'. It set priority on the environmental crimes of modifying or forging the automatic monitoring data or interfering with the automatic monitoring facilities. It also extended examinations of third-party monitoring institutions, comparing their monitoring reports by cross-checking, and set severe punishments for environmental crimes of providing false testing reports or distorted proof documents. Recently, the State Market Regulatory Administration, the Ministry of Natural Resources, the Ministry of Public Security and the MEE jointly announced a nationwide inspection of all testing and monitoring institutions through double-blind random sampling in September and October 2022, the results of which will be made public (China News Network 2022).

On 13 July 2022, just before the first anniversary of the China ETS, the National Carbon Market Construction Conference was held, at which the MEE announced that the emphasis of the scheme's next phase will be on the management of data quality, speeding up capacity expansion and establishing a robust daily quality-control mechanism for carbon market data (MEE 2022). We can see that China is taking seriously the environmental data issue, and improvements will probably be apparent soon.

Summary

Based on previous data and analysis, there are at least two major similarities between the China ETS and the EU ETS:

1. A large and unified market. High levels of energy consumption and GHG emissions allow large trading volumes for emissions allowances. According to the theory of economy of scale, once more countries have joined the EU ETS and the China ETS covers more sectors, we can expect better efficiency of the carbon markets. However, how to regulate a larger ETS—from data quality to the MRV process—is a new subject for policymakers.

2. Strong political motivation. Market mechanisms have advantages over the Pigovian tax regime and are more transparent. The European Union has a strong desire to be a leader on climate change issues, and China aims to be an 'environmentally friendly civilisation'. Political motivations push the progress of emissions-trading markets. Given the current climate crisis, management of GHG emissions and corresponding trading schemes will likely be an increasingly important subject in international politics.

Conclusions and further discussion

This chapter summarises the history and development of global emissions-trading markets and discusses two of the major markets, the European Union and China. Although the two regions have different economic and political backgrounds, their ETSs are successful and have huge potential.

Other countries and regions with high levels of GHG emissions, such as India and the United States, should accept their major climate action responsibilities and set an agenda to build their own ETS. International institutions, like the UN Environment Programme and the Intergovernmental Panel on Climate Change, should encourage dialogue and cooperation between different regions on ETSs and create a roadmap towards a possible global ETS. Climate change is a challenge for all countries on Earth, so no-one should avoid their respective duty to address it, including through emissions trading.

References

Aither. 2022. *EU ETS: Phase 4 in a Glimpse*. 13 May. Aither. Available from: www.aither.com/eu-ets-phase-4-in-a-glimpse/.

Burtraw, Dallas and Sarah Jo Fueyo Szambelan. 2009. *U.S. emissions trading markets for SO² and NOˣ*. RFF Discussion Paper. Washington, DC: Resources for the Future. doi.org/10.2139/ssrn.1490037.

China News Network. 2022. 'Eight Departments: Carry Out the Supervision and Random Inspection of Inspection and Testing Institutions in 2022.' [In Chinese]. *Qianlong News*, [Beijing], 3 September. Available from: china.qianlong.com/2022/0903/7588126.shtml.

Crocker, T.D. 1966. 'The Structuring of Atmospheric Pollution Control Systems.' *The Economics of Air Pollution* 61: 81–84.

Dales, J.H. 1968. *Pollution, Property & Prices: An Essay in Policy-Making and Economics*. Toronto, ON: University of Toronto Press.

European Commission (EC). n.d. Market Stability Reserve. *EU Emissions Trading System (EU ETS)*. Brussels: EC. Available from: ec.europa.eu/clima/eu-action/eu-emissions-trading-system-eu-ets/market-stability-reserve_en.

European Commission (EC). 2022. 'ETS Market Stability Reserve to Reduce Auction Volume by over 347 Million Allowances between September 2022 and August 2023 (Update).' *News Article*, 12 May. Brussels: Directorate-General for Climate Action. Available from: climate.ec.europa.eu/news-your-voice/news/ets-market-stability-reserve-reduce-auction-volume-over-347-million-allowances-between-september-2022-05-12_en.

International Carbon Action Partnership (ICAP). 2019. *Emissions Trading Worldwide: Status Report 2019*. Berlin: ICAP.

International Carbon Action Partnership (ICAP). 2020. *Emissions Trading Worldwide: Status Report 2020*. Berlin: ICAP.

International Carbon Action Partnership (ICAP). 2022. *China National ETS*. September. Berlin: ICAP. Available from: icapcarbonaction.com/en/ets/china-national-ets.

Ministry of Ecology and Environment (MEE). 2022. 'National Carbon Market Construction Work Conference Held in Beijing.' *Shanghai Observer*, 16 July. Available from: sghexport. shobserver.com/html/baijiahao/2022/07/16/799615.html.

Slater, H., D. De Boer, G. Qian and W. Shu. 2022. *2021 China Carbon Pricing Survey*. Beijing: ICF. Available from: www.chinacarbon.info/wp-content/uploads/2022/02/EN_ 2021-China-Carbon-Pricing-Survey-Report.pdf.

Song, Min, Fang-Fang Tang and Zhang Sheng (eds). 2020. *Green Finance*. [In Chinese]. Wuhan, China: Wuhan University Press.

Tang, Fang-Fang and Xu Yongsheng (eds). 2019. *Carbon Finance: Theory and Practice*. [In Chinese]. Wuhan, China: Wuhan University Press.

The Paper. 2022. 'With the Proliferation of Fraudulent Testing Data, What Will Be the Focus of the Upcoming Annual Inspection Agency Supervision and Spot Check?' *The Paper*, [Shanghai], 6 September. Available from: www.thepaper.cn/newsDetail_ forward_19788284.

Trading Economics. 2022. *EU Carbon Permits*. New York, NY: Trading Economics. Available from: tradingeconomics.com/commodity/carbon.

Union of Concerned Scientists (UCS). 2022. *Each Country's Share of CO_2 Emissions*. 16 July 2008 [Updated 14 January 2022]. Cambridge, MA: UCS. Available from: www.ucsusa.org/resources/each-countrys-share-co2-emissions.

United Nations Framework Convention on Climate Change (UNFCCC). n.d. *The Doha Amendment*. Bonn, Germany: UNFCCC. Available from: unfccc.int/process/the-kyoto-protocol/the-doha-amendment.

Varsani, Hitendra D. and Rohit Gupta. 2022. *Introducing the Carbon Market Age*. [Blog], 8 June. New York, NY: MSCI. Available from: www.msci.com/www/blog-posts/ introducing-the-carbon-market/03227158119.

World Bank. 2022. *Carbon Pricing Dashboard*. [Online]. 10 September. Washington, DC: World Bank Group. Available from: carbonpricingdashboard.worldbank.org/map_data.

12

The transition to carbon neutrality in China and its impacts on Australia

Xiujian Peng, Xunpeng Shi, Shenghao Feng
and James Laurenceson

As the world's largest developing country, China is marching towards ambitious climate goals of achieving peak carbon by 2030 and carbon neutrality by 2060. Given that China is the largest buyer of Australia's iron ore and one of the largest buyers of Australia's coal and liquefied natural gas (LNG), such climate efforts could be expected to impact Australia profoundly. This chapter examines how China's transition to carbon neutrality will affect the Australian economy at the national and state levels and by industry. Our simulation shows that although China's imports of Australian fossil fuels will fall significantly, the impact of those changes on the national economy is negligible. However, the mining sector and those states and territories that rely on fossil fuel production will suffer relatively larger effects.

Introduction

In September 2020, the Chinese Government announced that China would adopt 'more vigorous policies and measures' to see carbon emissions peak before 2030 and strive to achieve carbon neutrality by 2060.[1] This was China's first commitment to achieving net zero emissions. Since this announcement, widespread attention has been devoted to exploring pathways for achieving these goals and their potential energy and economic implications for China (for example, He et al. 2020; EFC

---

1   The two targets are sometimes referred as the 'double carbon targets' or the '3060 targets'.

2020). As the world's largest carbon dioxide emitter, China's ambition to reach net zero carbon emissions in less than four decades will require substantial structural change in the energy and economic sectors, imposing significant challenges on its economy.

Moreover, the resulting economic impacts and emissions changes could vary significantly across its trading partners, caused by the differences in production and trade structures, trade volumes and sectoral emissions intensities (Liu et al. 2016; Meng et al. 2018). Australia is an example of a country that might appear particularly vulnerable to the cross-border impact of China's climate policy change. In late 2007 China overtook Japan to become Australia's largest trading partner, and in 2009 became Australia's largest export market (Australian Government Department of Foreign Affairs and Trade 2022a). Goods exports to China grew from A$6.0 billion in 2000 to A$149 billion in 2019, accounting for 38.2 per cent of Australia's total exports in 2019, while goods imports from China grew from A$9.1 billion to A$79.5 billion over the same period, accounting for 24.7 per cent of total imports (DFAT 2020).

Understanding the impacts of climate action at home and abroad is plainly relevant to Australia's interests. First, the revenue from its world-leading role as an LNG and coal exporter is being challenged by the transition away from fossil fuels to renewable energies in other parts of the world, especially its major fossil fuel customers: China, Japan and South Korea. Second, understanding the impacts can inform Australia's policies to achieve a just energy transition domestically (UN 2021). Under Australia's federal system, a just energy transition will involve supporting vulnerable regional communities that are negatively and disproportionately affected, such as those where fossil fuel extraction industries have been concentrated (Carley et al. 2018). If a significant number of communities are dissatisfied with the energy transition, the national agenda will experience significant headwinds. Studying the impacts is timely given that the new Australian Labor government has legislated a 43 per cent cut in carbon emissions by 2030 (compared with 2005 levels). This is significantly higher than the previous government's 26 per cent target and is binding. The unprecedented suspension of the National Electricity Market (NEM)—a wholesale electricity market and the physical power system—in June 2022 was a reminder of the potential of a disorderly energy transition to cause severe disruptions to public life (AEMO 2022).

While there are many studies of the emissions relations between Australia and China, there has yet to be an investigation of how China's carbon-neutral transition will affect the Australian economy, its industries and regions, as well as critical non–fossil fuel exports such as iron ore. Most studies of the Australia–China emissions issues focus on embodied emissions, such as Chen et al. (2016), Wang et al. (2019) and Huang et al. (2020). Only a few general equilibrium studies, such as Xiang et al. (2017) and Tian et al. (2022), focus on economic and trade policy. One study that is close to this is Kemp et al. (2021), which estimates the impacts of changes in China's, Japan's and South Korea's demand for fossil fuel imports from Australia. However, most studies in the literature have discussed neither how China's climate policy change could affect Australia's iron ore exports nor the impact on Australia's regions and sectors.

This chapter investigates the effects of China's carbon neutrality on Australia from 2023 to 2060 by undertaking a computable general equilibrium (CGE) modelling exercise. Specifically, it examines the impact of China's changing import demand for some key Australian energy and mineral exports, including coal, LNG, iron ore and nonferrous ores, on the Australian economy. The results have potential to inform policymakers at federal and state levels, as well as industry and community leaders.

This chapter is organised as follows: section two provides an overview of China's climate policy from an Australian perspective. Section three briefly explains the research methodology. The policy shocks and simulation results of China's import demand changes for Australian fossil fuels and minerals under carbon-neutrality action will be presented in section four, while conclusions and policy implications are discussed in section five.

China's climate policy: An Australian perspective

Since 2006, China has been the world's largest emitter of carbon dioxide. However, in 2009, China dramatically changed its climate policy when, before the Copenhagen Conference of Parties (COP) to the UN Framework Convention on Climate Change (UNFCCC) (Watts 2009), it announced its first carbon emissions reduction goal: to lower 'carbon intensity' by 40–45 per cent from 2005 levels by 2020. In 2015, China pledged in its Intended Nationally Determined Contributions submitted to the Paris Agreement to reduce its emissions intensity by 60–65 per cent from 2005 levels by 2030. In 2020, China committed to achieving carbon neutrality by 2060 (Shi et al. 2021b). China's long-awaited national emissions-trading scheme (ETS) made its debut in July 2021. In a policy planning document released in October 2021, China explicitly nominated that, by 2030, carbon dioxide emissions per unit of GDP would drop by more than 65 per cent compared with 2005 levels, the share of non–fossil fuel energy consumption would reach about 25 per cent and the total installed capacity of wind and solar power would reach more than 1,200 gigawatts (Government of the PRC 2021). By 2060, the share of non–fossil fuel energy will be more than 80 per cent of China's total energy consumption. In November 2021, the Chinese Communist Party released its third resolution on the major achievements and experiences over its 100-year history with the 'dual carbon' targets marked as a major achievement in its pursuit of an 'ecological civilisation' (Xinhua 2021).

China has domestic interests in and international pressure to embrace early and strong mitigation actions. Since domestic air, water and soil pollution are closely related to energy consumption, it has been estimated that strong climate policies could reduce the number of deaths related to China's particulate matter (PM) 2.5 and ozone by 23 per cent by 2030, compared with a baseline scenario (Yang et al. 2021). Green growth, through innovation and creation of quality jobs, could become a new aggregate growth driver (Stern and Xie 2022). A green recovery from the Covid-19 pandemic could also encourage strong near-term actions against climate change. The continuing pandemic also creates a low-interest environment that is suited to boosting economic growth through public-funded infrastructure; green infrastructure investment kills two birds with one stone (ADB 2022; IEA 2020; EAF Editorial Board 2020). Global political economy is another factor that can stimulate China's climate actions. China holds important investment portfolios in the power sector of many Belt and Road Initiative countries, many of which have also announced their net-zero ambitions. Chinese President Xi Jinping recently announced a policy of no new investment in coal-fired power generation abroad. Given these potential gains, some have called for China to peak emissions during the period of the Fourteenth Five-Year Plan (2021–25)—some five years ahead of its earlier-announced target (Yu et al. 2018).

Amid such calls, calls for an immediate cessation of new coal power generation construction has been particularly heightened (Morgan et al. 2022). China's industrial policy on coal indeed indicates its attitude towards climate action. Along with the increasing efforts to control carbon emissions, the Chinese Government has been promoting coal capacity cuts since 2016 as a part of its supply-side reform agenda (Shi et al. 2020; Wang et al. 2022). Additionally, there have been increased penalties for workplace safety violations, frequent checks by the Central Supervision Office of Ecological and Environmental Protection and a corruption probe focused on the coal industry in the PRC's largest coal-producing province—all of which have greatly reduced previously unreported coal production (Shi and Yang 2022).

Meanwhile, China is poised to take significant strides in the development of large, non–fossil fuel infrastructure projects in the power sector. A total of 11 new nuclear energy projects, comprising 21 units, have been approved since 2019. In the wake of regional power shortages in the summer of 2022, the National Energy Administration has been actively promoting the approval of new nuclear energy projects; the construction of new hydropower projects, on the Jinsha, Lancang and Yellow rivers; as well as interprovincial power transmission channels (NEA 2022).

Local government leaders are likely to adopt overly aggressive emissions reduction policies for at least two reasons. First, since emissions reduction has become a political mission and there are no criteria for the appropriate level, central government agencies will not risk either adjusting targets or easing the pressure applied to achieve them. Second, local government leaders will tend to overdeliver on the targets to protect their interests, as the costs will be borne by the factories whose emissions are curbed, which have little power to push back against political decisions. As a large and centralised country, China's national policy goals are often decomposed to lower levels of government through the hierarchy of province, city and county. Since China committed to peak carbon emissions by 2030 and carbon neutrality by 2060, many cities, companies and institutions have proposed radical emissions reduction plans (Shi et al. 2021b). However, peaking carbon locally as early as possible may not be the best scenario for China. Due to China's vast size and the notable provincial disparities in socioeconomic development and energy systems, some provinces are unlikely to keep pace in peaking carbon emissions (Shi et al. 2021b). Interregional competition has led to forceful 'campaign-style' carbon reduction policies that harm local economies . In recognising the presence of overly aggressive moves to cut emissions, China's top decision-making body called on the country to 'rectify' campaign-style activities (You 2021).

Despite the harms of over-aggressiveness, it is important to recognise that neither early emissions peaking nor timely carbon neutrality can be taken for granted. Although a portion of China's Covid-19 stimulus has been poured into 5G, high-speed rail and ultra-high-voltage power transmission projects, which could arguably reduce emissions, 206 gigawatts of new coal-fired capacity were also given the green light in early 2020 (Gosens and Jotzo 2020). Recent power shortages are further testing policymakers' resolve. In the winter of 2021–22 and the summer of 2022, several localities endured severe power shortages. A combination of unfortunate weather (severe snow or drought, very high or very low temperatures, little wind or sunshine), retirement of coal-fired power plants and lack of timely and affordable coal supply has contributed to such difficulties (Shi and Yang 2022). There seems to be a tug-of-war between energy security needs and low-carbon development needs. The policy inclination is clear: whenever the former is at risk, the latter must concede, at least in the short term. In the first quarter of 2022, China's provincial governments approved plans to add a total 8.63 gigawatts (GW) of new coal power (Greenpeace East Asia, 2022). Technological breakthroughs and supply chain management could pose serious challenges for the dual carbon targets, too. It has been reported that experts enlisted by China's Ministry of Science and Technology have identified a list of critical technologies in support of these targets, among which 36 per cent are in the demonstration phase and 50 per cent are either still in the research and development phase or remain as concepts (He 2022). Some of the rare-earth minerals needed for wind power installations, such as neodymium, praseodymium and dysprosium, could face supply shortages. China's reserves of lithium, cobalt, nickel and manganese, which are important for lithium battery production for electric vehicles, could also hit development bottlenecks (He 2022).

Alongside these challenges, there seems to be momentum worldwide to replan the energy transition due to last year's energy price surge, the power crunch in late 2021 and the ongoing crisis in Ukraine. The 2022 National People's Congress (NPC) reiterated the importance of coal as a vital part of China's energy strategy. While President Xi announced in April 2021 that China would start cutting coal consumption from 2026, in March 2022, he said China could not simply 'slam the brakes' on coal as the green transition would be a long and arduous process. Premier Li Keqiang's report to the NPC also announced that the energy targets for the Fourteenth Five-Year Plan period would no longer be assessed annually and flexibility would be allowed (Shi 2022). Nevertheless, China's adjustments do not necessarily jeopardise its climate commitments. Since there is no prior experience for a major and fast-growing developing country to achieve peak carbon amid various uncertainties, trial and error are perhaps not surprising. A rational and pragmatic action plan is more sustainable than a radical one (Shi 2022).

As the world's second-largest economy, China's efforts to reduce emissions will inevitably affect other countries' economies and associated carbon dioxide emissions through the supply chain, especially those countries that have close economic connections. Australia's heavy dependence on Chinese markets for its commodity exports makes it outstanding among the countries likely to be impacted. In 2019, iron ore, nonferrous ores, coal and LNG accounted for more than three-quarters of Australia's total goods exports. For these four goods, China bought 82 per cent, 35 per cent, 21 per cent and 32 per cent of Australia's exports, respectively (Table 12.1).

Table 12.1 Share of Australia's exports to China (per cent)

	2017	2018	2019	2020	2021	Shares of individual exports in total Australian exports in 2019
Iron ore	81.88	81.22	82.16	80.92	81.96	52.9
Nonferrous ores	31.24	34.59	35.47	32.26	18.23	4.4
Coal	20.64	21.41	21.44	20.60	0.04	9.2
LNG	26.31	31.23	32.43	32.38	36.10	10.9

Source: DFAT (2022b).

Most studies of Australia–China environmental issues focus on embodied emissions, not climate policies. Chen et al. (2016) showed that Hong Kong and Beijing import large amounts of carbon dioxide emissions from many cities in both China and Australia. Wang et al. (2019) simulated the embodied carbon dioxide emissions in trade between China and Australia under four different policy scenarios and the results showed that a 'research and development–focused' scenario could reduce the embodied carbon significantly. Huang et al. (2020) estimate the embodied carbon dioxide emissions in trade between China and Australia and find that the increased trade volume has led to growth in these embodied emissions, while declining emissions intensity mitigates this growth.

General equilibrium studies that are relevant to Australia and China have examined economic or trade policy, but not net zero carbon policies. Xiang et al. (2017) analyse the impacts of the China–Australia Free-Trade Agreement (ChAFTA) based on a computable partial equilibrium model and the simulation results show that ChAFTA will increase coal exports from Australia to China by 35.7 per cent and coal exports from China to Australia by 19.9 per cent. Jayanthakumaran and Liu (2016) and Tan et al. (2013) indicate that Sino-Australian trade contributes significantly to global carbon dioxide emissions reduction. Tian et al. (2022) estimate that the Regional Comprehensive Economic Partnership Agreement (RCEP), which covers both China and Australia, among other countries, would increase global emissions by about 3.1 per cent. Shi et al. (2021a) examine the economic and emissions impacts of rerouting supply chains using Australia–China trade as an example. They found net zero emissions in these two countries would result in a significant decline in Australia's coal exports and a more modest decline in its LNG exports, while the impact on Australia's GDP would be relatively small.

Methodology

This chapter investigates how change in China's imports of Australia's four most important commodity exports (Table 12.1) will affect the Australian economy and regional development. We use a multiregional model of Australia, the Victoria University Regional Model (VURM), with the latest 2018 database, to explore the economic implications for Australia if China's demands for fossil fuel and mineral imports adjust during its transition to carbon neutrality by 2060. The changes in China's import demands are extracted from the carbon-neutrality simulation using the CHINAGEM-E model. As discussed in Feng et al. (2021), CHINAGEM-E is an extension of the CHINAGEM model, a dynamic CGE model of the Chinese economy.[2] The CHINAGEM-E model was developed to analyse energy and climate change–related issues in China. It features disaggregated energy sectors, a detailed and updated database, a new power generation nesting structure, energy and carbon emission accounts, a carbon tax and a carbon capture and storage (CCS) mechanism. Feng et al. (2021) discuss in detail the assumptions used in these scenarios, including the macroeconomic closure, the energy efficiency and preference shocks, the CCS assumptions and the carbon emissions pathways. Although these assumptions are made by consulting the literature, they are subject to uncertainties. Conducting a thorough analysis of each of these assumptions, however, is beyond the scope of a scenario analysis like that of Feng et al. (2021). Instead, Feng et al. (2021) tested 14 alternative carbon-neutrality scenarios by

---

2   Please refer to Peng (forthcoming) for the details of the CHINAGEM model.

varying the key underlying assumptions. They found that the core simulation scenario results, which are used in the current study, are robust within reasonable variations in the tested assumptions.

The VURM was developed by the Centre of Policy Studies at Victoria University, Australia. As explained in Adams and Dixon (2015) and Adams (2021), the VURM is a bottom-up model of Australia's six states and two territories. In this model, each regional economy is modelled as an economy in its own right, with region-specific households, industries, prices and so on. The regions are linked via model-determined changes in interstate trade and movement of labour and capital.

In the VURM, investment is allocated across industries to maximise rates of return to investors (households, firms). Capital creators assemble, in a cost-minimising manner, units of industry-specific capital for each industry. In the version of the VURM used for this study, there are 83 industry sectors. Each state has a single representative household and a state government. There is also a federal government. Finally, there are foreigners, whose behaviour is summarised by export demand curves for the products of each state and by supply curves for international imports to each state.

As is standard in CGE models, the VURM determines the supply and demand for each regionally produced commodity as the outcomes of optimising the behaviour of economic agents. Regional industries choose labour, capital and land to maximise their profits while operating in a competitive market. In each region, a representative household purchases a particular bundle of goods in accordance with the household's preferences, relative prices and its disposable income. Interregional trade, interregional migration and capital movements link each regional economy. Governments operate within a federal fiscal framework.

The VURM provides results for economic variables on a year-on-year basis. The results for a particular year are used to update the database for the commencement of the next year. In particular, the model contains a series of equations that connect capital stocks to past-year capital stocks and net investment. Similarly, debt is linked to past and present borrowing/saving and the regional population is related to natural growth and international and interstate migration.

Finally, in addition to its economic core, the VURM contains several enhancements to facilitate the modelling of environmental issues. These include:

1. an accounting module for energy and greenhouse-gas emissions that covers each emitting agent, fuel and region recognised in the model
2. quantity-specific carbon taxes or prices
3. equations for interfuel substitution in transport and stationary energy

4. a representation of Australia's National Electricity Market (NEM)

5. equations that allow for the adoption of abatement measures (for combustion and non-combustion emissions) as functions of the price of greenhouse gas emissions.

The VURM also includes a top-down facility for generating base-case prospects and the effects of decarbonisation on real gross regional product (GRP) and regional employment for 88 Statistical Area Level 4 (SA4) regions. SA4 are designed for the output of a variety of regional data, including from the 2021 Australian Census of Population and Housing. For the details of the top-down mechanism, please refer to Adams (2021).

We use Australia's Zero-Emissions Scenario (AZES) from Adams (2021) as a baseline scenario. Adams (2021) modelled the impacts on the Australian economy of changes necessary for Australia to achieve net zero greenhouse gas emissions by 2050. He simulated two scenarios from 2021 to 2050. The first is a 'base case scenario', which models the future development of the Australian economy under business-as-usual assumptions. The second is a 'zero-emissions scenario' that deviates from the base case due to Australia and parts of the rest of the world acting to progressively reduce net emissions to zero by 2050. Since the VURM is a single-country model, it takes into account the rest of the world (RoW) by having exogenously positioned export demand schedules for goods and services and exogenously imposed foreign currency prices for imports. For international trade, in the base case scenario, Adams (2021) assumes that RoW demands for Australian products grow in line with recent trends. In the AZES, Adams (2021) assumes that most of Australia's major trading partners pursue a course to zero emissions. However, he excluded China and India, assuming they took only limited steps. Yet, given the official statements and policy actions already taken by Beijing, which will be summarised in the next section, this assumption will be revised, at least with respect to China.

This study tries to fill the gap by shocking China's import demand changes during its net-zero transition on top of the AZES. Specifically, we make the AZES our new base, while China's Carbon-Neutrality Scenario (CCNS) is our new policy scenario. The differences between the two simulation results are the impacts of China's carbon-neutrality transition on Australia.

Impacts of China's carbon-neutrality transition on the Australian economy, industries and regions

China's carbon-neutrality transition and Australian exports of fossil fuels and minerals

We examine the economic impacts on Australia of changes in China's import demand in its net-zero transition. We take the import demand changes from our recent research into China's decarbonisation efforts over the period 2020–60 using the CHINAGEM-E model. To investigate the economic effects of China's carbon-neutrality efforts, Feng et al. (2021) first designed a business-as-usual (BAU) scenario to serve as the benchmark against which policy results are compared, and a core policy scenario, the Carbon-Neutrality Scenario (CNS)[3].

Simulation results of the CNS from Feng et al. (2021) show that reaching carbon neutrality requires China's energy structure to significantly change. Coal's share in primary energy consumption will decline from 57 per cent in 2020 to 12.3 per cent in 2060, while the share of non–fossil fuels will nearly quadruple, reaching 74 per cent. Among the non–fossil fuel energy sources, solar and wind power will increase the most, with their shares increasing from less than 1 per cent and 3 per cent in 2020, respectively, to 31 per cent and 22 per cent, in 2060. Total electricity output is higher in the CNS, with non–fossil fuel energy contributing the most. For instance, 62 per cent of total electricity is from coal-fired power generation in 2020; this share will fall to 11.5 per cent, while the contributions of solar and wind power generation will increase to 36 per cent and 25 per cent, respectively, by 2060. The share of bioenergy will also double, from 2 per cent to 4 per cent. The remaining non–fossil fuel electricity will come from traditional hydropower and nuclear power (Figure 12.1).

Such transformation in the energy system is accompanied by changes in China's economic structure. Fossil fuel and energy-intensive sectors will contract considerably, while non–fossil fuel energy sectors will boom.

While Feng et al.'s (2021) simulations project significant structural change, the effects of carbon neutrality on the macroeconomy are mild. By 2060, real GDP in China will be approximately 1.4 per cent lower than in the baseline scenario. In other words, from 2020 to 2060, with climate action, China's real GDP will grow at 3.56 per cent per annum compared with 3.61 per cent per annum without climate action.

---

3   CNS is the policy scenario in the CHINAGEM-E model while CCNS is the policy scenario in the VURM model.

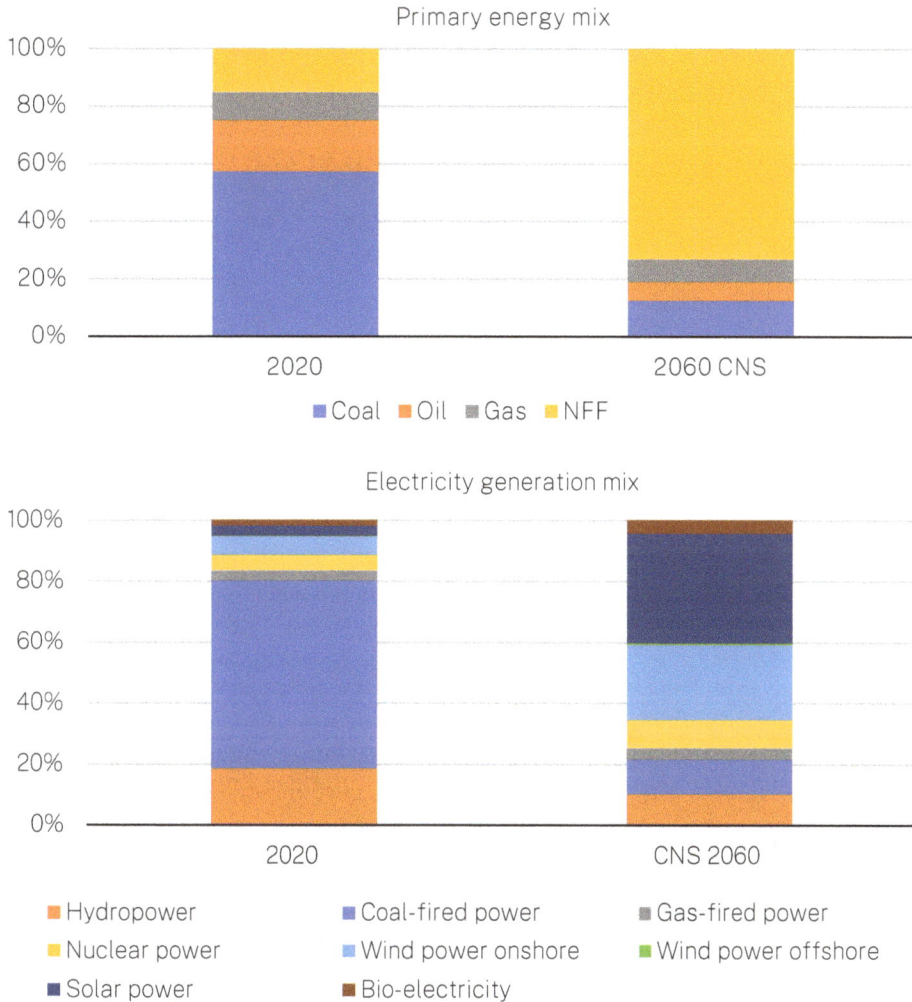

Figure 12.1 China's changing energy mix in the carbon-neutrality scenario
Notes: CNS is the Carbon-Neutrality Scenario in Feng et al. (2021); NFF is non–fossil fuel.
Source: CHINAGEM-E carbon-neutrality simulation results (Feng et al. 2021).

The substantial changes in China's energy mix imply significant changes to its fossil fuel imports. China's import demand for coal, crude oil and gas will fall sharply. By 2050, China's imports of coal will be nearly 60 per cent lower, gas will be more than 47 per cent lower and oil imports will be nearly 35 per cent lower than they were in the baseline scenario. By 2060, China's imports of coal and gas will be more than 60 per cent lower and its oil imports will be nearly 50 per cent lower (Figure 12.2).

Imports of fossil fuels - cumulative deviation from BAU (per cent)

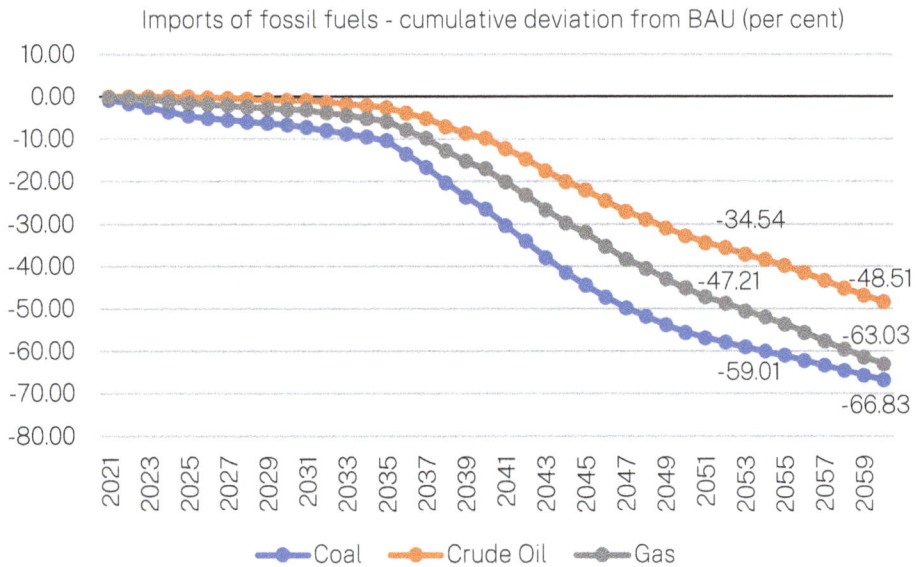

Figure 12.2 Significant decline in China's fossil fuel imports

Source: CHINAGEM-E carbon-neutrality simulation results (Feng et al. 2021).

China's import demand for iron ore and nonferrous ores, however, may fall not as much or at all. China's investment will remain strong with carbon-neutrality actions. The steel smelting industry sells a large portion of its outputs to the construction sector, which in turn sells a large portion of its outputs to firms engaged in investment. As the output of the construction sector falls only a little, the steel smelting sector also suffers only a minor loss in output (–0.96 per cent in 2050 and –0.85 per cent in 2060) (Figure 12.3a).[4] Since the steel smelting sector is the largest user of iron ore in China, the iron ore sector will also suffer a minor loss. At the same time, the price of domestically produced iron ore increases due to a rise in domestic price levels caused by prices on carbon emissions. There is thus a price-induced substitution effect for China to demand more imported iron ore. Our simulation results show that, by 2050, domestic iron ore production will be 3.56 per cent lower, while imports will be only 0.11 per cent lower relative to the BAU scenario (Figures 12.3a and 12.3b). By 2060, domestic production of iron ore will be 3.07 per cent lower (Figure 12.3a) while imports of iron ore will be 0.04 per cent higher than in the BAU scenario (Figure 12.3b).[5]

---

4   In China's carbon-neutrality scenario, for the steel smelting industry, we did not consider green steel production and the possible increase in the use of scrap steel.

5   The application of carbon capture and storage (CCS) mitigates the cost of carbon in the steel smelting industry. As a result, steel smelting production stops declining near the end of the 2040s. By the end of 2060, the output of steel smelting is 0.85 per cent lower than the BAU scenario. As its upper stream, the domestic iron ore industry also stops declining around the same time and, by 2060, its output is 3.07 per cent lower. The increase in the domestic iron ore price caused by the increasing carbon price drives iron ore users to look overseas for ore. Therefore, imports of iron ore are 0.04 per cent higher than in the BAU scenario in 2060 (Figure 12.3b).

Domestic production - cumulative deviation from baseline (per cent)

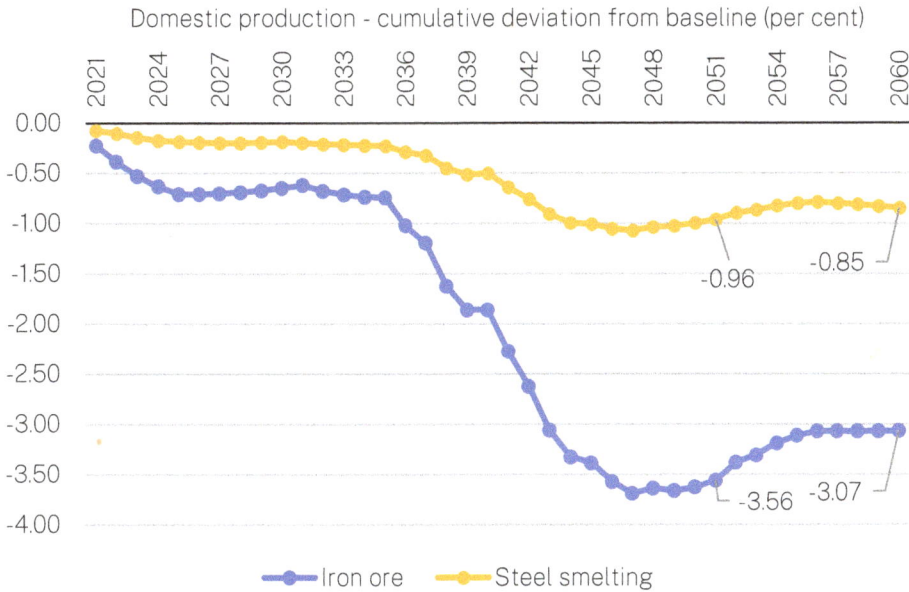

Figure 12.3a Declining production of iron ore in China

Iron ore imports - cumulative deviation from baseline (per cent)

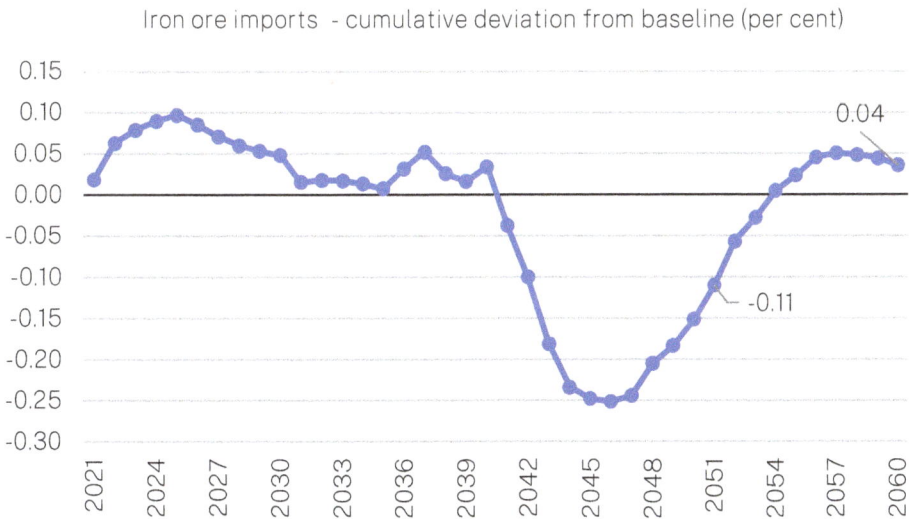

Figure 12.3b China's demand for imported iron ore

Source: CHINAGEM-E carbon-neutrality simulation results (Feng et al. 2021).

There is a similar story for nonferrous ore imports. As the main downstream industries for nonferrous ores, nonferrous smelting (–1.64 per cent in 2050 and –0.94 per cent in 2060) is hardly affected by carbon-neutrality action (Figure 12.4a). The carbon tax forces domestic nonferrous ore production to drop (by –3.31 per cent in 2050 and –2.69 per cent in 2060) and imports to rise (by 1.2 per cent in 2050 and 2.85 per cent in 2060) relative to the BAU scenario (Figure 12.4b).

Domestic production - cumulative deviation from baseline (per cent)

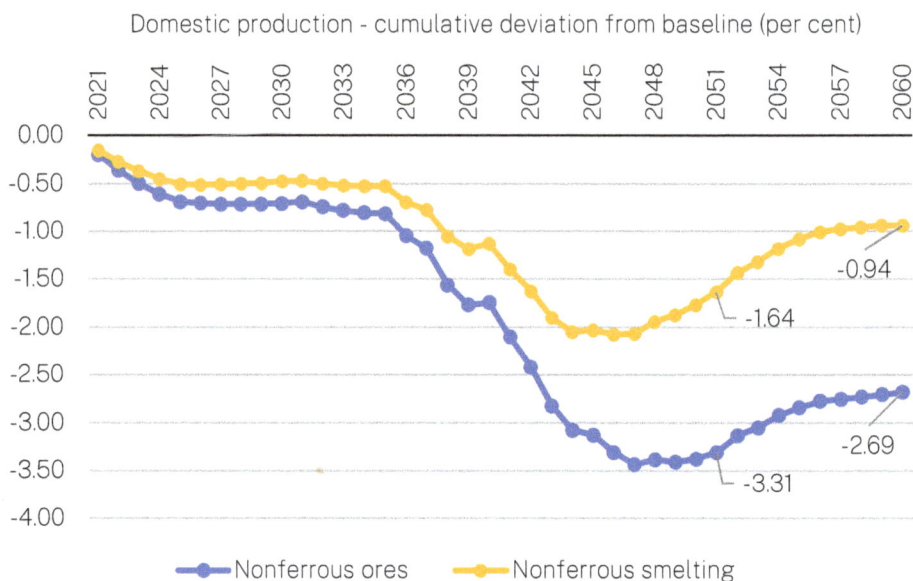

Figure 12.4a Declining production of nonferrous ores in China

Imports of nonferrous ores - cumulative deviation from baseline (per cent)

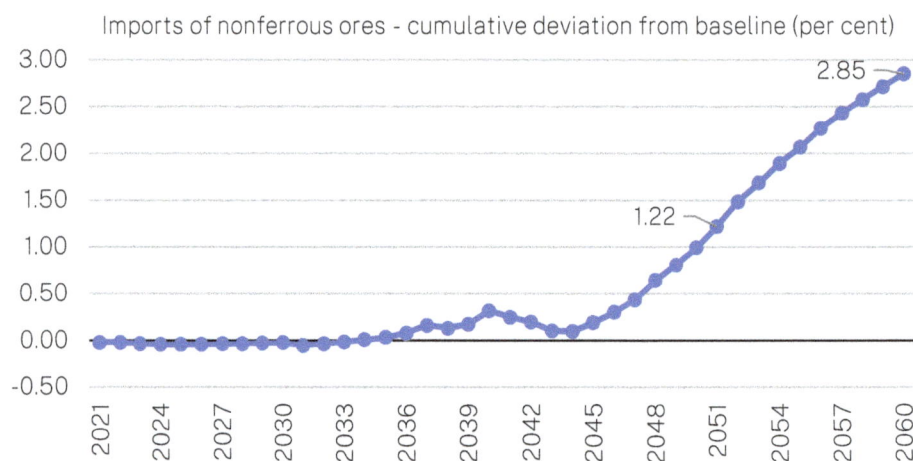

Figure 12.4b China's increasing demand for imported nonferrous ores
Source: CHINAGEM-E carbon-neutrality simulation results (Feng et al. 2021).

In this study, we assume that Australia's shares of exports to China will remain at their 2019 levels.[6] Using the shares in 2019, presented in Table 12.1, and the import demand changes simulated from the CNS using the CHINAGEM-E model, we calculated the annual changes in China's import demand for the four Australian

---

6   International trade was interrupted by Covid-19 between 2020 and 2022 and there was some trade friction between China and Australia from 2020, which particularly affected Australia's coal exports to China. We therefore chose 2019 shares in our study.

products from 2023 to 2050. These are then translated to export demand shocks to Australia and implemented as shifts in the corresponding export demand schedules in the VURM model.

We must point out that in this study we use only the results of the core policy scenario, CNS, from Feng et al. (2021), which has 14 alternative carbon-neutrality scenarios. However, the results of the import demand changes for Australia's energy products we are investigating—coal, natural gas, iron ore and nonferrous ores—are very similar among these 14 scenarios with those in the CNS.[7]

China's carbon-neutrality transition and Australian exports of fossil fuels and minerals

Our simulation shows that China's pursuit of carbon neutrality will slow the growth of most of Australia's mining exports (Figure 12.5). In the CCNS, Australia's exports of coal, LNG and iron ore will be 15.9 per cent, 18.4 per cent and 0.14 per cent lower, respectively, than in the base case (AZES)[8] by 2050. An exception is nonferrous ores, whose exports will be 0.44 per cent higher by 2050.

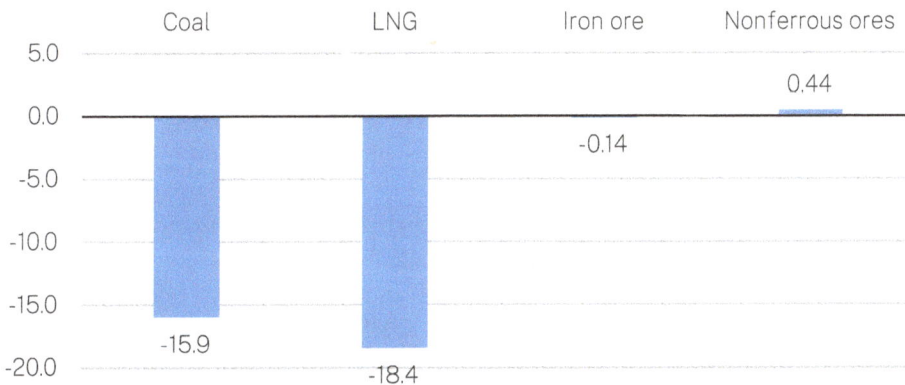

Figure 12.5 Australia's main fossil fuel and mineral exports in the CCNS: Cumulative deviation from AZES, 2050 (per cent)
Source: VURM simulation results.

---

7   Among these 14 scenarios, in the Border Adjustment Mechanism (BAM) scenario (which assumes that China implements carbon tariffs on energy-intensive imports, such as chemicals, cement and steel, to maintain its domestic goods' price competitiveness) and the Global Mitigation Efforts (GME) scenario (which assumes that world prices for energy-intensive goods such as chemicals, cement and steel change by the same percentage as China's domestic prices), the import demands for chemicals, cement and steel reduce substantially compared with the CNS. Since the carbon tariff in the BAM scenario and the import price change in the GME scenario are not applied on coal, natural gas, iron ore and nonferrous ores, the results of the import demand changes in these two scenarios are very similar to those in the CNS.

8   As we explained, the AZES does not assume China and India are on the path to their carbon-neutrality targets. In the AZES, exports of Australia's coal and LNG will continue to increase at a rate of 0.88 per cent and 3.96 per cent, respectively, annually from 2021 to 2050. But with the CCNS, the growth of Australia's coal and LNG exports will reduce to 0.2 per cent and 2.28 per cent, respectively, annually.

The decreased demand for Australia's coal, LNG and iron ore caused by China's carbon-neutrality action reduces Australia's terms of trade. Figure 12.6 shows that in the middle of this century, Australia's terms of trade will be 2.92 per cent lower in the CCNS than in the AZES.[9]

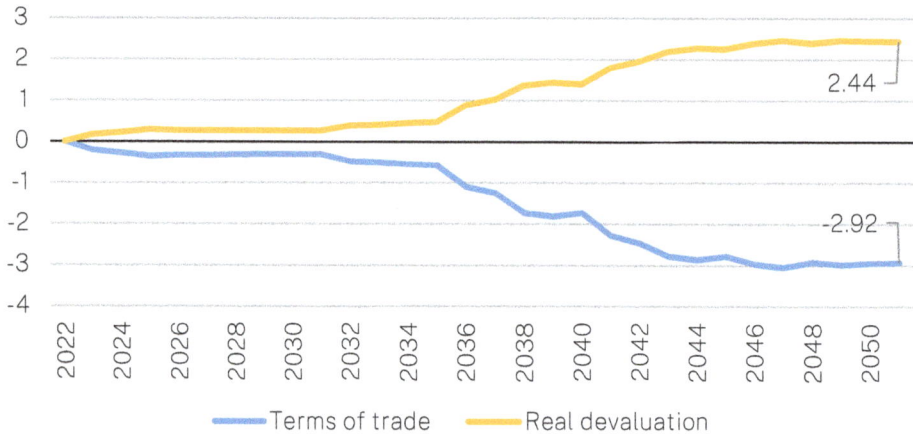

Figure 12.6 Changes in terms of trade and real devaluation: Cumulative deviation from AZES (per cent)

Source: VURM simulation results.

Impacts of China's demand changes on the Australian macroeconomy

The macroeconomic impact on Australia of changing import demand from China's carbon-neutrality action is marginal. Figure 12.7 shows the percentage deviations from the base case (AZES) values for real GDP and its components from the income side. Real GDP is 0.17 per cent lower in the CCNS by the end of 2050. The decline in real GDP is mainly because of the lower growth of capital stock. Figure 12.7 shows that capital stock is 0.43 per cent lower in the CCNS than in the AZES. This decline is due to the deterioration of the terms of trade, which causes structural effects on capital, investment and real GDP.[10] Lower capital growth means lower investment (–0.85 per cent in Figure 12.8). Given fixed employment,[11] the real wage rate drops (–0.55 per cent; Figure 12.7), reflecting the decrease in the capital–labour (K/L) ratio and the consequent decline in the marginal product of labour.

9   Positive change in real devaluation for the currency means the value of the Australian dollar in the international market becomes lower.

10   Please refer to Dixon and Rimmer (2002) for a detailed explanation of the structural effects caused by the terms of trade.

11   In the CCNS, we assume that, in the long term, national employment is exogenous and remains at the same level as in the baseline scenario, therefore there is no change in employment.

The impact of China's carbon-neutrality action on national real household and government consumption (C+G) is larger than on real GDP. Figure 12.8 shows that real household and government consumption is 0.49 per cent lower in the CCNS than in the AZES. The larger drop in real consumption compared with real GDP is because of the decline in the terms of trade affecting household income.

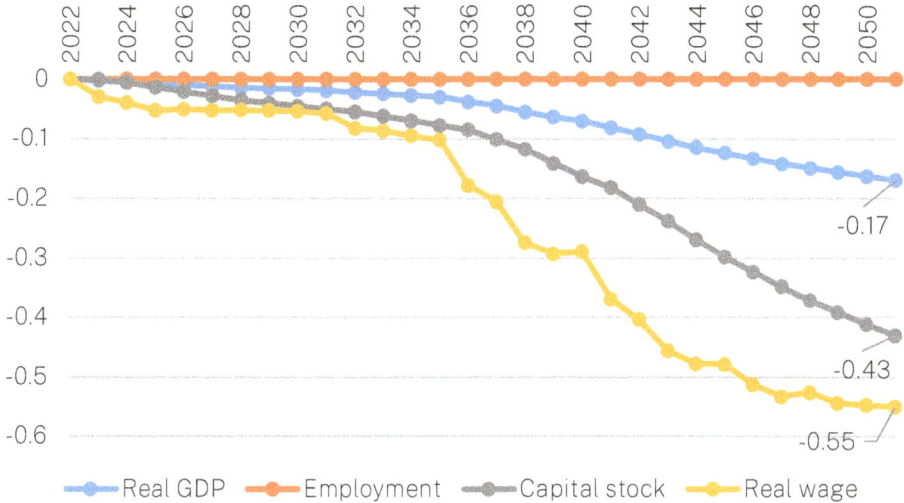

Figure 12.7 Real GDP and other macro-variables: Cumulative deviation from AZES (per cent)

Source: VURM simulation results.

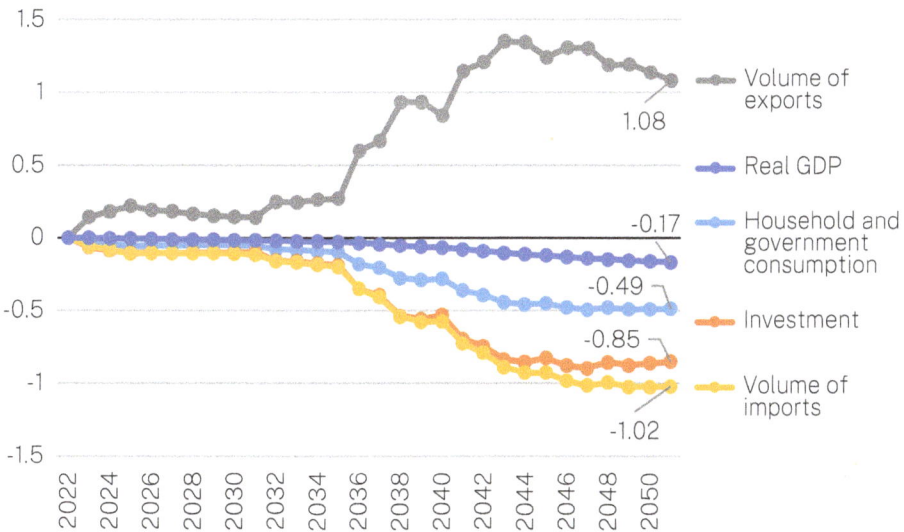

Figure 12.8 Real GDP and its components from the expenditure side: Cumulative deviation from AZES (per cent)

Source: VURM simulation results.

Real domestic final demand (C + G + I) drops more relative to real GDP (Y), leading to an improvement in trade balance (Export–Import).[12] This is accompanied by a real devaluation in the Australian dollar and an increase in the competitiveness of Australia's trade-exposed products. In 2050, the real exchange rate is 2.44 per cent below its baseline value (Figure 12.6).[13] In that year, exports have increased by 1.08 per cent while imports have fallen by 1.02 per cent (Figure 12.8).

The impacts of China's demand changes on Australian industries' production and employment

Australia's coal, LNG and iron ore industries will suffer from China's carbon-neutrality transition, while nonferrous ore industries will benefit slightly. Meanwhile, as discussed in the previous subsection, the real devaluation stimulates exports and increases the competitiveness of import-competing industries on local markets, therefore, export-oriented industries (except coal, LNG and iron ore) and import-competing industries will benefit from China's carbon-neutrality transition. Figure 12.9 shows the percentage deviations from the base case (AZES) values for exports of 81 commodities.[14] Except for coal and LNG, almost all the commodities that have overseas markets experience an expansion in their exports.

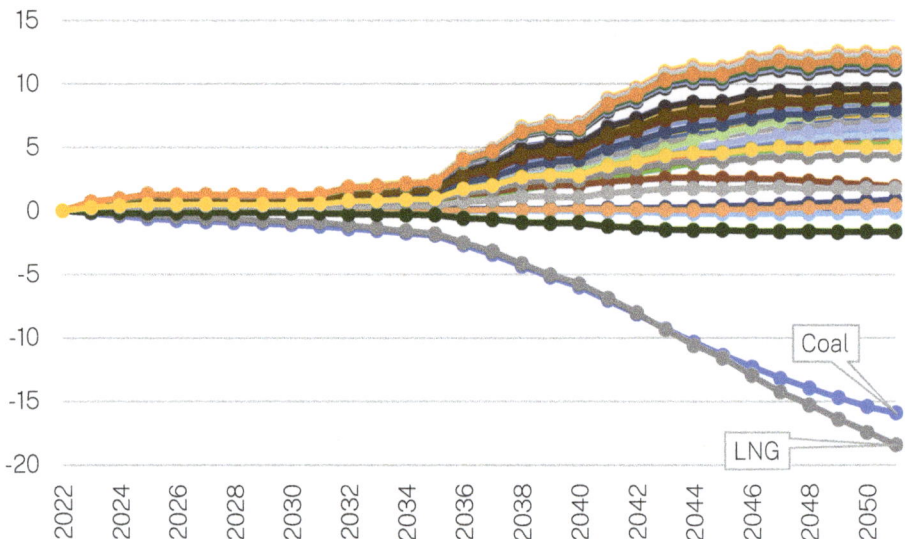

Figure 12.9 Changes in Australia's exports by commodity in CCNS: Cumulative deviation from AZES (per cent)

Source: VURM simulation results.

---

12   Recall the basic GDP identity: Y = C + I + G + (X – M).

13   The positive change of real devaluation in Figure 12.6 means a decline in the real exchange rate of the Australian dollar.

14   Please refer to the Appendix for the list of commodities in the VURM model used in this research.

Table 12.2 shows deviations from the baseline values for national production and employment by Australian and New Zealand Standard Industrial Classification (ANZSIC) division in the final year of the simulation period, 2050. Percentage deviations in production are shown in the first column; the second and third columns relate to employment. Percentage deviations in employed hours are shown first; absolute changes in the number of people employed expressed in units of 1,000 are shown second. Note that a change in hours can be accommodated by a mix of changes in the number of people employed and in hours worked per person. In our modelling, we allow for both.

Table 12.2 ANZSIC divisions: Production and employment in 2050

ANZSIC division	Percentage deviation in production	Percentage deviation in employment (hours)	Absolute deviation in employment (1,000 persons)
A. Agriculture, forestry, fishing	1.47	2.32	2.40
B. Mining	–3.94	–4.65	–6.62
C. Manufacturing	2.38	2.60	2.68
D. Utilities	–0.32	–0.12	–0.44
E. Construction	–1.03	–0.98	–0.63
F. Wholesale trade	0.45	0.51	0.60
G. Retail trade	0.06	0.13	0.15
H. Accommodation	0.25	0.24	0.27
I. Transport	–0.05	0.13	0.31
J. Information media	–0.09	0.00	0.04
K. Financial services	–0.28	–0.28	–0.27
L. Rental services	–0.70	–0.79	–0.94
M. Professional services	0.07	0.12	0.11
N. Administrative services	0.09	0.10	0.13
O. Public administration	–0.44	–0.43	–0.44
P. Education	–0.03	–0.02	–0.04
Q. Health	–0.33	–0.32	–0.28
R. Arts and recreation	–0.17	–0.11	–0.11
S. Other services	–0.37	–0.35	–0.28
T. Dwelling ownership	–0.08	0.00	0.00

Source: VURM simulation results.

Changes in production in most industries are in line with real GDP. In this section, we only discuss the industries with notably large changes compared with real GDP.

It is not surprising that mining (B) suffers the most because the slight increase in the exports of nonferrous ores cannot offset the significant decline of coal and LNG. Mining industry production drops significantly and there are 6,620 fewer jobs—a 4.65 per cent decline in total sectoral employment. Since construction (E) sells most of its outputs to investment-related services and investment overall declines relative to its baseline level (Figure 12.8), construction also suffers.

Agriculture, forestry and fishing (A) has a significant export share. As discussed in the previous section, China's decarbonisation decreases the real value of the Australian dollar, which increases the competitiveness of internationally traded industries. Therefore, agriculture, forestry and fishing (A) is projected to experience an increase in production (1.47 per cent) primarily due to increased sales to overseas markets. With an increase in production, employment also increases (2.32 per cent, or 2,400 additional jobs).

Accommodation (H) comprises industries that produce hotel, restaurant and food services. It also has a significant export share, reflecting sales in Australia to foreign visitors. With a devaluation of the Australian currency, the accommodation division is expected to see an increase in production (0.25 per cent) primarily due to increased sales to overseas visitors. Sectoral employment is thus projected to grow by 0.24 per cent, or 270 jobs.

Manufacturing (C) comprises some industries that are exported-oriented and some that are import-competing. The real devaluation of the Australian dollar also stimulates the expansion of manufacturing: production increases by 2.38 per cent and employment increases by 2.6 per cent, or 2,680 jobs.

The impacts of China's demand changes on Australian regions

Real gross state product (GSP) falls relative to the baseline scenario (AZES) in Queensland (QLD), Western Australia (WA), the Northern Territory (NT) and the Australian Capital Territory (ACT), and rises in Victoria (VIC), Tasmania (TAS), South Australia (SA) and New South Wales (NSW). Figure 12.10 shows projected percentage deviations from base-case levels for real GSP. Percentage deviations in production and employment (hours) in 2050 are given in Table 12.3, which also shows the absolute change in the number of employed persons in 2050.

The pattern of impacts on real GSP reflects the pattern on industries. Just as some industries experience output gains relative to the AZES scenario and some experience output losses, state results vary due to differences in industrial composition.

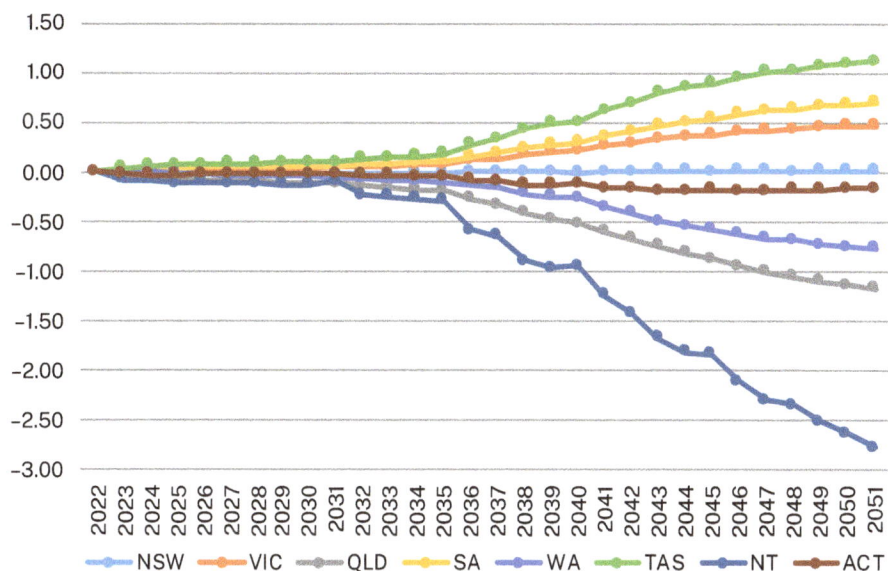

Figure 12.10 Real gross state product: Percentage cumulative deviations from AZES values

Source: VURM simulation results.

Table 12.3 State and territory production and employment in 2050

State/territory	Percentage deviation in real GSP	Percentage deviation in employment (hours)	Absolute deviation in employment (1,000 persons)
New South Wales	0.01	0.14	0.16
Victoria	0.47	0.67	0.72
Queensland	−1.18	−1.07	−0.92
South Australia	0.70	0.91	0.99
Western Australia	−0.77	−0.47	−0.67
Tasmania	1.11	1.30	1.26
Northern Territory	−2.77	−2.79	−2.35
Australian Capital Territory	−0.17	−0.12	−0.02

Source: VURM simulation results.

Queensland has a large representation of coalmining, which is the main reason China's decarbonisation is expected to reduce its share in the national economy. In 2050, Queensland is projected to have a real GSP 1.18 per cent lower than in the baseline scenario; employment is down by 1.07 per cent—equivalent to 920 fewer jobs.

The Northern Territory is also projected to contract in output—down by 2.77 per cent relative to the baseline levels (AZES) in 2050. The main negative influence for the Northern Territory is a large representation of gas extraction and LNG manufacturing. Its employment will be 2.79 per cent lower or 2,350 job losses.

In Western Australia, although gas and iron ore mining and LNG manufacturing drive its state production down, its exports of other minerals will partially offset the negative effects. The combined effects are that its real GSP is projected to fall slightly (by 0.77 per cent, or 670 jobs lost) relative to the baseline. New South Wales will also have a slight loss in its output, mainly because of its coal production.

The Australian Capital Territory's economy is almost entirely service-oriented and therefore the fall in its production and employment is consistent with the national picture.

By contrast, Tasmania, Victoria and South Australia do not have or only have small amounts of coal and LNG production. They benefit slightly from the expansion of their export-oriented and import-competing industries. Though New South Wales suffers from the decline of its coal production, it will benefit from the expansion of its export-oriented and import-competing industries. The combined effects are that New South Wales will have a slight increase in its output.

Conclusion

China's decarbonisation will cause significant changes in its energy and economic structures, which will have important implications for many Australian industries and commodities. Applying the multiregional model of the Australian economy (VURM), this research explores the implications of China's changing import demand for the Australian economy through impacts on Australia's main fossil fuel and mineral exports. Our simulation shows that though the substantial decline of China's energy imports will reduce Australia's exports of fossil fuels, it will increase other Australian exports, including of nonferrous ores, and the overall impacts on the national economy are negligible.

The key results of our analysis can be summarised as follows: first, by the middle of the century, Australia's coal and LNG exports will decline by nearly 16 per cent and 19 per cent, respectively, compared with a scenario that does not consider China's carbon-neutrality actions. Second, Australia's iron ore exports will suffer a minor decline. Exports of nonferrous ores could increase slightly given the assumption that China will not increase the use of scrap steel and switch to 'green steel' production. Third, declining demand for fossil fuels in China will cause Australia's terms of trade to fall, leading to negative structural effects on capital, investment and real GDP. Fourth, the slight devaluation of real exchange rate increases Australia's competitiveness. As a result, Australia's exports are 1.08 per cent higher and its imports are 1.02 per cent lower in the middle of the century. Fifth, the effects of China's net-zero transition on Australian industries are a mixed story with fossil fuel industries losing, while some other industries, especially export-oriented ones, gain. Sixth, the regions with high coal and LNG industry concentrations, such as the Northern Territory and Queensland, are disproportionately and negatively affected. The slight increase in other mineral exports in the case of Western Australia cannot fully offset the negative effects of the decline in LNG and iron ore exports.

This chapter has several caveats. First, the impacts of China's carbon-neutrality transition are simulated by demand changes in just four products: coal, LNG, iron ore and nonferrous ores. Impacts through trade of other products in both directions, and the response of the Australian economy, have not been considered. We also have not considered the increasing use of scrap steel. If these assumptions are changed, export of iron ore might decline further and the increasing demand for Australia's nonferrous ores could also change. Another limitation is that while Australia can benefit from decarbonisation in China and elsewhere through its development of critical minerals and hydrogen, the current versions of both the CHINAGEM-E and the VURM models have not included these emerging industries that will potentially play an important role in both countries' carbon-neutrality transitions. Taking the steel industry as an example, replacing coking coal with hydrogen in steelmaking will affect Australia's coal exports, but it could benefit from exporting hydrogen-related energy-intensive products. By processing iron ore using hydrogen for the early stages of steelmaking, Australia could export to China more processed iron (ingot) rather than iron ore (Garnaut 2019). The third limitation is that these results do not consider the effects of China's efforts to diversify the sources of fossil fuel and iron ore imports. We assumed that the shares of Australia's main exports to China are the same as their 2019 levels. A further argument for improvement is that using a global model instead of the CHINAGEM-E could capture more nuanced impacts through interactions in global trade.

References

Adams, P. 2021. *Zero greenhouse gas emissions by 2050: What it means for the Australian economy, industries and regions.* Centre of Policy Studies Working Paper No. G-324, November. Melbourne: Victoria University.

Adams, P. and J. Dixon. 2015. *The Victoria University Regional Model (VURM): Technical documentation, Version 1.0.* Centre of Policy Studies Working Paper. Melbourne: Victoria University.

Asian Development Bank (ADB). 2022. *Implementing a Green Recovery in Southeast Asia.* Manila: ADB.

Australian Bureau of Statistics (ABS). 2020. *Australia's Trade in Goods with China in 2020.* [Online]. 3 September. Canberra: ABS. Available from: www.abs.gov.au/articles/australias-trade-goods-china-2020#:~:text=Australianexportsofgoods to,disruptionscausedbyCyclone Damien.&text=Year-on-year%2Cexports,July2020weredown16%25.

Australian Energy Market Operator (AEMO). 2022. 'AEMO Suspends NEM Wholesale Market.' Media release, 15 June. Melbourne: AEMO. Available from: aemo.com.au/newsroom/media-release/aemo-suspends-nem-wholesale-market.

Carley, S., T.P. Evans, M. Graff and D.M. Konisky. 2018. 'A Framework for Evaluating Geographic Disparities in Energy Transition Vulnerability.' *Nature Energy* 3: 621–27. doi.org/10.1038/s41560-018-0142-z.

Chen, G., T. Wiedmann, Y. Wang and M. Hadjikakou. 2016. 'Transnational City Carbon Footprint Networks: Exploring Carbon Links between Australian and Chinese Cities.' *Applied Energy* 184[SI]: 1082–92. doi.org/10.1016/J.APENERGY.2016.08.053.

Den Elzen, M., H. Fekete, N. Höhne, A. Admiraal, N. Forsell, A.F. Hof, J.G.J. Olivier, M. Roelfsema and H. van Soest. 2016. 'Greenhouse Gas Emissions from Current and Enhanced Policies of China until 2030: Can Emissions Peak Before 2030?' *Energy Policy* 89: 224–36. doi.org/10.1016/j.enpol.2015.11.030.

Department of Foreign Affairs and Trade (DFAT). 2020. *Trade Time Series Data.* [Online]. Canberra: Australian Government. Available from: www.dfat.gov.au/trade/resources/trade-statistics/trade-time-series-data.

Department of Foreign Affairs and Trade (DFAT). 2022a. *China Country Brief.* Canberra: Australian Government. Available from: www.dfat.gov.au/geo/china/china-country-brief.

Department of Foreign Affairs and Trade (DFAT). 2022b. *Trade, Investment and Economic Statistics.* [Online]. Canberra: Australian Government. Available from: www.dfat.gov.au/trade/resources/trade-statistics/trade-statistics.

Dixon, P.B. and M.T. Rimmer. 2002. *Dynamic General Equilibrium Modelling for Forecasting and Policy: a Practical Guide and Documentation of MONASH, Volume 256.* Amsterdam: North-Holland Publishing Company. doi.org/10.1108/S0573-8555(2001)256.

East Asia Forum (EAF) Editorial Board. 2020. 'Don't Waste Fiscal Stimulus, Invest It in Mitigating Climate Change.' *East Asia Forum*, 23 March. Available from: www.eastasiaforum.org/2020/03/23/dont-waste-fiscal-stimulus-invest-it-in-mitigating-climate-change/.

Energy Foundation China (EFC). 2020. *Synthesis Report 2020 on China's Carbon Neutrality: China's New Growth Pathway—From the 14th Five Year Plan to Carbon Neutrality.* Beijing: EFC.

Feng, S., X. Peng and P. Adams. 2021. *Energy and economic implications of carbon neutrality in China: a dynamic general equilibrium analysis.* Centre of Policy Studies Working Paper No. G-324, August. Melbourne: Victoria University. doi.org/10.2139/ssrn.3985229.

Garnaut, R. 2019. *Super-Power: Australia's Low-Carbon Opportunity*. Melbourne: La Trobe University Press.

Gosens, J. and F. Jotzo. 2020. 'How Green is China's Post-COVID-19 "New Infrastructure" Stimulus Spending?' *East Asia Forum*, 5 May. Available from: www.eastasiaforum.org/2020/05/05/how-green-is-chinas-post-covid-19-new-infrastructure-stimulus-spending/.

Government of the People's Republic of China (PRC). 2021. 'Opinions of the Central Committee of the Communist Party of China and the State Council on Completely and Accurately Implementing the New Development Concept and Doing a Good Job on Carbon Peak and Carbon Neutrality [关于完整准确全面贯彻新发展理念做好碳达峰碳中和工作的意见].' *Xinhua News Agency*, [Beijing], 24 October. Available from: www.gov.cn/zhengce/2021-10/24/content_5644613.htm.

Greenpeace East Asia, 2022. Plans for new coal plants in China rebound, with 8.63 GW approved in the first quarter of 2022. Available from: www.greenpeace.org/eastasia/press/7488/plans-for-new-coal-plants-in-china-rebound-with-8-63-gw-approved-in-the-first-quarter-of-2022/.

He, J., Z. Li, X. Zhang, H. Wang, W. Dong, S. Chang, X. Ou, S. Guo, Z. Tian, A. Gu, F. Teng, X. Yang, S. Chen, M. Yao, Z. Yuan, L. Zhou and X. Zhao. 2020. 'Comprehensive Report on China's Long-Term Low-Carbon Development Strategies and Pathways.' *Chinese Journal of Population, Resources and Environment* 18(4): 263–95. doi.org/10.1016/j.cjpre.2021.04.004.

He, K. 2022. Carbon Neutrality and Green, High Quality Development, Presentation to 2022 Seashell Finance Digital Economy Summit, August 3, 2022, Beijing.

Huang, R., G. Chen, G. Lv, A. Malik, X. Shi and X. Xie. 2020. 'The Effect of Technology Spillover on CO_2 Emissions Embodied in China–Australia Trade.' *Energy Policy* 144: 111544. doi.org/10.1016/j.enpol.2020.111544.

International Energy Agency (IEA). 2020. *Sustainable Recovery*. World Energy Outlook Special Report, June. Paris: IEA. Available from: www.iea.org/reports/sustainable-recovery.

Jayanthakumaran, K. and Y. Liu. 2016. 'Bi-Lateral CO_2 Emissions Embodied in Australia–China Trade.' *Energy Policy* 92: 205–13. doi.org/10.1016/J.ENPOL.2016.02.011.

Kemp, J., M. McCowage and F. Wang. 2021. 'Towards Net Zero: Implications for Australia of Energy Policies in East Asia.' *Reserve Bank of Australia Bulletin*, September: 30–40. Available from: www.rba.gov.au/publications/bulletin/2021/sep/pdf/bulletin-2021-09.pdf.

Laurenceson, J. and M. Zhou. 2020. *COVID-19 and the Australia–China Relationship's Zombie Economic Idea*. Sydney: Australia–China Relations Institute, University of Technology Sydney. Available from: www.australiachinarelations.org/sites/default/files/20200507%20Australia-China%20Relations%20Institute%20report_COVID-19%20and%20the%20Australia-China%20relationship%E2%80%99s%20zombie%20economic%20idea_James%20Laurenceson%20Michael%20Zhou.pdf.

Liu, Y., B. Meng, K. Hubacek, J. Xue, K. Feng and Y. Gao. 2016. '"Made in China": A Reevaluation of Embodied CO_2 Emissions in Chinese Exports using Firm Heterogeneity Information.' *Applied Energy* 184: 1106–13. doi.org/10.1016/j.apenergy.2016.06.088.

Meng, J., Z. Mi, D. Guan, J. Li, S. Tao, Y. Li, K. Feng, J. Liu, Z. Liu, X. Wang, Q. Zhang and S.J. Davis. 2018. 'The Rise of South–South Trade and its Effect on Global CO_2 Emissions.' *Nature Communications* 9(1871). doi.org/10.1038/s41467-018-04337-y.

Morgan, R.E., R. Cui, M. Bindl, N. Hultman, K. Mathur, H. McJeon, G. Iyer, J. Song and A. Zhao. 2022. 'Quantifying the Regional Stranded Asset Risks from New Coal Plants under 1.5°C.' *Environmental Research Letters* 17(2). doi.org/10.1088/1748-9326/ac4ec2.

National Energy Administration (NEA). 2022. 'The National Energy Administration Remobilised and Rearranged the Power Supply during the Peak Summer Season.' [In Chinese]. Media release, July. Beijing: NEA.

Peng, X. forthcoming. *CHINAGEM: A Dynamic General Equilibrium Model of China— Theory, Data and Applications*. Berlin: Springer.

Shi, X. 2022. 'China's Changing Climate Action Roadmap.' *East Asia Forum*, 11 May. Available from: www.eastasiaforum.org/2022/05/11/chinas-changing-climate-action-roadmap/.

Shi, X., T.S. Cheong and M. Zhou. 2021a. 'COVID-19 and Global Supply Chain Configuration: Economic and Emissions Impacts of Australia–China Trade Disruptions.' *Frontiers in Public Health* 9: 1–13. doi.org/10.3389/fpubh.2021.752481.

Shi, X., Y. Sun and Y. Shen. 2021b. 'China's Ambitious Energy Transition Plans.' *Science* 373(6551): 170. doi.org/10.1126/science.abj8773.

Shi, X., K. Wang, Y. Shen, Y. Sheng and Y. Zhang. 2020. 'A Permit Trading Scheme for Facilitating Energy Transition: a Case Study of Coal Capacity Control in China.' *Journal of Cleaner Production* 256: 120472. doi.org/10.1016/j.jclepro.2020.120472.

Shi, X. and M. Yang. 2022. 'China's Coal Phase-Out Faces a Rocky and Winding Road.' *Oxford Energy Forum* 131: 9–12.

Stern, N. and C. Xie. 2022. 'China's New Growth Story: Linking the 14th Five-Year Plan with the 2060 Carbon Neutrality Pledge.' *Journal of Chinese Economic and Business Studies*: 1–21. doi.org/10.1080/14765284.2022.2073172.

Tan, H., A. Sun and H. Lau. 2013. 'CO_2 Embodiment in China–Australia Trade: The Drivers and Implications.' *Energy Policy* 61: 1212–20. doi.org/10.1016/J.ENPOL.2013.06.048.

Tan, W. 2021. 'China Restricted Imports from Australia. Now Australia is Selling Elsewhere.' *CNBC*, [Englewood Cliffs, NJ], 2 June. Available from: www.cnbc.com/2021/06/03/australia-finds-new-markets-for-coal-barley-amid-china-trade-fight.html.

Tian, K., Y. Zhang, Y. Li, X. Ming, S. Jiang, H. Duan, C. Yang and S. Wang. 2022. 'Regional Trade Agreement Burdens Global Carbon Emissions Mitigation.' *Nature Communications* 13: 408. doi.org/10.1038/s41467-022-28004-5.

United Nations (UN). 2021. *Transforming Extractive Industries for Sustainable Development.* Policy Brief, May. New York, NY: UN. Available from: www.un.org/sites/un2.un.org/files/sg_policy_brief_extractives.pdf.

Wang, S., Y. Zhao and T. Wiedmann. 2019. 'Carbon Emissions Embodied in China–Australia Trade: a Scenario Analysis Based on Input–Output Analysis and Panel Regression Models.' *Journal of Cleaner Production* 220: 721–31. doi.org/10.1016/J.JCLEPRO.2019.02.071.

Wang, Y., D. Wang and X. Shi. 2022. 'Exploring the Multidimensional Effects of China's Coal De-Capacity Policy: A Regression Discontinuity Design.' *Resources Policy* 75: 102504. doi.org/10.1016/j.resourpol.2021.102504.

Watts, J. 2009. 'China Sets First Targets to Curb World's Largest Carbon Footprint.' *The Guardian*, [London], 26 November. Available from: www.theguardian.com/environment/2009/nov/26/china-targets-cut-carbon-footprint.

Xiang, H., Y. Kuang and C. Li. 2017. 'Impact of the China–Australia FTA on Global Coal Production and Trade.' *Journal of Policy Modeling* 39(1): 65–78. doi.org/10.1016/J.JPOLMOD.2017.01.001.

Xinhua. 2021. 'Resolution of the CPC Central Committee on the Major Achievements and Historical Experience of the Party over the Past Century.' *Xinhua*, November 16 2021.

Yang, J., Y. Zhao, J. Cao and C.P. Nielsen. 2021. 'Co-Benefits of Carbon and Pollution Control Policies on Air Quality and Health till 2030 in China.' *Environment International* 152: 106482. doi.org/10.1016/j.envint.2021.106482.

You, X. 2021. 'China Issues New "Single-Game" Instructions to Guide its Climate Action.' *Carbon Brief*, [London], 4 August. Available from: www.carbonbrief.org/china-issues-new-single-game-instructions-to-guide-its-climate-action/.

Yu, S., S. Zheng, X. Li and L. Li. 2018. 'China Can Peak its Energy-Related Carbon Emissions before 2025: Evidence from Industry Restructuring.' *Energy Economics* 73: 91–107. doi.org/10.1016/j.eneco.2018.05.012.

Zheng, H., M. Song and Z. Shen. 2021. 'The Evolution of Renewable Energy and its Impact on Carbon Reduction in China.' *Energy* 237: 121639. doi.org/10.1016/j.energy.2021.121639.

Appendix

Table A12.1 List of commodities and industries in the VURM model, 2019 version

1 SheepCattle	Sheep and beef cattle
2 Grains	Grains production
3 DairyCattle	Dairy cattle
4 OtherCrops	Other crop production
5 SugarCane	Sugarcane production
6 Cotton	Raw cotton and ginning
7 OtherAg	Other agriculture
8 FishHuntTrap	Fishing, hunting and trapping
9 Forestry	Forestry and logging
10 AgSrv	Agricultural services
11 Coal	Coalmining
12 Oil	Oil extraction
13 GAS	Gas extraction
14 LNG	LNG production
15 IronOre	Iron ore mining
16 OthNonFeOre	Nonferrous metal ore mining
17 NonMetMins	Non-metallic ore mining
18 MiningSrv	Exploration and mining support services
19 MeatProds	Meat products
20 DairyProds	Dairy products
21 SugarManuf	Refined sugar processing
22 OthFoodProds	Other food products
23 DrinkProds	Beverages and tobacco
24 TCF	Textiles, clothing and footwear
25 WoodProds	Wood products
26 PaperProds	Pulp and paper products, printing
27 PetrolRefine	Petroleum refinery products
28 OtherChems	Other chemical products
29 NonMetCement	Non-metallic mineral products
30 IronSteel	Iron and steel manufacturing
31 Alumina	Alumina smelting
32 Aluminium	Aluminium refining
33 OtherMetals	Other non-ferrous metals
34 MotorVehicle	Motor vehicles and parts
35 OtherTranEqp	Other transport equipment
36 OtherMan	Other manufacturing
37 ElecCoal	Electricity generation: coal
38 ElecGas	Electricity generation: gas
39 ElecHydro	Electricity generation: hydro

40 ElecOther	Electricity generation: non-hydro renewable
41 ElecSupply	Electricity supply
42 GasSupply	Gas supply and products
43 WaterSupply	Water and drainage products
44 ResidBuildng	Residential construction
45 NonResBld	Non-residential construction
46 CvlEngCnstct	Civil engineering
47 ConstrucSrvc	Construction services
48 WholeTrade	Wholesale trade services
49 RetailTrade	Retail trade services
50 Accommodation	Accommodation services
51 Restaurant	Restaurant and food services
52 RoadFreight	Road freight transport
53 RoadPassngr	Road passenger transport
54 RailFreight	Rail freight transport
55 RailPass	Rail passenger transport
56 AirTrans	Air transport services
57 OthTrans	Water and other transport services
58 Commun	Communication services
59 BankFinance	Banking services
60 Insurance	Insurance services
61 Superann	Superannuation services
62 RentHire	Non–real estate rental and hiring services
63 OwnerDwellng	Ownership of dwellings
64 RealEstateSr	Real estate business services
65 LegalSrv	Legal services
66 ProfSciTech	Professional, scientific and technical services
67 AdminSupport	Other business services
68 PubAdminReg	Public administration
69 Defence	Defence services
70 PreSchool	Preschool education services
71 PrimSchool	Primary school education services
72 SecdrySchool	Secondary school education services
73 TechVocOthEd	Technical education services
74 TertiaryEdu	Tertiary education services
75 HealthSrv	Healthcare services
76 ResidCare	Residential care services
77 ChildCareSrv	Childcare services
78 OthSocAsst	Other care services
79 ArtsRecreate	Arts and recreational services
80 Gambling	Gambling services
81 OtherSrv	Other services

13

Cooperation, conflict and 'Quad' exports to China

Vishesh Agarwal, Jane Golley and Tunye Qiu

Introduction

China's integration into the global economy during the past four decades has delivered substantial economic benefits to China and its trading and investment partners. As one of, if not the major, beneficiaries of this globalisation process, China's wealth has grown at an extraordinary pace, transforming it from a poor developing country into a global economic superpower. In line with its rising power, the Chinese Government has shown an increased capacity and willingness to use economic tools such as trade policy to achieve its broader foreign policy objectives—that is, to engage in economic statecraft or what is now commonly referred to as geoeconomics (Blackwill and Harris 2016; Baru 2013). While some of these tools, like the capital flows embodied in the Belt and Road Initiative (BRI), are portrayed by the Chinese Government as 'win-win' mechanisms for promoting global development and prosperity, not everyone is convinced. Some depict the BRI, for example, as an exercise in 'debt-trap diplomacy' (despite ample evidence to the contrary),[1] while others fear the Chinese Government's growing power to manipulate the domestic and foreign policies of partner countries through the coercive use of trade and investment policy.

China is certainly not the first great power to engage in economic statecraft; it has been a persistent feature of international relations for centuries (Davis et al. 2019). In some cases, trade relations have been based on the premise that trade will prove to be 'a bond of friendship between nations' (Hirschman 1980: 7), while in others

---

1   See, for example, Jones and Hameiri (2020); Van Grieken and Kantorowicz (2021); and Brautigam (2020).

they have been pursued with 'dependence, influence, and even domination' in mind (Hirschman 1980: 13). Regardless of whether the stronger relative power in any bilateral relationship exerts that power to 'win-win' or 'win-lose' effect, trade patterns in the past have been shown to closely reflect political relations in a variety of contexts (Long 2008)—for example, rising in times when 'bonds of friendship' strengthen and contracting in times of conflict. However, it has also been observed that most of the variation in political relations between nations in recent decades has been moderate and short-lived, with limited if any impact on trade between the disputing nations (Heilmann 2016; Du et al. 2017).

There are sound theoretical reasons to expect the effects of political shocks on trade outcomes to be minimal and short-lived. Du et al. (2017: 212) describe the dynamics between trade and conflict as an infinitely repeated game with a 'Pareto perfect equilibrium' (that is, none of the players has any incentive to deviate from their strategies) in which bilateral relations consist of a 'combination of healthy trade and peaceful political relations'. In this context, moderate shocks in political relations are understood as 'accidental' deviations from the equilibrium and players have an incentive to settle disputes and return to the earlier Pareto superior combination of trade and peace.

In this chapter, we ask to what extent did moderate shocks in political relations (hereinafter 'political shocks') affect the exports to China of four of its major trading partners—Australia, India, Japan and the United States—between 2001 and 2020? During this period, China experienced frequent episodes of both political cooperation and political conflict with each of these trading partners. This provides the necessary variation in political relations required to quantify the effects of moderate political shocks on exports to China. We select them in part because, in 2017, these four countries revived the Quadrilateral Security Dialogue (the 'Quad') that was initiated in 2007 and involves high-level political and military cooperation between democracies. Some have argued that this is to ensure that an authoritarian China does not leverage its growing economic resources as coercive tools to achieve foreign policy objectives in the Indo-Pacific region (Medcalf 2020), while others have called it 'containment by any other name' (Raby 2020: 138). Whichever is the case, this revival seems to indicate that a less cooperative and more confrontational period of bilateral and quadrilateral relations with China lies ahead.

The Quad countries also make for an interesting set of nations to analyse because the drivers of political conflict with China have been different for each of them. Japan and India have historical border disputes with China, which tie into complex, and at times antagonistic, histories tracing back thousands of years. In contrast, the relatively short history of the US–China relationship has evolved rapidly in the past decade, shifting from a relatively symbiotic one to one that is increasingly antagonist and defined by great-power rivalry. This rivalry has, in turn, added fuel to the rapidly deteriorating relationship between Australia and China, which has reached its lowest point since diplomatic relations were established in 1972 (Raby 2020). Variations in these different bilateral *political* relationships are, in turn, shown to generate different impacts on aggregate export growth for each Quad country.

In a related study, Agarwal and Golley (2022) find that deteriorating political relations had short and long-run effects on India's aggregate export growth to China only between 1998 and 2018; for Australia, Japan and the United States, they report no effects of political relations on trade. Disaggregating by five-year subperiods, they find that long-term effects (lasting up to two years) are significant for India and Japan for the subperiod 1998–2002, while in all other subperiods there are no significant effects for any of the Quad countries. Golley et al. (2022) conducted a similar study for the period 2001–20, concentrating on Sino-Australian relations, and found no long-run effects of political relations on Australia's aggregate export growth to China. Both these studies also conducted product disaggregated analysis and reported heterogeneous short-run effects across sectors and periods.

This chapter extends the analysis of the effects of political relations on exports to China beyond our earlier focus on the perspective of government actors by constructing a political relations index (PRI) from the perspective of military actors and analysing the effects of a shock to this military index—as well as the government index—on Quad export growth. With two of the results below revealing long-term effects on export growth arising from a military shock (for Australia, over the period 2001–20, and for India, over the period 2016–20), we also disaggregate the composite index of military political relations, which adds together cooperation and conflict events, into separate cooperation and conflict effects. The results indicate that political relations and trade between the four Quad countries and China are connected (or not connected) in different ways; there is no 'one size fits all' for understanding this complex politics–trade nexus.

The rest of the chapter is structured as follows. The next section summarises China's rising economic power and its changing trade relationships with the Quad countries, before presenting a series of bilateral government and military PRIs, constructed using the Global Database of Events, Language and Tone (GDELT). We couple this with a case study of a period of conflict between China and India, centred on a military standoff in the disputed region of Doklam (known as Donglang in China) in June 2017. We then describe the empirical model used to identify the dynamic effects of political shocks on Quad nations' exports to China, before discussing the main results. The conclusions summarise our key findings.

Measuring bilateral trade and political relations with China

Figure 13.1 highlights three significant trends in the increasing capacity of China to use trade policy as a tool of economic statecraft. First, on the y-axis is the value of a country's trade with China as a share of total trade. This indicator reflects the 'vulnerability' aspect of partner countries' trading relationship with China (Gasiorowski 1986; Mansfield and Pollins 2009). Between 2000 and 2020, all Quad countries saw an upward shift, implying an increase in their China share of trade. The largest percentage point increase was for Australia, with China's share in its total trade increasing from 6.6 per cent in 2000 to 34 per cent in 2020 (a fivefold increase). China's share of trade for the United States increased from 6 per cent in 2000 to almost 15 per cent in 2020 but is notably still much lower than for Australia.

Second, the x-axis shows the value of each country's trade with China as a share of its own GDP. This indicator reflects the 'sensitivity' aspect of partner countries' trading relationship with China (Gasiorowski 1986; Mansfield and Pollins 2009). Between 2000 and 2020, all Quad countries experienced a rightward shift, implying an increase in trade with China as a share of GDP. Again, Australia experienced the largest percentage point increase, with the China trade-to-GDP ratio rising from approximately 2 per cent in 2000 to 11 per cent in 2020.

Third, the size of the partner country bubbles, reflecting each country's GDP relative to China's GDP, has continually decreased in the past two decades. The significant change in the relative size of the Chinese economy is attributable to the faster rate of economic growth in China than in other countries. The largest change in relative economic size has been for Japan, from more than four times the size of the Chinese economy in 2000 to less than half the size of the Chinese economy in 2020. The relative size of the US economy has also declined about sixfold, from 8.5 in 2000 to 1.4 in 2020. The decline in relative GDP is smaller for India, which has experienced rapid economic growth comparable with China's in the past two decades.

None of these facts provides evidence that China has utilised tools of economic statecraft to 'punish' partner countries in times of deteriorating political relations, nor that it has used them to reward partner countries when political relations improve. Rather, the point is that China's capacity to engage in economic statecraft, should it so choose, has increased significantly over time as a consequence of its rising relative economic power and its rising importance as a trading partner—most prominently for Australia.

Unlike economic indicators such as trade flows, which are objectively quantifiable, political relations between countries are difficult to both define and measure. The raw political events data for China and the Quad countries in the analysis that follows are extracted from the GDELT. The GDELT uses an automated machine-coding system to classify daily reports of events from 11 global news outlets according to the actors involved and events recorded and is considered the most comprehensive event dataset of its kind (Leetaru and Schrodt 2013). The events are indexed according to the 'Goldstein score', which ranges from –10 (for extreme hostility) to +10 (for extreme cooperation). For example, in the case of conflict, the use of military force would be weighted more heavily than expelling a country's diplomats or verbal criticism, while in the case of cooperation, signing a treaty would receive a higher weighting than diplomatic negotiations.

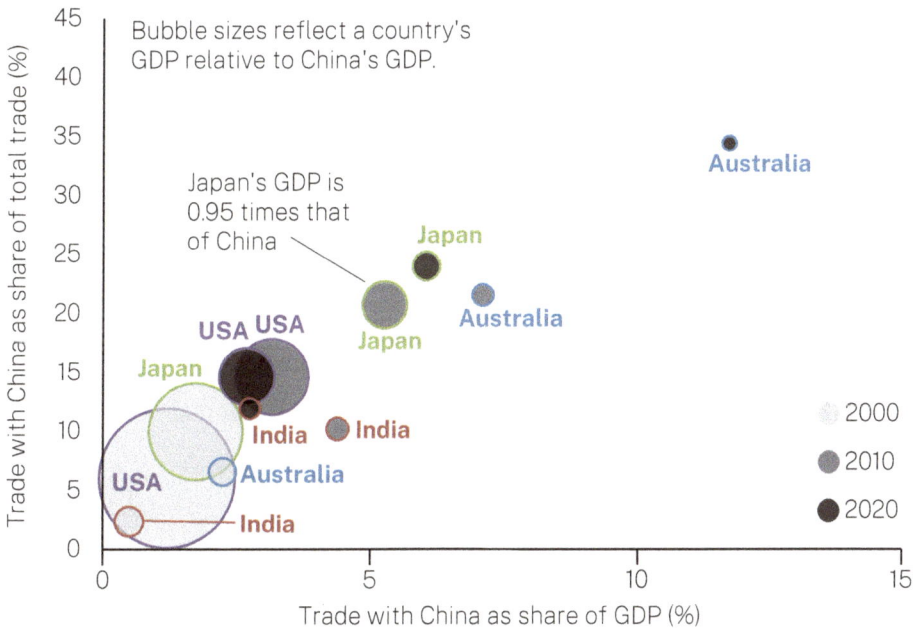

Figure 13.1 China's relative economic growth and trade integration with Quad economies, 2000–20

Sources: CEIC and authors' calculations.

We focus only on state actors, which can be separated into 'government' and 'military' actors. Table 13.1 illustrates a range of Goldstein scores allocated to a sample of military and government 'messaging' from one country to another, encompassing both cooperation events (with a positive Goldstein score) and conflict events (with a negative score). For example, the highest 'conflict' event is deemed to be a military attack, clash or assault, with a Goldstein score of –10 (the lowest possible score) that would feature in the military PRI, while extending economic aid is an example of a cooperative event, which would register a score of 7.4 on the government PRI. Both cooperation events and conflict events are aggregated to construct two indicators of bilateral political relations at the monthly frequency: a government PRI and a military PRI.

Table 13.1 Goldstein scores for a range of cooperation and conflict events

Event	Goldstein score
Military attack, clash, assault	–10.0
Armed force mobilisation, exercise, display, military buildup	–7.6
Break diplomatic relations	–7.0
Cancel or postpone planned event	–2.2
Urge or suggest action or policy	–0.1
Explain or state policy	0.0
Yield position, retreat, evacuate	0.6
Grant privilege, diplomatic recognition, de facto relations	5.4
Make substantive agreement	6.5
Extend economic aid; give, buy, sell, loan, borrow	7.4
Extend military assistance	8.3

Source: Extracted from GDELT by the authors.

PRI series constructed in this way still include trade-related events that occur between state actors—for example, the signing of a free-trade agreement or the imposition of tariffs on certain goods. To remove the effects of such trade-related events, we use the residuals of the following regression (Equation 13.1) to construct a 'trade-filtered' version of the PRIs. Since all subsequent data and analysis will be trade filtered, we call this simply the 'PRI'.

Equation 13.1

$$\log(PRI_{j,m}) = \alpha_0 + \alpha_1 \left(\frac{\#trade_{j,m}}{\#events_{j,m}} \right) + \varepsilon_{j,m}$$

In Equation 13.1, $PRI_{j,m}$ is the (government or military trade-filtered) PRI measure of country j towards China in month m; is the total number of events recorded between country j and China in month m; $\#trade_{j,m}$ is the total number of events in which the term 'trade' appears in the event descriptions recorded between country j and China in month m; $\#events_{j,m}$ is the total number of events recorded between country j and China in month m; and $\varepsilon_{j,t}$ are the residuals for country j in month m. Normalising the trade event count by the total number of events reported in a given month removes nominal effects, such as seasonality and increasing media coverage, from the PRI series.

Figure 13.2 plots the long-run trends[2] in political relations from the perspective of Quad nation governments between January 2000 and December 2020, with January 2000 levels indexed to 100 for all countries. Indexation allows for the graph to be interpreted as changes in the levels of political relations for a given trading partner. For example, the average monthly Goldstein score of trade-filtered events for the

---

2   Trends here refer to the monthly smoothed PRI series using local polynomial regression fitting or 'Loess' smoothing, a similar technique is used in Heilmann (2016).

Chinese–Indian government political relationship—that is, events for which Indian government (non-military) actors are the 'sender' and the Chinese Government (non-military) is the 'target'[3]—increased by about 9 percentage points between 2001 and mid-2012, followed by a fairly rapid decline through to mid-2020, taking it close to the January 2001 level. Similarly, the China–Australia relationship improved by about 5 percentage points between 2001 and 2014, followed by a drop of 13 percentage points between 2015 and 2020.

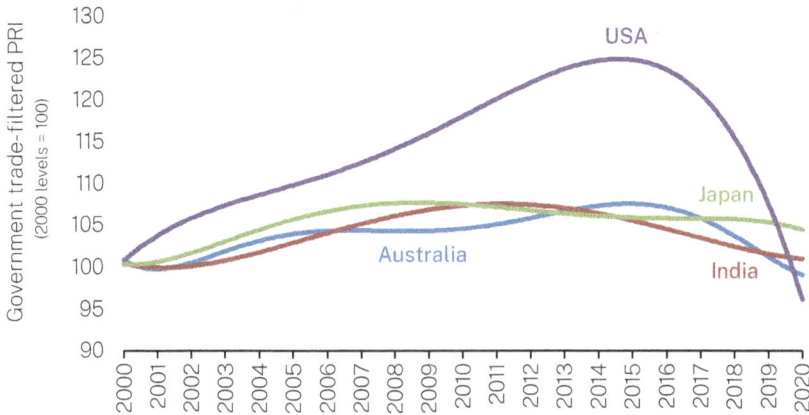

Figure 13.2 Long-run trends in government political relations with China, 2001–20
Source: CEIC and authors' calculations.

These long-run trends reveal an inverted-U shape for Australia, India and the United States, with political relations peaking in different years: around the GFC in 2008–09 for the United States, in 2012 for India and in 2014 for Australia. China–Japan relations are seen to stabilise after 2012, while the deterioration in political relations between China and United States has been consistent—and dramatic—since 2014, with political relations between the world's two largest economies in 2020 far below 2001 levels. The deteriorations for Australia–China and India–China relations are also notable.

The long-run trends depicted in Figure 13.2 smooth out the data, masking the significant events that underpin them. These are evident in Figure 13.3, which illustrates the average annual government and military PRIs for each of the Quad countries. One point that is apparent from this figure is that there are greater fluctuations in the government PRIs for all countries compared with the military PRIs. In general, it would also appear that the downward trend in recent years evident in Figure 13.2 has largely been driven by deterioration at the government-to-government level. However, these annual data obscure events that have shorter-term implications, as the case study below attests.

---

3   Examples of this are the Indian Government's announcements that it would not participate in the Belt and Road Initiative and would ban the use of TikTok and WeChat.

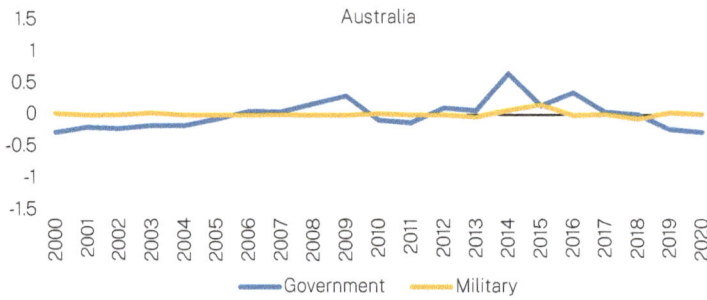

Figure 13.3a Australia

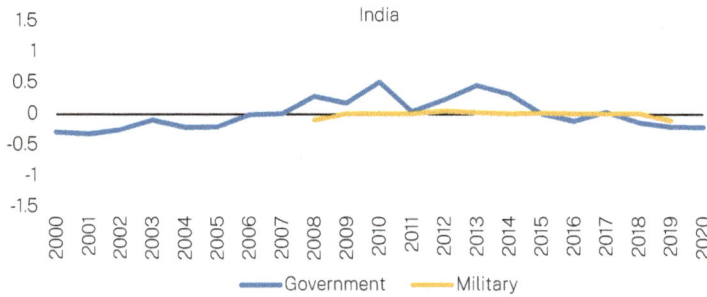

Figure 13.3b India

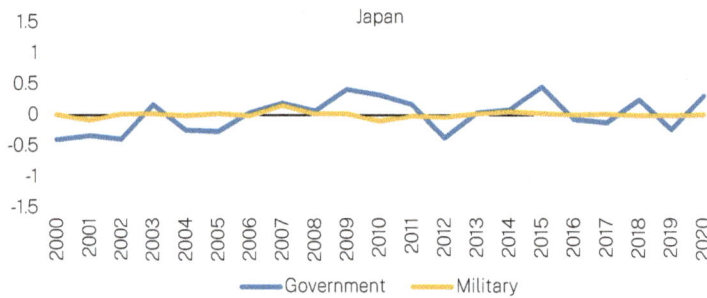

Figure 13.3c Japan

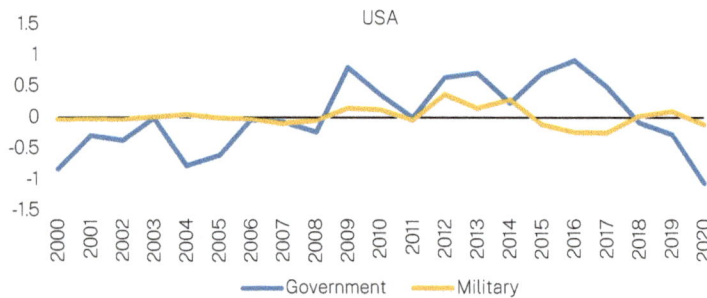

Figure 13.3d USA

Figure 13.3 Average annual government and military trade-filtered political relations with China, 2001–20

Note: Military events data are only available for India–China from 2008.

Source: Authors' calculations using GDELT data.

Case study: China–India Doklam standoff

India and China have a long history of border disputes, beginning with India gaining independence from British rule in 1947 and the formation of the People's Republic of China in 1949. The two countries fought a war in late 1961 over the 'ill-demarcated frontier along Eastern Ladakh and North-Eastern Frontier Agency (NEFA, which in 1987 became Arunachal Pradesh)' (Roy 2021: 83). After the war, relations between the two countries were suspended until the late 1980s when India's then prime minister visited Beijing in a bid to normalise political relations. Since the early 1990s, there has been much deeper engagement between the two countries, particularly in the economic domain, with a large increase in trade and investment ties, while political relations have remained stable with the occasional dispute arising due to unresolved border issues.

In June 2017, India and China were involved in one of the most significant military standoffs between the two countries in recent years in the disputed region of Doklam, which lies in the Sikkim sector of the India–China border and forms a triple junction between India, China and Bhutan (Ratha 2020: 196–97). The conflict began with the construction of a road by the Chinese People's Liberation Army in the Doklam region, which Bhutan and India saw as a security threat. The construction was first opposed by the Royal Bhutanese Army, which tried to push back the Chinese construction party, failing which Indian troops intervened and a standoff ensued between China and India.

Despite a sharp rise in political tensions in June, by August, both countries had agreed to disengage to avoid further escalation. The fact there was little public support in either country for a protraction of the issue, alongside pressure from the United States to reach a swift diplomatic solution and the need for a successful BRICS (Brazil, Russia, India, China and South Africa) Summit, possibly helped ease tensions between the two Asian powers (Ratha 2020). In 2018, China and India held an informal summit in Wuhan, China, where Chinese President Xi Jinping emphasised 'the importance of constructing an open and pluralist global economic order in which all countries can take part without restraint to pursue their development' and reiterated the necessity for India and China to work together given they had convergent interests in areas of global governance (Ratha 2020: 210).

Figure 13.4 shows the logged values of the government and military (trade-filtered) PRI indicators for China and India two years before and after the Doklam standoff in June 2017. The first panel, which focuses on government actors, is more volatile and there is a slight dip in the PRI in the few months before and after the standoff. However, the deterioration in political relations in this period does not stand out when the entire two years before and after the incident are considered, with much larger decreases in political relations seen in the latter half of 2016, at the end of

2017, in the second half of 2018 and in the first half of 2019. Overall, this panel suggests that political relations from the perspective of government actors remained largely stable during the standoff.

The second panel of Figure 13.4 shows political relations from the perspective of Indian military actors towards Chinese military actors. Here we see a sharp decrease in the PRI in the month of June 2017 when the standoff took place, which correlates with the anecdotal evidence that the standoff was an event largely involving military actors. Before the standoff, we observe an increase in the PRI, in the latter half of 2016, followed by the sharp decrease in the PRI in June. However, in line with the anecdotal evidence that suggests that relations between the countries stabilised soon thereafter as military disengagement took place, the military PRI stabilises in the next two months with relatively smaller dips in political relations seen in early 2018.

Broadly speaking, Figure 13.4 illustrates episodes of both cooperation and conflict between government and military actors in India and China, with sufficient variation at the monthly level for the empirical analysis that follows.

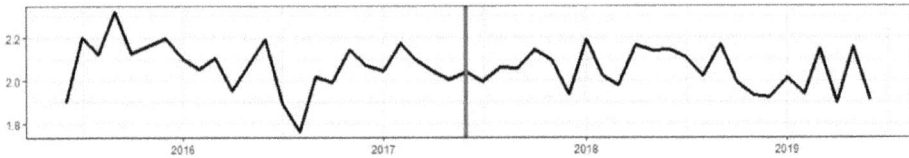

Figure 13.4a Government relations

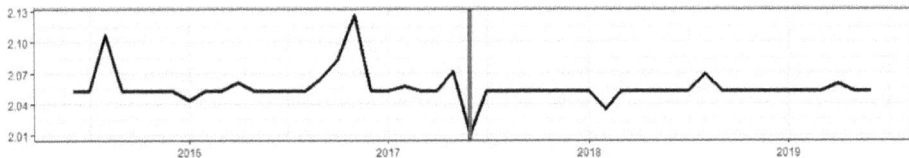

Figure 13.4b Military relations

Figure 13.4 Doklam standoff
Notes: The y-axis shows the logged values of PRI. The red line marks the month of June 2017 when the Doklam incident occurred.
Source: Authors' calculations using GDELT data.

Empirical model, data and results

Most empirical studies that quantify the effects of political determinants on trade do so within the context of a gravity model (Anderson and van Wincoop 2003; Du et al. 2017: 218). The empirical approach in this chapter follows Du et al. (2017) and Agarwal and Golley (2022) by situating the gravity model of trade within a vector auto-regression (VAR) framework. The flexible nature of this framework allows for the endogenous treatment of trade and political relations along with the covariates considered (Du et al. 2017: 218). Moreover, a VAR framework allows for quantification of the dynamic effects of political shocks on trade—that is, short-run effects that last for months and long-run effects that last for years—enabling inferences to be made about the dynamic impact of the shocks. Formally, the model estimated is Equations 13.2 and 13.3.

Equation 13.2

$$x_{j.m} = \alpha_0 + \sum_{I=1}^{n} A_{j,i}(x_{j.m-i}) + e_{j.m}$$

Equation 13.3

$$x_{j.m} = (\Delta ex_{j,m}, \Delta PRI_{j,m}, \Delta y_{c,m}, \Delta y_{j,m}, \Delta reer_{j,m})'$$

In these equations, the subscript j represents partner countries (Australia, India, Japan and the United States), m represents the month (January 2001 ... December 2020). The column vector $x_{j,m}$ contains: 1) the percentage change in partner j's exports to China at time m ($\Delta ex_{j,m}$); 2) the percentage change in partner j's trade-filtered PRI towards China at time m ($\Delta PRI_{j,m}$); 3) the percentage change in China's industrial production index at time m ($\Delta y_{c,m}$); 4) the percentage change in partner j's industrial production index at time m ($\Delta y_{j,m}$); and 5) the percentage change in the ratio of partner j's real effective exchange rate to China's real effective exchange rate at time m ($\Delta reer_{j,m}$). The trade data are from CEIC, the political events data are from the GDELT, as described in the earlier section, the international investment position data are from the World Bank General Economic Monitor and the OECD Statistics Database and the real exchange rate data are from the Bruegel database.

The $A_{j,i}$s in the model are *5x5* matrices that contain the VAR model coefficients and E[ee'] is the *5x5* variance–covariance matrix of contemporaneous error terms. The lag order, n, is selected using the Schwarz Information Selection Criterion. Estimation of the model in differences is necessary because the PRI series is found to be non-stationary in levels but stationary in first differences for most partners. All other data series are also found to be first-order integrated. As discussed in Sims (1980), estimation of VAR models requires *a priori* assumptions regarding the causal ordering of contemporaneous shocks between system variables. We consider political shocks as the most exogenous, followed in order of appearance by terms-of-trade shocks, export shocks and industrial production shocks. From a narrative perspective, these shocks can be interpreted as follows, respectively: an exogenous moderate political conflict event is initiated by China's partners; with a lag of one month, China retaliates through an attempt to change the terms of trade (measured as real exchange rates) in its favour; subsequently, the changes in terms of trade impact trade flows, which in turn lead to changes in consumption for both countries.[4]

---

4   Agarwal (2022) provides a theoretical basis for this narrative by constructing a game-theory model of political relations and trade.

The model is estimated using data aggregated at the monthly level rather than annually, because political shocks tend to be short-lived, so aggregating data at the annual level in such work can lead to inappropriate inferences regarding the extent and timing of the effects of political shocks on trade (for further details, see Du et al. 2017; Agarwal 2022; Agarwal and Golley 2022).

The dynamic effects of political shocks on exports to China can be measured using orthogonalised impulse response functions (OIFs) generated using the VAR model described by Equation 13.2. OIFs are derived from a Choleski decomposition of the error variance–covariance matrix under the assumptions regarding the causal ordering of shocks. They illustrate the changes over time due to a shock on one variable in the system on all other system variables (Sims 1980; Du et al. 2017).

Our primary interest here is whether these OIFs reveal significant short and long-term effects of political shocks on export growth from each Quad country to China. We implement a *positive* shock to the PRI (which can be interpreted as an increase in cooperation or a decrease in conflict) and can identify four *a priori* possibilities:[5]

1. A positive shock to the PRI has no significant short or long-run effects (suggesting that politics and trade are decoupled, in what we call the 'globalisation' hypothesis).
2. A positive shock has positive significant short and long-run effects. This can be interpreted as either an *increase* in political cooperation leading to *higher* export growth or an *increase* in conflict leading to *lower* export growth (in its simplest terms, the 'politics affects trade' hypothesis).
3. A positive shock to the PRI will have only short-run positive effects on export growth, consistent with the expectations of the 'accidental deviations hypothesis'.
4. A positive shock to the PRI will have a negative effect on export growth in the short or long run. This could be interpreted either as an *increase* in political cooperation leading to *lower* export growth or an *increase* in conflict leading to *higher* export growth.

While the last of these possibilities might sound counterintuitive, in the results presented below and elsewhere, we provide evidence that is consistent with this hypothesis. In brief, the logic behind it is that when high-level political relations deteriorate (in either the government or the military sphere), it is plausible that behind-the-scenes efforts by bureaucrats and/or companies engaged in trade not only compensate for the political deterioration, they could also overcompensate to

---

[5]   In a companion paper (Golley et al. 2022), we discuss the theoretical underpinnings of these hypotheses in more detail.

the extent that export growth rises. We call this the 'doubling down' hypothesis.[6] If the effect on exports is only evident in the short run, this hypothesis becomes a subset of the 'accidental deviations' hypothesis, although it may not then be quite as 'accidental' as the name implies. If there is evidence consistent with this hypothesis holding in the longer run, it challenges the logic behind mainstream notions of why politics affects trade—reflected in the second hypothesis. In what follows, we find evidence in support of each hypothesis, depending on the index used, the period analysed and the country in question.

Results: 2001–20

Figure 13.5 displays the OIFs associated with a one standard deviation positive shock to the government PRI series on export growth to China for the Quad countries between 2001 and 2020. The red dotted lines show 90 per cent confidence bands using a bootstrap method. We illustrate the results of a positive shock, noting that a negative shock produces export effects of the same magnitude, but with the opposite sign. For all four countries, this figure reveals that there are no short-run effects of a political shock on export growth. Despite this common finding, note that the dynamic pattern of the impact of the shock does differ across countries, which is to be expected because of differences in industrial structure and in the duration of contracts across industries and firms in each country, which are not explicitly modelled (Du et al. 2017: 219).

As an alternative way of presenting the results, Table 13.2 presents the effects of a positive one standard deviation shock to the government/military PRI on export growth for each country, with significant effects shown in bold for each month in which they occur. No significant effects are found beyond eight months, hence our reporting of the results through to this point. The results for the government PRI shock confirm the results presented in Figure 13.5: there are no short-term effects on export growth for any country. Turning to the military PRI, we see significant positive effects for Australia and the United States in the first month, with the latter implying an increase of 1.85 per cent in export growth from the United States to China following a positive one standard deviation shock (that is, a rise in cooperation). Conversely, this could be interpreted as a 1.84 per cent reduction in export growth following a negative shock (that is, a rise in conflict).

---

6   A complementary possibility to this is that in times of rising cooperation, export growth may in fact fall, which we term the 'dropping the ball' hypothesis. Our results below are not consistent with this hypothesis, so we simply footnote it here, referring interested readers to the companion paper in the previous note for further discussion.

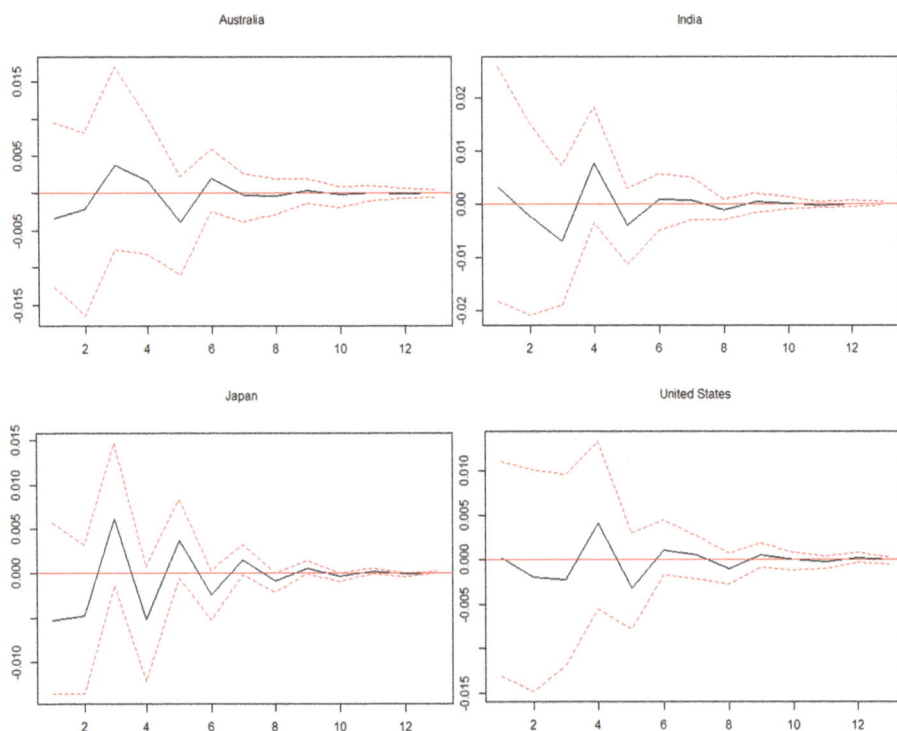

Figure 13.5 Short-run effects of government PRI shocks on export growth to China, 2001–20

Notes: This figure depicts the dynamic effects of a one standard deviation positive shock to the government PRI series on a country's export growth to China as implied by the VAR model (Equation 13.2). The red lines show the upper and lower limits at a 90 per cent confidence interval using a bootstrap method.

Source: Authors' calculations.

We then compute the cumulative long-run effects of PRI shocks on export growth between 2001 and 2020 implied by the VAR model over a time horizon of two years. The final column of Table 13.2 shows the results, confirming that there are no long-run effects for any country following a shock to the government PRI (consistent with the first globalisation hypothesis above). For the military PRI, a significant positive long-term effect is found for Australia and China, with a one standard deviation positive shock in the military PRI associated with a 0.49 per cent increase in export growth two years after the shock. Again, this could be interpreted as an *increase* in cooperation driving an *increase* in export growth, or an *increase* in conflict driving a *decrease* in export growth. This is consistent with the second hypothesis.

Table 13.2 Effects of government and military political shocks on exports to China, 2001–20 (per cent)

Country	Short-run effects								Long-run effects
	Months after political shock								
	1	2	3	4	5	6	7	8	
Government PRI									
Australia	−0.34	−0.21	0.38	0.17	−0.39	0.20	−0.03	−0.04	−0.23
India	0.57	−0.12	−0.05	0.07	−0.04	0.02	−0.01	0.00	0.44
Japan	−0.53	−0.47	0.62	−0.52	0.37	−0.24	0.15	−0.09	−0.68
United States	0.02	−0.20	−0.22	0.41	−0.32	0.10	0.06	−0.10	−0.21
Military PRI									
Australia	**0.74**	0.30	0.52	−0.80	0.67	−0.13	−0.29	**0.31**	**0.49***
India	n.a.	n.a.	n.a.	n.a.	n.a.	n.a.	n.a.	n.a.	n.a.
Japan	0.56	−0.35	0.01	0.07	−0.05	0.04	−0.01	−0.03	0.26
United States	**1.85**	−1.29	−0.14	0.82	−0.63	0.22	0.05	**−0.11**	0.01

Notes: This table displays the cumulative effects of a one standard deviation positive shock to the trade-filtered PRI series on each country's export growth to China implied by the VAR models. The long-term horizon is two years. n.a: not available, as the Indian Military PRI series only starts in 2008 onwards.

Results: 2016–2020

Next, we focus on the period 2016–20, in part to see whether Chinese behaviour changed in recent years in line with its growing economic resources, but also because this represents a period of increasing conflict—or at least falling cooperation—with the four Quad countries. As seen in Table 13.3, for Australia, no short or long-term effects are found in this subperiod for the government or military PRIs. For Japan, significant short-run effects for the government PRI begin with a positive shock but, overall, there are no long-term effects. For the United States, a relatively large positive coefficient on export growth appears to follow a shock to the military PRI, but this rebounds soon after, with no evidence of a long-term effect. Thus, for Australia, there is no evidence of a relationship between (deteriorating) political relations and aggregate[7] Australian exports during this period, while the results for the United States and Japan are consistent with the accidental deviations hypothesis.

---

7   In Golley et al. (2022), we disaggregate exports into 20 HS2 sectors, revealing heterogeneous results across sectors—some with significant short- and long-run results, in contrast with the insignificance in the aggregated data.

Table 13.3 Effects of government and military political shocks on exports to China, 2016–20 (per cent)

Country	Short-run effects									Long-run effects
	Months after political shock									
	1	2	3	4	5	6	7	8	9	
Government PRI										
Australia	0.94	–0.17	–0.49	0.67	–0.51	0.27	–0.09	0.00	0.02	0.01
India	–0.24	–2.13	1.28	–0.68	0.38	–0.23	0.14	–0.08	0.04	–0.02
Japan	–0.47	–1.13	1.79	–1.83	1.57	–1.21	0.87	–0.59	0.38	–0.01
United States	1.53	0.85	–0.70	0.36	–0.12	0.03	0.00	0.00	0.00	0.02
Military PRI										
Australia	–1.22	0.17	0.36	–0.39	0.24	–0.10	0.03	0.01	–0.01	–0.01
India	–5.13	–3.58	2.30	–0.88	0.28	–0.08	0.02	–0.01	0.00	–0.07*
Japan	1.27	–0.11	–0.65	0.39	0.16	–0.49	0.49	–0.25	–0.04	0.01
United States	2.06	–2.08	1.35	–0.85	0.49	–0.29	0.16	–0.09	0.05	0.01

Notes: This table displays the cumulative effects of a one standard deviation positive shock to the PRI series on each country's export growth to China implied by the VAR models. The long-term horizon is two years.

India's results are the most intriguing. For the period 2016–20, there are no significant effects for the government shock. However, for the military shock, there is a negative effect in the second month after a positive shock—and this is substantial enough to generate a long-run negative effect (although, again, the magnitude is low).

Conflict and cooperation

In this section, we unpack the finding for India of a significant *negative* long-run effect on export growth following a positive shock to the military PRI for the period between 2016 and 2020. The Doklam case study presented above provides one clear case of a rise in military conflict between China and India during this period, while a deadly clash between Indian and Chinese soldiers in June 2020 in Ladakh, in the disputed border region in the Himalaya, provides another. The 2017 revival of the Quad, which calls for high-level military cooperation between the four member countries (and, by implication, an assumption of deteriorating military cooperation with China), further suggests that it makes sense to interpret this as a period of deteriorating bilateral political relations between China and India more broadly (evident in Figure 13.1). Here, we seek to investigate whether that negative coefficient was driven by shocks to cooperation, shocks to conflict, or both. To do this, we create two separate indices for cooperation and conflict in terms of

Indian military actors 'messaging' to China, calculated using only the positive and the negative Goldstein scores, respectively. Using the same method applied above, Table 13.4 reports the results for a positive shock to each of these indices.

Note that, according to hypotheses two and three above, the *a priori* expectation is that a *decrease* in political cooperation will result in *lower* export growth, as will an *increase* in conflict. In the case of cooperation, interpreting the results here remains straightforward: positive short and long-run coefficients would be consistent with hypothesis two, and positive short-run coefficients only are consistent with hypothesis three—the accidental deviations hypothesis. However, instead, we find a coefficient of –2.25 occurring in the third month (that is, a one standard deviation positive shock to PRI leads to a 2.25 per cent decrease in export growth), which is consistent with our doubling down hypothesis: a reduction in cooperation being associated with a rise in export growth.

Interpreting the shocks to the conflict index requires a little more care, because a positive shock to the PRI implies a *decrease* in conflict. In this case, a negative coefficient on export growth (as we find for the second month) means that a *decrease* in conflict is associated with a *decrease* in export growth; or, conversely (and more critically given the period in question), an *increase* in conflict is associated with an *increase* in export growth. This, too, is consistent with the doubling down hypothesis presented above.

In combination, the results presented in Table 13.4 suggest that the negative long-run effect of a military shock is driven by both the cooperation and the conflict indices, with both indices working against the mainstream expectation that periods of higher conflict (or reduced cooperation) will result in lower export growth. We do not wish to oversell this finding, given that there are no long-run effects for either of these indexes—and the long-run effect when they are combined is small. It does, however, suggest that the relationship between political relations and trade is far from straightforward, and we should be open to expecting the unexpected.

Table 13.4 Effects of military shocks on Indian export growth to China, conflict and cooperation (per cent)

Military PRI			Short-run effects									Long-run effects
			Months after political shock									
Country	Time	Index	1	2	3	4	5	6	7	8	9	
India	2016–20	Cooperation	4.83	2.69	–2.25	1.17	–0.53	0.24	–0.11	0.05	–6.07	4.83
		Conflict	–5.10	–3.33	2.42	–1.06	0.39	–0.14	0.05	–0.02	–6.87	–5.10

Notes: This table displays the cumulative effects of a one standard deviation positive shock to the trade-filtered PRI series on India's export growth to China implied by the VAR models. The long-term horizon is two years. Notice that these short turn effects are not statistically significant.

Concluding thoughts

There is a burgeoning empirical literature that investigates the extent to which moderate shocks in political relations affect trade outcomes. The evidence on this political–trade nexus is mixed but can generally be divided into three categories: those finding that trade strengthens when 'bonds of friendship' (or political cooperation) strengthen, in the short run only (suggesting accidental deviations from a Pareto optimal equilibrium in which there is no long-term relationship) or in both the short and the long runs (suggesting that politics has significant and lasting impacts on trade); those that find trade weakens in times of conflict (in the short and/or the long runs); and those that find no evidence of political relations impacting on trade in either of these two ways. This chapter makes several contributions to this empirical literature, including some findings that run counter to those presented in the literature to date.

First, we provide estimates of the dynamic effects of moderate political shocks on the merchandise exports of Quad countries to China between 2001 and 2020, using two constructed measures of political shocks—based on Quad country government and military actors' 'messaging' to China, made possible using GDELT data. The analysis suggests that government shocks had no significant short- or long-run effects on any of the four countries' exports over this period. In contrast, we found evidence of small, positive short-term effects following a shock to the military PRI for Australia and the United States, with Australian exports further experiencing a long-term positive effect as well. For Japan and India, there were no short or long-term significant coefficients for either of the two PRIs.

We then focused on the most recent period, 2016–20, in which all Quad countries experienced downward trends in their political relations with China (although to differing degrees), using the Doklam military standoff between China and India in mid-2017 to demonstrate an episode of reasonably significant conflict. In this period, for the government PRI, no countries experienced statistically significant short-run or long-run effects. For the military PRI, export growth from the United States to China was shown to be positively associated with a positive shock, although neither the short-run nor the long-run effects are statistically significant, although neither the short-run and the long-run coefficients are statistically significant.

We unpacked the results for India one step further, by separating the PRI into separate 'cooperation' and 'conflict' indexes for the period 2016–20. Our findings were consistent with a 'doubling down' hypothesis, which suggests that periods of rising conflict can in fact be associated with rising export growth—in both the short and the long runs. We do not seek to claim that these results provide concrete evidence in support of this hypothesis. Rather, as we have detailed extensively in a companion article focused on the Australia–China relationship (Golley et al. 2022), we argue that there is a possibility that when high-level political (in this case, military) relations deteriorate, bureaucrats working behind the scenes in Delhi and Beijing may couple with the determination of Indian companies to ensure that their lucrative access to China's markets are preserved. The key point here is that trade is overwhelmingly undertaken by companies that are principally motivated by economic considerations, such as profits, costs and quality. In turn, these considerations reflect cross-country variation in production complementarities and purchasing power. These economic fundamentals may not only create a separation between these actors and those strategists in country capitals preoccupied with geopolitical alignment, they may also go further to ensure that trading links are strengthened even as political relations decline.

The evidence presented in this chapter does not allow us to answer this question definitively, but it does lead us to conclude that the relationship between politics and trade is far from straightforward, with a spectrum of possibilities hinging on the nature and definition of political relations, the actors involved in defining those relationships (government or military) and the heterogeneous responses of companies and households across countries in the wake of shocks to those relationships. China has the opportunity to be a responsible, inclusive and cooperative global power. As President Xi (2022) consistently stresses in his annual addresses to the World Economic Forum in Davos and elsewhere, cooperation is the best way to 'make economic globalisation more open, inclusive, balanced and beneficial for all', while 'confrontation does not solve problems; it only invites catastrophic consequences'. As the Russia–Ukraine war continues with devastating effects and as tensions rise across the Taiwan Strait, it is crucial to ensure that this rhetoric is consistently reflected in the reality of China's global economic and other interactions. For the Quad countries as well, finding ways to advance cooperation and minimise conflict wherever possible in the years ahead will play an important role in reducing the possibility that the Pareto superior combination of trade and peace becomes only a distant memory.

References

Agarwal, V. 2022. 'The effects of political shocks on international trade: evidence from China and major partners, 1998-2018.' PhD thesis. The Australian National University, Canberra. doi.org/10.25911/DZSH-DA40.

Agarwal, V. and J. Golley. 2022. 'Do Political Relations Affect Exports to China? Evidence from the "Quad".' *The World Economy* 45(9): 2882–901. doi.org/10.1111/twec.13252.

Anderson, J.E. and E. van Wincoop. 2003. 'Gravity with Gravitas: A Solution to the Border Puzzle.' *American Economic Review* 93(1): 170–92. doi.org/10.1257/000282803321455214.

Baru, S. 2012. 'Geo-Economics and Strategy.' *Survival* 54(3): 47–58. doi.org/10.1080/00396338.2012.690978.

Baru, S. 2013. 'India and the World: A Geoeconomics Perspective.' *Economic and Political Weekly*: 37–41.

Blackwill, R.D. and J.M. Harris. 2016. *War by Other Means*. Cambridge, MA: Harvard University Press. doi.org/10.4159/9780674545960.

Brautigam, D. 2020. 'A Critical Look at Chinese "Debt-Trap Diplomacy": The Rise of a Meme.' *Area Development and Policy* 5(1): 1–14. doi.org/10.1080/23792949.2019.1689828.

Bräutigam, D. and T. Xiaoyang. 2012. 'Economic Statecraft in China's New Overseas Special Economic Zones: Soft Power, Business or Resource Security?' *International Affairs* 88(4): 799–816. doi.org/10.1111/j.1468-2346.2012.01102.x.

Chubb, A. 2021. 'The Sino-Indian Border Crisis:Chinese Perceptions of Indian Nationalism.' In *Crisis: The China Story Yearbook 2020*. ANU Press, Canberra: 222–237. doi.org/10.22459/CSY.2021.08.

Dalzell, S., J. Snape and T.D. Landgrafft. 2020. 'Tonnes of Australian Lobsters Stuck in Chinese Airports amid Trade Tensions.' *ABC News*, 2 November. Available from: www.abc.net.au/news/2020-11-02/australian-lobster-exports-caught-in-china-trade-tensions/12837700.

Davis, C.L., A. Fuchs and K. Johnson. 2019. 'State Control and the Effects of Foreign Relations on Bilateral Trade.' *Journal of Conflict Resolution* 63(2): 405–38. doi.org/10.1177/0022002717739087.

Du, Y., J. Ju, C.D. Ramirez and X. Yao. 2017. 'Bilateral Trade and Shocks in Political Relations: Evidence from China and Some of its Major Trading Partners, 1990–2013.' *Journal of International Economics*, 108: 211–25. doi.org/10.1016/j.jinteco.2017.07.002.

Ferguson, V. 2020. 'China Sours on Australia's Wine.' *The Interpreter*, 1 September. Available from: www.lowyinstitute.org/the-interpreter/china-sours-australia-s-wine.

Gasiorowski, M.J. 1986. 'Economic Interdependence and International Conflict: Some Cross-National Evidence.' *International Studies Quarterly* 30(1): 23–38. doi.org/10.2307/2600435.

Golley, J., V. Agarwal, J. Laurenceson and T. Qiu. 2022. 'For Better or Worse, in Sickness and in Health: Australia–China Political Relations and Trade.' *China Economic Journal*: 1–20. doi.org/10.1080/17538963.2022.2117180.

Heilmann, K. 2016. 'Does Political Conflict Hurt Trade? Evidence from Consumer Boycotts.' *Journal of International Economics* 99: 179–91. doi.org/10.1016/j.jinteco.2015.11.008.

Hirschman, A.O. 1980 [1945]. *National Power and the Structure of Foreign Trade*. Berkeley, CA: University of California Press.

Jones, L. and S. Hameiri. 2020. *Debunking the myth of 'debt-trap diplomacy': How recipient countries shape China's Belt and Road Initiative*. Asia-Pacific Programme Research Paper. London: Chatham House.

Leetaru, K. and P.A. Schrodt. 2013. 'GDELT: Global Data on Events, Location, and Tone, 1979–2012.' *ISA Annual Convention* 2(4): 1–49.

Lim, D. and V. Ferguson. 2020. 'In Beef over Barley, Chinese Economic Coercion Cuts against the Grain.' *The Interpreter*, 13 May. Available from: www.lowyinstitute.org/the-interpreter/beef-over-barley-chinese-economic-coercion-cuts-against-grain.

Long, A.G. 2008. 'Bilateral Trade in the Shadow of Armed Conflict.' *International Studies Quarterly* 52(1): 81–101. doi.org/10.1111/j.1468-2478.2007.00492.x.

Mansfield, E.D. and B.M. Pollins (eds). 2009. *Economic Interdependence and International Conflict: New Perspectives on an Enduring Debate*. Ann Arbor, MI: University of Michigan Press.

Medcalf, R. 2020. *Contest for the Indo-Pacific: Why China Won't Map the Future*. Melbourne: Black Inc.

Pfaff, B. 2008. 'VAR, SVAR and SVEC Models: Implementation within R Package Vars.' *Journal of Statistical Software* 27(4): 1–32. doi.org/10.18637/jss.v027.i04.

Raby, G. 2020. *China's Grand Strategy and Australia's Future in the New Global Order*. Melbourne: Melbourne University Press.

Ratha, K.C. 2020. 'Deciphering the Doklam Standoff: The Context of the Contest.' *Jadavpur Journal of International Relations* 24(2): 196–215. doi.org/10.1177/0973598420939685.

Roy, K. 2021. 'Focusing on India's Look East Policy: India–China Relationship from 1947 to 2020.' *International Area Studies Review* 24(2): 79–96. doi.org/10.1177/22338659211018324.

Sims, C.A. 1980. 'Macroeconomics and Reality.' *Econometrica: Journal of the Econometric Society*: 1–48. doi.org/10.2307/1912017.

Van Grieken, B.J. and J. Kantorowicz. 2021. 'Debunking Myths about China: The Determinants of China's Official Financing in the Pacific.' *Geopolitics* 26(3): 861–88. doi.org/10.1080/14650045.2019.1654459.

Xi, Jinping. 2022. 'President Xi Jinping's Message to the Davos Agenda in Full.' World Economic Forum, Davos, Switzerland, 17 January. Available from: www.weforum.org/agenda/2022/01/address-chinese-president-xi-jinping-2022-world-economic-forum-virtual-session/.

14

US–China relations: How to stop the economic damage from de-globalisation

Wing Thye Woo

US–China economic decoupling: On course for acceleration?

The economic welfare of both the United States and China has been increasingly hurt by the continuation of the economic decoupling of the two countries, even after Donald Trump was booted out of the White House on 20 January 2022. And it seems highly likely that the pace of economic decoupling will quicken in the medium term because US–China relations are on course to worsen due to the ratcheting up of the geostrategic and technological competition between them.[1]

In this chapter, we argue that the potential economic damage for these two countries and the rest of the world can be prevented if China and the United States share a realistic definition of what constitutes national security in a multipolar world. Specifically, we can construct institutional arrangements between the United States and China that will address their national security concerns without negatively impacting their economic interaction so long as: 1) neither country believes its national security is guaranteed only when it has military dominance over the other country; and 2) each country deems its national security is safeguarded when there is only minimal probability that the other side can undertake a successful first attack that ensures victory.

---

1   The economic reasons for the US–China trade war are examined in Woo (2008), Liu and Woo (2018), and Swenson and Woo (2019).

This chapter is organised as follows. Section two outlines the geostrategic competition between the United States and China, while section three outlines their technological competition. Section four suggests institutional arrangements that can keep geostrategic and technological competition from causing a downward spiral in economic ties that ends globalisation.

As we will show later, these same institutional arrangements that define the three types of competition—economic, geostrategic and technological—can become the basis of US–China cooperation to coordinate the supply of global public goods to ensure common global prosperity in a harmonious world that achieves the United Nations' 17 Sustainable Development Goals (SDGs) of the 2030 Development Agenda and the 1.5°C target of the Paris climate treaty. Our analysis will point out that it is wrong to view the quests for national security and technological prowess as zero-sum games. They can yield win-win outcomes, as can economic competition, when appropriate guardrails are put in place.

The scaling up of geostrategic competition

Geostrategic competition took a violent turn in Europe when Russia invaded Ukraine on 24 February 2022. The war began shortly after Russian President Vladimir Putin returned from a visit to China, where both nations had declared a friendship with 'no limits' on 4 February 2022. The North Atlantic Treaty Organization (NATO), led by the United States, is the biggest supplier of weapons to Ukraine, and China is the biggest buyer of the Russian oil that has been sanctioned by the United States and its allies.

The geostrategic competition in East Asia heated up when the Speaker of the US House of Representatives and third highest-ranking member of the US Government, Nancy Pelosi, landed in Taiwan on 2 August 2022 after the Chinese Ministry of Foreign Affairs had warned that the Chinese military would not 'sit idly by' if her rumoured visit were to occur (Reuters 2022). In a telephone conversation with US President Joe Biden on 28 July 2022, Chinese President Xi Jinping had said: 'Public opinion shall not be violated. And if you play with fire, you get burned. [I h]ope the US side can see this clearly' (White House 2022; Al Jazeera 2022).

The outcome was predictable. The Chinese military conducted live-fire exercises in six zones around Taiwan immediately after Pelosi's departure from the island (Everington 2022). China sent aircraft and ships past the midway line in the Taiwan Strait for the first time and launched missiles over Taipei and into a part of the Pacific Ocean that is in the Exclusive Economic Zone of Japan—a close military ally of the United States.[2]

---

2   China took non-military action as well, including the suspension of climate talks with the United States and the cessation of cooperation in fighting narcotic flows. See Joselow (2022); Lo (2022).

What deserves immediate attention is that the likelihood of further escalation in US–China tensions over Taiwan has since increased. In an interview with Scott Pelley on 18 September 2022, President Biden agreed with Pelley's summary of the US position as: 'US forces, US men and women, would defend Taiwan in the event of a Chinese invasion' (Pelley 2022).

As this was the fourth time President Biden had said his country would defend Taiwan against China, it is clear the United States has abandoned its policy of 'strategic ambiguity' and embraced one of 'strategic clarity' as the more effective way to deter a Chinese invasion.

Furthermore, this interview was notable in that President Biden, unlike previous US presidents, did not oppose a formal declaration of independence by Taiwan:

> Scott Pelley [interviewer]: What should Chinese President Xi know about your commitment to Taiwan?
>
> President Biden: We agree with what we signed on to a long time ago. And that [is that] there's [the] One-China Policy, and Taiwan makes their own judgments about their independence. We are not … encouraging their being independent … [T]hat's their decision. (Pelly 2022)

While it is possible President Biden misspoke on the matter of Taiwan's independence (it was the first time he had expressed this opinion in public, unlike the four times in which he committed US troops to defend Taiwan), it seems too much of a coincidence that Pelosi had expressed a similar opinion on 21 July 2022 that the United States supported the right of Taiwan to decide on its independence: 'It's important for us to show support for Taiwan. I also think that none of us has ever said we're for independence when it comes to Taiwan. That's up to Taiwan to decide' (Sprunt and Feng 2022).

In addition to this inflaming of the perennially contentious issue of Taiwan, US–China disagreement on the legitimacy of China's claim of sovereignty over the large portion of the South China Sea bounded by China's Nine-Dash Line has translated into military action. The Quadrilateral Security Dialogue (Quad) of four big democracies—India, Australia, Japan and the United States—which was initiated in May 2007 in response to China's increased naval activities in the South China Sea and became dormant in January 2008 after Australia changed its mind about the matter, was revived by President Trump in 2017 (Buchan and Rimland 2020; Marlow 2022).

And, on 15 September 2021, Australia, the United Kingdom and the United States formed the AUKUS alliance to transfer nuclear submarine technology to Australia to render it a more muscular 'deputy sheriff' in patrolling the South Pacific.[3]

Cold War 2.0 is here. This development is well captured by the fact that NATO identified China as a systemic threat for the first time in 2022 (Kyodo News Agency 2022). NATO (2022) lumped Russia and China together and described China's behaviour as a threat to global law and order:

> The People's Republic of China's (PRC) stated ambitions and coercive policies challenge our interests, security and values … The PRC's malicious hybrid and cyber operations and its confrontational rhetoric and disinformation target Allies and harm Alliance security. The PRC seeks to control key technological and industrial sectors, critical infrastructure, and strategic materials and supply chains. It uses its economic leverage to create strategic dependencies and enhance its influence. It strives to subvert the rules-based international order, including in the space, cyber and maritime domains. The deepening strategic partnership between the People's Republic of China and the Russian Federation and their mutually reinforcing attempts to undercut the rules-based international order run counter to our values and interests …

> We will work together responsibly, as Allies, to address the systemic challenges posed by the PRC to Euro-Atlantic security … We will boost our shared awareness, enhance our resilience and preparedness, and protect against the PRC's coercive tactics and efforts to divide the Alliance. We will stand up for our shared values and the rules-based international order, including freedom of navigation. (NATO 2022)

The atmosphere is presently thick with mutual suspicions about the intentions of the other side. On 22 April 2022, US National Security Council Coordinator for the Indo-Pacific Kurt Campbell arrived helter-skelter in Honiara, the capital of Solomon Islands, in the wake of that country signing a security pact with China. Honiara is 9,843 kilometres (or 16 flying hours) from Los Angeles, yet the increased potential presence of China there was seen as an immediate threat to the national security of the United States, in the same way that the potential NATO membership of Ukraine was seen as a grave threat to the national security of Russia.[4]

The dogs of war, having driven the doves of peace from the fields of Ukraine, were now swimming in the stretch of water between Taiwan and Solomon Islands.

---

3   There is debate about the origin of the use of 'Deputy Sheriff' to describe Australia's relationship with the United States. According to the BBC (2003), Australian Prime Minister John Howard used this term in a 1999 interview with *The Bulletin* magazine to characterise Australia's role. Esther Pan (2006), however, says it was a term *The Bulletin* coined to depict Howard's attitude.

4   US Secretary of State Antony Blinken announced an aid package of US$810 million for Pacific Island nations on 29 September 2022. See Magnier (2022). For the US view on islands in the Indo-Pacific, see Campbell (2022).

The intensification of technological competition

Despite China's much-lauded rapid economic growth since 1978, in 2021, it is still technologically far behind the United States. China's GDP per capita is 18.1 per cent or 27.9 per cent of that of the United States depending on whether the market exchange rate or the purchasing power parity (PPP) exchange rate is used.

It has therefore been natural for China to actively seek to upgrade its technological capacity in addition to continuing the process begun in 1978 of economic reform and opening. The latter was confirmed by the 2013 decision of Xi Jinping's new administration to restructure the economic system 'to allow the market [forces] to play a "decisive role" in the allocation of resources' (Huang 2023).

A significant step forward in technological upgrading occurred with the launch of the Made in China 2025 (MIC 2025) program in 2015 to undergird the Thirteenth (2016–20) and Fourteenth (2021–25) Five-Year plans. The MIC 2025 policy:

> calls for breakthroughs in 10 sectors and supports a range of sector-specific plans …
>
> MIC 2025 sets goals for each sector to increase the share of production by Chinese firms … China seeks to lead at each point in the value chain. In semiconductors, for example, China seeks to build a globally competitive industry in design, operating systems, manufacturing, packaging, testing, equipment and materials. (Congressional Research Service 2020)

China committed about US$300 billion in 2018 to support MIC 2025 (Wikipedia 2022). In the subsequent Covid-19 stimulus package in 2020, it allocated US$1.4 trillion to be spent on new infrastructure by 2025 to further deepen 'integration of the Internet of Things and the real economy' (Trivedi 2020).

Inevitably, many analysts have seen a contradiction between the 2013 policy pledge to give the market a 'decisive role' in resource allocation and the 2015 policy of direct government support to induce the emergence of the 10 high-tech industries in Figure 14.1 (for example, aerospace, high-end computerised machines and robots and energy equipment). This contradiction between stated policy principle and subsequent policy action is particularly severe because the targeted amount of local content in most of these high-tech products is very high. Figure 14.2 reports that local content will be more than 90 per cent in agricultural machinery and 80 per cent in high-performance computers, high-tech maritime vessels and electric vehicles, batteries and engines.

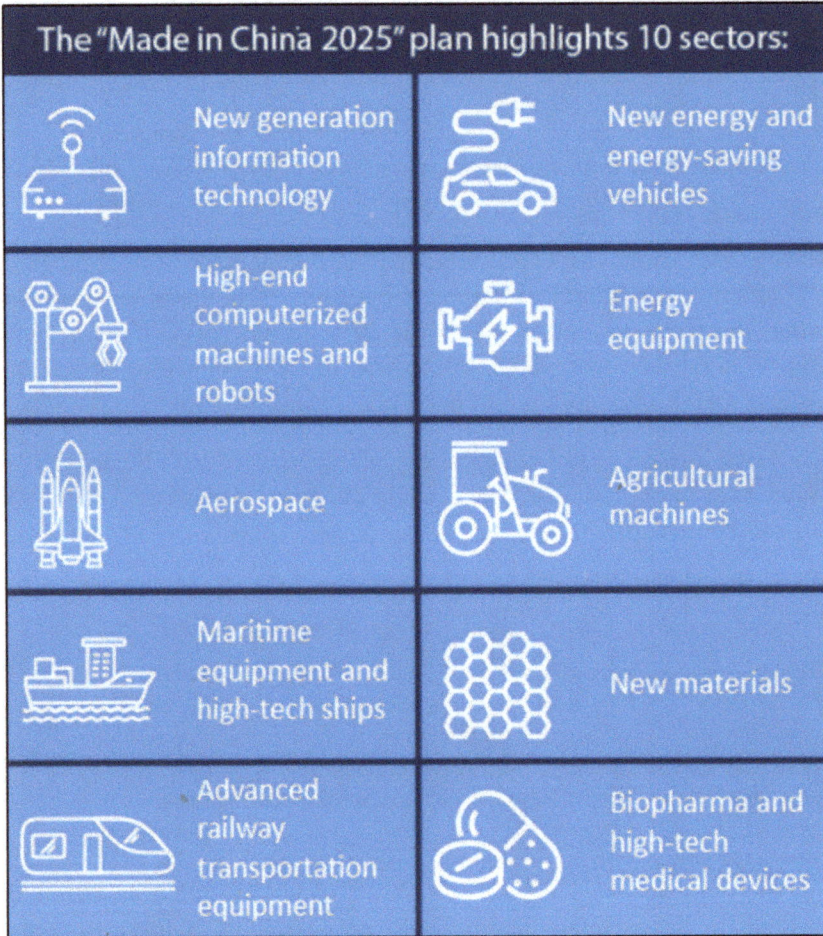

The "Made in China 2025" plan highlights 10 sectors:

New generation information technology	New energy and energy-saving vehicles
High-end computerized machines and robots	Energy equipment
Aerospace	Agricultural machines
Maritime equipment and high-tech ships	New materials
Advanced railway transportation equipment	Biopharma and high-tech medical devices

Figure 14.1 China's industrial priorities, 2015–25

Source: Congressional Research Service (2020).

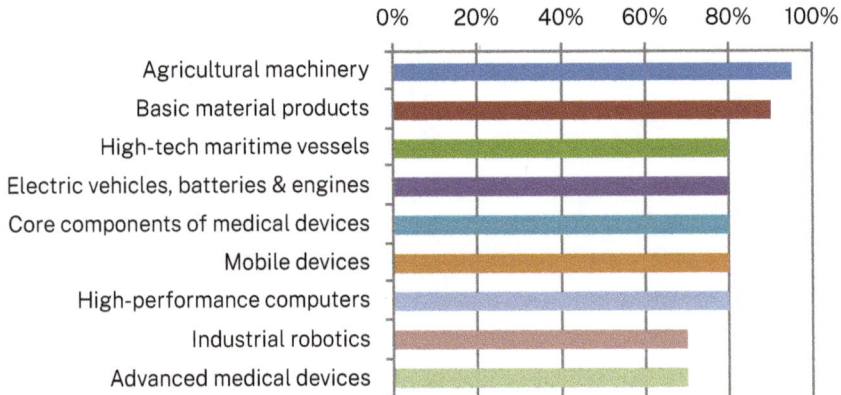

Figure 14.2 Selected MIC 2025 domestic content goals

Source: Congressional Research Service (2020).

The contradiction is deepened given state funding is usually given to state-owned enterprises to deliver advanced technology. As Feigenbaum (2018) notes:

> If Beijing is serious about making the market 'decisive,' then, by definition, the state must retreat. But in the five years since the plenum, the reverse seems to have happened in many areas. Above all, state-owned enterprises (SOEs) have been consolidated and strengthened. And Party committees within these firms have been strengthened too.

However, Feigenbaum (2018) then astutely points out that the 2013 pledge and the 2015 action are contradictory only when seen from the interests of foreign firms and not those of domestic firms:

> The fact is, China could very well increase *domestic* competition while retaining high walls, strong barriers, and non-tariff protectionist obstacles to foreign competition … In many sectors, … Beijing will try to hold off opening its markets until domestic competitors have been so strengthened that they can dominate foreign rivals in the Chinese market, even without the same levels of government support …

> [W]e sometimes put this point pretty bluntly when kicking it around in our office chatter: Deng Xiaoping's policy was 'reform and opening up' (*gaige kaifang*); by contrast, Xi's policy aims to decouple reform from opening up.

Here, we recognise that there is a clash in China's technological modernisation project between the interests of the foreign high-tech entrepreneurs who want China to be the market for their products and the interests of Chinese entrepreneurs who desire higher future profits by moving up the value-added ladder. There is no clash between the interests of the foreign and domestic entrepreneurs, and when China's economic welfare is lowered, only if the infant industry assumption turns out to be untrue in most cases in China. While the development experiences of China's immediate neighbours, Japan and South Korea, would support the case for infant industry protection, the uniform experience in Latin America and South-East Asia has been that their infant industries seldom matured and then entrenched these countries in the middle-income trap.

Foreign concerns about future income losses from China's industrial policy were further heightened in 2018 when China announced that it would begin drawing up the 'China Standards 2035' plan to enable Chinese firms to set global standards on emerging technologies like quantum computing, artificial intelligence (AI), the Internet of Things and green technology. The official rationale for this new state initiative is often given in the dictum 'third-tier companies make products [三流企做品]; second-tier companies make technology [二流企做技]; first-tier companies make standards [一流企做准]' (Morgan Stanley Research 2021: 5).

According to this line of thinking, China is currently home to mostly third-tier companies—those that produce designs originally created abroad. Made in China 2025, a key industrial policy for the development of tech in China, seeks to foster second-tier companies that are leaders in design and innovation.

As such, the China Standards 2035 project endorses and builds upon Made in China 2025. In effect, the goal of the latter—to transform China into a leading tech innovator and producer—is a stepping-stone in achieving the former …

A major benefit of leading standards is being able to influence them in a way that benefits one's own strengths and ambitions. In this way, if China were to lead standard setting, they may be used to privilege domestic companies, such as the telecommunications giant Huawei.

Besides influencing the direction of standards, however, is the more basic issue of licensing fees. Because most proprietary standards in the tech industry are created by foreign companies, China is the world's second largest payer of licensing fees in the world. China Standards 2035, then, seeks to reverse this relationship and make China a net recipient of licensing fees. (Koty 2020)

In short, MIC 2025 and China Standards 2035 will together temporarily decouple China's high-tech firms from the global marketplace, fund them generously to learn from the rest of the world and to become better than their teachers, and then release them to dominate global markets. It was inevitable that China's technological strategy would be perceived as predatory by many foreign observers and would excite newspaper headlines like 'China's "Standards 2035" Project Could Result in a Technological Cold War' (Gargeyas 2021).

The outcome is that US firms and US society at large have now become concerned about the implications of China's technology strategy for future US economic prosperity, technological innovation and national security. The validity of these concerns was boosted by three aspects of China's growth that marked it as different from that of other large developing economies.

The first aspect is the exceptional speed with which China is closing the development gap with the United States. Table 14.1 reports that China's development gap was reduced by 16.8 percentage points to 23.8 percentage points in the 1990–21 period compared with a reduction of 1.7 percentage points to 5.6 percentage points for India and –4.8 to –0.1 percentage points for Brazil. The standards of living in both Brazil and India were higher than in China in 1990 but China was substantially richer than both in 2021.[5]

5   China's GDP per capita went from about 82 per cent to 86 per cent of India's to 264–551 per cent, and from 12 per cent to 15 per cent of Brazil's to 120–167 per cent.

Table 14.1 Growth and trade performance of China in comparative perspective

Part A: Growth in standard of living							
	Current US$ using market exchange rate					Current international $ using PPP exchange rate		
	US	China	India	Brazil		China	India	Brazil
A.1: GDP per capita (amount)								
1990	23,888.6	317.9	367.6	2,622.3		981.4	1,200.3	6,693.6
2021	69,287.5	12,556.3	2,277.4	7,518.8		19,338.2	7,333.5	16,056.0
A.2: GDP per capita as percentage of US								
1990		1.3	1.5	11.0		4.1	5.0	28.0
2021		18.1	3.3	10.9		27.9	10.6	23.2
A.3: Development Gap with the US reduced in 1990–2021* (percentage points)								
		16.8	1.7	−0.1		23.8	5.6	−4.8
Part B: Transformation in world trade (% of world exports)								
Year	US	China	Hong Kong	India	Brazil			
1990	22.47	1.18	2.15	0.52	0.40			
2020	13.50	10.01	3.42	1.72	0.91			

* The development gap is obtained from Section A.2 by deducting the value in 1990 from the value in 2021.

Sources: Part A data from World Bank Open Data (available from: data.worldbank.org/); Part B data from World Integrated Trade Solution (available from: wits.worldbank.org/CountryProfile/en/Country/WLD/Year/1990/TradeFlow/Export).

The second noteworthy aspect about China's fast growth is that it now makes the largest footprint on the world economy. In terms of foreign economic interaction, Part B of Table 1 shows that China's share of global exports had increased from 1.18 per cent in 1991 to 10.01 per cent in 2021 while the US share had declined from 22.47 per cent to 13.50 per cent. Furthermore, China's GDP measured in PPP$ has been larger than US GDP since 2016.

The point from our comparison of US and Chinese data on exports and GDP is that today's world is a bipolar world, and that it runs the risk of bipolar disorder if any one of the two countries defines its national security as military dominance over the other country.

The third distinctive aspect about China's growth is that China has world-class capacity in an unusually large range of high-tech products. Huawei is still the world's leading 5G company despite strong US efforts to cripple it since 2017 when Trump took office. And, of the 277,500 international patents filed in 2021, China topped the list with 69,540 Patent Cooperation Treaty (PCT) filings, followed by the United States (59,570), Japan (50,260), South Korea (20,678) and Germany (17,322):[6]

---

6   China has been the top filer since 2019, when it overtook the United States. International patents fall into several categories, the main category of which are Patent Cooperation Treaty (PCT) filings.

> [For] the fifth consecutive year, China-based telecoms giant Huawei Technologies topped the global ranking, with 6,952 PCT applications … followed by US firm Qualcomm at 3,931; South Korea's Samsung Electronics at 3,041 and LG Electronics at 2,855; and Mitsubishi Electric Corp of Japan at 2,673. (AFP 2022)

> Chinese firms have filed approximately 75 per cent of global artificial intelligence patents in the past decade and 40 per cent of all 6G patents, while the United States accounted for only 35 per cent of the latter. (Sworn and Harjani 2022)

Some observers, like Sworn and Harjani (2022), do not regard the possibility that China is producing more knowledge than the United States as indicative of China winning the technological race. They deem US innovation to be of much higher quality than Chinese innovation and will hence continue to earn a larger total amount of technological rents. Sworn and Harjani (2022) regard Huawei as an outlier in a Chinese 'corporate environment lacking high-quality IP filings' and they characterise most of the state-favoured technology companies as 'being inefficient and debt-laden'.[7]

Mainstream thinking in the United States does not share this sceptical attitude about China's technological prowess. For example, a recent report by the US National Security Commission on Artificial Intelligence (NSCAI 2021) warned:

> America is not prepared to defend or compete in the AI era … AI is an inspiring technology. It will be the most powerful tool in generations for benefiting humanity. Scientists have already made astonishing progress in fields ranging from biology and medicine to astrophysics by leveraging AI … (p. 1)

> We should embrace the AI competition … [W]e must win the AI competition that is intensifying strategic competition with China. China's plans, resources, and progress should concern all Americans. It is an AI peer in many areas and an AI leader in some applications. We take seriously China's ambition to surpass the United States as the world's AI leader within a decade.

> The AI competition is also a values competition. China's domestic use of AI is a chilling precedent for anyone around the world who cherishes individual liberty. Its employment of AI as a tool of repression and surveillance—at home and, increasingly, abroad—is a powerful counterpoint to how we believe AI should be used. The AI future can be democratic, but we have learned enough about the power of technology to strengthen authoritarianism abroad and fuel extremism at home to know that we must not take for granted that future technology trends will reinforce rather than erode democracy … (p. 2)

---

7   For example, the case of Tsingha Unigroup. See Zhang et al. (2021).

China possesses the might, talent, and ambition to surpass the United States as the world's leader in AI in the next decade if current trends do not change … (p. 7)

China is organized, resourced, and determined to win this contest. (p. 11)

The above report was chaired by Eric Schmidt, a co-founder of Google, who funded a follow-up report that called China a 'technology peer' and made an even more urgent call to the US Government to respond forcefully to China's effort to win the AI race:

At stake is the future of free societies, open markets, democratic government, and a world rooted in freedom not coercion … China uses its techno-economic advantage for political leverage. Nations—including U.S. allies—reliant on China's tech swing into the PRC's political orbit … Authoritarian regimes sell the case that they are masters of the modern world … An open internet is compromised … The U.S. military's technological edge erodes. The PRC annexes Taiwan … The PRC cuts off the supply of microelectronics and other critical technology inputs. (SCSP 2022: 9, 16, 17, 18)

The thrust of the above report goes beyond calling for state intervention to ensure that the United States wins the AI race to recommending large-scale state funding for a comprehensive industrial policy to support public–private partnerships in technological innovations to counter China's industrial policies.

Given the clamour for retaliatory action against unfair Chinese trade practices from some of America's biggest internet companies, such as Google, Facebook, Twitter and WhatsApp, and against Chinese militarisation of the South China Sea from traditional US allies, the Obama administration reacted to the former with tariffs on selected products (for example, tyres and solar panels) and to the latter with its 'Pivot to Asia' policy in 2011.

The Trump administration launched a trade war against China in 2018, a blockade of Huawei[8] and a vigorous counterintelligence campaign against Chinese spying on US industries. In the words of Christopher Wray (2022), Chinese espionage is the greatest threat to the economic vitality of the United States and is so pervasive that the Federal Bureau of Investigation (FBI) has been finding two cases of it every day.[9] A common target of FBI investigations are ethnic Chinese working in US research universities.[10]

---

8   A Trump rule came into effect in September 2020 that blocked 'companies around the world from using American-made machinery and software to design or produce chips for Huawei or its entities' (Swanson 2020).

9   'The greatest long-term threat to our nation's information and intellectual property, and to our economic vitality, is the counterintelligence and economic espionage threat from China … It's the people of the United States who are the victims of what amounts to Chinese theft on a scale so massive that it represents one of the largest transfers of wealth in human history … We've now reached the point where the FBI is opening a new China-related counterintelligence case about every 10 hours. Of the nearly 5,000 active FBI counterintelligence cases currently under way across the country, almost half are related to China' (Wray 2020).

10   The enthusiasm of the FBI in its duties has unfortunately resulted in many miscarriages of justice. See Apuzzo (2017); Barry and Benner (2022); Benner (2021); Lewis-Kraus (2022).

US–China technological competition has continued to intensify under the Biden administration. On 9 August 2022, President Biden signed the bipartisan *CHIPS* [Creating Helpful Incentives to Produce Semiconductors] *and Science Act 2022*, which provides, among many commitments: 1) US$54.7 billion for US semiconductor research, development, manufacturing and workforce development and the promotion and deployment of wireless technologies; and 2) a 25 per cent investment tax credit for capital expenses for manufacturing semiconductors and related equipment.

And on 31 August 2022, Biden restricted US sales of sophisticated microchips to China and Russia:

> Limits were placed on high-end GPUs [graphic processing units] that power supercomputers and artificial intelligence, said Nvidia and AMD, two Silicon Valley chip makers … [The] scope of the U.S. government's actions appears to go beyond Nvidia and AMD. Other companies that make tool[s] or design software have received similar letters in recent weeks informing them that the high-end technologies they export to China have been restricted. (Clark and Swanson 2022)

Additional trade and investment regulations were being drawn up in October 2022 to 'block any firm that uses America-made technologies … from selling to Chinese entities [such as firms and universities] that are targeted' by the US Government, to broaden the range of microchips that cannot be sold to China, to restrict the 'sale of cutting-edge U.S.-made tools to China's domestic semiconductor industry' and to 'scrutinize the investments that U.S. companies made abroad for national security risks' (Mozur et al. 2022). These new rules are expected to hit the fast-growing Chinese market for supercomputers and data centres very hard.

Reversing the downward spiral in US–China relations

The tensions in US–China relations have been increasing because of a vicious cycle created by the interaction of disagreements over three types of competition: economic, technological and geostrategic. A self-reinforcing process of escalation can occur when a conflict in the geostrategic sphere spills over into the economic sphere in the form of trade barriers—for example: China refuses to buy seafood from the 'offending' party, Country A, and Country A retaliates in the technological sphere such as by reducing academic research collaboration with China. Country B, a strategic ally of Country A, then offers to arm Country A with a powerful game-changing weapon, exacerbating the tensions between China and Country A in the geostrategic sphere and making the tit-for-tat process an explosive one, ricocheting from one type of competition into another.

With a few more rounds of 'righteous' actions by each side, the multilateral free-trade system would be shredded and global supply chains reconfigured to reduce reliance on the other, 'clearly hostile' side. The result would be a lower level of economic welfare on both sides of the dispute, with questionable improvements in the national security of either one. This final suboptimal outcome is most likely unintended and unexpected by any side at the outset.

How can we stop this vicious cycle in US–China relations from unravelling economic globalisation and undermining the cooperation needed to fight future pandemics and climate change? Our answer to this question is that the three types of competition—economic, technological and geostrategic—must be segmented to stop spillovers from one sphere into the other two.

Specifically, the instruments that are used in each type of competition should be kept distinct. For example, when Geely overtakes Tesla in producing electric cars, the United States should not blockade Chinese ports to prevent Geely's electric cars from dominating global markets. Any US blockade of Chinese ports is an act that should be reserved solely for the geostrategic competition sphere—for example, if China was engaging in nuclear proliferation or international terrorism.

Geostrategic competition should be settled by diplomatic means rather than economic instruments. Countries should seek national security through direct negotiations on arms control (for example, about the amount and type of missiles and their location from one another's borders) rather than through limiting exports of high-tech microchips to the other country.

And, spying on Country A by the security agencies of Country C should be confined to military matters and not conducted on commercial enterprises in Country A to benefit commercial enterprises in Country C. While commercial espionage is 'normal' (subject to legal penalties when caught), this task must not be outsourced to a country's security agencies.

Technological competition should be separated from economic competition. First-World governments and economists must acknowledge that every country is entitled to move up the value-added chain in production by extending temporary state support to particular sub-sets of economic activities. A government would be failing in its responsibilities if it does not promote sustainable economic development.

The United States has a plethora of science promotion programs, innovation incentives and defence procurement practices to inspire and inculpate new technologies. The WTO should convene an international conference to formulate an international treaty on the use of industrial policies covering issues such as the maximum size and duration of state support to any domestic industry.

Negotiated agreements on arms control and spying practices would also partition technological and geostrategic competition. The imposition of restrictions on international academic exchanges to fight technological competition is futile and slows global technological progress to the long-run detriment of all parties.

The reality is that building up one's technological and innovation capability is a more effective way to win the technological competition than holding the other side down with actions like denials of visas to foreign students and restricting exports of high-tech products. It is much easier for a country to strengthen knowledge-generation mechanisms within its own borders than to retard such mechanisms located beyond its borders.

The best way for a country to improve its hand in technological competition is to invest more in its research universities, offer more incentives to the private sector to conduct R&D, provide more funding to expand and strengthen all levels of education and make the country more attractive as a migration destination for foreign talent.

How can we get China and the United States to agree to adopt these sensible rules of engagement? Trust is obviously the prerequisite for a durable agreement between both countries, and trust, in turn, is more easily given when it is undergirded by mutual benefit.

We believe other Asian-Pacific countries can play an important role in the creation of the kind of trust that is needed for such an agreement. South Korea, Japan, Australia and New Zealand are trusted US strategic allies and important economic partners of China. They, along with the rest of the Asia-Pacific, will benefit more from being friends of both countries than from supporting one side only or from being bystanders to Cold War 2.0.

Our suggestion is that Asian-Pacific countries should work to deepen regional integration, with the European Union and Norman Angell's mechanism of peace as models. In 1909, Angell (1913) predicted that a Europe-wide war was no longer possible because no country would find life liveable without international trade. The unleashing of the dogs of war in August 1914 could be seen as refutation of Angell's hypothesis, but instead, Konrad Adenauer of Germany, Alcide De Gasperi of Italy and Robert Schuman of France concluded that European economic integration in 1914 was not deep enough to render militarism completely unappealing. This led to the 1957 Treaty of Rome, which established the European Economic Community, and finally, the birth of the European Union (EU) and EU citizenship in 1993, along with an expanding list of supranational institutions such as the European Commission, European Parliament and a common currency.[11]

---

11 The EU project is admittedly an ongoing process and has been repeatedly predicted by some prominent economists to fail in the future—for example, Friedman (1977); Feldstein (1977, 2012).

With EU-style deep regional economic integration, a united Asia-Pacific—let's call it the Pacific Asia Union (PAU)—would not only be difficult to manipulate to participate in a proxy war, it would also not accept a subservient relationship to any big power. The PAU would be big enough to be a persuasive voice in moderating US–China tensions and to work with multilateral institutions (chiefly, the United Nations and its agencies) to help develop sensible rules for US–China engagement.

Furthermore, the PAU would promote the expansion of beneficial economic globalisation, guarding against the globalisation agenda promoted by the biggest multinational corporations. For example, high finance disingenuously portrays unrestricted capital flows and tax havens as the gold standard of market economics.

A recent egregious example of the selective use of free-trade principles to benefit Western corporations was the United States' support for infant milk formula manufacturers to suppress public health information campaigns by the World Health Organization (WHO) and its member countries to promote breastfeeding. In 2018, at a WHO meeting:

> American officials sought to water down the resolution by removing language that called on governments to 'protect, promote and support breast-feeding' and another passage that called on policymakers to restrict the promotion of food products that many experts say can have deleterious effects on young children. (Jacobs 2018)

When Ecuador moved to implement the WHO resolution, the US ambassador to that country, Todd Chapman, told the government that if it did not drop the resolution, 'Washington would unleash punishing trade measures and withdraw crucial military aid'. The Ecuadorean Government reversed its decision to promote breastfeeding (Jacobs 2018).

The efforts of US and Western European governments to exempt the products of their firms from regulation in foreign markets and to extend their monopoly status to foreign markets are why they are claiming that the gold standard in trade agreements are extreme free-market policies in selective areas. The trade negotiators of highly developed countries frequently serve the interest of their oligarchs by opposing government subsidies and regulations in developing economies and (yet!) insisting that developing countries impose stringent and long-lasting protection on intellectual property rights owned by the oligarchs. This selective use of free-market policies in trade agreements constitutes economic bullying because these policies are optimal only in a technologically stationary world with no market failures and no human-induced climate change.

Of more immediate practical relevance, the PAU must begin working hard to strengthen US–China cooperation on the supply of global public goods—such as maintaining multilateral free trade, preventing nuclear proliferation and mobilising adequate development assistance to developing countries—that would accelerate achievement of the SDGs and the Paris climate target. Successful US–China cooperation based on the United Nations' SDG framework would build the trust needed for good-faith adherence to sensible rules partitioning economic, technological and geostrategic competition.

The first step in the journey to reverse the downward spiral in US–China relations is for Australia and the Association of Southeast Asian Nations (ASEAN) to encourage the Asian-Pacific community to merge the overlapping economic blocs of RCEP, CPTPP and the Indo-Pacific Economic Framework to form the Pacific Asia Union. The second step is for the PAU to work with the United Nations and its agencies to formulate guidelines for US–China relations that would segment their economic, technological and geostrategic competition.

References

Agence France-Presse (AFP). 2022. 'Global Patent Filings Surged to Record High in 2021, Up 23% from Singapore: UN Report.' *Straits Times*, [Singapore], 11 February. Available from: www.straitstimes.com/business/economy/global-patent-filings-surged-to-record-high-in-2021-up-23-from-singapore-un-report.

Al Jazeera. 2022. '"If She Dares": China Warns Nancy Pelosi against Visiting Taiwan.' *Al Jazeera*, 1 August. Available from: www.aljazeera.com/news/2022/8/1/china-warns-pelosi-against-visiting-taiwan.

Angell, Norman. 1913. *The Great Illusion: A Study of the Relation of Military Power to National Advantage*. 4th rev. edn. New York, NY: G.P. Putnam's & Sons. Available from: www.gutenberg.org/files/38535/38535-h/38535-h.htm.

Apuzzo, Matt. 2017. 'Former Espionage Suspect Sues, Accusing F.B.I. of Falsifying Evidence.' *The New York Times*, 10 May. Available from: www.nytimes.com/2017/05/10/us/politics/fbi-xi-xiaoxing.html?action=click&module=RelatedLinks&pgtype=Article.

Barry, Ellen and Katie Benner. 2022. 'U.S. Drops Its Case against M.I.T. Scientist Accused of Hiding China Links.' *The New York Times*, 20 January. Available from: www.nytimes.com/2022/01/20/science/gang-chen-mit-china-initiative.html.

Benner, Katie. 2021. 'U.S. Moves to Drop Cases against Chinese Researchers Accused of Hiding Military Ties.' *The New York Times*, 24 July. Available from: www.nytimes.com/2021/07/24/us/politics/chinese-researchers-justice-dept.html.

BBC. 2003. 'Bush Hails "Sheriff" Australia.' *BBC News*, 16 October. Available from: news.bbc.co.uk/2/hi/asia-pacific/3196524.stm.

Buchan, Patrick Gerard and Benjamin Rimland. 2020. 'Defining the Diamond: The Past, Present, and Future of the Quadrilateral Security Dialogue', *CSIS Briefs*, 16 March. Available from: www.csis.org/analysis/defining-diamond-past-present-and-future-quadrilateral-security-dialogue.

Campbell, Kurt. 2022. 'Closing Plenary: U.S. View on Islands in the Indo-Pacific.' *YouTube*, 19 September. Available from: www.youtube.com/watch?v=V2qLuZSPi-w&t=29s.

Clark, Don and Ana Swanson. 2022. 'U.S. Restricts Sales of Sophisticated Chips to China and Russia.' *The New York Times*, 31 August. Available from: www.nytimes.com/2022/08/31/technology/gpu-chips-china-russia.html#:~:text=The%20Biden%20administration%20has%20imposed,performance%20computing%20and%20artificial%20intelligence.

Congressional Research Service. 2020. ' "Made in China 2025" Industrial Policies: Issues for Congress', 11 August 2020. Available from: sgp.fas.org/crs/row/IF10964.pdf.

Everington, Keoni. 2022. 'China Announces Live-Fire Drills in 6 Zones Surrounding Taiwan.' *Taiwan News*, 3 August. Available from: www.taiwannews.com.tw/en/news/4614648.

Feigenbaum, Evan. 2018. *A Chinese Puzzle: Why Economic 'Reform' in Xi's China Has More Meanings than Market Liberalization*. 26 February. Washington, DC: Carnegie Endowment for International Peace. Available from: carnegieendowment.org/2018/02/26/chinese-puzzle-why-economic-reform-in-xi-s-china-has-more-meanings-than-market-liberalization-pub-75668.

Feldstein, Martin. 1997. 'The Political Economy of the European Economic and Monetary Union: Political Sources of an Economic Liability.' *Journal of Economic Perspectives* 11(4): 23–42. doi.org/10.1257/jep.11.4.23.

Feldstein, Martin. 2012. 'The Failure of the Euro: The Little Currency that Couldn't.' *Foreign Affairs*, January–February. Available from: www.foreignaffairs.com/articles/europe/2012-01-01/failure-euro.

Friedman, Milton. 1997. 'The Euro: Monetary Unity to Political Disunity?' *Project Syndicate*, [Prague], 28 August. Available from: www.project-syndicate.org/commentary/the-euro--monetary-unity-to-political-disunity.

Gargeyas, Arjun. 2021. 'China's "Standards 2035" Project Could Result in a Technological Cold War.' *The Diplomat*, 18 September. Available from: thediplomat.com/2021/09/chinas-standards-2035-project-could-result-in-a-technological-cold-war/.

Huang, Cary. 2013. 'Party's Third Plenum Pledges "Decisive Role" for Markets in China's Economy.' *South China Morning Post*, [Hong Kong], 12 November. Available from: www.scmp.com/news/china/article/1354411/chinas-leadership-approves-key-reform-package-close-third-plenum.

Jacobs, Andrew. 2018. 'Opposition to Breast-Feeding Resolution by U.S. Stuns World Health Officials.' *The New York Times*, 8 July. Available from: www.nytimes.com/2018/07/08/health/world-health-breastfeeding-ecuador-trump.html.

Joselow, Maxine. 2022. '5 Things to Know about the Suspension of U.S.–China Climate Talks.' *The Washington Post*, 24 August. Available from: www.washingtonpost.com/politics/2022/08/24/5-things-know-about-suspension-us-china-climate-talks/.

Koty, Alexander Chipman. 2020. 'What is the China Standards 2035 Plan and How Will it Impact Emerging Industries?' *China Briefing*, 2 July. Hong Kong: Dezan Shira & Associates. Available from: www.china-briefing.com/news/what-is-china-standards-2035-plan-how-will-it-impact-emerging-technologies-what-is-link-made-in-china-2025-goals/.

Kyodo News Agency. 2022. 'NATO Strategy Document Mentions China Challenge for 1st Time.' *Nikkei Asia*, [Tokyo], 30 June. Available from: asia.nikkei.com/Politics/International-relations/NATO-strategy-document-mentions-China-challenge-for-1st-time.

Lewis-Kraus, Gideon. 2022. 'Have Chinese Spies Infiltrated American Campuses?' *The New Yorker*, 14 March. Available from: www.newyorker.com/magazine/2022/03/21/have-chinese-spies-infiltrated-american-campuses.

Liu, Tao and Wing Thye Woo. 2018. 'Understanding the US-China Trade War', *China Economic Journal* 11(3): 319–340.

Lo, Kinling. 2022. 'White House Confirms China Has Stopped Anti-Drug Cooperation.' *South China Morning Post*, [Hong Kong], 29 September. Available from: scmp.com/news/china/diplomacy/article/3194183/white-house-confirms-china-has-stopped-cooperating-anti-drug.

Magnier, Mark. 2022. 'US Seeks to Reassure Pacific Island Nations with US$810 Million Package.' *South China Morning Post*, [Hong Kong], 29 September. Available from: www.scmp.com/news/china/diplomacy/article/3194307/us-seeks-reassure-pacific-island-nations-us810-million-package.

Marlow, Iain. 2022. 'What Is the 'Quad' and Should China Fear It?', *Bloomberg*, 19 May. Available from: www.bloomberg.com/news/articles/2022-05-19/what-is-the-quad-and-should-china-fear-it-quicktake-l3dcbtou?leadSource=uverify wall.

Morgan Stanley Research. 2021. *China Standards 2035: Poised to Reshape a Multipolar World.* Global Technology, 6 May. New York, NY: Morgan Stanley. Available from: advisor.morganstanley.com/the-elrod-runyan-group/documents/field/e/el/elrod-%26-runyan-group/Artificial%20Intelligence.pdf.

Mozur, Paul, Ana Swanson and Edward Wong. 2022. 'U.S. Said to Plan New Limits on China's A.I. and Supercomputing Firms.' *The New York Times*, 3 October. Available from: www.nytimes.com/2022/10/03/business/us-limits-chinas-supercomputing.html.

National Security Commission on Artificial Intelligence (NSCAI). 2021. *National Security Commission on Artificial Intelligence: Final Report.* 1 March. Washington, DC: NSCAI. Available from: www.nscai.gov/wp-content/uploads/2021/03/Full-Report-Digital-1.pdf.

North Atlantic Treat Organization (NATO). 2022. *NATO 2022 Strategic Concept.* 29 June. Available from: www.nato.int/nato_static_fl2014/assets/pdf/2022/6/pdf/290622-strategic-concept.pdf.

Pan, Esther. 2006. 'Australia's Security Role in the Pacific.' *Backgrounder*, 18 June. New York, NY: Council for Foreign Relations. Available from: www.cfr.org/backgrounder/australias-security-role-pacific.

Pelley, Scott. 2022. 'President Joe Biden: The 2022 60 Minutes Interview.' *60 Minutes*, [CBS News], 18 September. Available from: www.cbsnews.com/news/president-joe-biden-60-minutes-interview-transcript-2022-09-18/.

Reuters. 2022. 'China Warns Its Military Will "Not Sit Idly By" if Pelosi Visits Taiwan.' *Reuters*, 1 August. Available from: www.reuters.com/world/asia-pacific/china-warns-its-military-will-not-sit-idly-by-if-pelosi-visits-taiwan-2022-08-01/.

Special Competitiveness Studies Project (SCSP). 2022. *Mid-Decade Challenges to National Competitiveness*. 12 September. Arlington, VA: SCSP. Available from: www.scsp.ai/wp-content/uploads/2022/09/SCSP-Mid-Decade-Challenges-to-National-Competitiveness.pdf.

Sprunt, Barbara and Emily Feng. 2022. 'Pelosi Has Landed in Taiwan. Here's Why That's A Big Deal.' *All Things Considered*, [National Public Radio], 2 August. Available from: www.npr.org/2022/08/02/1114852740/pelosi-is-about-to-land-in-taiwan-heres-why-thats-a-big-deal.

Swanson, Ana. 2020. 'U.S. Delivers Another Blow to Huawei with New Tech Restrictions.' *The New York Times*, 15 May. Available from: www.nytimes.com/2020/05/15/business/economy/commerce-department-huawei.html.

Swenson, Deborah and Wing Thye Woo. 2019. 'The Politics and Economics of the US-China Trade War', *Asian Economic Papers* 18(3).

Sworn, Hannah Elyse and Manoj Harjani. 2022. 'US–China Economic Competition Rests on Intellectual Property.' *East Asia Forum*, 29 June. Available from: www.eastasiaforum.org/2022/06/29/us-china-economic-competition-rests-on-intellectual-property/#:~:text=In%202021%2C%20China%20was%20the,per%20cent%20of%20the%20latter.

Trivedi, Anjani. 2020. 'China Is Winning the Trillion-Dollar 5G War.' *The Washington Post*, 13 July. Available from: www.washingtonpost.com/business/china-is-winning-the-trillion-dollar-5g-war/2020/07/12/876cb2f6-c493-11ea-a825-8722004e4150_story.html.

White House. 2022. 'Background Press Call on President Biden's Call with President Xi Jinping of the People's Republic of China', *Press Briefings*, 28 July.

Wikipedia. 2022. 'Made in China 2025.' *Wikipedia*. Available from: en.wikipedia.org/wiki/Made_in_China_2025.

Woo, Wing Thye. 2008. 'Understanding the Sources of Friction in U.S.-China Trade Relations: The Exchange Rate Debate Diverts Attention Away from Optimum Adjustment', *Asian Economic Papers* 7(3).

Wray, Christopher. 2020. 'The threat posed by the Chinese Government and the Chinese Communist Party to the economic and national security of the United States.' Speech at Hudson Institute Video Event: China's Attempt to Influence US Institutions— A Conversation with FBI Director Christopher Wray, Washington, DC, 7 July. Available from: www.fbi.gov/news/speeches/the-threat-posed-by-the-chinese-government-and-the-chinese-communist-party-to-the-economic-and-national-security-of-the-united-states.

Zhang, Erchi, Qu Yunxu, Peng Qinqin and Han Wei. 2021. 'Rescuing China's Would-Be Chipmaking Champion.' *Nikkei Asia Weekly*, [Tokyo], 7 September. Available from: asia.nikkei.com/Spotlight/Caixin/Rescuing-China-s-would-be-chipmaking-champion.

Index

A page number containing 'n.' indicates a reference appearing in a footnote on that page.

www.ingramcontent.com/pod-product-compliance
Lightning Source LLC
Chambersburg PA
CBHW050236220326
41598CB00044B/7407